The Vegetable Gardener's BIBLE

SECOND EDITION

Discover Ed's High-Yield
W-O-R-D System for All North
American Gardening Regions

Edward C. Smith

Storey Publishing

DEDICATION

To my darling Sylvia,
with whom I have gardened joyously
for more than thirty years.

The mission of Storey Publishing is to serve our customers by
publishing practical information that encourages
personal independence in harmony with the environment.

Edited by Carleen Madigan and Gwen Steege
Art direction and book design by Jessica Armstrong

Front cover photography by © Storey Publishing/Giles Prett (author)
    and © Walter Chandoha (background)
Back cover photography by © Sylvia Ferry Smith (author, carrots, cauliflower, radishes),
    and © Storey Publishing/Giles Prett (squash and tomatoes)
Interior photography credits appear on page 340
Illustrations by Beverly Duncan, except for: Brigita Fuhrmann 166, 167, 178 (leaf miner, mite, snail);
    Kurt Musfeldt 175–177, 178 (Mexican bean beetle, slug), 179; © Elayne Sears 83

Indexed by Christine R. Lindemer, Boston Road Communications

Storey Publishing
210 MASS MoCA Way
North Adams, MA 01247
www.storey.com

Printed in the United States by R.R. Donnelley
10 9 8 7 6 5 4 3 2 1

LIBRARY OF CONGRESS CATALOGING-IN-PUBLICATION DATA

Smith, Edward C. (Edward Clarke), 1941–
    The vegetable gardener's bible / Edward C. Smith. — 2nd ed.
      p. cm.
  First ed. published in 2000.
  Includes index.
  ISBN 978-1-60342-475-2 (pbk. : alk. paper)
  ISBN 978-1-60342-476-9 (hardcover : alk. paper)
  1. Vegetable gardening. 2. Organic gardening. I. Title.
SB324.3.S62 2010
635—dc22
                                        2009023862

CONTENTS

ACKNOWLEDGMENTS

This book is a revised and expanded version of the 2000 edition of *The Vegetable Gardener's Bible*; it exists in large part because of the help I received creating that earlier edition. Thank you again, Maggie Lydic, Deborah E. Burns, Gwen W. Steege, Giles Prett, Charles W. G. Smith, Lindsey and Nathaniel, and, most important, Sylvia Ferry Smith. This time around, I've had the help of a fine editor, Carleen Madigan, and art director Jessica Armstrong. Once again, Sylvia Ferry Smith has created the garden and recreated it in photographic images; this book would not exist were it not for her gardening skill and artist's eye. Thanks, too, to gardening friends who shared ideas and/or let us photograph their gardens: Susan Carpenter, David Carpenter, Lee Blackwell, Ruth Richards, Ann Miller, Richard Wiswall, Henry Homeyer, Shane Smith, and Christy Aucoin.

In the Garden

Many years ago, when Sylvia and I began our life together, we decided to heed the sound of a different drummer. We wanted to live close to the earth, building our home from wood that was locally harvested and milled, heating it with wood from our own land, heating water and producing electricity with solar power, and — most important — growing as much of our own food as we could from our own garden. *The Vegetable Gardener's Bible* is in many ways a report on the evolution of that garden.

Sylvia and I have had a garden every year of our marriage, over 30 gardens now. The first one was small, about 120 square feet. Each year since then, the garden has become bigger (now it's about 1,500 square feet) as we've grown more and more of our own food. As the garden grew, so did the amount of work and time it required. There was and still is, though, the rest of life to deal with — children, work, a house to finish, and other buildings to keep up with (a garage, a shed, a couple of greenhouses, a woodworking shop). So we had to figure out how to garden with less work and do it in ways that gave us good, nutritious food; depended very little on fossil-fueled machines or fossil-fuel-derived fertilizers; and left the soil in better condition than it was when we started. Gardening organically, maintaining soil fertility, and nurturing soil life ensures not only that we will have a bountiful and healthful harvest but also that our children and their children will, too. That's what *The Vegetable Gardener's Bible* is all about.

Over the ten years since the first printing of *The Vegetable Gardener's Bible,* I've continued to learn about how to make my vegetable garden more productive. (Folk wisdom notwithstanding, old dogs — and old gardeners — can learn new tricks. They can also abandon old ones that no longer work.) I've figured out or learned from other gardeners better ways to do things. I've questioned how I've done things and sometimes learned that such doings were either not really effective or not worth the time and effort for the effect they had. I've heard from readers who had good suggestions or questions I hadn't thought to ask. I've also experimented with growing new vegetables and growing old standbys using different methods. All of this new knowledge and more, I'd like to share with you, in hopes that your garden will become a slice of paradise in your backyard.

After all, Eden was a garden. For Sylvia and me, the garden is a place to go for quiet contemplation, a source not only of food but also of spiritual renewal and intimate contact with life's most basic processes. In the garden, we are participants in life. As Masanobu Fukuoka wrote in *The One-Straw Revolution,* "The ultimate goal of farming is not the growing of crops, but the cultivation and perfection of human beings."

— Ed Smith

PART ONE

FROM SEED TO HARVEST
Higher Yields with Less Work

CHAPTER 1

A New Way to Garden: Wide, Deep, Raised Beds

MY FIRST VEGETABLE GARDEN, when I was eight, was very traditional: the vegetables were arranged in narrow rows separated by wide paths. That was the way my parents gardened, and every year we gathered what looked like a pretty good harvest. When I moved to Vermont, my address changed, but the way I gardened stayed the same. It hadn't yet occurred to me that gardening could be, or needed to be, improved.

The more I gardened, the more I learned. I tried wide rows and liked the results. It wasn't just that I grew more in less space; the plants actually grew better in wide rows than they did in narrow ones. From wide rows I tried wide raised beds, and again there was a noticeable improvement. After more investigation, I began using wide, deep, raised beds and growing my best gardens ever. I noticed that whenever a plant's growing space gets wider or deeper or both, its growth improves. I asked why. The answer led me to a new system of gardening. It has to do with roots.

A Radical View of Roots

There's a saying here in the Northeast Kingdom of Vermont that the worst part of ignorance isn't what we don't know; it's that so much of what we do know just isn't so. The truth of that adage has, as we put it in this part of the country, hit me right upside the head a number of times in my life. But it was never truer than it was in my garden. For a lot of my gardening life, my decisions about how best to grow plants were informed by some ideas about plant root systems that just weren't so.

WHAT I KNEW ABOUT CARROT ROOTS

The box on the next page shows two drawings of carrots. The one on the left represents what I thought I knew about carrot roots, and it's what guided my

▲ Give 'em stretching room. *This wide, deeply dug bed of carrots thrives because its roots have room to stretch and find the nutrients and moisture they need.*

decisions about how best to grow carrots. The root system, of which there isn't a whole lot, extends outward a few inches and downward about the same amount. It covers about the same area belowground as the foliage does aboveground. I rather suspect that I'm not the only gardener to see things more or less this way. I've often seen drawings very much like this in books.

With this narrow view of roots to guide me, it made perfect sense to grow carrots in narrow, shallow beds. I believed that all the carrot really needed was a band of loosened soil about 8 inches (20 cm) wide and about the same depth, just what it gets in the traditional garden.

I further assumed that what was true for carrots was also true for the other vegetable plants. If they had a band of loose soil about as wide as the reach of their foliage and as deep as my tiller could till, vegetable plants had all the space they really needed. That's the space they get in a traditional row-based garden, so it made good sense to garden that way.

BUT IT JUST ISN'T SO

I remember the moment I first really *saw* a drawing similar to the one on the right in the box. I'd looked at it before, but I hadn't really seen it. I felt that a bulb lit up in my head, illuminating the reason my plants preferred these wider rows and deeper beds.

The drawing on the right, rather than that on the left, shows the way carrot roots really grow, or more precisely, how carrot roots can grow if they get enough loose soil to grow in. Carrot roots can extend as much as 1½ feet (45 cm) on all sides and as much as 3 feet (90 cm) downward. In other words, the roots extend outward much farther than the foliage does.

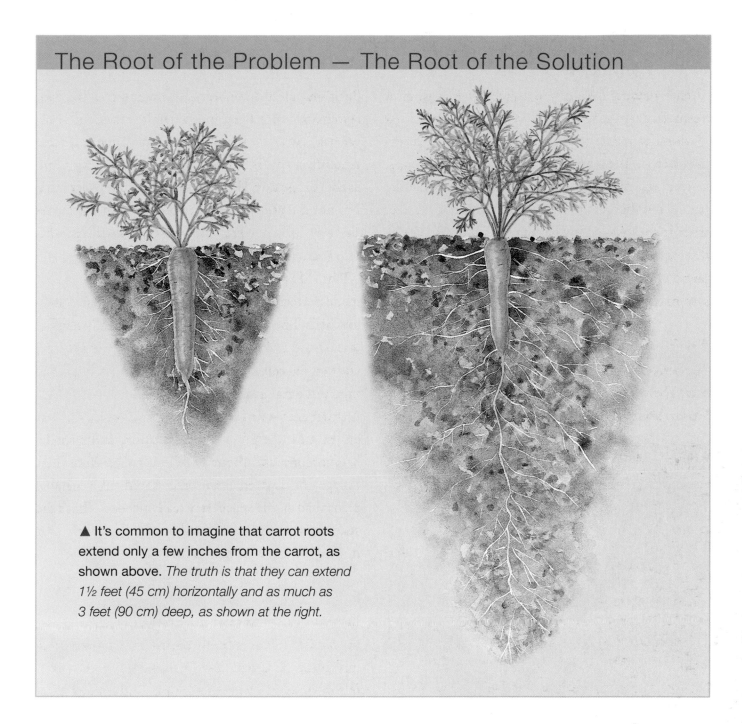

▲ It's common to imagine that carrot roots extend only a few inches from the carrot, as shown above. *The truth is that they can extend 1½ feet (45 cm) horizontally and as much as 3 feet (90 cm) deep, as shown at the right.*

What is true for carrots is also true for all the other vegetable plants in the garden. Even so-called shallow-rooted sorts like celery or onions can grow much more extensive root systems than we usually imagine, and all of them grow better with a lot more room than they get in a traditional narrow, shallow row.

From that moment, I set about designing a garden bed that gives plant roots substantially more room to grow and at the same time can be easily built and maintained. Unlike the traditional garden, in which each foot (30 cm) of row provides plant roots with about ⅔ of a cubic foot (20 cm³) of growing space, a wide, deep, raised bed provides over 5 cubic feet (1.5 m³) per row foot, almost eight times more space. This is why the vegetables I grow in my wide, deep, raised beds are the most vigorous, healthy, and productive I've ever grown.

Raised Beds = Less Compacted Soil

A garden contains two kinds of space — space for plants to grow, and space for a gardener to walk while tending the plants. Walking on garden soil exerts pressures of as much as 10 pounds per square inch (4.5 kg per 2.5 cm²), quite enough to force soil particles together and compress the spaces between them. The result is compacted soil which, although it still contains all the nutrients it did before, no longer allows air and water to enter and move about and can no longer support abundant root growth. Roots, particularly the tiny, delicate root hairs that absorb moisture and nutrients, grow in the spaces between soil particles. They grow poorly or not at all where such spaces are absent or not sufficiently numerous. The part of the plant we see aboveground is entirely dependent on the part we don't see beneath the ground. A stunted, poorly developed root system leads inevitably to a stunted and poorly developed plant.

In a typical narrow-row garden, over half the soil is compacted into walkways for the gardener. If the gardener favors power tilling and cultivating machines, as much as three-quarters of the garden becomes inhospitable to plants.

In a garden with wide, deep, raised beds like the ones I use, plants get the lion's share of the space, and they get the lion's share of the soil. In my garden, about three-quarters of the garden space is used to grow plants, and only about a quarter is used for walkways.

A traditional garden puts the needs of the cultivator first. A garden based on wide, deep, raised beds puts the needs of the cultivar first.

▲ Spring: After the cover-up. *These wide beds received their winter blankets of straw mulch in October. Now, in early spring, they've been uncovered so that the strengthening sun can warm the soil. The first peas are sprouting at the trellis base, and lettuce transplants grow beneath.*

▲ Midsummer: Weed-free, plant-friendly soil. *As the long days of summer spur the garden into full growth, wide, deep, raised beds provide good drainage; closely planted crops shade out weeds and keep moisture from evaporating; and mulched paths provide walking and working areas while protecting the soil from compaction.*

GARDENING OUT OF THE BOX

Most gardeners grow plants in narrow, single rows separated by wide walkways. Why? If we go back far enough in the history of gardening, the answer we finally reach is: "So there'll be room for my horse (or my tractor, or my rototiller) to get between the rows." The actual reason for planting the way most gardeners do today has very little to do with the nature and growth requirements of vegetable plants.

▲ Late summer: The path to a successful harvest. *The abundant harvest from efficiently planted wide, deep, raised beds will convince even skeptical gardeners that this is the path to gardening success.*

Grow More in Less Space with Less Work

Wide, deep, raised-bed planting has many practical advantages in addition to offering a better growing environment. Because of the high ratio of bed space to walking space, you can grow substantially more vegetables in substantially less space. Switching from gardener-centered to plant-centered spacing results in dramatic savings. Raised beds are also less work because they're easier to weed, water, and fertilize. And after the first year, weeding is almost a thing of the past.

SPACE SAVERS

Walkways are narrower in a bed-based garden because they are used just for walking, not for wide cultivating machines. There are also fewer walkways because they do not occur between every row. In a traditional garden, the recommended spacing between rows is determined more by the needs of the cultivator than it is by the needs of the cultivar. In beds, most vegetables can be grown much closer together, resulting in a further saving of space.

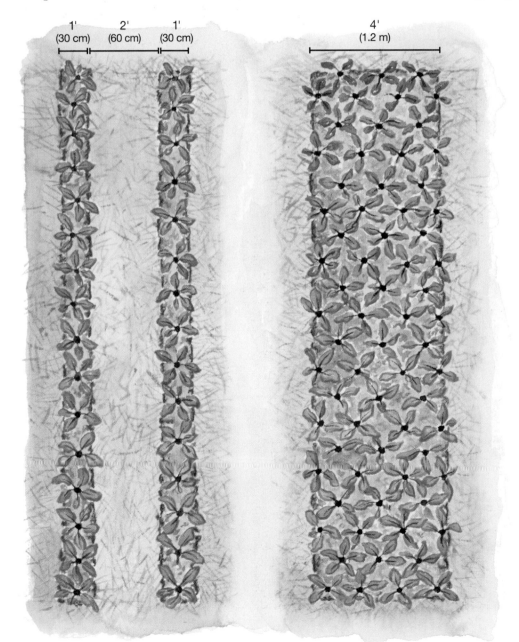

◀ **Two ways to plant beets.** *In the garden at the far left, only about 15 plants fit in each of two traditional narrow rows, because of the walkway between. In a wide-bed garden that takes up the same amount of space, it's possible to fit about 70 plants in staggered rows.*

WORK SAVERS

Once you've created a garden bed, it's permanent; you'll need to loosen and aerate the soil and add compost, fertilizer, and other amendments, but only in the bed, not in the adjoining walkways. That saves time, it saves the work of making extra compost, and it saves the expense of extra fertilizer and rock powders.

Watering, too, can be concentrated where it will do the most good. Efficient systems, such as soaker hoses or drip irrigators, are easy to install in wide beds and allow you to direct the water right to the plants, not to the walkways. Deep beds provide a reservoir for water, making more water available to plants; you'll need to water less frequently.

Fewer walkways also means less of a very tedious form of weeding: digging weeds out of the hard-packed soil of walkways. And when you grow plants in beds so that their leaves just barely touch when the plants are mature, you create a microclimate that not only saves water because there's less evaporation but also inhibits weeds because soil is shaded.

▲ Less walking space, more growing space. *Narrow, straw-mulched walkways need little care, and more space is left for growing plants.*

◄ A built-in umbrella. *As the plants grow, their foliage shades the ground beneath so that it stays moist, and with little sun to encourage growth, any weeds are thin, spindly, and easily removed.*

The Bed: A Basic Garden Module

A bed can be any width or length, supported by sides or not. And a garden is one or more (often many, many more) beds. Step one toward creating a bed garden is deciding how big you want your beds.

GETTING THE SIZE RIGHT

How wide and deep does a bed have to be for the plants to grow their best and simultaneously allow me to enjoy the garden? The rule here is simple: Let the width of the bed be determined by your own comfort, its depth by the plants' needs.

HOW WIDE IS WIDE ENOUGH?

How wide you make a bed depends on how wide a bed you can comfortably tend without having to walk or kneel in the bed soil. You need to be able to reach easily to its center to plant, weed, cultivate, prune, and harvest. For me, that's about 18 inches (45 cm), so a bed width of about 3 feet (90 cm) is just right. For trellised or staked plants, I like a slightly narrower bed of about 30 inches (75 cm). Applying this "rule of comfort," different gardeners are likely to come up with different answers. I know gardeners who like beds 4 or even 5 feet (1.2 to 1.5 m) wide, while others prefer narrower ones.

HOW LONG IS LONG ENOUGH?

Bed length is pretty much arbitrary and depends partly on how much space you have. Where I have the space, I prefer beds that are about 15 feet (4.6 m) long. One reason for this is purely psychological. I usually assign myself garden work "by the bed," and I become overwhelmed at the prospect of coping with a bed much longer than 15 feet (4.6 m). I have another, more practical reason, too. I build trellises for many of my crops, and the lumber I use for them comes in 8-foot (2.4 m) lengths. If my beds are 15 feet

(4.6 m), the trellises are easy to construct, using two boards with some overlap (see pages 78–79).

HOW DEEP IS DEEP ENOUGH?

Bed depth is determined not by what's comfortable for the gardener but what is best for plants. Increasing the depth more than the standard 8 inches (20 cm) requires some work. If you're building supported beds, it also means additional materials and money. But once you do it, you'll have better results and much less work in following years. Using the designs and techniques in this book, I combine deep tilling with raising the soil level to achieve beds with about 18 inches (45 cm) of loosened soil. The plants might like even more, but they don't really need it. I'm quite satisfied with the results I get.

▲ **Keep off the beds.** *Easy to tend, these 3-foot-wide (90 cm) garlic beds never get compacted because I don't have to step into them to weed or harvest.*

Let Your Creativity Come Out and Play

No rule says that all the beds need to be lined up next to one another, or even that they have to be all squares or rectangles. A garden made of wide, raised, deep beds allows you to go beyond the traditional grid system of so many vegetable gardens.

- **Scatter beds around your yard,** wherever optimum growing conditions exist. Or, like flower beds, let them be part of your landscape plan, their shapes and locations determined in part by aesthetic considerations.

- **If you like squares or circles, go for it.** I sometimes wonder why flowers get most of us thinking in free-form designs for beds, while vegetables confine us to straight lines and right angles.

▲ **What an angle!** *Garden beds can be any shape your imagination dreams up, even triangles.*

▲ **Good things come in small packages.** *These two beds each measure just 3 feet by 3 feet but offer enough space for a bounty of tomatoes, basil, lettuce, parsley, zucchinis, and cucumbers.*

Where Does Your Garden Grow?

Before getting "down and dirty" and actually making a few beds, let's figure out where to put them. What's a good place for a garden? With enough time, work, and materials, you can probably create a productive garden almost anywhere, but you can save a lot of work and expense if you start with a site that already has most of what your garden will need. Ancient cultures tried to explain how everything works by referring to four basic elements: sun, wind, water, and earth. That's not a bad starting point for figuring out where to put a garden.

It All Starts with the Sun

All life depends on solar energy. For many life-forms, that's a dilemma, because many life-forms can't utilize solar energy directly. We human beings, for example, are dependent on solar energy, but we don't have means to capture and use it. Enter green plants. Green plants, like those we grow in our gardens, can do what no other living thing can do: they can capture solar energy and convert it into forms they can use. That captured energy can then be used by plant-consuming creatures and the creatures that, in turn, consume them. This "capture and convert" process is called *photosynthesis:* literally, "putting together with light." Solar energy combines hydrogen from water (drawn from the earth by plant roots) with carbon (from carbon dioxide in the air) to form *carbohydrates,* the building blocks from which all living things are made. As gardeners, we want our plants to have the best possible chance to capture solar energy and work their photosynthetic miracle.

LET THE SUN SHINE IN

If there is a most important consideration in planning a garden, it is sunshine. You can't have photosynthesis without the "photo" part. (See It All Starts with the Sun, below left.) Some plants do thrive in deep shade, but none of them are vegetable plants. Although some vegetable plants (usually those grown for their leaves) can tolerate partial shade, most need full, unobstructed sunlight for at least six hours a day to produce the best yields, and many (tomatoes and peppers) do better with more than six hours. The minimum ration doesn't offer much of a buffer against nature's fickle ways. There are many days in most summers when very little sunlight gets through the clouds. When the sunny days finally arrive, extra hours of sunlight beyond the minimum can make a big difference as plants make up for the photosynthesis they couldn't accomplish during the cloudy times. Morning sun is particularly helpful because it dries the dew from leaves and thereby inhibits fungal diseases.

Observe your potential garden spot in spring every hour or so, marking the areas of shadow with stakes and recording the times. If you don't end up

THE ROOT OF THE PROBLEM

Some of the things that cause shade — trees and large bushes, for instance — can create other problems for the garden even if they're along a northern border and don't block the sunlight. They have roots, lots of roots with a very long reach, and it won't take long for those roots to find the rich soil of your garden beds and start sucking up the nutrients and water you'd rather have in your vegetable plants.

with at least six hours of sun over the whole garden-to-be, consider the following:

- **Clear the decks.** Remove whatever causes the extra shade, if possible.

- **Change its shape.** Consider changing the shape of your garden to match the full-sun area. One of the advantages of gardening in beds is that you aren't limited to the traditional straight lines of a narrow-row garden. You can vary the arrangement of your beds and even their shapes to match different situations.

- **Smaller can be better.** Create several smaller gardens instead of one large one. Put as much of the garden as you can in the largest sunny area and, if possible, scatter two or three others where they can take advantage of other small sunny spots.

◀ **By dawn's early light.** *Throughout the season, observe patterns of light and shadow in your garden. Here, in late August, beds are sunlit by 10 A.M. For best results, you need six hours of direct sun.*

◀ **As shadows lengthen.** *In June, the time of year when the sun is most directly overhead, you can see shadows from neighboring trees beginning to creep toward the beds about 4 o'clock in the afternoon.*

THE ANSWER IS BLOWING IN THE WIND

Wind can be a friend or a foe. Gentle, consistent movement of the air benefits a garden by mixing different pockets of air together. This helps prevent extremes of hot and cold and modifies very humid or dry air, making mildews less likely. But frequent high winds can steal moisture from the leaves and damage plants by breaking stems, tearing leaves, or damaging trellises.

It's sometimes difficult to know if winds will be a problem, but here are some clues. If your garden has a beautiful long-range view, it may also be windy. Places on the coasts of lakes or oceans or with northern or western exposures tend to be windy. If you have a windy site, put the garden where there is already a windbreak, or plan on creating one. Trellised crops like peas or pole beans can fit the bill here.

Effects of Air Movement and Sun on Sloping Gardens

- **Air movement.** Cold air moves downhill and will collect in low areas or where dense plant growth, fences, or buildings block its movement. Frosts will be less of a problem in gardens on slopes where cold air can move over and past the garden rather than settling in it.

- **Sun.** In northern regions, a site that slopes to the south will warm more quickly in spring and stay warm longer in fall. In milder regions, a gentle northern slope will be less likely to overheat in summer.

▼ **Fruits of protection.** *Situated on a beautiful hillside, this vegetable garden is protected from strong westerly winds by a pea trellis. This barrier not only blocks the wind, but it provides a bonus crop of delicious peas as well.*

WATER, WATER, EVERYWHERE

Goldilocks wanted her porridge neither too hot nor too cold, but just right. And so it is with the garden and water: things need to be just right. Too little water, and the plants will suffer stress; they'll droop, sag, and finally expire. Even if they appear to recover, the lack of water has had an effect, and they'll never be as healthy and productive as they could have been. But too much water is just as bad. With too much water, there's not enough room in the soil for the air that is essential to plant roots and to the many soil-dwelling creatures that help plants to grow.

Nobody Likes Wet Feet

You can't grow vegetables in a swamp, but in the spring or after a rainy spell swamps can look dry compared to some folks' gardens. If you have no choice but to garden in a too-wet site, you may be able to correct the problem (See Making the Best of a Bad Situation, below), but most people's swampy garden problems come from putting their gardens in a site that looks dry most of the time but whose natural preference is being wet.

If you suspect your potential garden site is too wet, look for these two clear signs of a site with poor drainage:

- **Slow drying.** The soil takes much longer to dry out after a rain than nearby soil. After drying, the soil often cracks or forms a crust.

- **Puddle-forming.** Rather than drying up and draining away, puddles remain for hours after rain. Standing water in early spring, shortly after the snow is gone, is okay, but if it's still there in late spring after the soil has completely thawed and it's time to start working in the garden, then the site is too wet.

Making the Best of a Bad Situation

It's not the end of the world if your only good garden spot is too wet. You may be able to dry the site enough with drainage ditches around the garden or by installing perforated drainage piping. And if the problem isn't too serious, particularly if it's seasonal (the soil takes too long to dry out in the spring, for instance), simply changing to a raised bed garden may solve the problem by "rising above" it.

▶ **Dry up!** *There are many types of garden soils, and each drains a little differently. Sandy soils drain and dry quickly. Loam drains well, forming puddles that quickly disappear after it stops raining. Silt and clay soils are most often associated with wet places and often harbor puddles hours after a storm.*

THE GOOD EARTH

A productive garden does need good soil and plenty of it, but one of the benefits of gardening in beds is that you don't need to start with good soil, or even with any soil. If the only place you have enough sunlight for a garden is where a gravel driveway used to be, you can put a garden there. There'll be some work involved, but it's possible.

If you are, though, lucky enough to have a choice of locations with enough sun, access to water, and moderate air movement, pick the spot with the best soil. I'll have a lot more to say about soil in chapter 6, but for now, "best" means soil that has a nice, dark brown color, that crumbles fairly easily, and that's already growing something — be that a lawn, a field of hay, or just a lush crop of weeds. Sparse vegetation is usually a sign of poor soil. If you have a choice, you'll have an easier time working with soil that's already able to support plants.

Words of Warning

In addition to poor soil, you'd be wise to be aware of areas that may be contaminated. If your house is old enough to have been painted with lead-based paint, or if the windows contain lead-based putty, the soil right near the house is likely to be contaminated with lead. Because lead can be taken up into plants (especially leafy greens), it's best to avoid planting in these areas.

If you want to put your garden where there is now lawn, and if that lawn has been treated with an herbicide or with one of those products that promises to fertilize the grass and simultaneously eliminate the dandelions and other broad-leaved plants, you have a problem. The herbicide that makes the dandelions disappear will also make most of your vegetable plants disappear. In such a case, remove the sod and use a deep, supported raised bed filled with compost and some uncontaminated soil.

HOME IS WHERE THE HEART IS

If you have a number of potential garden sites with enough sunlight, good air circulation, enough water (but not too much) and decent soil, put the garden or gardens closer to rather than farther away from the house. Lettuce is more likely to become a salad if fetching it does not involve a hike. Watering is easier to do when the garden is near the spigot, and general garden care is more enjoyable when your time is

Tips for Choosing a Garden Location

- Sun, sun, sun

- A gentle southern slope, for sunlight and air movement

- Some sort of windbreak if occasional high winds are a problem

- No barriers where you don't need windbreaks, so neither hot nor cold air becomes trapped in the garden

- Good water drainage

- Easy access to water for irrigation when needed

- As close to home as you can (But a garden at your neighbor's, or a shared community garden on an otherwise vacant lot, is better by far than no garden at all.)

spent actually caring for the garden instead of walking back and forth from the house to the garden. A garden that is close to your house is likely to be close to your heart.

We have two gardens, each where it is because of what's growing in it. The large garden, where we grow mostly vegetables for storage and winter use, is a short walk from the house, while the smaller kitchen garden, where we grow most of what we eat fresh in summer, is only a few steps from the front door. Both gardens are visible from the house, and this is a nice plus. For me the vegetable garden is as much a part of our home's landscape as are the flowers and trees. I enjoy just contemplating the garden from inside the house, particularly on a rainy summer day, or imagining the garden-to-be while gazing at the snow that covers it in winter.

Bigger Isn't Necessarily Better

Here's a good rule that helps keep vegetable gardening enjoyable: Start with a garden small enough so it feels manageable. There's no quicker way to extinguish the spark that ignites the joy of gardening than by taking on too much too soon. Later on, if you're longing to work in the garden but there doesn't seem to be anything to do, then it's probably time to expand. But if this is your first vegetable garden, make it a size that you think you can take care of, and remember that whatever size you choose, a wide, deep, raised-bed garden will give you more food than a row-style garden of the same size, requiring about the same amount of work, so you'll grow more in less space anyway.

The Joy of Garden Tools

"One feels so kindly towards the thing which allows the hand to obey the brain." These words, written by the garden author Gertrude Jekyll (1843–1932) about her gardening tools, capture for me a very important part of the enjoyment I experience in the garden. A good tool allows me to do exactly — not approximately, but exactly — what I want to do, and it allows me to do it easily and comfortably. It was created by a tool designer and craftsman who were striving, as I am, to do the best they could. And if form dictated by function is part of what makes something beautiful, then a good tool is also a worthy object of contemplation. I spend a lot of time in the garden, and for much of that time I have a tool in my hand; when that tool is a good one, I enjoy my garden time more.

This isn't to say that you can't enjoy your garden unless you have lots of expensive tools. Gardeners have managed to grow food with no more than a pointed stick. If there's no flex in the budget, you can make a fine garden with a shovel, a rake, and a hoe from a tag sale. But when you can afford a new garden tool, buy quality; good tools last longer, work better, and add to the pleasure of garden hours.

Tools for Bed Building

If your garden is small — a single bed or just a few beds — you may choose to dig it by hand. In this case, you'll need a spade and a stout garden fork. A crowbar will be handy if you encounter rocks. Although both spades and shovels are used for digging and the words are often used interchangeably, shovels and spades are quite different tools.

- **Spade.** With its flat, rectangular blade, a spade allows you to cut a straight edge around a bed or to cut out neat squares of sod and peel them off evenly at the root line.

- **Shovel.** The convex, pointed blade of a shovel makes it a good tool for moving soil — from walkway to bed, for instance — and for digging holes.

- **Steel rake.** The rake head should attach to its handle by a hoop. Use it with the tines down to draw soil from walkways into beds and to move soil within beds. Flip it over and use the flat side to smooth the bed surface.

- **Garden fork.** This is the tool to use for loosening compacted soil. A well-made garden fork has thick, somewhat narrow tines about a foot long (30 cm) and ⅜ inch (10 mm) square. Such tines are strong and won't bend when working in the soil or when they encounter a large rock, but they're narrow enough to move easily through the soil when loosening clods of dirt. What I don't want here is a flat-tined tool often called a "potato fork," the tines of which bend easily in compacted or rocky soil.

- **Broadfork or deep spader (optional).** At one time, it was possible to buy a stout broadfork — essentially a big, wide garden fork — to deeply loosen the soil. It makes the soil-loosening job quicker. Most of the broadforks I've tried in recent years aren't up to the task of breaking new ground, but there is a similar tool called a deep spader (18 inches [45 cm] wide, with 16-inch [40 cm] tines), which can do the same job without bending tines. (See Suppliers, page 337.)

YOU GET WHAT YOU PAY FOR

I don't buy cheap tools because I've found that, in the long run, they always end up costing more — in money and in frustration and wasted time — than the expensive ones. Cheap tools are often poorly designed, sacrificing utility for a lower price. At best, such tools make gardening more work. At worst, they don't do the job right or they end up hurting you. They make your back ache, they make your muscles sore, or they give you blisters. And by and by, they break. By the time you've bought a second cheap tool to replace the broken one, you'll probably have spent more than one good tool would have cost in the first place. The trouble is that at first glance a lot of cheap tools can look like expensive ones. On more careful inspection you can see that the cheap tools are made from inferior materials or put together poorly.

Sometimes you can tell that you will like a tool just by looking at it or seeing a picture of it, but usually you need to hold it. Check to see if the fit is comfortable: Is there room for your hands within enclosed handles? Is the surface smooth and welcoming to your skin? Does the handle fill, but not overfill, your hand? Next, how does it balance? It should be easiest to hold in just the way you'll hold it when at work. At the same time, notice its weight. You don't want a tool that's too heavy, but a tool can also be too light. For digging tools in particular, you may want a slightly heavier tool to provide some of its own inertia to get the job done.

TOOL BUYER'S CRITERIA:

- Forged steel
- Comfortable grip
- Smooth surfaces
- Good balance
- Appropriate weight

Judging a Shovel's Merits

The forged steel shovel on the right is much stronger than the pressed steel shovel on the left. Forged steel is thicker and must be heated in order to shape it by hammering; pressed steel is simply bent to shape. Note that on the shovel on the right, the socket is forged as part of the tool head and then welded closed. The handles of tools with a pressed socket loosen after use. Look for this construction when you purchase a shovel, spade, or garden fork.

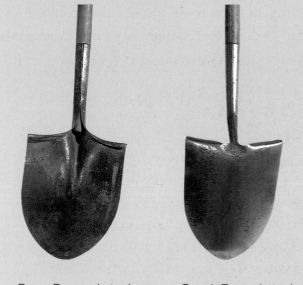

Poor: Pressed steel   *Good: Forged steel*

▲ **Comfort for the gardener.** *This sturdy trowel has a number of good points. Its stainless-steel head will not rust, and although it's harder to sharpen than softer metals, stainless steel keeps its edge longer. I also like the wooden handle. It's pleasing to the eye and hand, and unlike plastic or metal, it doesn't feel cold in chilly spring weather or hot when it's been left in the summer sun.*

The Search for a Perfect Rectangle

Regardless of what style garden you prefer, from tight and formal to loose and free-form, there are some skills that you need to know so you can plan and create the garden of your dreams. The first steps in creating a wide, deep, raised-bed garden are the same as those you'd take when starting any garden.

Laying out beds is something I'm fussy about. Once I've decided on rectangular beds, I want rectangles, not parallelograms. You don't have to be this particular, but making accurate rectangular beds is really pretty easy, and it's fun. All you need are five stakes, some twine, a steel measuring tape, and the only thing I remember from geometry class: magic triangles (see the box below).

Before you begin, mow the garden area, leaving the grass clippings where they fall. You'll be digging them into the soil in a later step.

You can reuse the stakes and string for any number of new beds. Use the string as a guide to outline the area with a sprinkling of lime or flour.

Customized Garden Beds

- **Custom size.** You can use this technique to make beds of any length. Simply change the 15-foot (4.6 m) measurement to whatever length suits your needs. Just be sure you have a 3-foot (0.9 m) "leg" and a 5-foot (1.5 m) "hypotenuse."

- **Custom style.** Use the method to lay out a single wide bed in a lawn area or, after tilling a large garden, multiple wide beds, within the entire space.

The Magic Triangle

About 4,000 years ago, the Egyptians used a simple mathematical formula to lay out the pyramids. They called it the "magic triangle," and it's still magic today. We can use it to help lay out our garden beds.

The formula is this: If one leg of a triangle is three units, the second leg is four units, and the hypotenuse is five units, then the angle between the legs is a right angle.

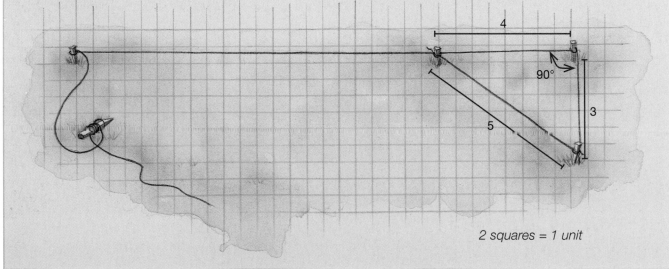

2 squares = 1 unit

Laying Out a Wide Bed

WHAT YOU'LL NEED

For a bed 3' × 15' (0.9 × 4.6 m):
- About 50 feet (15.2 m) of garden twine
- Five 1-foot (30 cm) stakes

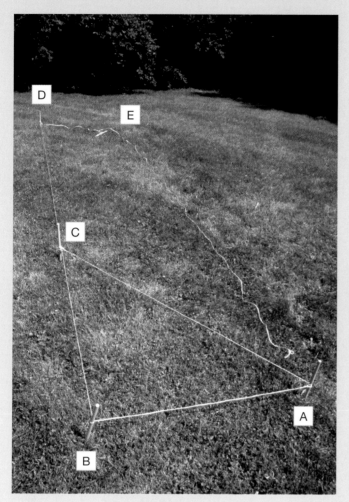

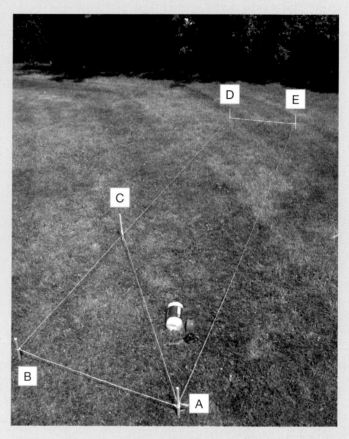

1 Attach stake A at one end of the twine; stake B, 3 feet (0.9 m) beyond that; stake C, 4 feet (1.2 m) beyond that; stake D, 11 feet (3.3 m) beyond that; and stake E, 3 feet (0.9 m) beyond that.

- Measure another 15 feet (4.6 m) of twine beyond that and cut the twine.

- Measure a 5-foot-long (1.5 m) piece of twine, and tie it to stake C.

- Following the pattern in the photo, position the stakes in the following order: first B and D, and then C so that the twine lies straight between B and D.

- Stretch the 5-foot-long (1.5 m) piece of twine from stake C to stake A, and position stake A so that the twine is taut on all sides.

2 Position stake E so that all the twine is taut. And there it is, a perfect 3' × 15' (0.9 × 4.6 m) rectangle! Leave the twine in place, or use a sprinkling of flour or lime to outline the area marked by the string and remove the stakes and string.

▶ **Stake out.** *Measure out your lengths of twine and prepare your stakes before you go out in the garden.*

Digging a New Wide-Bed Garden

Wherever you live, preparing a new garden involves three things: dealing with whatever is already growing there (usually grass), loosening the soil that lies beneath whatever is growing there, and improving the soil by adding organic matter. You can do these things whenever you have the motivation and time to do it, but the best time for your new garden is in late summer or fall the year before you plan to plant.

FALL START-UP

Starting in fall means that you do your share of the work of soil improvement, but you also get a lot of volunteer help from worms and other creatures living in the soil. These little garden leprechauns will work through the colder months and digest a lot of organic matter while simultaneously aerating and loosening the soil. This extra help provides a couple of added bonuses that save you work: You can leave the sod in the bed where it will decompose, rather than having to remove it, and you can add uncomposted or partly composted organic materials, such as chopped leaves, instead of completed compost.

SPRING START-UP

If you start a new bed in spring, on the other hand, there won't be time for your volunteer helpers to decompose the sod before you plant, so you'll have to remove it instead of turning it into the bed. Save the sod and add it to your compost pile, sandwiching it between layers of other organic matter, or compost it separately by stacking it in a pile, root-side up. The sod will take about a year to break down and turn into a rich brown compost. Then bring it back to the garden and turn it into the soil.

Begin by laying out the area you plan to dig, following the steps on page 27.

WHEN SPRING COMES . . .

If you dug your new bed in the fall, remove the mulch as soon as you can in the spring, so the soil can warm. As soon as the soil is dry enough to work, spread an inch (2.5 cm) or so of compost and work it into the soil with a garden fork. Try to accomplish this without walking in the bed.

Preparing New Garden Beds with a Rototiller

It's possible to use hand tools to dig a new garden, especially if you're an Olympic weight lifter or your garden is small, but I like to use a big rear-tine rototiller when I'm starting a large, new garden. Tilling, however it is accomplished, is a three-step process:

1. Cut the sod free and into small pieces that will be easy for soil organisms to break down.

2. Loosen and aerate the soil.

3. Mix the sod and other organic material evenly into the loosened soil.

Using a rototiller for this process is a lot less work than digging a big garden by hand, and the tiller does a better job of chopping sod and other organic matter into small pieces and distributing them throughout the top 9 inches (22.5 cm) or so of the soil. If I manage to schedule time for it, I like to prepare the ground in the fall, because that's when there are lots of leaves to till in.

Step-by-Step to a Simple Wide Bed

1 After selecting a good site and laying out the bed with stakes and string (see page 27), cut around the edges with a sharp spade or edging tool.

2 Holding your spade at a low angle to the ground, cut out blocks of soil about 12 inches (30cm) square. Peel the sod squares back with your spade.

3 If you're starting a garden in fall, simply turn the squares over and chop them into the soil with your spade. If you're starting in spring, lift the squares of sod, bang them against the tines of a garden fork to remove as much soil as possible, and put them in the compost pile.

FAST MULCH TIP

Leaves are particularly good for the garden because tree roots reach deep into the subsoil and absorb trace minerals, which then appear in the leaves. If you're planning to work leaves into your garden beds to enrich the soil, put them through a shredder or spread them on an area of lawn where you can mow them with a power mower to chop them up. You'll find it's easier to work them in, and they'll break down more quickly after you add them to the soil.

4 Loosen the soil deeply (see page 31) and work about 2 inches of well-rotted manure or compost into the soil.

Deeper Beds for Super-High Yields

A simple wide-bed garden will give you a very big advantage over a traditional row-style garden, because you're providing 5 to 10 times more uncompacted soil to your plants for root growth in the same amount of space. But with a little more work, you can get even greater increases in plant vigor and yield. Look again at the drawing of plant roots (page 11) that indicates the need for wider and deeper growing spaces. As you can see, roots can grow deeper than the 9 inches (22.5 cm) or so of soil that you loosen with a tiller. You can provide for this additional growing depth by working the soil either by double-digging or deep-forking. I prefer deep-forking, because double-digging involves a lot more work for no more gain.

GETTING TO THE BOTTOM OF THINGS

Loosening the soil farther down usually involves getting into a different kind of soil — subsoil, as distinct from topsoil. Although subsoil contains very little organic material and therefore few of the nutrients plants need most, it often contains various other nutrients (micronutrients) that plants need in smaller amounts, which are often not present in the topsoil. In addition, by loosening subsoil you can increase its capacity to receive and store water; this can become critical to plants' health during dry times. You initiate a process whereby plant roots and worms can enter the area much more easily and continue the loosening and aerating process. They will slowly improve the subsoil structure and build capillaries to connect it with the topsoil.

DOUBLE-DIGGING

Double-digging is often seen as the defining technique of Biodynamic/French Intensive gardening, as described by John Jeavons (see Further Reading on page 338). Its advantage is a very thorough loosening of the subsoil. The disadvantages are that it takes a lot of time and work; it also results in more mixing of soil layers than does broadforking. You'll need a spade and a garden fork to double-dig. Here's how to do it:

Dig a trench about the width of your spade and about a foot (30 cm) deep across the width of the bed, putting the soil you're removing in a wheelbarrow. (You'll need it at the far end of the bed.) Loosen the exposed subsoil. If compaction is not too severe, just insert the garden fork and pry downward on its handle. If the soil is really packed, break it up first with the spade and then work it with the fork. Now dig the top layer of soil from one side of the trench and put it on top of the loosened subsoil in the first trench. Continue to the end of the bed. Fill in the last trench with the soil from the wheelbarrow.

How Loosening Subsoil Benefits Your Plants

- Subsoil contains small amounts of certain nutrients (micronutrients) that aren't always available elsewhere.
- Subsoil can serve as a reservoir for moisture.
- Roots and worms can enter the area much more easily and continue the loosening and aerating process.

Four Ways to Get Deep Soil

Using a sturdy broadfork or deep spader. The long tines on these allow for deep penetration into the soil. To avoid compacting the soil with your feet, stand in the walkway, rather than in the bed, while using any kind of digging tool.

Using a garden fork. If you don't have a deep spader, you can get something of the same effect using a garden fork. Thrust the fork down into the soil as deep as you can get it, then rock it back and forth to loosen the subsoil.

Raising the level of the bed. Although this doesn't loosen the subsoil of the garden, it does provide more soil depth for plant roots to grow down into.

Double-digging. This labor-intensive method does loosen subsoil and incorporate nutrient-rich compost deep into the bed. But it also mixes up the natural layers of the soil, with potentially adverse effects on soil life.

Pile It On: Another Way to Add Depth

Loosening the subsoil with a garden fork (or deep spader) or by double-digging are two ways to get a deeper bed, but you can also provide more depth for root growth by adding topsoil to the bed. If your beds are bordered by lawn or you left grass walkways, this option involves importing some soil. If, however, you are building beds in the midst of a larger area of prepared soil, the material you need, fully enriched and loosened, is already there in what will become the walkways between the beds. It would be a shame to waste this beautiful stuff growing weeds that you'll later have to grub out of the walkways, when all you have to do is rake or shovel it out of the walkway area and over the beds!

Because there is less area in walkways than in beds, and because you won't be taking all the topsoil in the walkways, bed depth will probably increase no more than 3 or 4 inches (7.5 to 10 cm), but even this is enough space for a lot of root growth. Just watch what happens when you plant carrots in a bed with this much more topsoil. The extra vigor and growth they exhibit will amaze you. Beds made this way will keep their shape without support if the sides have a gentle slope.

After the area is tilled, rake it smooth and then follow the steps on page 27 to outline each bed. Leave about 1½ feet (45 cm) for the walkways between each bed.

▼ **Better garden beds equal better gardens.** *The plants below are growing in wide, deep, raised beds. With room for their roots to grow, these vegetables are amazingly vigorous and healthy.*

Raising the Bed Level

1 Standing on one side of the bed, shovel 4 or 5 inches (10 to 12.5 cm) of topsoil from the walkway and put it on the bed. Work down the length of the bed, then move to the opposite side and repeat the process. Remove the guide string when the bed is shaped.

2 Rake the top of the bed as level as possible, then use the back side of the rake to smooth the length of the bed.

3 If you didn't add compost or manure when you tilled the area, spread 1 or 2 inches (2.5 to 5 cm) over the bed now and work it in as you smooth. This is also a good time to add other soil amendments, such as greensand.

4 To make your walkways carefree, cover them with three to six layers of newspaper, followed by a layer of clean, seed-free straw or hay. (Don't use the glossy, colored sections of the paper. The other parts are okay because the inks used are soy-based.)

Supporting Your Raised Beds

Deep-digging methods give you about 18 inches (45 cm) of cultivated soil. If you bring in more soil, you'll probably need to provide some support for it, such as boards, timbers, or cement blocks. This step involves a substantial increase in time, labor, and probably money, but the result is neat-looking beds. Supported raised beds are especially appropriate if your beds are in a lawn or you have limited garden space.

A supported raised bed is surrounded by a retaining structure about 8 to 12 inches (20 to 30 cm) high, of sufficient strength to hold that amount of soil. You can use wood — anything from boards or planks to timbers or even logs — as well as stones, bricks, or cement blocks. (See the box on page 36 for the advantages and disadvantages of other materials.) The photos here show how to build a raised bed supported by boards.

▲ Pack it in. *This 4' × 12' (1.2 × 3.7 m) raised bed made of spruce boards provides a good quantity and impressive variety of crops for a small family. As shown, it offers celery, cabbages, cherry tomatoes, and two kinds of peppers (Italian frying peppers and a handsome purple variety). Pink snapdragons add a spark of color.*

"Treated" Wood?

Wood rots. Some wood rots more slowly than other wood, but it all rots eventually, and it rots more quickly when it is wet and in contact with soil, which is what happens when you build supported garden beds with it. You can buy so-called "treated wood," which resists rot, meaning that it takes much longer to rot than untreated wood. Is it a good choice for garden beds? I don't think so. The "treatment" involved in treated wood consists of saturating it with poisons (chromium, copper, and arsenic), which stop rot by poisoning the organisms — soil-dwelling fungi and bacteria — that do the rotting. I don't want to poison soil-dwelling organisms, many of which improve the health of garden soil and have beneficial relationships with garden plants. Over time, more and more of those poisons will migrate from the treated wood to the surrounding soil. Over a long time (treated wood is supposed to last 40 years or so, not forever), all of that poison will end up in my garden soil, capable of killing off myriad soil microbes. Chromium, copper, and arsenic are also capable of poisoning human beings.

When I build supported raised beds I use either a fairly rot-resistant wood like cedar or plastic, cement blocks, or stone.

Creating a Raised Bed with Plank Sides

WHAT YOU'LL NEED

For sides
- Two 12-foot (3.7 m) pieces of 2" × 12" (5 × 30 cm) lumber

For ends
- Two 4-foot (1.2 m) pieces of 2" × 12" (5 × 30 cm) lumber

For stabilizers
- Two 3-foot, 9-inch (1.14 m) pieces of 2" × 2" (5 × 5 cm) lumber

For corner supports
- Four 1-foot (30 cm) pieces of 2" × 2" (5 × 5 cm) lumber
- 1 lb. (454 g) of 10d nails or 1 box of 3-inch (7.5 cm) galvanized deck screws

1 Screw or nail one end piece to one of the side pieces, butting the side piece against the end piece. Screw or nail the second side piece in the same manner. Repeat at the other end to create a box. Use three fasteners at each corner. Use a carpenter's angle to make sure that each corner is square.

2 Measure and mark 4-foot (3.7 m) intervals on each side for the placement of the two stabilizers. The stabilizers will be at the bottom of the raised bed when you put it in place.

3 Set one stabilizer so it is flush with the edge at each side. Screw or nail in place.

4 Set one of the corner supports at the inside of a corner. Screw or nail it in place from the outside, at both the end and the side. Repeat with the remaining corners.

(continued on next page)

5 Place the completed wood frame on your planting site. Sprinkle lime or flour around the outer edge of the frame to mark the area to be dug. (You can also mark the area with stakes and string.) Set the frame to one side.

6 Using a sharp garden spade, cut around a section of sod about 1 foot square (30 cm²). With the spade held at a very low angle to the ground (about 10°), cut into the marked section just beneath the root zone of the grass. Remove the sod and place it on a tarp. Continue to remove all the sod in the bed area.

SOME FACTS ABOUT RAISED-BED MATERIALS

Material	Advantages	Disadvantages
Planks (1½–2"; 4–5 cm, thick)	▪ Easy to handle	▪ Require support at corners and every 4 feet (1.2 m) or so ▪ Will rot
Timbers (4"×4" to 8"×8") (10×10 cm to 20×20 cm)	▪ Longer-lasting than planks ▪ Larger ones hold back soil even if partly rotted ▪ 6"×6" (15×15 cm) and larger don't need support ▪ Provide a place to sit while tending plants	▪ Expensive ▪ Will rot eventually ▪ Smaller sizes require support at corners
Logs	▪ Inexpensive if you already own some surplus trees and have a way to move them to the garden ▪ Lasts many seasons	▪ Cumbersome and heavy, especially the larger sizes
Cement blocks	▪ If leveled with some care, won't require additional support ▪ Retain heat, allowing soil to warm more quickly and stay warmer	▪ Most expensive ▪ Can be unattractive ▪ Not comfortable to sit on

7 Using a garden fork, loosen the soil about 8 inches (20 cm) deep over the entire bed. You don't need to turn over the soil; just rock the fork back and forth to break it up evenly over the entire bed.

8 Put the frame on the bed. Replace the sod *upside down,* breaking it up with a garden fork or spade as you lay it on.

9 Spread a layer about 1 inch (2.5 cm) deep of compost and/or well-composted manure into the loose sod. Work this into the surface with the garden fork.

10 Fill the frame with a mixture of good topsoil and more compost. You'll probably want to bring the soil to within 1 to 2 inches (2.5 to 5 cm) of the top of the frame.

11 Rake the area, breaking up any clumps as you go. Allow the bed to settle for a week before planting.

CHAPTER 2

Planning Your Garden, Growing Your Plan

I<small>T'S LATE IN DECEMBER.</small> The temperature is way below freezing; the days are short and seldom sunny. Today, summer seems more a dream than a memory, and the garden beds are just humps in the blanket of snow. I'm bundled to the ears, trudging through drifts to get the mail. I open the box, and there it is. The first seed catalog!

For me, that shivering movement in front of the mailbox is the beginning of the end of winter. Spring is still a long way ahead, and there will be many days yet just as cold and snowy as this one. But from here on in, I'm no longer moving further away from last year's garden; I'm moving closer to next year's garden. We'll begin the journey tonight, in front of the fire, with this first seed catalog and a big sheet of paper titled, "Garden Plan."

Selecting Savory Seed Catalogs

Open the January issue of any popular gardening magazine and turn to the section where all the seed companies are listed. Page after page after page! And dozens of seed company ads. How are you ever going to winnow that list down to the half-dozen or so you'll actually end up doing business with? This is how I've gone about it.

STICK PRETTY CLOSE TO HOME

Most of my longtime favorite seed companies are based in the northeastern part of the country, which is also where I live and garden. That's no accident.

Although a seed company may or may not have grown its seeds in the same area the company is located, it usually carries only seeds that will grow well in that region. Most of the companies I trade with maintain trial gardens to ensure this.

Some vegetable varieties grow well almost anywhere, but others do well only in particular climates. I have the best chance of getting varieties that grow well in my garden if they have been tested in gardens with a similar climate.

▲ It's not just about selling seeds. *My favorite seed catalogs are full of the information I need for a successful garden.*

SOME KERNELS OF WISDOM WITH YOUR KERNELS OF CORN

Just as I'll patronize a store where the salespeople know their products and can help me make informed decisions, I'll buy from seed companies whose catalogs give me the facts I need to choose seeds and plants wisely and the cultural information I need to ensure a successful harvest. In this regard, there are some very big differences among catalogs.

In one catalog a typical bush bean description says the beans are tasty and tender and that the seeds should be planted after the last frost because they need to grow in warm soil. That's all.

A second catalog sells the same variety of bush bean but with a whole lot more useful information as a bonus. The bean is described as somewhat more tender than a currently popular variety, tasty when used fresh, but not very good for canning or freezing. I also get germination temperature, pH preference, disease resistance, and a definition of "warm soil" as being at least 60°F (16°C). As I flip through the pages, I notice that I also get cultural information, such as a plant's soil fertility needs, its ability to tolerate heat or cold, harvest and storage hints, and whether that plant will grow well in a container.

The second catalog makes it much easier for me to choose among bean varieties and helps me succeed with whatever I decide to plant. My favorite seed catalogs really have a place among my favorite garden books. I refer to them often for information on planting, growing, harvesting, and pest and disease control. I patronize seed companies whose catalogs help me garden, even if the seeds cost more; I'm willing to pay my share of the extra costs involved in producing a really useful catalog.

THE PRICE IS RIGHT

I won't choose one seed company over another because of 5- or 10-cent price differences. But all other considerations being equal, when one company charges $1.80 and another charges $.80 for the same size packet, I'm likely to patronize the latter.

Some seed houses offer smaller packets of seeds for similarly smaller prices. That's not much help when I'm buying carrot or radish seeds because I usually plant all I get in a standard packet. But I use only two or three of the 20 or 30 seeds in a standard packet of any summer squash. If I can buy small packets, I can then afford to buy several different varieties. Similarly, I much prefer being able to get a half-dozen small packets of different tomato varieties rather than a single, large pack of just one kind.

The Safe Seed Pledge

Many of the vegetables listed in catalogs are *hybrid* plants — a new tomato, for example is created by cross-pollinating two different kinds of tomato (see page 42 for more information). Contrast this with what are known as *genetically modified organisms* (GMOs) — these plants are created by inserting unrelated genetic material into a plant. For example, some varieties of corn have been modified to contain genes from the bacterium *Bacillus thuringiensis* in order to make the corn more pest-resistant.

The debate about GMO safety is ongoing, but many people are concerned enough to avoid them entirely. The Council for Responsible Genetics has created a Safe Seed Pledge, which some seed companies take, agreeing not to buy or sell genetically modified seeds or plants. I buy only from seed companies that have signed the Safe Seed Pledge.

SUPPORT DIVERSITY

In a few instances these rules don't apply. I will go on trading indefinitely with some companies for other reasons. For example, sometimes a particular seed company is my only source of a favorite variety. In another instance a company may have very large selections of vegetables I like to experiment with, like lettuces, tomatoes, or beans. Then there are some small companies that carry hard-to-find varieties. One such company I buy from every year sells local heirloom varieties. Another caters to short-season gardeners with a wide selection of early varieties. There are also some interesting companies that specialize in preserving not just heirloom but historic varieties. I like to send at least some business to these companies every year, just so they'll be there when I need them.

▲ **These take the prize.** *The catalog said, "These beans are surefire blue-ribbon winners." A bit of hyperbole, perhaps? Not this time; ours actually did win First Prize at the Tunbridge World's Fair.*

Seed Catalogs as Garden Tools

A tool is anything that helps you accomplish a task or purpose. By that definition, a good seed catalog can be a very useful garden tool to help you decide which crops and varieties to grow in the garden. But having a good tool is only half the battle; you also have to know how to use it. Here's a sample catalog entry for Big Beef tomatoes, and here's how to use it.

F1 VERSUS OP

The varieties in seed catalogs are commonly of two types: F1 hybrids or open-pollinated (OP).

Open-pollinated varieties. These varieties are genetically stable, which means that seed collected from OP plants will produce offspring essentially the same as the parents. Open-pollinated varieties, which include heirlooms — old-time varieties — often taste better and may be better suited to particular growing conditions.

If you want to save seeds or if you are concerned about keeping heirloom varieties available, choose open-pollinated seeds.

F1 varieties. These first-generation hybrids are offspring from two genetically pure parents. Hybrids often outproduce open-pollinated varieties and are generally more resistant to disease. The downside is that these fine qualities last only one generation. Seeds collected from F1 hybrids usually produce weak, inferior plants.

CRACKING THE CODES

Along with straightforward descriptions of each vegetable variety, you'll often find a lot of information contained in icons or enclosed in tables. For instance, instead of mentioning cold tolerance, a catalog might use a snowflake icon, or a flowerpot icon to identify a good container plant. The All-America Selections (AAS) Winner identifies varieties that have been recognized for superior qualities by this nonprofit gardening organization. Look for keys to this information in both the catalog general introduction and the introductions to each catalog section.

SAMPLE CATALOG ENTRY

Big Beef (F1): 73 days
(AS, F2, L, N, TMV, V)

A beefsteak-type tomato with meaty, tasty fruit and an old-time tomato flavor. Early maturity and superior disease tolerance. Large (avg. 8–10 oz.; 0.2–0.3 kg), mostly blemish-free globe-shaped red fruit. Produces well, even under adverse conditions. Indeterminate. Organically grown seeds.

PKT $2.20; 1/16 oz. $9.90

WEATHER TOLERANCE

This category includes things such as cold tolerance or resistance to flowering (bolting) in hot weather. If your growing season is relatively short, choose a cold-tolerant tomato variety such as Oregon Spring or Valley Girl. You can have lettuce salads further into the summer if you choose a bolt-resistant variety like Deer Tongue or Buttercrunch.

DAYS TO MATURITY

The number listed as "days to maturity" tells how long it takes from sowing the seed to harvest. For some long-season crops that are started indoors, this number is calculated from transplanting rather than sowing. Be sure you know to which starting point the catalog is referring.

Days-to-maturity numbers can be very helpful estimates when you are planning your planting and harvesting schedules. They are especially important for gardeners like me who live in an area with a short growing season. A variety that takes longer to mature than the number of frost-free days I'm likely to have is probably not a good choice for my garden.

You'll find variations in maturity dates from catalog to catalog, due to differences in growing season, soil fertility, and other conditions where they were tested. Likewise, after you've gardened for a few years, you'll notice that maturity times in your garden may differ from those in the catalogs; in fact, maturity times in your garden will vary from year to year. The moral of the story? Days to maturity is an educated guess about what is likely to happen most years in most gardens, but it's not a guarantee of a certain outcome; it's most useful when comparing different varieties in the same catalog. You may not know for sure how long Sugar Buns sweet corn (70 to 80 days) takes to ripen, but you can be sure that it will ripen quite a bit sooner than Silver Queen (88 days).

DISEASE RESISTANCE

Disease resistance may be mentioned in the variety description or identified by means of letters or numbers. (The code may appear in the general catalog introduction or at the beginning of each catalog section.) The code letters here indicate that Big Boy tomato plants are resistant to verticillium wilt (V), fusarium wilt (races 1 and 2 [F2]), nematodes (N), tobacco mosaic virus (TMV), alternaria stem canker (AS), grey leaf spot (L). After you've narrowed your planting list by using qualities such as flavor, whittle it down more by including only those varieties with resistance to diseases they're likely to encounter in your gardening area. (Your gardening neighbors and your own experience will guide you here.)

ORGANICALLY GROWN SEEDS

When I have the option, I choose organically grown seeds even if they cost more. (They usually do.) I don't know whether organically grown seeds produce better plants, although I suspect they might because their parents were plants that could grow well without chemical fertilizers and pesticides. What I do know, though, is that organic growing methods build and improve agricultural soils rather than deplete and degrade them. Choosing organically grown seeds is one way to support an agricultural ethic I believe in.

DESCRIPTION

I've found that reading seed catalogs is a little like reading used-car ads: What is not said is sometimes more important than what is said. Up here in snow and road-salt country, if a car is free of rust, the ad will say so. If it doesn't say so, the car is very likely rusty. With this in mind, I look for what isn't said when I'm trying to decide on this year's varieties. If I need a bean that freezes well and the description doesn't mention this, then I assume it doesn't freeze well. When I'm choosing tomatoes, flavor is my prime concern, so I like it when flavor is the first thing mentioned, not an afterthought. What I avoid is a variety that brags about color, firmness, yield, size, freedom from blemishes, or ability to ship well. These are all important qualities to commercial growers who need to ship their produce and sell it to a fussy public, but they're not of much interest to me. All I have to worry about is getting my tomato from the garden to the table, so I look for flavor first. Keep in mind, though, that catalog descriptions (like ripe tomatoes) are best taken with a grain of salt.

Deciding What to Plant

Okay, time to get serious. I can't order every variety in every catalog. Like a kid in a candy store, I've got to make some choices. What to plant? That question really has two parts, one hidden behind the other: What vegetables will I grow? And what varieties of those vegetables will I grow? Here's how I figure out what goes in the garden each year.

GROW WHAT YOU'LL EAT

This one is deceptively simple. I often find that I'm violating this rule while appearing to follow it. We may, for instance, eat some of everything we grow, but not all of everything we grow. Any food that ends up in the compost pile instead of on the table is a waste of precious garden space and gardening effort.

The beet goes on. Until a few years ago, we always grew quite a few beets, mostly varieties that stored well in the root cellar, but we used only about a tenth of what we'd stored; the rest went to the compost

▲ **Lock out.** *It's said that in some towns August is the only time folks lock their car doors . . . to keep over-blessed gardeners from dumping extra zucchini in them.*

pile in spring. We finally accepted that beets are not a favorite winter food for us. On the other hand, we do like beets during the summer but we were growing too few of varieties that taste best harvested young. We replaced the large planting of storage beets with small succession plantings of summer beets — varieties that are especially good when eaten young and fresh, often with their greens. Now we eat the beets we grow.

The ever-prolific zucchini. We learned another lesson from zucchini. We always grew three or four zucchini plants each year. You know the rest of that story. We ate zucchini. We froze zucchini. We pickled zucchini. When we couldn't eat or freeze or pickle any more, the chickens and the turkeys ate zucchini. And when we and the birds had all had our fill, the plants went right on producing yet more zucchini. Now I grow one zucchini plant each year. That satisfies all our needs. The garden space we've saved is now planted to other summer squash, maybe to some variety we've never tried before. We gardeners too often grow certain vegetables in certain amounts just because that's the way we've always done it, or the way our parents did it, or our neighbors. By making sure we grow what we really like to eat, in amounts that we really will eat, we increase the useful yield of our gardens with no additional effort.

GROW WHAT YOU CAN'T BUY

I can buy Russet or Kennebec potatoes at the grocery store or farmers' market, but can I buy French Fingerling or Russian Banana? Probably not. But I can grow them. I can buy corn, cantaloupes, and lettuce at the store, but I can't buy corn as fresh, cantaloupes as perfectly ripe, or lettuce of as many kinds, colors, and flavors.

GROW WHAT SAVES YOU MONEY

I can buy garlic at the store, but only if I've remembered to stuff my wallet well before leaving home. Now that I'm raising enough garlic to save some for seed, it costs me nothing but the labor of growing it.

GROW WHAT THE NEIGHBORS GROW

The growing conditions most like those in your garden are likely to be the growing conditions in your neighbors' gardens. If it works for them, there's a pretty good chance it will work for you. Most of our neighbors swear by Jet Star tomatoes, and all the local nurseries have a large number in stock. Sure enough, Jet Star has come to be our favorite too — the one variety we can always count on regardless of what Mother Nature sends our way.

TRY SOMETHING NEW

Like many gardeners, I'm a creature of habit. Sometimes this is good, but when routine becomes a rut, it's a good idea to give yourself a boot and try something new. Fortunately, trying something new in the garden has never been easier. Each spring I find vegetables in the seed catalogs that I've never heard of before, such as edamame, cardoons, scorzonera, or vegetable amaranth. Or new and colorful varieties of old favorites: purple cauliflower, purple peppers and purple carrots; white eggplants and squash; green-striped tomatoes; and bright red turnips. A few years ago, vegetables from Europe, Japan, and Africa weren't available in North America. They are now, and each year brings more. And there are more and more varieties of tomatoes, sweet corn, and peppers. Twenty years ago the catalogs and area garden centers carried less than half a dozen tomato varieties. Today my favorite seed catalog lists 40 tomato varieties, and another catalog lists well over 300! Even the local garden center grows two dozen varieties, including some heirlooms. It's not hard to find something new to grow in the garden every year.

I don't try every new variety that comes down the pike, but I do grow at least one or two new varieties and one or two new vegetables each year. I have to remind myself not to fall in love with a new variety right away. I grow it in the garden for a year or two and see how well it performs. If I like it, then I grow more of it the next season.

▲ **New kids on the block.** *With all the colorful varieties available, why stick to the same ones you're familiar with? Give these a go: Graffiti cauliflower, multicolored carrots, and red-veined sorrel.*

Time to Plan Is Time Well Spent

The robins are singing! Spring is here! The garden beds are all ready. I have all my seeds. Time to get going! It's very tempting to pull on a pair of boots, grab a trowel or a hoe, and starting planting. And sometimes that's just what I do. A garden planned as a by-product of spring fever often works out fine. But sometimes it doesn't. Spring is not an easy time to be patient, but a bit of patient planning can make the rest of the garden season much more productive and much more fun.

Part of this planning involves figuring out which crops benefit from (or really don't benefit from) following other kinds of vegetables in the garden (see Rotation Guidelines, opposite). Another important consideration is siting plants next to garden partners who won't shade them out or compete too much for nutrients. Giving plants plenty of room to grow and amiable neighbors will help them flourish and produce a bountiful harvest.

Let the Sun Shine In... Most of the Time

Most of the plants in the garden do best with at least six hours a day of full sun, some even more. To make best use of the sun, I put tall plants like corn and trellised tomatoes, beans, and peas toward the northern side of the garden. You'll notice that your garden gets the most sun at about the time of the summer solstice. In fact, at 10 a.m. in mid-June a 6-foot (1.8 m) pole placed in the middle of one bed will barely cast a shadow to the center of the next bed. But the sun's angle gets progressively steeper as the summer wears on, and tall crops can sometimes produce enough shade to hurt their neighbors. It can be even more of a problem if your garden is already shady for a significant part of the day. It's best to keep tall plants on the northern side.

▼ **Move to the rear, please.** *I keep trellised plants and corn on the north side of the garden so that these tall crops don't shade lower-growing vegetables.*

Crop Rotation: Musical Chairs in the Garden

When I make garden plans each year, I check my records of the past few years and make sure I don't plant any crop, or even one of the same family (for plant families, see the chart on page 336), in the same place two years in a row. Any break in the cycle is good, and longer breaks are even better. Two or three years between similar crops are better than one, and it may take five or even seven years to starve out a disease like clubroot. Crop rotation is standard practice for farmers, but the technique is equally important and beneficial for home gardeners, for both soil nutrition and for pest and disease control.

BEEF UP THAT SOIL: ROTATION AND NUTRITION

Each kind of plant takes from the soil a particular combination of nutrients in particular amounts. The same crop, grown in the same spot year after year, uses up some of those nutrients, and even the best soil-maintenance practices won't always restore all the nutrients to the levels that crop requires. The longer they grow in the same spot, the more the condition of the soil worsens and the greater the resulting stress on the plants. Depleted soil equals defeated plants.

HIDE-AND-SEEK: ROTATION TO AVOID DISEASE OR PESTS

Many pests winter in the soil as eggs or larvae. When they emerge in spring, they would like to find their favorite food growing nearby. No need to cruise around for burgers when the friendly gardener dependably provides those burgers when and where they're needed. If the food isn't there, the bugs have to roam around to find out where it is. The farther a hungry bug has to go in search of a proper meal, the less likely it is to find it and the more likely it is to become a meal itself for some bug predator.

Soilborne diseases, too, can stay dormant over the winter and even for many years, but most cannot survive for long if the plants they thrive upon have left the neighborhood.

The Case of the Cucumber Beetles

The mystery of the cucumber beetles began a while back when a friend asked me what to do about a major striped cucumber beetle infestation in his winter squash. He had been adding compost and rotted manure to the soil for years and had enviable results with most crops but not winter squash. In the course of discussion, he mentioned that, although he'd moved other crops around the garden from year to year, the squash patch, in a handy spot at one edge of the garden, had been in the same place for over 20 years. Bingo! That was making it all too easy for the cucumber beetles to build up their populations and devastate the squash. The solution? Rotate the squash. Case closed. (No, that didn't eliminate *all* the cucumber beetles, but it did reduce their population and make the remaining problem a lot easier to deal with.)

ROTATION GUIDELINES

- Follow heavy-feeding plants with light feeders.

- Put deep-rooted vegetables where shallow-rooted plants previously grew.

- Avoid rotating plants of the same family within the same bed. (They tend to have similar nutritional needs and are often prey to the same pests and diseases.)

TWO SAMPLE ROTATIONS

On paper a rotation plan could have different plants moving from one bed to the next around the garden until they arrived back at their starting point. In a real garden with real plants it's not that easy, especially if you combine companion planting and rotation, as I do. For instance, real-life crop rotation may find onions and radishes appearing just about anywhere.

When you begin to plan a rotation scheme, one of the first things you realize is that not all the beds in a garden are really available to all the plants. If I put the corn or the trellis-grown tomatoes, peas, and beans along the southern edge of the garden, the plants in the next few beds would have to grow in the shade for a good part of the day. Some of them would find this acceptable, but most would not. It's

good planning to restrict all the tall plants and those growing on trellises to the northern and northeastern sides of the garden, as much as possible. The way I manage this is to have two rotations, one for low-growing plants and one for sun blockers.

The sun-blocker rotation includes corn, as well as the plants I grow on a trellis or poles (tomatoes and beans or peas). I also include squashes and squash family crops here. Although I often grow the cucumbers on trellises, the other squash relatives aren't particularly tall. These squashes tend to spread, however, so I usually plant them along the northern and eastern edges of the garden, the same area where the sun blockers live. I don't have to worry about related plants following one another, since none of these plants is in the same family.

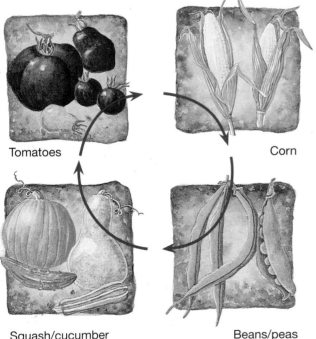

Tomatoes

Corn

Squash/cucumber

Beans/peas

▲ A sun-blocker rotation. *Trellised tomatoes, beans, peas, and cucumbers, along with corn, can grow 8 to 10 feet (2.4 to 3 m) tall. To avoid these taller plantings casting shade on other crops, I keep these in one rotation on the northeastern side of the garden.*

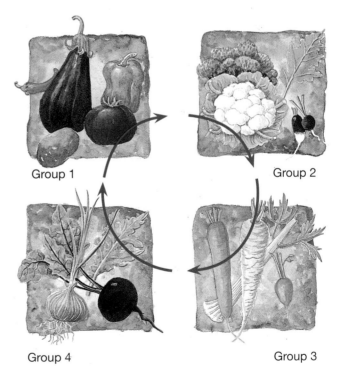

Group 1

Group 2

Group 4

Group 3

▲ A low-grower rotation. *This scheme groups family members to make the rotations. Group 1 consists of potatoes, peppers, eggplants, and/ or determinate tomatoes. Group 2 is any member of the cabbage family. Group 3 is the carrot family, including carrots, parsnips, and celery. Group 4 covers everything else.*

SUCCESS WITH SUCCESSION PLANTING

Spring is often called the "planting season," but it's a mistake to think of spring as the only season when planting can happen. By midsummer, a spring-planted garden is full of holes where short-season crops have ripened and been harvested. That's a lot of wasted space and wasted productivity. There's a way to fill those empty spaces: it's called succession planting. Make sure that all the space in your garden is growing something all the time. Whenever a hole appears, fill it with something that will mature and be ready to harvest in whatever time is left in the garden year.

SUCCESSION PLANTING GROUND RULES

- **Do** refresh the soil by spreading a layer of compost and working it into the soil with a rake.

- **Don't** plant the same crop (or one of the same family) in the same place more than once a season.

OPPORTUNISTIC SUCCESSION PLANTING

In our garden, a lot of succession planting happens without a whole lot of planning. Whenever we harvest some spinach for salad, we thereby create a small hole in the garden to be filled with radishes, lettuce, or perhaps arugula.

We've learned that some natural successions are quite reliable. For instance, where we are, in Zone 4, garlic planted the previous fall is ready for harvest in late July. We replace it with lettuce, spinach, radicchio, or Chinese cabbage, all of which can be sown in July and harvested in the fall. Similarly, early lettuce and spinach crops occupy the space that will be filled later by storage crops of carrots and beets. Bush beans are succeeded by sowings of kale for fall and early-winter harvest. And the peas are done producing just about the time we need space to plant strawberry runners.

Waste Not, Want Not: Using Green Manures

Whenever you have a space in your garden that you can't fill with a crop for the table, sow a crop "for the garden." Here are two ways to do this:

- **Peas.** If you have some leftover pea seeds, broadcast them over one of these unused spaces in the late-summer garden. Poke the seeds in with your finger where they fall. At the least, you have a nitrogen-fixing green-manure crop to till in or to harvest for the compost pile. At best you get all the preceding and a bunch of tasty peas later in the fall.

- **Green manures.** Buckwheat, winter rye, and annual alfalfa are known as "green manures." Green manures add organic matter to the soil and increase its nutrient content. Before the green manure crop is killed by frost (or, in the case of buckwheat, just as it begins to flower), chop it into the soil with a sharp hoe or cut it down and add it to the compost pile.

▲ **Feeding time for the garden.** *Wait until buckwheat is just beginning to flower, and then turn it into the soil as green manure.*

Buddy System for Plants: Companion Planting

When I planted my garden in rows, it never occurred to me to plant more than one kind of vegetable in any row. That's just not the way it's done. But when I started planting in beds, it seemed reasonable to consider mixing different sorts of plants in a bed. I like the notion in a general way, because it's closer to the way things occur in the natural world. Nature tends to mix things up instead of planting big blocks of just one kind of plant.

Over the years that people have gardened, many gardeners have reported that there appears to be a synergistic relationship among certain plants. One or both of them appear to grow better, yield more, and sometimes even taste better when they grow near one another. These are often called "companion plants." In other cases, plant partnerships have negative effects — one plant inhibits another's growth.

Very little is known about why some of these relationships exist. It is clear, for instance, why carrots might benefit from having onions, leeks, rosemary, wormwood, or sage nearby: Carrot flies, whose larvae attack young carrot roots, may be repelled by the aromas these plants give off. But why do some gardeners report that carrots grow with tomatoes or lettuce to mutual benefit? Why do celery, parsnips, and dill seem to inhibit carrots? Nobody knows for certain, and most of the "evidence" is anecdotal. Consider all the advice, including the suggestions in this book, as a starting point, not gospel. Keep track of the results and compile your own list of garden companions.

SOME GARDEN FRIENDS AND ADVERSARIES		
Plant	**Garden Friend(s)**	**Garden Adversary(ies)**
Asparagus	Basil, nasturtium, parsley, tomato	Garlic, onion
Bean, bush	Beet, cabbage, carrot, cauliflower, celeriac, celery, chard, corn, cucumber, eggplant, leek, marigold, parsnip, pea, potato, radish, rosemary, strawberry, sunflower	Basil, fennel, kohlrabi, onion family
Bean, pole	Carrot, cauliflower, chard, corn, cucumber, eggplant, marigold, pea, potato, rosemary, strawberry	Basil, beet, cabbage, fennel, kohlrabi, onion family, radish, sunflower
Beet	Bush bean, cabbage family, corn, leek, lettuce, lima bean, onion, radish	Mustard, pole bean
Broccoli	Beet, bush bean, carrot, celery, chard, cucumber, dill, kale, lettuce, mint, nasturtium, onion family, oregano, potato, rosemary, sage, spinach, tomato	Lima, pole, and snap bean, strawberry
Brussels sprout	Beet, bush bean, carrot, celery, cucumber, lettuce, nasturtium, onion family, pea, potato, radish, spinach, tomato	Kohlrabi, pole bean, strawberry
Cabbage	Beet, bush bean, carrot, celery, cucumber, dill, kale, lettuce, mint, nasturtium, onion family, potato, rosemary, sage, spinach, thyme, tomato	Pole bean, strawberry
Cantaloupe	Corn	Potato
Carrot	Bean, Brussels sprouts, cabbage, chive, leaf lettuce, leek, onion, pea, pepper, red radish, rosemary, sage, tomato	Celery, dill, parsnip

\multicolumn{3}{c}{**SOME GARDEN FRIENDS AND ADVERSARIES**}
Plant	**Garden Friend(s)**	**Garden Adversary(ies)**
Cauliflower	Beet, bush bean, carrot, celery, cucumber, dill, kale, lettuce, mint, nasturtium, onion family, potato, rosemary, sage, spinach, tomato	Pole bean, strawberry
Celery	Bush bean, cabbage family (especially cauliflower), leek, parsley, pea, tomato	Carrot, parsnip
Corn	Beet, bush bean, cabbage, cantaloupe, cucumber, morning glory, parsley, pumpkin, squash	Tomato
Cucumber	Bush bean, cabbage family, corn, dill, eggplant, lettuce, nasturtium, pea, radish, sunflower, tomato	Potato, sage
Eggplant	Bush bean, pea, pepper, potato	None
Kale	Beet, bush bean, cabbage, celery, cucumber, lettuce, nasturtium, onion, potato, spinach, tomato	Pole bean
Kohlrabi	Beet, bush bean, celery, cucumber, lettuce, nasturtium, onion, potato, tomato	Pole bean
Leek	Beet, bush bean, carrot, celeriac, celery, onion, parsley, tomato	Bean, pea
Lettuce	Everything, but especially carrot, garlic, onion family, and radish	None
Lima bean	Beet, radish	None
Onion family	Beet, cabbage family, carrot, kohlrabi, leek, early lettuce, parsnip, pepper, spinach, strawberry, tomato, turnip	Asparagus, bean, pea, sage
Parsley	Asparagus, corn, tomato	None
Parsnip	Bush bean, garlic, onion, pea, pepper, potato, radish	Caraway, carrot, celery
Pea	Bean, carrot, celery, chicory, corn, cucumber, eggplant, parsley, radish, spinach, strawberry, sweet pepper, turnip	Onion family
Pepper	Carrot, eggplant, onion, parsnip, pea, tomato	Fennel, kohlrabi
Potato	Bush bean, cabbage family, corn, eggplant (as trap crop), marigold, parsnip, pea	Cucumber, pumpkin, raspberry, rutabaga, squash family, sunflower, tomato, turnip
Pumpkin	Corn, eggplant, nasturtium, radish	Potato
Radish	Bean, beet, cabbage family, carrot, chervil, corn, cucumber, leaf lettuce, melon, nasturtium, parsnip, pea, spinach, squash family, sweet potato, tomato	Hyssop
Rutabaga	Nasturtium, onion family, pea	Potato
Spinach	Cabbage family, celery, legumes, lettuce, onion, pea, radish, strawberry	Potato
Squash	Celeriac, celery, corn, dill, melon, nasturtium, onion, radish	Potato
Strawberry	Bean, borage, lettuce, onion, pea, spinach	Cabbage family
Tomato	Asparagus, basil, bee balm, bush bean, cabbage family, carrot, celery, chive, cucumber, garlic, head lettuce, marigold, mint, nasturtium, onion, parsley, pepper, pot marigold	Dill, fennel, pole bean, potato
Turnip	Onion family, pea	Potato

Giving Your Plants Elbow Room

The primary reason to garden in beds rather than in single rows is to provide plant roots with the room they need to grow, but wide, raised-bed planting also saves garden space. Many plants can be grown much closer together in beds than in rows, with the result that a bed-based garden can be much smaller than a row-based garden while still producing the same yield. (See the drawing on page 53.)

HOW TO DETERMINE PLANT SPACING

Most seed catalogs and seed packets give recommended spacing for seeds and transplants. But this spacing is based on planting in rows, since that's the method most gardeners have used in recent years. We lack data for making rules about spacing in wide beds. In addition, not all beds are equal. You can grow plants a lot closer together in a bed 5 feet (1.5 m) wide, 2 feet (0.6 m) deep, and full of compost-enriched soil than you can in a bed 2 feet (0.6 m) wide and 8 inches (20 cm) deep with a marginally fertile soil.

In part 3, as part of the cultural information for each vegetable, you'll find suggestions for spacing in beds. You may have to experiment to customize these recommendations for your own situation. The recommendations are good starting points if your beds are at least a couple of feet (60 cm) wide, deeply dug, and have at least 8 inches (20 cm) of topsoil with good nutrient balance and high organic-matter content. If you can't provide these conditions, space your plants a little farther apart. As you make your decisions, be sure to consider two important factors: how you're providing for your plants' access to sunlight and how much nutrients and moisture they'll receive.

- **Sunlight.** Garden plants need sunlight. It is what drives the life-sustaining process of photosynthesis. Plants can grow close enough so that their leaves barely touch, but no closer, lest they shade one another. When you plan spacing, you need to know how large an area the plant's foliage will occupy when mature.

- **Nutrients and moisture.** Plant roots do not compete for environmental resources the same way plant foliage does. Leaves cannot share space without shading one another, but roots can intermingle in their quest for nutrients. The limiting factor is not the size of plant root systems but the number of plants compared to the amount of nutrients available. Although at a certain point plant size will be restricted by lack of nutrients, you can compensate either by decreasing the number of competing plants or by increasing the supply of nutrients.

◄ Don't touch. *As these beets and broccoli plants grow, we thin them so that their leaves just touch but don't crowd each other. The onions are about ready to harvest as scallions.*

MAKING A GARDEN PLAN

A garden plan doesn't have to be complex. In fact, it probably shouldn't be, or it won't get done in the first place. These drawings show my kitchen garden first in early summer, and then later when the fast-growing crops are replaced by succession plantings. Each plant is identified at the right by a number.

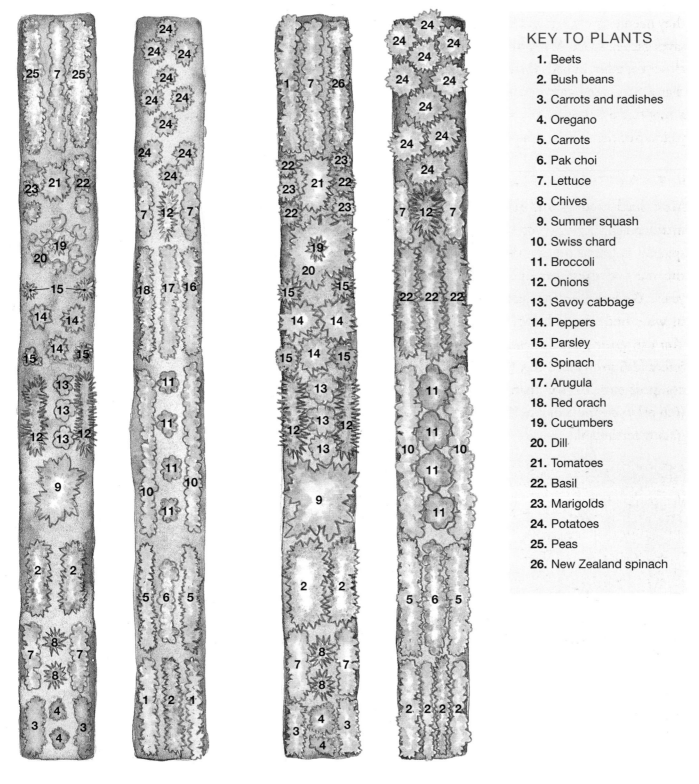

KEY TO PLANTS

1. Beets
2. Bush beans
3. Carrots and radishes
4. Oregano
5. Carrots
6. Pak choi
7. Lettuce
8. Chives
9. Summer squash
10. Swiss chard
11. Broccoli
12. Onions
13. Savoy cabbage
14. Peppers
15. Parsley
16. Spinach
17. Arugula
18. Red orach
19. Cucumbers
20. Dill
21. Tomatoes
22. Basil
23. Marigolds
24. Potatoes
25. Peas
26. New Zealand spinach

Early Summer

Late Summer

Plans for Small Gardens

Whether your garden is large or small, a garden plan is important to its success. The two commercially made raised beds pictured on page 17 are only 3' × 3' (0.9 × 0.9 m), but with a plan for succession planting, they can provide a steady supply of good-tasting vegetables from spring through late fall. Not only that, but the herbs and flowers look great!

You could adapt the plans shown here to grow the vegetables you and your family like most. Instead of celery, you might like to try more herbs, such as oregano and dill. Herbs make great fillers in a small garden like this. You could even use them instead of the flowers. In summer, plant New Zealand spinach or eggplant instead of some, or all, of the peppers. Be sure to plant tomatoes, or any other tall-growing crop, on the north side of the garden so that they don't cast shade on the other plants.

You can either stake the tomatoes or use a trellis similar to the one on pages 78–79. It's especially easy to install trellises in a raised bed: Simply fasten the posts to the inner sides of the wooden bed with a metal strap. Remember to prune your tomatoes when they reach the top of their support so that they don't slouch over the other plants.

Garden Journal

Good books about gardening can be a big help. Along with general information about soil temperature, soil moisture, pH, air temperature, and day length, they often contain new ideas as well as inspiration that can add to the challenge and pleasure of gardening. But what may come to be your most helpful gardening book isn't available in any bookstore. It's the one you write yourself — your garden journal. This is the best possible garden book because it's all about your garden and how your garden is unique. A well-kept garden journal can be one of the best gardening tools you'll ever own.

Among the things I think worth noting in a garden journal are these:

- Soil and air temperature at particular times of the day, including daily maximums and minimums, and degrees of frost, if any

- Temperatures under row covers and beneath plastic mulches

- Weather, especially unusual occurrences such as heavy storms, extended droughts, or long periods of either very hot or very cool weather

- Watering record

- Planting or transplanting dates, germination dates, and harvest dates for each crop, including cover crops

- Starting and finishing dates for compost piles

- "Rogues' Gallery" — insect pests and/or diseases. What? When? How many bugs? How bad the disease? What did I do, and how well did it work?

- Harvest notes — How much? How plentiful?

- Soil maintenance and development —When and how much? Compost? Leaf mold? Rock powders? Other supplements?

KEY TO PLANTS

1. Spinach
2. Beets
3. Lettuce
4. Radishes
5. Celery
6. Garlic
7. Leeks
8. Parsley
9. Marigolds
10. Nasturtiums
11. Tomatoes
12. Peppers
13. Basil
14. Kale

Mid-May Garden

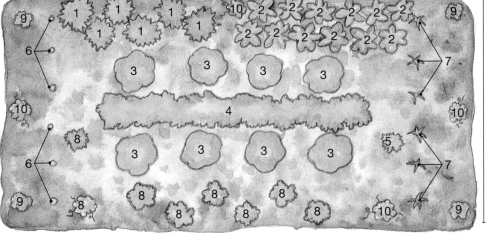

3' (0.9 m)

6' (1.8 m)

Mid-July Garden

Early September Garden

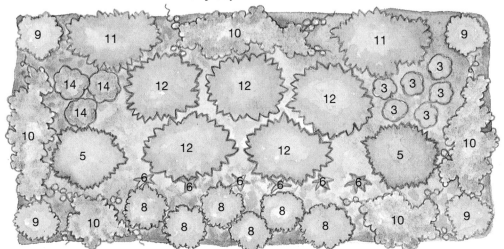

CHAPTER 3

Jump-Starting Your Garden

WHAT WILL END AS THE HARVEST STARTS with the seeds, and the seeds start out in one of three places: indoors, in the cold frame, or right in the garden.

Plants that need a long growing season — tomatoes, peppers, onions, celery, eggplant, melons, and winter squash — begin life on a sunny windowsill or in the greenhouse. These plants are joined by a few cabbage, broccoli, lettuce, and basil plants. They don't need a head start, but I start a few indoors anyway to get an early harvest.

The rest of the cabbage and broccoli, along with cauliflower and Brussels sprouts, are nursed along in the cold frame. When they're little, these plants can have a rough time competing with weeds and surviving attacks from leaf-loving pests. Once the plants are big enough to fend for themselves, I transplant them to the garden.

The remainder of the seeds, from corn to radishes, and beets to carrots, wait in the seed packet until conditions are just right, and then I sow them right in the garden.

Starting Seeds Indoors

Most seeds are easy to get along with and don't demand much from us. Wherever they start life, whether in a seed flat or sown in the garden, seeds have the best chance of becoming vigorous, productive plants if you give them what they need:

- A loose, disease-free planting mixture, kept evenly moist

- A complete, low-analysis fertilizer

- A seed-starting container with good drainage

- The appropriate amount of light

- The right germination temperature

For advice about soil temperature, planting depth, germination times, and so on, refer to specific vegetables in part 3.

GETTING THE PLANTING MIXTURE RIGHT

From the germination period until the first few true leaves emerge, the crops you're most likely to start indoors are very susceptible to diseases. Since most of these diseases are soilborne, the best way to keep young seedlings healthy is to use a pasteurized or sterilized soilless seed-starting mixture rather than garden soil.

Soilless mixtures typically contain about 40 percent milled sphagnum peat moss, 50 percent medium-grade vermiculite, and about 10 percent horticultural-grade perlite. The finished mix is fine and light, and it holds moisture well. Many soilless mixtures also contain fertilizer or compost, which gives the seedlings a boost that lasts for a few weeks. If your mix doesn't contain this nutrient charge, fertilize the seedlings once their first true leaves have emerged. I use fish emulsion or fish-and-seaweed liquid fertilizer at half strength once a week.

SEED-STARTING CONTAINERS

You'll find many kinds of seed-starting containers, including trays, trays segmented into cells, plastic pots, peat pots, clay pots, and soil blocks. The good news is that you can't make a bad choice, as long as the container has drainage holes in the bottom. Some seem to work better than others, and over time I have acquired a favorite.

I like to use a compartmented foam seed-starting kit. Each seedling grows in a small Styrofoam cell, which protects against wide temperature fluctuations because it's well insulated. At the bottom of each cell is a large drainage hole that puts the growing medium in contact with a capillary mat (a feltlike cloth that absorbs water like a thin sponge). One end of the mat sits in a water-filled reservoir, so that the seedlings get a continuous supply of water from below, keeping them just-moist at all times. The whole thing is topped by a transparent plastic lid, creating a mini greenhouse, which also helps maintain proper temperature and moisture levels during germination and just after the plants emerge.

RENEW, REUSE, RECYCLE

The seed-starting kits I use, as well as other store-bought units, work well and are fun to use, but they're not your only option. Many, many tomato plants begin productive lives every year in cutoff milk cartons or foam cups. I've yet to find anything better for starting celery than the plastic trays that tofu comes in. Remember to poke drainage holes in the bottom of whatever container you use: "If the pot doesn't drain, the plant doesn't grow."

Sowing Seeds in Containers

1 Pour about 6 quarts (6 L) of soilless seed-starting mixture into a large waterproof container. Use warm water to make a mixture that is evenly moist but not soggy. Fill the seedling container with the soilless mixture.

2 Press the pegged stand gently but firmly into the planting compartments. This ensures that each compartment is filled to the bottom, so that the planting mixture contacts the capillary mat, which will wick a steady supply of moisture to it.

3 Sow two seeds in each cell and cover them lightly with the seed-starting mixture as recommended under specific vegetables in part 3.

4 Dip the capillary mat in water to wet it thoroughly. The mat will conduct an even, steady flow of water to the cells in the seed tray. Place the mat on top of the pegged stand. Fill the plastic-lined reservoir with warm (80°F; 27°C) water.

5 Set the seed tray on the pegged stand and cover it with the plastic lid. Place the seed tray atop a refrigerator or a radiator to keep it warm. Monitor both the planting mix and the surrounding air temperatures with soil and air thermometers.

CARING FOR SEEDLINGS

Light. After the seeds have germinated, they do best with 12 to 16 hours of light a day. When the seedlings are up, move the setup to a sunny window. On cold nights, protect them from drafts. If you don't have a sunny spot, rig up adjustable fluorescent lights about 3 inches (7.5 cm) above the tops of the plants.

Heat. Try to keep the temperature near the recommended optimum for the plant's growth.

Water. Make sure the planting mix never dries out. If you can't arrange bottom watering, use a watering can that provides a fine stream (see page 74) to avoid damaging the tender seedlings.

Fertilizer. Once a week, water your seedlings with a half-strength mixture of organic fertilizer.

Moving Your Plants Along

Shortly after the first set of true leaves appears (see True or False? in the box below), transplant tomatoes, peppers, and eggplant into 4-inch (10 cm) pots. Onions, celery, and lettuce can stay in the flats.

When I prepare the planting mix for these transplants, I use a combination of one-half soilless seed-starting mix and one-half compost. The stems and leaves of these plants grow quickly, and their roots grow even faster. Moving the plants into this larger growing space prevents the roots from becoming cramped, which can slow down or even stop growth. The larger pots also encourage the plants to produce sturdier stems. Because you've included compost in your potting mix, you shouldn't need to fertilize; just make sure the plants always have enough water and light.

True or False?

Seeds are a miracle of miniaturization. Each one contains all the bits and pieces of an entire plant. Of course, the seed doesn't look like a plant when we sow it. But even when the plant first emerges from the soil, we can't usually recognize what kind it is until it grows the kind of leaves we're familiar with — its true leaves.

Seedlings generally have two types of leaves. The first to appear we call seed leaves or cotyledons. After these, the first set of true leaves develops and expands above the seed leaves. For example, with broad-leaved vegetables such as beans or squash, the arched stem of the seedling emerges first, followed by a pair of thick seed leaves, often with the seed coat still attached, and finally the first pair of true leaves.

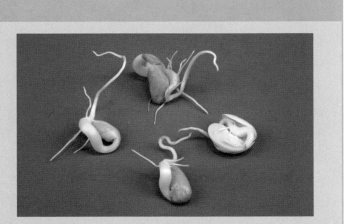

▲ Sprouting bean seeds

There are some exceptions to this pattern:

- **Peas.** When peas germinate, the seed leaves stay underground, so the first leaves you see are true leaves.

- **Narrow-leaved vegetables.** Some crops, such as corn and onions, produce only one seed leaf instead of two, and the seed leaf is very similar to the true leaf. The best way to tell if true leaves are emerging from narrow-leaved vegetable seedlings is to count the leaves. If there are two or more leaves on a seedling, then true leaves have formed. Corn and onions have another interesting complication: The true leaf forms beneath the seed leaf, rather than above it as in broad-leaved vegetables.

Seed leaves   "True" leaf

Transplanting Seedlings into Larger Containers

NEVER HANDLE A SEEDLING BY ITS STEM

Once damaged, a stem usually doesn't recover, and the plant may die. If you bruise or break a piece of leaf, on the other hand, the plant will survive.

Follow this method for safe handling: Cradle the rootball in your hand and steady the plant by gently holding a leaf between your fingers.

1 Mix together one part each of planting mix, compost, and garden soil and moisten well with warm water. It should be evenly moist but not soggy.

2 Fill 4-inch (10 cm) containers with the planting mixture. Use a trowel or other tool to make a hole in the center of the soil mix.

3 Loosen the seedling from the original container and lift the rootball gently into the prepared containers. I find that this job is best accomplished with a pair of kitchen spoons or forks. They work well and don't damage the seedlings or the roots. Press soil gently but firmly around the rootball. Water again to moisten thoroughly.

The Cold Hard Facts about Cold Frames

A cold frame is one of those tools I didn't know I needed until I got one. Now that I have one, I don't know how I got along without it.

This garden tool isn't complicated. It's just a box with no bottom and with a top that lets in light and can be opened or removed. Its purpose is to create a friendly environment outdoors where plants grow faster and healthier than in unprotected garden beds.

READY-MADE COLD FRAMES

My Juwel cold frame has held up very well for more than 10 years, and I use it all year long. At about 9 square feet (2.7 sq m), it isn't big. It's made of aluminum, which means that it's lightweight yet strong, and I can easily carry it around from one garden assignment to the next.

Both side and top panels are made of double-wall translucent polycarbonate. The sides of most cold frames are opaque, so plants receive light only through the top. But the Juwel frame's translucent sides allow more light inside the box, with the result that plants are stronger and stockier. The double-wall glazing reduces heat loss and cuts down on condensation.

A House of Straw for Your Garden

If you have four bales of hay or straw and an old storm window, you have the makings of a basic cold frame. Although this frame can't do all the things a more refined unit can, it works very well both for starting some of your seeds and for hardening off transplants in spring. You'll use it again in fall to provide frost protection for low-growing plants, so that you can keep some of the more cold-tolerant vegetables and herbs (hardy lettuce, kale, and parsley, for instance) growing late into fall.

Arrange four straw bales around a prepared seedbed, with the straw laid vertically. Be sure to overlap the ends with the sides, to avoid exposure at the corners.

Check to be sure your storm window will rest securely over the opening. Storm windows have glass, and it's easy to accidentally break the panes and end up with shards in your plants. To avoid such a mess, remove the glass and then cover the frame with 4 or 6 mil clear plastic and staple it in place.

Please note: If you suspect that a storm window contains lead-based putty or paint, it's best not to use it around food plants. Many of the storm windows old enough to be candidates for cold frame tops are also old enough to have lead-based paint and/or lead-based putty holding in the glass.

Starting Seeds in a Cold Frame

1 Seedlings will emerge faster and be healthier if you first supercharge the seedbed with some compost. Spread about an inch (2.5 cm) of compost on the soil and work it into the top 3 inches (7.5 cm) or so. This will help keep the soil loose and improve moisture retention as well as provide the nutrients the seedlings will need.

2 After seeds germinate, thin them to stand about 2 inches (5 cm) apart. Because the plants will still be fairly small when they leave the cold frame, you can grow them this close together and still leave enough room for them to develop healthy root systems.

AVOID FRIED SEEDLINGS!

Leave the cover off your cold frame when temperature permits, so that plants don't get too hot on sunny days and so that they get moisture when it rains.

Juwel cold frame

3 Monitor the temperature in the cold frame and open or close the top to keep temperatures within the range each crop prefers. An automatic vent opener is a real help here, especially if you are often away from home. Cold frames can easily overheat on sunny days, even in cold weather. Automatic opening devices require no electricity and operate using thermal energy.

A YEAR IN THE LIFE OF A COLD FRAME

Here's how we've learned to keep our cold frame in action all year long: When the garden is full of snow in late winter, our cold frame is full of delicious spinach. After growing these greens until spring, we use the cold frame to harden off tomatoes and peppers. In early summer it does the job of a mini greenhouse, boosting the growth of heat-loving peppers. Then, as the cold returns, it becomes home to late-fall lettuce and winter spinach.

Turn Winter into Summer: Greenhouse Growing

Late in March, with snow still hiding the grass, I raise the top on the cold frame — and everything is green. Deep green spinach, medium green kale, and light greens on lettuces and claytonia. Perhaps I can find a pill like the one Alice in Wonderland took, to shrink me down so I can spend the rest of the day in among the warmth and greenery and forget the winter for a while. Or failing that, perhaps I could find a cold frame big enough so I could fit inside. And that is what I did. Our solar greenhouse is a cold frame big enough for our whole family to fit inside among the beds full of salad greens. We spend hours there, puttering among the plants or just reading or playing cards, forgetful of winter, unmindful of the cold and barren snow. With such a greenhouse, the joys of vegetable gardening have expanded to fill the whole year.

A BIG GARDEN BED WITH A COVER

Rather than install tables in our greenhouse, we created an inground bed by deeply loosening the soil, then raising the soil from the walkway. Supported by wood sides, the U-shaped bed runs along both sides of the greenhouse and across the short end opposite the door. Down the middle, we constructed a simple walkway of 18-inch-square (45 cm) cast-concrete pavers.

Built from a kit, the greenhouse itself is an aluminum-framed shedlike design with walls and roof of double-wall resilient plastic. Anyone fairly handy with construction tools could build a suitable structure from scratch and cover it with greenhouse plastic. A good solar greenhouse handles heat well, both capturing and holding it and letting it go.

A YEAR-ROUND GARDEN TOOL

The greenhouse has its greatest impact during winter, keeping fresh greens on our table and smiles on our faces, but it's an important part of the garden every

▲ The heart of the garden. *Our greenhouse, with all of its potential, has changed the way we garden and also given us the chance to enjoy fresh produce throughout the year.*

◄ You don't have to be Alice. *Walking into our greenhouse on a snowy winter day, we're engulfed by the color and scents of summer.*

day of the year. It's great for starting heat-loving, cold-sensitive plants (tomatoes, peppers, basil, and squashes) that will later live in the outdoor garden. We sow them both in flats and right in the inground beds. We also use the greenhouse in spring and summer for these crops:

- **Cabbage family.** Cabbages and their kin stay in the greenhouse until they're big enough to survive the rigors of outdoor life.

- **Eggplant and basil.** Particularly fussy sorts like eggplants and basils, which do not like even short periods of cool temperatures, grow better in the greenhouse then they do outdoors.

- **Tomatoes.** We grow a few tomatoes inside the greenhouse all summer, so that we can have tomatoes even after the first fall frosts.

- **Spinach, claytonia, and winter lettuce.** Before the last tomato leaves the vine, the first seedlings of the winter garden emerge — spinach, claytonia, and all sorts of winter lettuces.

- **Garden transplants.** As the summer vegetables finish, we transplant lettuces, kale, and chard from outdoors and get the greenhouse ready to feed our bodies and spirits through late fall and winter.

But They'll Freeze!

In December, January, and February, night temperatures in our greenhouse dip well below 0°F (–17°C), and all the plants therein freeze solid. If we pick them while they're frozen, the result more closely resembles mush than salad. But if we wait until the sun has warmed the soil and thawed the leaves, we have a salad that has even more depth of taste than any in the summer can produce. The secret? Don't water the plants during the coldest months (mid-December to mid-March in our region). If there's too much water inside the plant cells, they freeze and burst, killing the plant.

▲ Winter salads. *Our fresh-picked winter salads from the greenhouse are even tastier than those we harvest from our summer garden.*

◄ Spring start-up. *The greenhouse is the perfect place to get seeds off to the right start. We start plants both in containers and directly in the ground.*

◄ Summer home. *Even in July and August, we keep some plants going inside the greenhouse. Here, we get an extra boost of heat for long-season melons.*

Just-Right Conditions for Sowing

You can sow many seeds directly in the garden, where they sprout and grow into vegetable plants. Even if the conditions are poor, some seeds usually come up. Yet for plants to be their strongest, the seeds they come from must germinate quickly and vigorously, and for that they need temperatures and moisture conditions to be just right. When the conditions in the garden match the requirements of the seed, it's time to sow. Refer to specific vegetables in part 3 for advice about the growing conditions for each crop.

KNOWING WHEN THE MOISTURE LEVEL'S RIGHT

Not only must soil temperature be right, the soil's moisture level must also be optimal for the best seed germination. Once temperature and moisture levels are reached, they must remain steady until the plants are well established. Proper moisture not only aids seed germination but helps protect the soil as we slice and dice it with hoes and trowels.

SOME LIKE IT HOT, SOME LIKE IT COLD

Many plants have definite soil temperature preferences. They'll germinate better and faster if they get what they need.

- **Spinach** takes about three weeks to germinate at 40°F (4°C) and only one week at 60°F (16°C).

- **Broccoli** takes about four weeks to germinate at 40°F (4°C), about three weeks at 50°F (10°C), and only one week at 70°F (21°C).

- **Peppers and eggplant** take about three weeks to germinate at 65°F (18°C), and they won't germinate at all below that temperature. They germinate best at 85° to 90°F (29° to 32°C).

- **Tomatoes, peppers, eggplant, onions, and leeks** like it hot. They can tolerate 75°F (24°C) but germinate and grow better above 80°F (27°C).

- **Most lettuce** varieties, which sprout and grow best in cool temperatures, won't germinate at all when the soil temperature is above 75°F (24°C), and germination is spotty above 65°F (18°C).

- **Most cool-season vegetables,** such as peas and radishes, really do like it cool. These plants do best if they start life around 65°F (18°C). Peas will germinate even in cooler soil, and most gardeners try to get at least some of the pea crop planted as soon as the soil can be worked. But peas germinate at a higher rate and faster in warmer soil; a later planting will usually catch up with an early planting, especially during cold, wet springs.

▶ Putting the squeeze on a soil wet test. *Take a handful of soil and squeeze it. If you squeeze out water, or if the soil compresses and stays that way when you loosen your grip and try to crumble the soil, it's too wet (A). If it just flows off your hand like talcum powder, it's too dry (B). Soil with proper moisture should compress and hold together but then crumble when worked gently between your fingers (C).*

JUST-RIGHT SOIL TEMPERATURES FOR GERMINATION

For each kind of seed, there is a "just-right" soil temperature for germination. When the soil is warmer or colder than that, fewer seeds germinate, and they take longer to do so. A long, slow germination subjects plants to severe stress right at the beginning of life. They don't grow as fast, and they aren't as able to cope with stresses like insects, fluctuations in temperature and moisture, and diseases like damping-off. If soil temperatures are way off the mark, none of this matters — the seeds probably won't germinate at all.

For the best germination and strongest seedlings, seeds need soil that not only starts out at the right temperature but also stays that way. One year, we planted the first batch of corn when the soil was 75°F (24°C). It stayed that way for a week, and the corn was up. At the end of that week, just before a cool snap, we planted another batch. The soil temperature suddenly dropped to 65°F (18°C), and the corn that eventually germinated took more than two weeks to come up.

Soil Thermometer

Mounted within a metal tube strong enough to withstand the rigors of being pushed into the soil repeatedly, this soil thermometer makes monitoring soil temperature easy. Push the thermometer 1 or 2 inches (2.5 to 5 cm) into the soil, and take a reading after the fluid stops moving, usually about a minute.

New-Fashioned Bed Warmers

To give seeds the warmth they need earlier than it occurs naturally, you can raise soil temperature by applying plastic mulch at least a week before you sow seeds or transplant. All plastic mulches are not created equal. They come in different colors, and each color differs in its ability to warm garden soil.

- **Clear plastic,** or builder's plastic, is inexpensive and warms soil very well. But because it allows all wavelengths of light to reach the soil, it also encourages weeds.

- **Black plastic mulch.** For years, this was the plastic of choice for heating up the soil while blocking weeds. It worked well and was quite inexpensive. It's still inexpensive, but now there are plastics that warm the soil even better.

- **IRT plastic mulch.** The initials stand for Infrared Transmitting. This brownish green plastic sheeting allows infrared light to pass through it to warm the soil, but blocks wavelengths of visible light that weeds need to grow. It warms the soil almost as well as clear plastic, though it costs a little more. IRT produces especially good results for melons but also works well for eggplant, corn, peppers, squash, and pumpkins.

Just-Right Temperatures for Growing

Once seeds have germinated, complications sometimes set in, because plants don't always grow best at the same soil temperatures at which they germinate best. And some actually prefer cooler growing temperatures than they need for germinating.

- **Cabbage and beans** grow best at 60° to 65°F (16° to 18°C), but cabbage germinates best at 85°F (29°C) and beans at 80°F (27°C).

- **Peppers** germinate best above 85°F (29°C) but grow best at 75°F (24°C).

- **Corn** germinates best at 80°F (27°C) but grows best below 75°F (24°C).

Most plants are pretty resilient and will sprout and survive even if you ignore these differences. They may even produce what looks like a decent crop. But they aren't as vigorous, healthy, or productive as they might be. For the biggest, best-tasting harvest as early as possible, provide your seeds and plants with the soil and air temperatures they prefer.

WARMING THEM UP . . .

When there is a wide gap between the ideal germination and growth temperatures of a plant, you can still give it what it needs. Here are two different ways you can accommodate a plant if the seedbed is at the right temperature for growth but too cool for optimum germination:

Indoor or cold frame environments. Start your plants indoors or in a cold frame, where proper germination temperatures can be more easily maintained. This works for many plants but is especially good for cabbage and peppers.

Plastic mulches and row covers. Warm the soil with plastic mulch before sowing, then use row covers to maintain proper temperature during germination. Let all the seedlings emerge, then remove the covers during the day. You can use a max-min thermometer (see the box on page 69) to determine whether night temperatures are dropping much below best growing temperatures.

▲ **Protected peppers.** *You can monitor and control both soil and air temperatures if you grow seedlings in a cold frame.*

▲ **A cozy situation.** *The seedlings in this mixed planting are protected from chilly nights, as well as insect pests, by a row cover that can be removed during the day.*

▲ **Summer coolers.** *Corn actually needs cooler temperatures when it's growing than when it's germinating. Applying a good mulch helps keep the soil cool.*

...OR COOLING THEM DOWN

If your challenge is a seedbed that is just right but growing conditions that are too warm, try the following:

Organic mulch. After the seedlings emerge, apply a thin layer of organic mulch to lower and moderate soil temperatures. Gradually increase the depth of the mulch as the plants grow. This works particularly well for corn.

GIVE JACK FROST THE COLD SHOULDER

After they emerge from the relative protection of the soil, plants must contend with the weather. If seeds are sown too early, the seedlings can be subjected to frosty mornings that they aren't prepared to deal with. Many of our favorite vegetable plants are either damaged or severely stressed by near-freezing temperatures. Many of these vegetables are the ones whose seed packets direct you to sow "after danger of frost has passed" (see box at the left).

Some plants are so sensitive to cool weather that they balk even at cool temperatures well above freezing. For some, 40°F (4°C) is too cool; for others, even 60°F (16°C) is chilly.

Your best tactic for managing these fussy plants is to monitor day and night temperatures with a max-min thermometer (see the box above) and delay sowing until temperatures are consistently within the preferred range for that crop. Sometimes patience is a gardener's best tool.

Providing the Cover-Up

You can give young, frost-sensitive plants some protection by covering them with floating fabric row covers or creating tents of plastic stretched over hoops. Row covers are pretty grand, and there is one for just about every purpose. Row covers can protect plants against insects as well as frost, or even create a mini greenhouse where you can grow things you otherwise have no business growing in your climate. Judicious use of row covers can make a big difference in how well you can provide for the needs of diverse garden plants. This, in turn, will make a difference in the size and quality of your harvest.

The most commonly used row covers are made of fabric. Reemay was the first of these covers, originally available in just one weight. Its success with gardeners has spawned a bunch of variations with different weights and subtly different applications. The lighter covers can rest right on top of most plants. If you use a heavier cover or your plants are delicate or pointy,

it's best to install supports for the cover. Garden suppliers sell hoops for this purpose, or you can make your own with ½-inch-diameter (1.3 cm), flexible PVC pipe, available at hardware stores.

As useful as row covers are, they can present some challenges all their own. Row covers need to be anchored so they don't blow away or tear in the wind. Yet they also need to be easily removed from the bed in order to weed or harvest plants. Although many experts have given a lot of advice on how to do this, I've never found a method that really worked and was practical. So I came up with one of my own that allows the row cover to be easily set in place and removed, even for one person. Once in place, the cover reliably stays put, even in windy weather. There's another benefit: The lengths of wood used to anchor the row covers also make them easy to store in winter.

ROW COVERS COMPARED			
Weight in oz./sq. yd. (gm/sq. m)	Light Transmission	Frost-Protection Value	Purpose
0.3 (6.7)	90%	Poor	Very effective control for cool-season vegetables (such as spinach and lettuce) against root maggots, flea beetles, leaf miners, aphids, thrips, and whiteflies without increase of temperature
0.5–0.6 (11–13)	85%	4°F (2.2°C)	Heats the soil, speeding up the growing season for heat lovers by two weeks or more
0.9 (20.2)	70%	4–6°F (2.2–3.3°C)	Primary use is for frost protection
1.5 (33.6)	50%	6°F (3.3°C)	A frost blanket; remove as soon as temperatures rise above freezing

Making Row Covers Manageable

1 Sandwich the long edges of the row cover between two thin slats of wood (such as lath). Use box nails to fasten the wood together and then turn the piece over and hammer down the protruding nail ends.

2 Set the supports in place. You'll need enough supports to place them about 3 or 4 feet (90 or 120 cm) apart along the length of the bed. Follow the manufacturer's instructions for purchased supports.

3 Lay one side of the row cover along one side of the bed, and then gently unroll the fabric and set the other side in place. Fasten the ends to the soil with U-shaped wires. When you need to tend the plants simply roll up the fabric around the wood strips.

OTHER PROTECTION AGAINST COLD WEATHER

If you have only a few, or scattered, plants, you may want to protect plants individually with "hot caps." Be sure to remove the hot caps before plants blossom: Tests show that yields are reduced if plants are not weaned from hot caps before blossom time.

◄ **For a homemade hot cap,** *cut the bottom off a plastic milk container and set this over the plant. Remove the cap on hot, sunny days.*

◄ **A very effective commercial hot cap** *is called Wall-O-Water, a teepee-shaped construction of plastic, water-filled cylinders. Here, it covers eggplant.*

Seeds: Putting Them in Their Place

In addition to its embryonic plant, each seed contains another important component. Within the seed is a small amount of stored energy, which the germinating plant uses to push through the soil into the sunlight. If the journey through the soil is too far because the seed was planted too deep, or too difficult because the soil is crusted or compacted, the little plant runs out of gas before it ever sees the light.

The smaller the seed, the smaller the embryonic plant and its energy reserves. And as a general rule, the smaller the seed, the closer to the surface the seed should be planted. To ensure vigorous seedlings and productive plants, follow the recommendations for planting depths for each vegetable in part 3.

When sown, most seeds should be covered with loose, compost-enriched soil to help keep the seeds moist and provide the darkness they need to germinate. The seeds of some plants, such as lettuce, are not only small but need light to germinate. Sow these seeds on the surface or cover them very lightly with screened compost or vermiculite. Avoid hoeing soil over the furrow, because it's hard to gauge how much soil ends up on top of the seeds. Be sure to keep the seedbed evenly moist until the seedlings emerge.

Seed-Sowing Tips

- **To plant large seeds,** like corn or beans, make the furrow a little less than the desired depth and push the seeds in level with the soil (A). This ensures that the seeds stay where you want them (for instance, sow beans with the "eye" down) and that they'll have good contact with the soil so they can absorb moisture quickly and evenly.

- **Plant peas in drills** by laying the seeds on the soil surface in the pattern you want and then poking each one in, to the first joint of your finger (B). Push soil gently into the holes and smooth it over.

- **To plant small seeds,** like carrots, roll them between your thumb and first two fingers. This makes spacing of the seed easier.

▲ **A.** *Planting beans in a furrow*

▲ **B.** *Planting peas in drills*

Sowing Seeds Outdoors

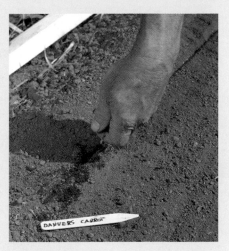

1 Use the back of a hoop rake to make the seedbed smooth and level. This makes it easier to place all the seeds at the same depth. Remove any pebbles or large bits of organic matter.

2 To make a furrow for sowing seeds, use a long piece of 1-inch (2.5 cm) square lumber. You can easily regulate depth and make a nice, straight row. Just lay the piece of wood along the bed where you want your row and gently press it into the soil to the desired depth.

3 After sowing, fill the furrow by dribbling a handful of soil into it, crumbling any lumps as you go. Gently pat the soil to make sure it contacts the seeds, but don't pack it down.

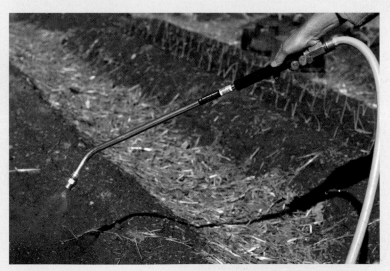

4 Label the row, so that you'll know what you planted and when you planted it.

5 Water the bed very gently, but evenly and thoroughly. Check the moisture daily and water again as necessary. The goal is to moisten the bed, not to make it soggy.

Bedtime for Young Seedlings

It's time to get the transplants you started indoors into the garden when the soil temperature meets their growing needs. Just as with sowing seeds, you can gain a bit of leeway here by using plastic mulch to warm the soil and row covers to warm the air. Transplanting on a cloudy day or in the evening will reduce transplant stress. If you must transplant on a windy day, cover plants with row covers after planting.

BEFORE YOU BEGIN

At least a week before you plan to transplant, prepare your planting bed and add any soil amendments. This will give the soil time to settle.

PLANTING DAY

Water the trays of seedlings thoroughly, and then let them stand for about an hour or until the planting mix is well drained. The mix should be moist enough to hold together, but not dripping. I like to water the plants the evening before I expect to plant. This ensures that the soil is moist and the seedlings are refreshed.

Hardening Off

At least a week before you plan to transplant your young crop outdoors in the garden, it's time to begin the process of "hardening off." This is like a little boot camp for vegetables. The plants learn to cope with direct sunlight, wind, and a wide range of temperatures. This is accomplished by exposing the plants to each one of these conditions, a little bit at first and then more and more as time goes on.

To harden off your seedlings, put them in a cold frame or shady spot in the yard for one hour the first day, then two hours the next day, and so on.

Tools for Transplanting

The only tools needed for transplanting are a trowel and watering can or hose.

- **Trowel.** Choose a trowel with a strong blade and shaft and a comfortable handle. You should be able to grasp it with either a "handshake" grip or what I call a "dagger" grip. When I'm transplanting, I use the dagger grip to plunge the blade straight down in the soil, make an opening by pulling back on the handle, and pop in the plant.

- **Watering Can.** When you choose a watering can, look for one that's well balanced when you tip it, so that it's easy to pour.

  Be sure the can has a rose. The rose attaches to the end of the nozzle and breaks the flow of water from a stream to a spray, so you don't wash away seeds or bludgeon little seedlings. The smaller the holes, the better. Haws cans, like this one, are designed so the rose directs the flow upward and the water comes down like gentle rain.

Rose

Transplanting Lettuce Seedlings

1 Just before planting, rake the seedbed to smooth the surface. Remove any stones, sticks, or other debris.

2 Mark the soil where you wish to put your transplants. When planting lettuces, you can stagger them in order to take full advantage of your wide bed.

3 Remove the seedling from its container by pushing up on it from below. Take care not to disturb the root system.

4 Plunge the blade of your trowel into the soil to a depth slightly deeper than the height of the rootball. Draw the blade back to make a hole about 1½ times the size of the rootball.

5 Gently put the seedling into place. Firm the soil around the base of the plant just enough to stabilize it, but don't pack it down hard.

CARING FOR NEW TRANSPLANTS

- Water newly planted seedlings frequently for the first few days after planting, especially in hot, sunny weather.

- For the first day or two after transplanting, use shade cloth or invert a plastic pot or a bushel basket over each seedling to give it protection against sun and wind.

Coming Up in the World: Vertical Gardening

Vertical gardening is just a fancy way to describe growing certain plants on a support of some sort, such as a stake, trellis, or fence. Although it's common to grow pole beans or peas this way, tomatoes, cucumbers, and even vining squash and melons can be grown vertically, saving space and improving the quality of the harvest.

SPACE

When they are allowed to wander at will, cucumbers, squash, and indeterminate tomatoes take up a lot more garden space than they need to. When these same plants climb a fence or trellis, lots of fertile garden space is freed up, which substantially increases your garden's productivity per square foot.

YIELD

Measured as the number of fruits produced, yield per plant may actually be somewhat less from a trellised plant. However, usable yield — the number of fruits that make it to the table in good condition — often increases because:

- **Tomatoes** on a trellis won't rot from contact with wet soil or be eaten by slugs. They're also less likely to be lost amid the foliage and overlooked until overripe.

- **Cucumbers** grow longer and straighter and are less likely to escape harvest. As soon as some of its fruits reach maturity, the cucumber plant calls it a job well done and stops producing, so fruits that escape harvest and reach maturity can reduce your total yield substantially.

▲ Teepees. *Whether commercially produced or home-made, teepees are effective traditional trellises for training green beans.*

▲ A-frames. *Filled with 7-inch (17.5 cm) netting, A-frame-style trellises provide reliable support for peas.*

A SIMPLE TRELLIS: VERTICAL GARDENING MADE EASY

The trellis I like best is fairly easy to build, provides good support, and can be used for peas, cucumbers, and even melons (on netting) or beans and tomatoes (on twine). The instructions that follow are for a 15-foot-long (4.6 m) trellis, about 5 feet (1.5 m) high in deeply loosened soil. Make the posts shorter if your soil is not that loose or longer if you want a higher trellis.

Use rot-resistant lumber. I like white cedar, which is available locally, but anything with some rot resistance will do. You can increase the wood's life span by applying a nontoxic wood preservative. Don't use pressure-treated wood or toxic preservatives. There is no way to keep those poisons out of the garden soil and out of the food that grows there. See page 78 for a recipe for a nontoxic wood preservative.

You'll need stakes to hold the netting down or anchor the lower end of the strings that support the tomatoes and beans. For stakes, I use wood scraps about 12" × 1" × ½" (30 × 2.5 × 1.3 cm), with an angled notch cut near the top.

▲ **Versatile homemade trellises.** *These sturdy structures can be fitted with twine for beans and tomatoes (above) or with netting for peas, cucumbers, or melons (right).*

Installing a Garden Trellis

WHAT YOU'LL NEED

For end posts
- Three 6½-foot (2 m) pieces of 2"×2" (5×5 cm) lumber

For top pieces
- Two 8-foot (2.4 m) pieces of 2"×2" (5×5 cm) lumber

For stakes
- Twelve 1-foot (0.3 m) pieces of 1"×1" (2.5×2.5 cm) lumber
- 1 pound (454 g) of common galvanized nails

1 Sharpen one end of each of the three posts to a point with an ax or hatchet.

2 Set the two end posts 15 feet (4.6 m) apart. Start the holes for the posts with a crowbar, and then drive them in with a sledgehammer until they don't wiggle. The posts need to be firmly set, as they'll be supporting a lot of weight. Take pains to strike the posts squarely with the sledgehammer, so you don't split the tops. Cutting a chamfer on the top of the post will also help prevent splintering.

HOMEMADE WOOD PRESERVATIVES

Nontoxic wood preservatives are available commercially. Or you can home-brew a batch: Melt 1 ounce (30 g) of paraffin in a double boiler. Remove from heat. Stir the melted paraffin into 3½ quarts (3.3 L) of turpentine. Stir ½ cup (120 ml) of linseed oil into the paraffin-turpentine mixture.

3 Line up the spot for the middle post, and start the hole with a crowbar. Drive the post in firmly, as in step 2. After it's in place, check whether the three posts are level. If not, adjust so that you'll be able to set the top pieces on fairly level.

4 Cut a 6-inch-long (15 cm) half-lap on one end of each top piece. This joint will lie on top of the center post. In step 6, you will drill right through both pieces to fasten them together and to the post.

5 Along the centerline of what will be the upper side of the top pieces, drive roofing nails at appropriate intervals to attach netting or twine.
- For twine, space nails about 15 inches (37.5 cm) apart.
- For 7-inch (17.5 cm) netting, set nails 7 inches (17.5 cm) apart. In addition, drive roofing nails at appropriate intervals into the two end posts.

6 Place a crosspiece so one end rests atop an end post and the end with the half-lap rests on the center post. Position this first crosspiece so that the second crosspiece will fit atop the half-lap. Position the second crosspiece. At each post, drill through the top into the post, and then drive a common galvanized nail through the hole into the post. Make the hole through the top slightly larger than the nail, so the top pieces can be removed easily.

7 If you're using twine, you'll need twelve 6½-foot (2 m) lengths. Tie one end of each length of twine to one of the nails on the crosspiece and the other end around one of the stakes. Pound each stake into the ground at a slight angle, directly below the corresponding nail. Adjust the twine to fit snugly.

8 If you're using netting, slip the top line of the netting over the nails on the crosspiece and the side lines over the nails on the posts. To keep the bottom snugly aligned, you can also drive stakes at intervals along the length of the bed and tuck the bottom line of netting into the notches in the stakes.

CHAPTER 4

Growing a Self-Sufficient Garden

O NE OF THE NICE THINGS ABOUT GARDENING is that plants are usually so forgiving. With a few fussy exceptions, vegetable plants will burst forth, grow, and yield at least something of a harvest, even when we gardeners just barely and intermittently meet their needs.

But the earliest, biggest, and best-tasting harvest comes from plants whose needs are fully met, on time. Plants do best when their growth, from germination right through maturity and harvest, is steady and uninterrupted. Just as stop-and-go driving is bad for the family car, stop-and-go growing is bad for garden plants.

We can ensure steady, uninterrupted growth in the garden by giving plants the food, moisture, and temperature they need when they need it and by protecting them from anything that hinders their growth, be it bug, disease, or weed. Much of our success in this endeavor depends on how we water, weed, and fertilize the garden.

Meeting the Needs of Your Plants

Once the last of your seedlings — the frost-sensitive sorts like tomatoes, basil, and squashes — are in the ground, your gardening focus changes from planting and transplanting to tending and nurturing. Unlike traditional gardeners who deal with problems as they crop up, our approach is to be proactive first and reactive second. First, and most important, we'll try to prevent or avoid problems. If that doesn't work, or doesn't work well enough, we'll investigate ways to correct or mitigate their effects.

WHAT PLANTS WANT

Whether it's a seedling or a ready-to-harvest crop, every plant needs the same things to thrive:

- Ample air, sunlight, and room to grow roots

- Enough, but not too much, water

- Soil and air temperatures within that plant's preferred range

- The right nutrients in the right amounts

▲ **Payoff.** *Early care leads to a healthy, plentiful harvest. If your aim is to give your plants all that they need for steady, uninterrupted growth, your reward will be a high-yield garden.*

Whenever a plant lacks one or more of these essentials for too long, it becomes stressed and growth slows or stops. When a plant moves from "growth mode" to "crisis mode," changes occur that affect both the size and the quality of its yield. Leaves become tougher and more fibrous and often develop a bitter taste; tubers and edible roots won't grow as big or taste as good; fruits won't be as sweet. Some plants may bolt or try to set fruit too soon. If stress continues, plants never catch up with others of the same age, resulting in lower yields.

As caretaker, your job is to supply additional water whenever nature doesn't supply enough; keep out the weeds that rob garden plants of the air, light, and moisture they need; apply mulches to help moderate soil and air temperature; and add nutrients to make up for what is not naturally available.

WATER, WATER, EVERYWHERE

Vegetable plants, like us and like most other living things, are made of mostly water. But that's not all there is to the water story.

- **Germination.** Water is one of the triggers that set off the miracle of germination. If water is absent or in short supply, seeds will simply sit there in the soil indefinitely without germinating.

- **Photosynthesis.** Water also supplies the hydrogen needed for photosynthesis; the H in H_2O becomes the H in the carbohydrates that plants manufacture.

- **Nutrient Transfer.** Water must surround the root hairs beneath the soil if nutrients are to pass from soil to plant. Whenever the soil immediately around any of a plant's root hairs becomes too dry, the transfer of nutrients slows, and the plant's growth slows as well.

- **Transpiration.** Last, and certainly not least, water, as it passes into and through the plant and exits from the leaves, is the means by which a plant circulates all sorts of matter within itself. When water exits from a plant through stomata in the leaves (a process called transpiration), it creates a partial vacuum that draws water from the soil and into the roots from whence it moves throughout the plant's tissues. For a plant, water's what makes the world go 'round.

- **Water Stress.** Whenever a plant has less water than it needs, it responds by slowing and finally stopping transpiration to prevent water loss from its tissues and subsequent wilting. But when transpiration slows or stops, growth slows or stops; the plant is in a condition of stress. It moves from growth mode to crisis mode, and a series of changes begins, each of which decreases the plant's ability to deal with other stresses and ultimately decreases its vigor, quality, and yield. Leaves toughen, blossoms appear too early, sugar content of fruits decreases, plants bolt and send up seed stalks, roots die, and leaves are shed. As if all of this weren't bad enough, plants in stress also become more attractive to pests and diseases. The extent of the damage depends on the extent and duration of the growth interruption, but some damage occurs every time a plant runs short of water. By the time a plant shows signs of needing water (like wilting), it's already in trouble; some damage has already occurred. In most cases, water-stressed plants do recover and go on growing — they'll usually produce a harvest — but water-stressed plants never really catch up, and the harvest won't be as good as it would have been. Prevention of water stress is much better than intervention after signs of water deprivation appear. The only really effective way to deal with water stress is to prevent it from happening in the first place.

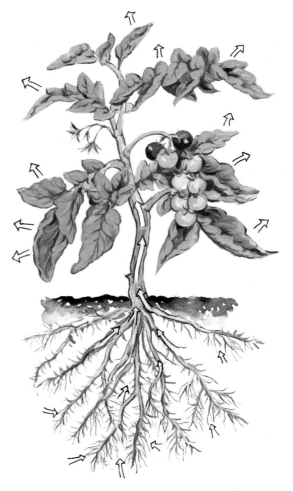

▲ **See what transpires.** *As water exits from the leaves of a plant, a force called transpirational pull is created, drawing water from the soil, through the roots, and into the stems and leaves.*

▲ **Off to the right start.** *Provide plenty of water from the time your plants are very young. The amount of water needed varies from plant to plant, so check part 3 for information about what you're growing.*

A WATERY SOLUTION

Ensuring sufficient water for plants involves a lot more than just turning on the hose or tipping the watering can, and most of what it involves happens long before you reach for either. You really start watering the garden when you prepare the soil and plant in wide, deep beds. In other words, many of the techniques that benefit your garden for other reasons also help create a garden that is less likely to have water problems at all.

THE WATER-FRIENDLY GARDEN

Deal with the water problem before it gets to be a problem by making your garden water friendly.

1. Garden in wide beds rather than single rows, to increase the volume of loose soil and decrease the volume of compacted soil. Loose soil can absorb and retain much more water than can compacted soil.

2. Loosen the subsoil to provide more space for water storage.

3. Add lots of organic matter, particularly compost, to increase the soil's ability to hold water. Compost can hold six times its weight in water. Organic matter also provides food for soil-dwelling organisms, from bacteria and fungi to worms, which in turn improve soil structure and increase the soil's ability both to accept and store moisture and to move it from moister to drier areas.

4. Use mulches and space your plants so that they shade the soil but not one another. This will reduce evaporation from the soil surface.

If your garden is "water friendly," you'll water less and you'll water less often.

▲ **Look for the silver lining.** *Nothing pleases a gardener more than a good soaking rain after several summer days of hot, dry weather. But your garden won't receive full benefits unless the soil is receptive to the dousing.*

MAKING THE MOST OF YOUR WATERING

Even with the best-prepared soil and most careful moisture conservation, most crops in most gardens will need at least some additional water from time to time in order to produce the highest yields. Most garden plants are surprisingly forgiving of watering mistakes. They'll go on growing and produce some sort of a crop even when their water needs are just barely satisfied. But there's a big difference between bare survival and luxuriant growth. My most successful gardens have resulted when I've watered better — not just more, but where and when it does the most good.

GIVE 'EM AN INCH . . . OR MORE

How do you know when and how much to water? Most garden books deal with the "When do I water?" question by noting that gardens need an inch of water a week; if it hasn't rained that much in a week, you should compensate with irrigation.

That's not really enough help. Different plants have very different water needs. Even the same plant has different water needs at each stage of its life cycle.

The kind of root system a plant has makes a difference, as well. An onion plant, with a relatively small and shallow root system, needs almost continually moist soil to thrive, especially when it is young and small. Whatever moisture-conserving tricks you choose, use them on the onions first. Even when nothing else in the garden needs water, check the onions.

A mature tomato plant, on the other hand, with roots ranging both deep and wide, won't be bothered by dry soil two or more inches down. Similarly, a wide planting of bush beans spaced to provide a "living mulch" will need water less often than the same number of plants growing in a single row and surrounded by bare earth.

Put the water where it is needed and when it is needed. It's that simple.

MULCH IS YOUR BEST FRIEND

Evaporation happens. You can't really stop it, but you can certainly slow it down by keeping the soil covered with some sort of mulch. What mulch to use and where to use it depends in part on what else you want to accomplish with the mulch.

- To keep soil cool, apply a layer of grass clippings, straw, or seed-free hay.

- To keep soil warm, use a plastic mulch or landscape fabric.

- To suppress weeds, use an opaque plastic mulch or a very thick organic mulch, with or without a layer of newspaper beneath it.

- For additional nutrients, if the crop you're mulching is a heavy feeder, use compost.

- To create a living mulch for plants that tolerate close spacing, thin so that the mature plants just touch their neighbors. This living mulch greatly reduces water loss from evaporation.

Plastic Mulches

Plastic mulches effectively conserve soil moisture, but they have some disadvantages compared to organic and living mulches: they cost money, need to be disposed of eventually, add nothing positive to the soil, and may prevent rainwater from soaking into the soil. If you're using an impermeable plastic mulch, install drip irrigation or a soaker hose beneath it.

▲ Soaker hose under red plastic mulch

Monitoring Soil Moisture

To anticipate a plant's water needs, pay attention to the soil rather than the plant. You can do this with two tools — your hand and a moisture meter available from a nursery or garden catalog.

1 Take up a handful of soil from the depth you're interested in and squeeze it.

2 Insert a moisture meter to the same depth.

HOW DO YOU KNOW WHEN TO WATER?

Don't wait until your plants wilt before you water. Plants showing signs of wilt have already absorbed the last of the water available to their root hairs and have begun to withdraw water from their extremities. This means they're already stressed, already in the first stages of crisis. It's not too late to save the plant but it is too late to prevent a growth interruption and some side effects you may not find out about until harvest. The trick here is to water the plant before it shows signs of water stress.

▲ **Too wet.** *If you can squeeze any water out, the soil is too wet. It's still a little too wet if a clod of soil comes apart in lumps, rather than crumbling.*

▲ **Too dry.** *Open your hand. If the clump just falls apart by itself, the soil is too dry.*

▲ **Just right.** *If it crumbles evenly into small granules, it's pretty close to just right.*

▲ **Calibrate it.** *Use a moisture meter to get a reading that indicates each condition. From then on, you can use the meter to perform spot checks on soil moisture at various depths and different locations.*

Watering Guidelines for Germinating Seeds

Seeds have to absorb moisture from the time they are sown until they germinate and emerge from the soil; the seedbed must be evenly and constantly moist throughout this period.

WATER NEEDS FOR THE SMALLEST SEEDS

The tiniest seeds — carrots, celery, and most of the cabbage family — are all planted about ¼ inch (6 mm) deep. Their seedbeds need to be constantly moist at least 1 inch (2.5 cm) down. This may require a light watering once a day or, in dry periods, twice or even three times a day. Until they have developed a minimal root system, small-seeded, shallow-rooted seedlings like these remain very sensitive to moisture deficiencies near the soil surface. For a week after emergence, continue monitoring and water as necessary so that no more than the top ¼ inch (6 mm) of the soil is dry.

PROVIDING FOR LARGE SEEDS

Although beans, peas, and other large-seeded plants are sown deeper, at 1 inch (2.5 cm) or more, their seeds are larger and therefore have to absorb a lot more water. They'll tolerate some dryness right at the soil surface but do best if their seedbed stays evenly moist during the entire germination period. Now is the worst time to skimp on water. Plants get off to the best start if germination happens as fast as it can. A germination process that drags on is itself a form of stress. If soil temperature is appropriate, germination problems are usually caused by insufficient soil moisture. In rainy periods, you may not need to water, but check to make sure the rain is penetrating deeply enough to reach the seeds. After the seedling emerges, keep the soil moist to at least 2 inches (5 cm) deep for the first week.

▲ **Steady does it.** *If you provide your seedlings with consistently moist soil, you'll be rewarded with healthy plants and a successful harvest.*

Caring for Cantankerous Carrots

Carrots are particularly fussy. If you don't keep their seedbed moist all the time, they'll just sit there and wait for rain. If they sit long enough, they won't come up at all. You can facilitate their germination by a simple trick.

Sow the carrot seeds as usual, water the bed, and then place a wide board or a piece of cardboard over the entire area. The cover protects the area from sun and drying winds and keeps the soil moist until the seeds germinate. After 7 to 10 days remove the board. Note: After about a week, check beneath the cover once or twice a day. If the seedlings emerge and grow for very long beneath the cover, they will die from lack of light.

Watering Guidelines for Seedlings

As vegetable plants grow from seeds to seedlings, their water needs change. Some plants, such as onions, naturally grow all their roots fairly close to the soil surface (see photo below). Others grow some roots close to the surface and also some farther down. And a few grow most of their roots deep into the soil, sometimes 3 feet (0.9 m), 4 feet (1.2 m), or more down. Let's look at particular plants:

• Onions, garlic, and celery have fairly compact root systems close to the soil surface. Especially when young, they need continually moist soil. Maintain a mulch of grass clippings or straw and monitor soil moisture during the first two or three weeks after planting.

• Cabbage family. Cabbages and other members of this family have both shallow and deep roots. They tolerate some dryness in the top 1 inch (2.5 cm) of soil, but they need moderate, even moisture deeper than that. Whenever you water, water deeply to encourage the growth of deep roots.

• Beets and carrots. Once they're established, beets and carrots begin developing a very wide, deep root system. They're not bothered by moisture changes in the top 1 or 2 inches (2.5 to 5 cm) of soil, and they may not need any extra water unless there is a long rainless period. When you do water, water deeply.

WATER NEEDS OF CLAY AND SANDY SOILS

Clay soils retain water well, but they also take it in more slowly. You will need to water less often but for a longer time.

Sandy soils absorb water quickly and, especially if they lack sufficient organic matter, lose it just as fast. Expect to water more often and for shorter periods. Monitor soil moisture frequently.

▲ **Coddle your onions.** *With their small, relatively shallow roots, onions are easily stressed if the soil is dry even 1 inch (2.5 cm) below the surface. Check every three or four days, and water to a depth of at least 3 inches (7.5 cm) whenever the top inch (2.5 cm) of soil gets even moderately dry. Keep onions mulched with grass clippings to preserve soil moisture.*

Checking Your Watering Technique

• Work your hand right into the soil near the edge of a bed before and after watering to be sure you're getting water down at least 6 inches (15 cm).

• Better still, purchase a moisture meter and use it not only to determine when to water but also to check the effectiveness of the job.

Watering Guidelines for Mature Plants

Shallow-rooted plants. As they mature, shallow-rooted plants such as corn can tolerate low moisture levels in the top couple of inches (5 cm) of soil, though most of them do better when they're mulched to maintain even moisture throughout the soil. Although these plants may seem shallow-rooted, many have some of their roots a foot (30 cm) or more down when they mature, so don't limit watering to just the top couple of inches. All mature plants need a good soaking whenever they get water.

Deep-rooted plants. Beets and other plants that naturally grow deep root systems actually benefit from a couple of inches (5 cm) of relatively dry soil near the surface. This is because too much surface moisture encourages the plant to grow extensive surface roots, which are then subject to stress if the soil does dry out later. In this case, the condition of the top few inches of the soil doesn't tell you about conditions down where the plants' roots are.

This is when the "inch a week" rule finally becomes useful. Whenever a week or so has passed without about an inch (2.5 cm) or so of rainfall, give the whole garden a good watering. Be sure to water the entire bed, not just the area right around each plant. Make sure the water permeates deeply (see page 88).

(see page 88)

CAUSES OF PUDDLING

What appears to be a problem of "too much watering" may really be something else, like inadequate drainage, compacted soil, or insufficient organic content. Chapter 6, Nurturing Vegetable-Friendly Soil, tells you how to correct each of these problems.

KNOWING WHEN TO STOP

Yes, it is possible to water too much, especially if your soil doesn't drain well in the first place. Plants need air as well as water, and they won't get enough air if too many of the spaces in the soil are filled with water. Plant growth stops when all the soil pores are filled with water for more than a few hours.

If water sits on the surface for more than 15 seconds without penetrating, stop watering. Check 12 hours later to assess whether the soil is adequately moist but not soggy. Adjust your timing based on what you find. For instance, if the soil is too dry after 12 hours, in the future you'll need to water until the surface water stays on for perhaps 20 seconds. If it's too wet, stop when the water takes only 10 seconds to penetrate.

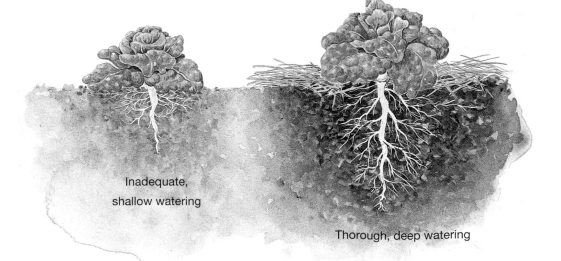

▶ **Bring them up right.** *In a well-prepared bed, most vegetable plants are able to grow extensive and far-reaching root systems, and they'll do so unless you train them to do otherwise by providing water and food in only a small circle right around the stem.*

Inadequate, shallow watering

Thorough, deep watering

CHOOSING THE BEST TIME OF DAY TO WATER

The earlier in the day you water, the more of that water will be lost to evaporation during the day. If you water too late in the day, however, plants may stay damp all night and be more susceptible to diseases such as mold and rot. For these reasons, I prefer to water in the late afternoon. My second choice is early morning. Still, your own garden soil, local weather patterns, or other factors may mean that another time is ideal for you. For instance, if it's very humid, you might want to avoid watering in late afternoon and water early in the morning instead. The fact that leaves dry quickly in the morning and shade the soil may offset the natural evaporation that occurs. Wherever you garden, you might want to give an extra watering to seedbeds and young seedlings in the morning to be sure they don't get too dry during the day.

COMMON-SENSE WATERING

Nature waters from above. Rain soaks the soil and also the plants. Usually gardeners are best off if they copy nature, but watering is an exception to the rule. Tomatoes, peas, beans, melons, and squash are all more susceptible to diseases like late blight when their leaves are wet, especially in muggy or humid weather. Overhead watering is also more wasteful, because most of the water that ends up on the leaves, rather than in the soil, is lost to evaporation. These are two good reasons to use watering methods that help you get the water where you want it — onto the soil and down to the root zone of the plant.

Like most people, I am not fond of tedious jobs. When watering the onions means hauling a watering can 500 feet (150 m) back and forth from the faucet to the garden, that's a tedious job, and a job I'm likely to skip, rush through, or do poorly. But if watering the onions means turning a spigot, picking up a hose, and waving a watering wand, the onions will get watered when they need it.

Watering Tools

Watering cans. I'm a sucker for good tools, and usually I don't regret buying them. Nice (and usually expensive) tools work better and are more fun to use. Nonetheless, I've recently replaced the ordinary galvanized watering can I bought years ago for five dollars at a yard sale. I wish I'd done it sooner, because there are subtle but important differences between an ordinary watering can and a very good watering can.

As described on page 74, my favorite watering can has a well-designed rose and good balance. Its long spout allows me to direct water beneath plant leaves, which moistens the soil while keeping the leaves dry. The large, well-shaped shield prevents water from splashing out when the watering can is very full. And its comfortable handle means I can hold it in one position as it empties, with no strain on my hand.

Haws watering can

Hoses. I thought I was saving money by not buying some extra hoses for the garden. By trying to save money, I diddled around and ended up doing too little watering, which reduced the harvest. Finally I broke down and got enough hoses to reach all over the garden. I sure wish I'd done it sooner. Save yourself frustration and do your garden a favor by getting enough hose to service the garden you're going to grow.

I've found that really cheap hoses aren't worth the little money they cost. But there's no need to go top-of-the-line either. Low-end commercial hoses, available from nursery and farm supply catalogs, are good enough and are sometimes cheaper than upper-end hoses from a garden center or hardware store. Look for a vinyl or rubber hose reinforced with polyester cords, which not only strengthen the hose but give it resistance to kinks as well. It should test to 500 psi, which means it will withstand pressure of up to 500 pounds per square inch (35 kg per cm²). Two 50-foot (15 m) hoses cost a little more than a single 100-footer (30 m), but they're a lot easier to roll up and carry around.

While you're shopping for hoses, you might want to consider some helpful attachments:

Shutoff valve

- **Shutoff valve.** This attaches to the business end of the hose so you can control the flow of water from there instead of racing back to the faucet. They're available in both brass and plastic. Plastic is less expensive, but brass lasts much longer.

- **Watering wand.** This device acts like a long spout on a watering can and lets you easily direct water onto the soil and below plant foliage, so that the soil gets moist but the leaves stay dry. It also means you can do your watering standing up.

▲ **The magic wand.** *Two hose attachments, a watering wand and a flaring rose, allow you to direct water right to the root zone.*

- **Assorted roses.** A flaring rose attaches to the end of the hose, or to the end of the watering wand, and breaks the water flow into a wide, Y-shaped, gentle spray that's easy on the plants and the soil while covering a wide swath. You can also purchase roses in other size and shapes. The round roses shown here direct the spray to more specific areas.

Flaring rose   *Round roses*

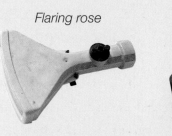

Mist nozzle

- **Automatic water timer.** An automatic timer allows you to regulate watering sessions to last between five minutes and two hours. It will even water while you're not home.

- **Moisture meter.** Insert a probe in the soil and get a moisture reading on a gauge. Guesswork over. (For photo, see page 88.)

- **Rain gauge.** You don't need to guess how much rain fell last week if you have one of these simple, inexpensive tools. Now you'll know if your garden really got that 1 inch (2.5 cm) of rain last week.

Rain gauge

Irrigation Systems

Inexpensive, do-it-yourself kits make both soaker hoses and drip irrigation systems a reasonable option for home gardeners. It's quite easy to install either of these in an hour or two, depending on the size of your garden. The only tool you'll need to complete the installation is a pair of scissors. Once you have an idea of how long it takes to reach the moisture level you want with either system, you can add an automatic timer to it to make your watering chores even easier.

Drip system. These kits allow you to customize your watering system to fit the size and layout of your garden. They come equipped with connectors, caps, and vinyl tubing with tiny perforations spaced about 1 foot (30 cm) apart along the entire length. When you turn the water on, it drips slowly out of each of these holes.

You may also see a variation on this system, which includes solid mainline tubing with narrow "spaghetti" tubing that you can space however needed. This type is especially useful when you have widely spaced plants (tomato plants, for instance); the perforated version is more appropriate for closely planted wide beds.

Soaker hose. Soaker hoses are designed to carry water and leak at the same time. They are made from a rubbery material that feels like a wetsuit. Soaker hoses are flexible and can be snaked over beds so each plant gets the water it needs. They can also be buried to provide water nearer the root zone. Some gardeners find that soaker hoses are less likely to clog than drip systems.

▲ **Easy does it.** *Before you begin your installation, lay out all the parts and plan the route your system will take through the garden.*

▶ Ready, set, water. *A drip setup like this one contains all the tubing, connecting Ts, and corner connectors you need to easily install an automatic watering system for your wide bed. Your hand-watering time will be reduced to a bare minimum.*

Installing a Drip Watering System

1 Beginning where you can connect with the water supply, run the tubing along one side of your garden at a right angle to the length of the beds. You will install driplines from this main line down each of the beds, using T and corner connectors as needed.

2 To install a dripline, lay out the parts needed to connect it to the main line. You'll need the T itself, as well as another length of tubing cut to the length of the bed.

3 Cut the main line where you want to make the joint. The dripline should lie along the center of the wide bed.

KEEP YOUR WATERING SYSTEM WORKING WELL

- **Winter care.** Be sure to take the entire system up and store it indoors over winter. Remove the caps and drain the lines before storing.

- **Clean up your act.** Flush the entire system with water before you install the caps. You should do this when you first install the system, as well as each time you put it in place after winter storage.

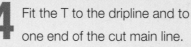
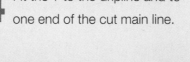

4 Fit the T to the dripline and to one end of the cut main line.

5 Complete the joint by fitting the other end of the cut main line to the second arm of the T.

6 Close off the ends of each of the driplines with the cap supplied in the kit.

Some Weed-Fighting Strategies

Weeds are plants growing where you don't want them to grow. Whether their seeds have arrived in your garden courtesy of the wind or were brought in by animals, or if runners have crept beneath the garden fence from other areas, these unwanted plants compete with garden plants for growing space, nutrients, water, and sunlight.

Garden plants are bred and selected by horticulturists for qualities such as taste, disease resistance, color, and size. Weeds, on the other hand, are bred and selected by nature for one quality — survival. In general, weeds germinate faster and grow faster than the garden plants they compete with. Garden plants may need some help from us to level the playing field.

▲ **A protective nursery.** *Growing young plants in a cold frame makes it easier to protect them from weeds until they're big enough to fend for themselves in the garden.*

You can deal with weeds by preventing them, by anticipating them, or by eradicating them. Although all garden plants are affected by competition from weeds, some are much more at risk than others, and all are much more vulnerable when they're young than when they're at or near maturity.

DON'T LET THEM GET STARTED

When I prepared my garden with a rototiller, I had terrible weed problems. What I didn't know was that the rototiller was actually planting a new crop of weed seeds as it agitated the soil and brought the seeds to the surface. The tool I thought was going to help my weed problem was making it worse. Now, the guiding principle for my weed-fighting strategy is to keep weeds from germinating in the first place. In my deeply dug, raised beds, protected by mulch each fall, the soil is hardly disturbed at planting time. I've found that since I've gardened this way, very few weeds appear — an unexpected benefit of wide-bed gardening.

GETTING A HEAD START ON THE WEEDS

When little weeds and little vegetable seedlings compete on even terms, the weeds win. You can tilt the playing field in favor of the vegetable plants by giving them a head start. Start weed-challenged plants like cabbage and its cousins indoors or in a cold frame, and transplant them to the growing bed when they are big enough to compete with the weeds.

A WHOLE LOT OF SEEDS

A cubic inch (16 cm³) of soil can contain as many as 5,000 weed seeds, many of which can remain viable for decades.

Tools for Weeding

Cape Cod weeder

Swan and colinear hoes. Swan and colinear hoes are real weed-killers! On each, a narrow blade is attached to the handle at about a 70° angle, allowing you to move the blade easily along the soil, parallel to the surface and just below it. You can sever or uproot weeds without disturbing the soil and bringing new weed seeds to the surface to germinate. For years I used a swan hoe. Its tapered shape makes it easy to use very near plants

Swan hoe

and among close plantings. Recently, I bought a stainless-steel colinear hoe, and it's my new favorite (there's also a version that is just plain steel; it's easier to sharpen, but it will rust if you don't keep it clean and dry). It's just as maneuverable as a swan hoe, but the blade is even thinner and easier to draw through the soil. Being stainless steel, it won't rust, and although it is harder to sharpen, it holds an edge longer.

Colinear hoe

Circle hoe. It doesn't look like any other hoe, and it looks as if it couldn't cover much ground. But especially on tough weeds close to plants whose roots I don't want to disturb, this is a favorite tool. And I find that I can work

Circle hoe

faster with a circle hoe, which makes up for the fact that I cover less ground with each stroke. It's available with either a long handle (for weeding standing up) or a short handle (for weeding on your knees).

Cape Cod and farmer's weeders. Intensive planting in wide beds saves space, but it can make weeding difficult because there isn't enough room between plants

for even a slim-bladed hoe. I've found the Cape Cod and farmer's weeders very helpful, each for a different kind of "close-in" weeding.

The Cape Cod weeder has a small blade held at right angles to a short handle. You draw this blade through the soil just below the surface to sever or uproot weeds and loosen the soil. This is Sylvia's favorite small weeder; I don't like it as much because I'm left-handed, and the tool is designed for right-handers.

When I go after long-rooted grasses like orchard grass or witchgrass, or deep-rooted dandelions or milkweed, I leave all the other weeding tools in the shed and take the farmer's weeder. This one's my favorite small weeder.

▲ **Dig it.** *Use a farmer's weeder to pry, grub, and cut roots as much as 8 inches (20 cm) down.*

▲ **Sweep away those weeds!** *You grasp and use a swan, colinear, or circle hoe much the way you hold a broom when sweeping the floor. It's important to keep the angle of the blade parallel to the ground, so don't extend your arms too far ahead of you. Instead of thinking of this tool as a hoe, I have found it useful to think of it as a knife on a long handle. I draw it through the soil with a sideways slicing action and picture the blade severing weed stems.*

Smart Clips

Vegetable plants are most sensitive to competition when they are little, with small and poorly developed root systems. This is also when they are most likely to be damaged or even uprooted when you are hoeing or pulling weeds near them. So change weapons. Put down the hoe, pick up a pair of scissors, and clip the weeds right at the soil surface. The roots probably won't have

enough strength to grow a new top, and when they shrivel and decompose, they leave air spaces behind and add a little bit of organic matter to the soil.

THE SHARPER THE BETTER

When most people say that something is "dull as a hoe," they mean it is very, very dull. But dull is not a word to describe a properly maintained hoe. The only job a dull hoe does well is to aggravate gardeners who are trying to use it. To do its job, a weeding hoe needs to be sharp so that it can sever weeds from their roots, not grub them from the earth, roots and all. You don't need to be able to shave with your hoe, but you should be able to peel little curls from a piece of pine lumber. See the box below for how to sharpen these tools.

SHARPENING A COLINEAR HOE

The procedure for sharpening a stainless-steel colinear hoe is the same as that for sharpening steel hoes, but because stainless steel is much harder than ordinary steel, you can't cut it with a file. Instead, I use a fine-grit diamond sharpening stone. Getting a good edge on a stainless-steel tool takes longer, but it also lasts a lot longer.

Sharpening Garden Hoes

1 The steel in most hoes is soft enough to be sharpened with an ordinary file. Hold the hoe firmly in a vise and file a bevel on the inside edge (the side facing toward the handle).

2 After you have a sharp edge, shift the hoe in the vise so that the other side is up and file it lightly to remove any large burrs.

Mulching for Weed Control

The effectiveness of mulches as weed suppressants depends on how well they prevent light from reaching the soil surface. A variety of mulches, both organic and inorganic (and even a "living" mulch), provide good choices for almost every garden.

ORGANIC MULCHES

This category includes any mulch comprised of dead plant material. It can be either in natural form, like straw, hay, grass clippings, pine needles, leaves, or bark, or in processed form, like cardboard or newspaper. Any of these spread in a thick enough layer to block light can suppress weeds. Note: Don't use the glossy, colored parts of the newspaper. Further note: Cardboard tends to be slippery underfoot, especially when used under straw.

▲ **Mulch you can eat.** *The fast-growing lettuce planted between these rows of corn keeps weeds down when the corn is young. In turn, the growing corn shades the lettuce during the hottest part of summer.*

PLASTIC MULCHES

Plastic mulches make effective weed fighters, although they don't have some of the side benefits of organic mulches. It's important to consider what effects the mulch may have in your garden in addition to weed control. For instance, plastic mulches, as well as black planter's paper, warm the soil. This is fine for heat-loving crops but detrimental for those that either grow slowly or decline in quality when the soil in their beds gets too hot. And some of the plastic mulches don't allow water to penetrate to the soil. Use the chart on page 98 to help guide your decisions.

LIVING MULCHES

You can place your plants so close together that nothing else can grow there. The plants can be all one crop or mixed. Good vegetables to plant densely include kale, spinach, and lettuce. It's not possible to treat all plants in this manner. For instance, beets will stunt one another if planted too closely. Cabbages and other mustard family members aren't very effective shade producers. Tomatoes and peppers aren't effective shade producers until they're mature. For plants that can't provide their own living mulch, interplant with other companionable vegetables. Try these combinations:

- Grow lettuce among carrots, corn, beets, or cabbage-family crops, where it provides a living mulch while benefiting from the cooling shade of the larger plants.

- Fast-growing lettuce and radishes can shade the soil between tomatoes or peppers until they mature enough to do it themselves.

Weed Control and Beyond: Organic Mulches

Organic mulches help control weeds, but that's not all they do. They also conserve soil moisture, moderate soil temperature, and provide food for soil-dwelling organisms; some even change soil pH.

- **Moisture.** Although organic mulches help conserve soil moisture, mulches like leaves, cardboard, and newspaper can make it harder for water to soak into the soil quickly, particularly during heavy rains when runoff is common. Other materials such as straw, hay, and grass clippings help with water absorption by soaking up any excess that the soil cannot absorb immediately.

- **Soil temperature.** Organic mulches, particularly those applied in thick layers, lower and moderate soil temperatures. Although sometimes desirable, it's not helpful when mulching retards soil warming in spring or prevents heat-loving plants from getting what they need.

- **Nutrients.** Because they come from plants in the first place, organic mulches provide food for soil-dwelling organisms and eventually become part of the soil, adding to its organic content.

- **Soil pH.** Pine needle mulches lower pH and should therefore be used only where this effect is desired.

◀ Clockwise from top left, leaves, straw, pine needles, bark chips, grass clippings.

WEED-KILLING INORGANIC MULCHES COMPARED

Type	Effectiveness	Other Factors
Clear (or builder's) plastic	Poor weed control, unless hot enough to fry weeds	Warms soil; prevents water from penetrating soil
Black plastic	Good weed control	Cheapest; warms soil; prevents water from penetrating soil
IRT (infrared transmitting) plastic	Good weed control by blocking visible light that weeds need for growth	Costs more than black plastic; warms soil better than black plastic; prevents water from penetrating soil
SRM (selective reflective mulch) plastic	Poor weed control	Warms soil; prevents water from penetrating soil
Planter's paper mulch	Good weed control	Water permeable; biodegradable
Landscaping fabric	Excellent weed control	Water and air permeable; moderates, but doesn't raise, soil temperature; four times more expensive than plastic; long-lasting
Ewe mulch (made from wool fibers)	Excellent weed control	Water permeable; moderates, but doesn't raise, soil temperature; costly

DEALING WITH CHRONIC WEED PROBLEMS

Sometimes weeds either start out in control of a new garden or become so much of a problem that simply hoeing or pulling can't keep ahead of them. Witchgrass, orchard grass, and purslane can fit in this category. Extreme measures are called for. Although this sometimes means you have to sacrifice a particular area of the garden for one growing season, it may be worth it in the long run. The three most effective ways to rid a garden bed of weeds are an organic mulch of newspaper and straw, black plastic mulch, and cover crops.

▲ **Extreme organic mulch.** *This method also works well as the first step for a new garden or garden extension: Cover the invaded area with cardboard or with at least two layers of newspaper. Cover this with a thick layer of straw. Leave it for a year. By the next spring, the weeds should be gone; the soil should also be richer and well worked by worms and other soil organisms.*

▲ **Extreme plastic mulch.** *Cover the area with black or IRT plastic for the growing season. Remove the plastic in the fall and mulch with leaves or straw for winter.*

◄ **Cover crops.** *To obliterate a really pernicious weed, plant a living mulch in the form of a cover crop that grows thick and heavy for one growing season. Buckwheat works well for this purpose. As soon as it begins to flower, I use a scythe to mow it down or till the plants into the soil as green manure. If you mow it, compost what you cut down. Make a second planting and then mow or till again. By the end of the season, those weeds should be gone. And as a bonus, there will be a lot more organic matter in your soil.*

FLAME WEEDERS

My reaction when I first read about flame weeders was that they may involve a bit of overkill. Using a propane-fueled torch to go after weeds seemed a little like using a 2 × 8 to swat houseflies. I reconsidered when I remembered my chronic problem with purslane. It grows like mad, and when you dig it out, half the time it reroots itself. If you chop it up, each piece becomes a new weed. When I put a flame weeder to this test, I was convinced that this tool is well worth adding to the weed-control arsenal, particularly if you have a big, weedy garden.

When you use a flame weeder, the objective is not to burn a weed completely to the ground, but just to heat it up so the cells burst and the plant dehydrates. It's very effective for eradicating small weeds in an unplanted bed, but because it doesn't distinguish between weeds and vegetable plants, and its heat can affect plants well beyond the visible flame, it's not for weeding in beds that have already been planted.

WALKWAY WEEDING

Weeding is not my favorite part of gardening, and weeding in the packed soil of the walkways is my least favorite kind of weeding. Pulling walkway weeds is futile; they usually break off instead of coming out, and the root left behind soon grows a new top. Hoeing with a swan or colinear hoe does not work very well either, because the soil is too compacted to let the hoe pass through it, and these hoes are not good hacking tools. Fortunately, however, a stirrup, or scuffle, hoe can handle walkway weeding.

▲ Firing up. *A flame weeder is most useful for tending paths or the sides of raised beds, where it's less likely to cause erosion than if you hoe or hand-pull the weeds. If these areas are mulched, be sure to wet the mulch very thoroughly before flaming the weeds, and work with a helper who has a hose at the ready to douse any fires that might get going in the mulch.*

An Ounce of Prevention Is Worth a Pound of Weeds

Even with the right tool, walkway weeding is not very high on my list of favorite ways to spend time in the garden. I'd much rather avoid the problem in the first place. So to prevent and control the problem, I mulch between and around all the garden beds with a two-layer mulch. The first layer, which consists of at least two thicknesses of newspaper or cardboard, blocks the light. The second layer of straw or mulch hay holds the first layer in place and provides something pleasant to walk on and look at. You can use water-permeable plastic mulch or landscape fabric for the first layer, but newspaper works as well and is a lot cheaper.

► Stirrup or scuffle hoe. *This handy tool has two sharpened edges, allowing it to cut on both its push and pull strokes, shearing weeds off slightly beneath the soil surface.*

More than One Way to Fertilize

I used to think that the phrases "weeding with a hoe" and "cultivating soil" meant pretty much the same thing. This isn't the case. In reality, soil cultivation involves more than just weed control. Its purpose is to introduce air into the soil, which in turn increases the activity rate of certain bacteria. This activity results in the release of soil nutrients. So gently agitating the soil surface with a hoe or curved-tine cultivator is actually one way of fertilizing your plants. Periodic cultivation is thus a good idea whether or not the garden is in need of a weeding.

The notion that fruitful gardens and regular side-dressing with fertilizer go hand in hand is an axiom for many gardeners. Let me suggest a heretical notion: Once you have good soil for growing vegetables, you'll get better yields and higher-quality vegetables if you don't fertilize plants at all during the growing period. Here's why: Plants grow fastest and best, are most vigorous and healthy, and produce the largest and best-tasting harvest if their growth is steady and uninterrupted. Whatever gardening techniques you use should be tested against the question: Does this promote steady, uninterrupted growth?

The key to avoiding growth interruptions is to keep the plant constantly supplied with the things it needs in order to grow. Growth slows in dry soil and speeds up in moist soil. Similarly, if the soil is too wet, growth slows, then resumes when the soil is again moist. If the soil is too hot or too cold, growth slows and then speeds up when temperatures return to the optimum range. If there aren't enough nutrients available to a plant, growth slows, and then it speeds up again when and if the nutrients become available. If you fertilize plants during the growing season, you encourage fluctuations in their growth

— an acceleration when the fertilizer is applied, gradual decrease as it is used up, then another acceleration when more fertilizer is applied.

▲ Killing two birds with one technique. *Gentle cultivation with a curved-tine cultivator like this one introduces air into the soil, which in turn releases soil nutrients.*

THE IDEAL: BALANCED NUTRITION

If a garden soil has plenty of organic matter in various stages of decomposition, sufficient major and minor nutrients, and a high level of biological activity, the plants living there will have all the food they need for growth, and this food will be supplied to them gradually and as they need it.

If you've been adding plenty of compost, paying attention to soil pH, and growing your plants in deep and wide beds, you won't need to (and shouldn't) add extra fertilizer, aside from a continually maintained layer of finished compost on the soil surface.

Making Compost Tea

For years, gardeners have recommended making compost tea by steeping compost or well-aged manure in water for four days. This was thought to be a quick-fix fertilizer for plants showing some degree of nutrient deficiency. For several reasons, I no longer recommend making compost tea in that way.

Steeping either compost or aged manure in water creates an anaerobic environment (one that is largely devoid of air). The beneficial bacteria and fungi in our garden soil need air. The microbes that grow and breed in anaerobic conditions are often harmful to plants. Furthermore, *E. coli* bacteria, many strains of which can make people very sick, are quite likely to be present in manure or in compost that hasn't heated high enough or long enough.

However, compost tea that has been properly made in an aerobic environment is valuable both as a quick-fix fertilizer and as a means of increasing the size and diversity of soil microbe populations, and this translates into healthy soil. Aerated compost tea has also been found to prevent or combat various diseases and to protect plants against some insect pests.

To make aerated compost tea you need good compost from a hot pile, water, and some way to keep air flowing through the water. The airflow facilitates the reproduction of "good" microbes. Aerobic compost brewers are available from some garden supply and seed catalogs (see Suppliers, page 337).

▶ **Steeping tea.** *Aerated compost tea is easy to make; just add a cloth sack of good compost to a bucket of water (left) and aerate the water using an aquarium pump (right).*

REALITY CHECK: TIME AND WORK

Unfortunately, gardens don't reach this blessed state overnight. It takes work, and it takes time. If you're starting a new garden or making the switch from traditional row-based gardens, your soil may not yet provide all the plants with all they need all season long. You'll probably have to supply some supplements. In addition, some plants require more food than others and will be more likely to need some extra help. In part 3, I make some suggestions for fertilizing the plants most likely to need it when growing conditions are short of optimum. If you're in doubt, fertilize. Little fluctuations in plant growth are a lot better than abrupt stops.

If your soil tests consistently indicate high fertility, however, and the less demanding plants are doing fine without supplements, it's okay to start the weaning process. Fertilize just part of a crop and see how things go. As you cut back on fertilizer, notice how the plants respond.

MORE THAN ONE FISH IN THE SEA: WHICH FERTILIZER?

Fish or fish-and-seaweed emulsions are well-balanced and fast-acting fertilizers for supplemental feedings, as is aerated compost tea. They provide the major nutrients and a wide spectrum of minor elements as well. Follow the manufacturer's directions for the amount and frequency of application, depending on the crop you are fertilizing. You have several choices of how to apply, including foliar feeding and sidedressing.

Use fish emulsion or aerated compost tea if you want a fast remedy. Foliar feed in the evening or on a cloudy day, because wet leaves, particularly if the moisture contains fertilizer, are easily damaged by sunlight. Label the spray bottle and use it just for fertilizing.

▲ Foliar feeding. *Mix the fertilizer with water according to instructions on the package, pour the mixture into a spray bottle, and then spray it directly onto the plant's foliage.*

▲ Sidedressing. *Following package directions for how much to use, sprinkle the fertilizer well beyond the plants' leaf line.*

CHAPTER 5

Enjoying the Harvest

Too often, a harvest that should have been bountiful falls short of the goal right at the end. We may tend the garden just as we should all season long and then miss the reward because we harvested too soon or too late, or made some mistake in curing or storing the crop. Timing and care at harvest can make the difference between bounty and mediocrity.

The slender filet bean that's perfect today is stringy tomorrow. Just a day changes peas from sweet and crisp to bland and mealy, and corn that's sweet picked before breakfast has a hint of starch if picked in the late afternoon.

Potatoes, gently dug, well cured, and stored at the right temperature and humidity will last into spring, as will garlic and onions, carrots and beets, cabbages and winter squash.

The choices we make at harvest determine whether our crops enrich the table or the compost pile.

Ripeness Is All: Timing the Harvest

Ripeness often means one thing to the vegetable plant and something quite different to the gardener. For plants, ripeness is a measure of how mature the seeds are. The closer the seeds are to maturity, the riper the fruit. A vegetable's standard for a successful life is to make seeds that will eventually sprout, grow, and carry on the family name. For gardeners, "ripe" means that whatever part of the plant we eat is at its most tasty and nutritious stage. Sometimes that is when the seeds are mature, sometimes not.

- **Tomatoes.** A ripe tomato has mature seeds, so it's ripe from the plant's point of view. It's also at its peak of flavor, so it's ripe by my definition too.

- **Beans.** When the seeds of a French filet bean are ripe and mature, the bean has more in common with a leather belt than it does with dinner. For me, a ripe filet bean is slender with tiny, immature seeds. Jacob's Cattle, Soldier, or Vermont Cranberry beans, plump and dry within crinkly dry pods, are perfectly ripe as far as either bean plant or bean gardener are concerned. Those beans are equally able to give rise to a new generation of bean plants or to a steaming crock of baked beans.

- **Squash.** Squash plants and I agree on ripeness for winter squash but not for summer squash. The former should have mature seeds, while the latter are best picked when small, with barely noticeable seeds.

- **Peppers.** Pepper plants agree with my notion of ripeness when my taste runs to red fruits but not when I prefer them green, when they are immature from the plant's point of view.

Plants That Are Tastiest When Their Seeds Are Ripe

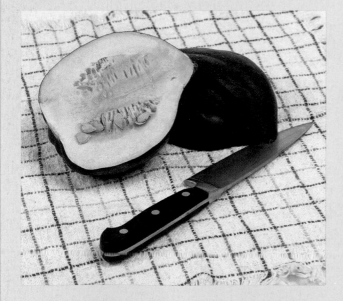

▲ **Winning winter squash.** *Unlike summer squash, which is best when its seeds are small and unformed, winter squash is most tasty when its seeds are mature.*

▲ Hot tomato! *When tomatoes are most juicy and flavorful, their seeds are also mature. Not only does a ripe tomato color up nicely, but it easily comes away from the vine when you gently tug it.*

WHEN RIPE IS RIPE

We harvest parts other than the fruits of some plants, such as onions, garlic, and potatoes. These crops are ripe when the plant dies back — signs that are pretty easy to see. But the signs of ripeness are not so dramatic and obvious with other plants, like tomatoes and melons, whose fruit we harvest. The signs of ripeness in these crops are much more subtle. Instead of affecting the entire plant, signals of the perfect time to pick are often restricted to the area right around the ripening fruit. For example, when a tomato or melon ripens on the vine, the plant is healthy, green, and vigorous, but the stem holding the ripe fruit begins to change, turning yellowish and loosening its grip on the fruit. A fully ripe tomato will slip loose from the plant if lifted gently. A ripe cantaloupe will come free from the plant with a gentle push of your thumb against the stem. One melon that gives a different readiness signal is the Chantais melon: You can tell that it's ripe when the small leaf next to the melon turns light brown.

▲ **Seedy and down at the heels.** *The oversized, seedy zucchini on the left doesn't compare in texture or flavor with the younger one on the right. As summer squash matures, the seeds enlarge and toughen, and the area around them becomes stringy, soft, and flavorless.*

Plants That Die Back When They Are Mature

▲ **Onion family signals.** *Hardneck garlic is ready to harvest when about one third of the leaves have started to turn brown.*

▲ **One potato, two potatoes.** *Dig your potatoes a couple of weeks after the tops wilt and die back.*

TWO KINDS OF RIPE

Sometimes ripe is simply a matter of personal taste. When is a pepper ripe? Or a green bean? Or a turnip? In each case, there's more than one right answer.

Peppers. Bell-type peppers are edible when they're green and immature, but they may be red, yellow, orange, purple, or brown when they mature, and they're edible everywhere between their green and fully colored states. Mature peppers are sweet, while green peppers are tangy. Harvest them when they taste good to you. Picking peppers at the green stage means you'll end up with a bigger crop per plant. If you keep picking the fruits before they fully ripen, the pepper plant goes on making new ones.

Green beans. Those that are to be eaten fresh or preserved by freezing or canning taste best fairly early in their development, long before the seeds within the pods are fully grown. Beans that grow much beyond the diameter of a pencil decline quickly in tenderness and taste; the bigger they get, the worse they taste. When they get really big ("ripe" from the bean plant's view of things), they are edible again. Now, however, it's not the pods you eat, but the seeds, which are very tasty as shell beans.

Root crops. Turnips, as well as beets and carrots, have multiple "ripenesses," depending on what you plan to do with them. Turnips and beets can be called ripe very early in life and cooked along with their greens. Turnips, beets, and carrots are all the most tender, tasty, and sweet at medium sizes, but they store better if they're bigger.

THE MORE YOU TAKE, THE MORE YOU GET

Call it the harvest paradox: The more summer squash, cucumbers, peas, or green and yellow beans you pick, the more you get to pick. A pea plant's goal in life is not to produce small, tender sweet peas to feed us, but to produce big, tough, starchy, inedible peas that will be the seeds for next year's pea plants. As soon as a pea plant succeeds in producing some seed-sized peas, its mission is accomplished, and it stops producing any more food-sized peas for you and me. The same is true of summer squash, cucumbers, and beans. An easy way to increase your harvest is to harvest regularly, when the fruits are young and tender.

▲ **Pick a peck.** *You can harvest and enjoy bell peppers throughout their growing stages. A young green pepper will have more of a tang than a fully mature, sweet red pepper.*

Jumping the Gun

You can harvest some onions (not garlic) and potatoes early in the season and provide yourself with special treats that only gardeners can usually enjoy:

- Plant some onion sets or plants very close together and then eat the thinnings as scallions or little creamed onions.

- Reach into the soil beneath a potato plant and filch a few when the peas are ready. A dish of new potatoes and tender young peas is a fine way to eat butter.

◀ It's a pea-pickin' thing. *If you diligently keep pea and bean vines picked, they will continue to produce.*

◀ Marbles, anyone? *Pull and refrigerate radishes when they're still small. They keep longer and their flavor is better.*

◀ Sunny side up. *Young carrots are one of those gourmet treats that keep gardeners going. These early carrots are at their most tender flavor stage, though carrots are higher in nutrients and store better when dug a bit later.*

SEIZE THE MOMENT

Carrots are tasty from the time they're as big as your little finger to when they're full-sized, so carrot harvest time spans most of the summer. The flavor and nutritional value of carrots changes over time. Baby carrots taste better, but big carrots are more nutritious. Some vegetables are another matter entirely. A French filet bean that was too small yesterday may be too big tomorrow, making its harvest time today and today only. If I want the best filet beans, I pick all the ripe ones every day. Ordinary beans, peas, and summer squash offer a bit larger window of opportunity, but I still check every day and pick at least every second day.

Salad radishes start tasting good to me as soon as they're the size of little marbles, but when they're the size of big marbles, they're just a day or two from splitting open and becoming infested with root maggots. I try to harvest them all before this happens and store them in the refrigerator. The radishes keep better there than they do in the ground.

Keeping the Harvest: Storage Options

In winter, when the taste of ripe tomatoes is but a memory, I'll still be eating winter squash, onions, potatoes, carrots, and beets from the garden . . . if I took time to store them correctly. The storage requirements of specific vegetables that can be saved for winter eating are given in part 3. The key to successful storage is finding or creating conditions that match these requirements.

MAKING USE OF WHAT YOU HAVE

For vegetables that like to be kept cool and dry, you may be able to locate a spot in your house that provides just what they need without customizing a special room. Put a thermometer in various nooks and crannies around the house — in closets, under beds, in rooms either unheated or underheated during the winter — and in different areas of the basement, if it's fairly dry. Note each vegetable's requirements and then see if any of the conditions you find matches these needs.

Sand or Sawdust?

Most garden books that deal with winter storage suggest bedding carrots and other roots in either damp sand or damp sawdust. I've had much better luck with sand. When I used sawdust, the roots began to shrivel after two months or so, because they gave up too much moisture to the sawdust, which in turn gave up too much to the air. Sand seems to stay moist all winter. I have problems with sand only if I make it too wet in the first place. The sand should be quite damp but not wet.

ROOT CELLARS

For the storage crops that want it cold and damp, you're not likely to find the right conditions unless you have an unheated basement. Even if you do, you may want to partition an area especially for food storage.

A root cellar that is perfectly adequate for most families' needs is large enough to store carrots, potatoes, beets, and other root vegetables, plus some cabbages. Sometimes the phrase *root cellar* conjures up visions of an immense underground cavern. It doesn't have to be huge, but it does need to be moist and cool: about 35 to 38°F (2 to 3°C) is ideal. If you store potatoes, it must also be dark.

Storing the Harvest

When you store your vegetables for winter use, remember that some crops prefer to be kept dry, whereas others like it moist. Garlic does best when you keep it cool but dry. Winter squash and dried beans need warm, dry spots. Store the following vegetables in a cool, moist place:

- Beets, in damp sand
- Brussels sprouts, on stems, in damp sand
- Cabbage, wrapped in newspaper
- Carrots, in damp sand
- Celeriac, in damp sand
- Celery, planted in a bucket of damp soil
- Jerusalem artichokes, in damp sand
- Onions, in baskets or braided
- Potatoes, in baskets
- Rutabaga, in damp sand
- Turnips, in damp sand

Winter Vegetable Hide and Seek

Different folks need different strokes, but you can usually find just the right storage conditions for all your winter vegetables somewhere in your house.

Warm, dry, with the possibility of sun. *Potted herbs can be overwintered in a warm, sunny windowsill. A spot like this is also good for ripening tomatoes from yellow-green to red. Dried herbs and beans cure best where it's warm but not too sunny.*

Cool and dry. *Onions, garlic, green tomatoes, pumpkins, and other winter squash store well in a dry spot that stays around 50°F, like this closet.*

Cold and moist. *If you've got a cold (just a couple of degrees above freezing), damp cellar, you've got the perfect spot to store Brussels sprouts (in a bucket of moist sand), carrots (buried in moist sand), potatoes, celery (potted up), and canned goods, among others.*

Cool and moderately moist. *Apples last the longest in a cool spot (just a couple of degrees above freezing is best) that's somewhat moist. Because they need to be stored separately from other produce, an insulated garage works very well.*

The Year-Round Garden

When I first started gardening, the growing season was pretty clearly defined. I followed the same traditions that gardeners had been using for generations. Gardening started in early spring when we planted the peas and a few leaf crops like lettuce. Then we paused to wait for the coming and going of the last frost, about Memorial Day in Vermont, when the rest of the plants went in. In fall, the first killing frost marked the end of the garden, and we all switched our attention to other things.

Now, however, things are very different. Row covers, cold frames, and garden greenhouses mean that we can keep something growing in the garden all year long. And it isn't just new hardware that helps create the year-round garden. Plant breeders have developed a number of frost-tolerant vegetable varieties that we can grow even in some of the unprotected parts of the garden long after the first "killing frost."

The first hard frost has been changed from an ending to a turning point. Although much of the garden does stop, some continues on. With the cold weather it's time for a change of focus, of keeping some things growing while also looking ahead to next year. What you do in the garden after the Big Frost is in one sense the ending and cleanup of the old garden, but in another it's the beginning of a new garden. What you do now in fall and early winter can have an important effect on what will happen in your garden next spring and summer.

Inground Storage

A few years ago at harvest time, I grew tired of digging carrots, clipping the tops, and bedding them in sand in the root cellar. I had about a third of a bed left, which I just covered with a thick mulch of straw topped with some chicken wire to keep the deer from digging up the carrots. I marked the corners of the bed with posts so I'd know where to dig after the snow had come. In early January, I went out to the garden and dug some carrots. Not only were they not frozen, they tasted better and sweeter than any I had stored in the root cellar. The key to success with this "lazy gardener storage system" is the thick mulch and a good covering of snow on top of it. The carrots won't survive in edible shape if the ground freezes around them. Since I've dug up perfectly good potatoes in the spring that I had missed when harvesting the fall before, it seems like this storage method would also work for potatoes and other root crops.

Spring Celery Bonus

Before the first hard frost in fall, I dig a half-dozen plants, replant them in sap buckets or large plastic buckets (in either case, be sure to provide drainage holes). I place them in the root cellar and water them whenever they begin to droop. If you're already growing your celery in containers, just move the containers indoors and keep them watered. We enjoy crisp, tasty celery all winter long. As spring approaches, the stalks will get pithy as the plant prepares to bolt.

Recycling the End-of-the-Garden Wastes

With less day-to-day work in the garden, you often have more time for some important long-range improvements to your garden soil. In part 2 you'll find some specific information on how to make compost and how to test and amend your soil. Here are some tips for things that are best to do right now.

RECOGNIZING THE HALF-FULL GLASS

A lot in life depends on how you view things. Are you more likely to see the half-full or the half-empty glass in certain situations? Looking at the garden right after the first really hard frost, some people see a mess to clean up. Others, seeing the same scene, find one final, glorious harvest, not for the table, but for the compost pile. Fall is the perfect time to start making the compost you'll need next spring and summer.

Much of what goes into compost piles in spring and summer is ready to compost without being chopped, ground, or otherwise reduced in size. This includes tender young weeds, grass clippings, high grass and weeds mowed from around the garden or beside the driveway, and the harvest from cover crops grown especially for compost.

▲ **The kindest cut.** *Tough stalks and overgrown vegetables will decompose more quickly if you chop them up before adding them to the compost pile.*

On the other hand, much of what remains in the garden in fall breaks down slowly and poorly unless it is chopped, shredded, or beaten to render it more edible by bacteria. For instance, broccoli, Brussels sprouts, and cauliflower plants — along with tomato vines, cornstalks, and melon and squash vines — all decompose faster if chopped into smaller pieces, exposing more surface area to the ravenous bacteria.

You need to take these additional steps in fall not only because the composting material itself is likely to be tougher but also because time is not on your side as the seasons slip toward winter. Cold temperatures of late fall and winter slow down bacterial activity. And once it gets really cold, the kinds of bacteria that prefer higher temperatures simply call it quits until spring.

FALL IS THE BEST TIME TO TEST AND AMEND YOUR SOIL

Like many gardeners, I sometimes test my soil in spring, because that's when I think of it. But fall is a better time, really a much better time, for this important activity.

- **Lead time.** If you discover problems, you have plenty of lead time to apply long-term solutions rather than quick fixes that don't last. For instance, rock powders, which are used to modify soil acidity and maintain nutrient levels, are more effective if given months to work rather than weeks. Giving them a whole winter to settle in is better than adding them in spring.

- **Ideal temperatures.** In early autumn, soil temperatures are optimum for biological activity — neither too cold, as in early spring, nor too hot. Because biological activity affects the availability of soil nutrients, tests for these nutrients are most accurate when soil life is most active.

Planning Ahead Can Improve Next Year's Garden

If everything has gone about as you had hoped, planning next year's garden involves no more than putting the plant rotations through one cycle. (For details about crop rotation, see pages 47–48.) If you're thinking about adding or dropping a vegetable or variety, now is a good time to make the decision so you can make proper preparations for the newcomers.

Many gardeners start the planning for the next year's garden in winter, when the seed catalogs start arriving in the mail, or even later, when the seeds themselves arrive. But there are some very good reasons to do a lot of the planning in fall, right after the garden has been put to bed and the last frosted remnants of summer's plants have been consigned to the compost pile:

- **For carrots.** If you decide in fall where next year's carrot patches will be, you can increase the chances for a terrific, good-tasting harvest by adding some autumn leaves or, even better, leaf mold to these beds. Just spread the leaves over the bed and chop them into the soil with a hoe. Soil creatures, such as earthworms, will spend the winter working on the leaves, breaking them down and liberating their nutrients for use by the carrots next summer.

- **For cabbage family crops.** If clubroot has attacked any of the cabbage family crops, add lime or wood ashes in the beds where they will be next year to raise the pH to a neutral (7.0) or even slightly alkaline level.

- **For acid-loving plants.** If pH levels are too high in any bed where acid-preferring plants will grow, work in some peat moss or sawdust. The months ahead give plenty of time for these to have some effects before you plant next year's garden.

- **For asparagus.** For such a skinny little vegetable, asparagus is hungry all the time. To supply this plant with the nutrients it needs, apply an inch (2.5 cm) of compost to this bed in fall and cover it with straw mulch to protect the asparagus roots from cold.

▲ **Fallen treasure.** *Autumn leaves add lots of organic matter and plant nutrients to garden soil. Shred them by running over them with a lawnmower, spread them on the garden, chop them into the soil, then add another layer to act as a winter mulch.*

Coverlets for the Garden Beds

Homes filled with people are generally well cared for, but nobody takes care of an empty house. Abandoned houses fall apart soon after people move out. The same is all too often true of gardens. Many folks abandon their gardens in winter and soon find out that bare soil is a lot like an abandoned house. It doesn't do well unless something — even a crop of weeds — is growing there. You can easily keep the garden alive and active in winter by sowing cover crops or applying organic mulches in fall.

WINTERING OVER WITH WINTER RYE

Sow a cover crop of winter rye in fall, and the garden will be a garden all winter long — and a whole lot better off. Winter rye sends out extensive roots that make the soil more friable. When the roots die and decompose, they leave behind countless spaces for air and water, along with lots of organic matter. Although winter rye doesn't add nitrogen to the soil, it does capture nitrogen already in the soil and prevent it from being leached away.

Mature winter rye can reach 4 feet (1.2 m) in height, but in the home garden it's best to harvest it earlier, while the stems are still young, tender, and easy to break down. Here are three ways to use it:

- At 8 to 16 inches (20 to 40 cm) high, work it into the soil by chopping with a hoe or tilling.

- Wait until flowering and mow it down for the compost pile.

- At flowering, mow and leave on the ground; mulch over it with straw.

WINTER MULCHING

Spreading a thick layer of organic mulch over the beds is the single best thing you can do for your whole garden as winter approaches. A good mulch insulates the soil, which either keeps it from freezing, or keeps it from freezing as deeply or quickly as it otherwise would. This has some very beneficial effects:

Soil that has gone through a deep freeze and thaw is more compacted in spring than it was in fall. Mulch mitigates the freeze cycles and helps maintain soil friability over winter.

Mulch applied after the first hard freeze, but before daytime temperatures stay below freezing, allows soil organisms (worms in particular) to go on working the soil for much longer than they otherwise could. And when freezing temperatures do invade the soil, the mulch slows the freezing process, allowing worms time to migrate deeper into the earth instead of being caught by a sudden cold spell and freezing to death.

I've found that leaf-mulched beds show even more worm activity in spring than do straw-mulched areas. I like to put down a layer of leaves for the worms and then top it off with some straw for extra insulation.

LOOKING AHEAD
As soon as the snow is gone in the spring:

- Rake back the mulch to let the soil begin to warm.

- Dig out the weeds you didn't get last fall (including the dandelions you left on purpose so you could harvest a mess of greens as the first meal from the garden).

- If you didn't do it in the fall, add compost, greensand, and rock phosphate (if you didn't add to your compost pile) and lime or wood ashes if you need to adjust soil acidity.

- Loosen the soil (but don't invert it or mix it up too much) with a broadfork or garden fork.

- Rake it smooth.

You're ready for another garden year.

PART TWO

THE HEALTHY GARDEN

Aboveground, Belowground

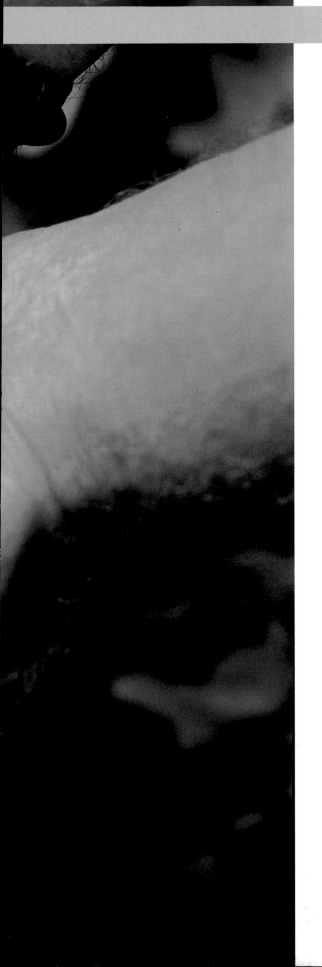

CHAPTER 6

Nurturing Vegetable-Friendly Soil

FOLK WISDOM HAS IT that a poor gardener grows weeds, a good gardener grows vegetables, and a very good gardener grows soil. Good soil is, indeed, the keystone in the arch that connects the seed's promise to the harvest's fulfillment. Improving your garden's soil is an investment not only in this year's harvest but also next year's harvest and the harvests of numberless years to come.

Good soil is not just "dirt" — not just sand and silt and clay. It is also the repository for a wide range of nutrients plants need for truly healthy growth. And it is also organic matter, the remains of plants and animals that have lived there. Most important, it comprises myriad living creatures ranging in size from relatively large and easily visible worms and beetles to microscopically small bacteria and fungi, all playing a part in creating an ecology where plants thrive. Good soil is not inert. It is, quite literally, alive.

Whatever you invest to improve your garden soil — adding plant nutrients, digging in compost, planting a cover crop of buckwheat, mulching — returns manyfold and for years to come in ever more bountiful harvests.

Nutrient-Rich Soil for Garden Success

To grow as well as they can, plants need many different nutrients. Nine of these — carbon, hydrogen, oxygen, nitrogen, phosphorus, potassium, calcium, magnesium, and sulfur — are required in relatively large amounts and are therefore called macronutrients. Among the others are iron, boron, manganese, copper, zinc, and molybdenum. These, called micronutrients, are needed in smaller amounts — sometimes very small.

To a vegetable plant, all the nutrients are important, but some are more likely to be in short supply, and these require more of the gardener's attention. For instance, carbon, hydrogen, and oxygen are free for the taking from air and water. Nitrogen, phosphorus, and potassium, on the other hand, are lacking to some degree in most soils. Even if they are present in sufficient amounts at the beginning of the gardening year, these elements may be used up and require replenishing each year or after each growing cycle and usually require supplementing, sometimes after each growing cycle. Calcium, magnesium, and sulfur are usually present in adequate amounts but not always.

To accurately evaluate your soil's nutrient content, you need to test your soil or have it tested (see how to do this on page 123). But the plants growing in it can also offer you clues to what it does — or doesn't — contain. The chart on the next page tells you how to read the messages your garden plants are sending. Notice that signs of excess are included along with signs of deficiency: "Moderation in all things" is as good a rule for plants as it is for people. Too much of some plant nutrients can be as bad as too little.

▲ It's great being green. *Healthy corn needs healthy soil with plenty of nitrogen to produce heavy crops and green leaves.*

▲ A pale shadow. *These corn seedlings, growing in nitrogen-deficient soil, are spindly and pale green to yellow in color.*

SOME CLUES TO WHICH NUTRIENTS YOUR PLANTS NEED

	Element/Symbol	Signs of Deficiency	Signs of Excess	Sources
Elements from water & air	Carbon/C	None known	None known	Air (carbon dioxide)
	Hydrogen/H	Wilting	Drowning	Water
	Oxygen/O	White areas in veins; high nitrates	None known	Air and water
Primary elements	Nitrogen/N	Light green to yellow leaves; growth stunted	Dark green leaves; excessive growth; maturity slowed; bud or fruit loss	Blood meal, fish emulsion, manure
	Phosphorus/P	Red or purple leaves; cell division slowed	Other essential elements sometimes tied up	Bonemeal, rock phosphate, superphosphate
	Potassium/K	Vigor reduced; susceptible to disease; thin skin; small fruits	Coarse, poor-colored fruit; intake of magnesium and calcium reduced	Greensand, muriate or sulfate of potash, seaweed, wood ashes
Secondary elements	Calcium/Ca	Growing point of plants damaged	Intake of potassium and magnesium reduced	Gypsum, limestone, oyster shells, slag
	Magnesium/Mg	Yield down; old leaves white or yellow	Intake of calcium and potassium slowed	Dolomite, magnesium sulfate (Epsom salts)
	Sulfur/S	Light green to yellow leaves; growth stunted	Combined with too-low pH, sulfur "burn"	Sulfur, superphosphate
Micronutrients	Boron/B	Small leaves; heart rot (corkiness); multiple buds	Yellowish red leaves	Borax
	Copper/Cu	Multiple buds; gum pockets	Intake of iron prevented; roots stunted	Copper sulfate, neutral copper
	Iron/Fe	Yellow leaves; veins remain green	None known	Chelated iron, iron sulfate (copperas)
	Manganese/Mn	Leaves mottled with yellow and white; growth stunted	Small dead areas with yellow borders on leaves	Manganese sulfate (Tecmangam)
	Molybdenum/Mo	Varied symptoms	Poisonous to livestock	Sodium molybdate
	Zinc/Zn	Small, thin, and yellow leaves; yield low	None known	Zinc sulfate

Let a Test Tube Be Your Crystal Ball

The ultimate test of any soil is the condition of the plants growing in it. Vigorous, healthy plants and a bountiful, tasty harvest mean the soil is just fine. Most gardens fall somewhat short of that goal, though, and would benefit from an addition of the right amendments in the right amounts. But before I can improve the soil, I need to know what's in it and what isn't. Some gardeners claim they can test soil by tasting it; I haven't tried that, so I can't say if it works or not. I do my "tasting" with a soil test. You can test your soil yourself or have it done at a laboratory, either through your state's Cooperative Extension Service or a private lab.

DO-IT-YOURSELF SOIL TESTS

Easy-to-use and inexpensive, do-it-yourself kits contain individual tests for pH, nitrogen, phosphorus, and potassium. With a do-it-yourself soil test, you get your results right away, rather than waiting for lab results. And you can test individual beds and

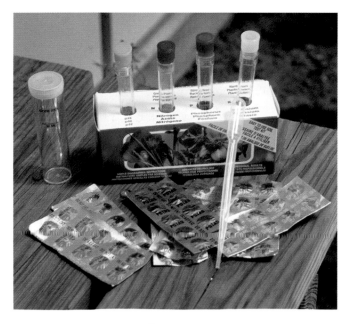

▲ Home-style chemistry. *Do-it-yourself kits are fun to use and provide a surprising amount of helpful information.*

fine-tune the soil for the vegetables you plan to grow there. Home test kits can be purchased at nurseries and garden centers as well as from mail-order suppliers. But DIY kits don't test for micronutrients, and they don't tell you anything about your soil's organic matter content.

LABORATORY SOIL TESTS

Compared to home tests, lab tests provide more information more accurately, including pH, nitrogen, phosphorus, and potassium levels, as well as values for secondary elements and micronutrients. Most labs can also test for the amount of organic matter, and some test for the amount and kind of biological activity going on in the soil.

That's a lot of very valuable information, but these benefits come at a cost, partly in money, partly in time. Soil tests by a state Extension Service are generally less expensive than those by private labs, depending on the range of the report. In either case you don't get instant results — particularly not in spring, when labs are often swamped with work from other gardeners and farmers.

THE BEST OF BOTH WORLDS

I use both kinds of tests. I test my soil with a kit at least once a year to monitor soil pH and major nutrient levels, and I test particular beds to match or adjust their characteristics to the needs of the plants I want to grow there.

When I'm starting a new garden or making a significant addition to an old one, I have a lab test done to make sure the soil doesn't have any major deficiencies. Ideally, I like to do this in fall, when labs are less busy. In addition, every three or four years I have a complete laboratory test done on the entire garden to make sure my soil improvement program is on track.

How to Take a Soil Sample for Testing

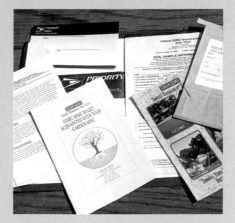

1 After scraping away any surface litter or mulch, use a trowel to dig a circular hole about 5 inches (12.5 cm) in diameter and as deep as the topsoil layer — 8 to 18 or more inches (20 to 45-plus cm), depending on how deeply the garden is dug.

2 Slice a strip of soil about ½ inch (13 mm) thick from the side of the hole and lay the sample on a sheet of newspaper. Take samples from at least 10 different places in your garden. Mix the samples well, breaking up any clumps and removing any stones or other litter.

3 Follow any further particular instructions for preparing the sample for home testing or shipment to the lab. For example, you may be asked to dry the sample to a particular degree before beginning tests or shipping.

SOIL-SAMPLING SAVVY

Any soil test is only as good as the sample of soil being tested. A sample that's not really typical of your garden soil, or one that is contaminated with anything other than garden soil, can't yield accurate results.

- Follow the test lab or test kit manufacturer's instructions carefully.

- Take samples before working the soil.

- Home tests involve mixing water with the soil sample. Use distilled water; it's pH neutral and contains no dissolved minerals that might affect test results.

- Use a clean trowel and wear clean latex gloves so you won't contaminate the samples.

- You'll get more accurate results, particularly for nitrogen tests, when the garden soil is warm and neither very dry nor very wet.

- Don't take samples from areas you know to be atypical, such as the spot where you piled the manure or compost before you spread it on other parts of the garden or a depression where runoff collects.

- Don't take samples within two weeks of adding fertilizers.

- Be sure to keep records of your results, including the date, weather conditions, and location of soil samples along with the readings.

Using Home Soil Test Kits

The two most popular types of home soil tests are chemical and electronic. Both are easy to use. Chemical kits are usually less expensive than electronic tests and offer good accuracy for the money. Both chemical kits and electronic testers can be purchased from local and mail-order garden supply companies.

Chemical kits. These supply different chemicals to measure soil pH along with phosphorus, nitrogen, and potassium levels. After mixing a small soil sample with distilled water, you add a chemical from the kit that changes the color of the solution. Then you compare the color of the solution with a color chart.

USING AN ELECTRONIC SOIL TESTER

With an electronic tester, you need only a trowel, distilled water, and the special cleaning pad supplied with the tester. To get a reading, you simply plunge the probes into wet soil and throw a switch. Move the switch one direction to get the pH value and the opposite way to measure fertility.

This device can be reused indefinitely, and it's somewhat faster to use than a chemical kit. On the other hand, while it can give you a fairly accurate reading of soil pH, its fertility reading doesn't tell you what nutrients your soil lacks.

Testing Your Soil pH with a Chemical Kit

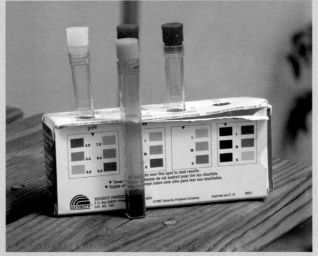

1 Following the package instructions, combine the soil sample and water with the chemical pH indicator supplied in the kit. Most kits supply test tubes for this purpose.

2 With the color chart placed so that a light source is behind it, hold the test tube about ½ inch (13 mm) away from the chart and compare the color reaction against the samples on the chart.

Soil pH: The Latch on Your Garden Gate

After you've tested your soil, you're left with a bunch of numbers that represent everything from pH to nutrients. What do they mean, and why do they matter? Let's start with pH, which I believe is the most important factor. My own garden experience a few decades back tells why.

Many years ago my wife, Sylvia, and I started a new garden in the Berkshire hills of western Massachusetts. It was the worst garden we have ever had. Most of the seeds didn't germinate at all, and many of those that did gave up quickly. The tomato plants grew to be 9 inches (22.5 cm) high and bore no fruit at all. The corn never got more than a foot (30 cm) tall.

All this trouble in soil that looked beautiful! It had wonderful tilth; a deep, dark brown color; plenty of organic matter. Soil tests showed no significant nutrient deficiencies. But what the tests did show was a pH of 4.5. With soil that acidic, none of the rest mattered. To be of any use to plants, nutrients in the soil must be available to them, which means they must dissolve in water. Most nutrients will not dissolve when the soil is either too acidic or too alkaline. And 4.5 is way too acidic.

The following year we added ground lime to the soil to bring the pH up to about 6.5. This single change allowed the nutrients to become available to the plants, and we had one of our best gardens ever. I have paid attention to pH levels ever since.

I should have been able to guess that the soil there would be very acidic: the whole area was rife with wild blueberries and what the locals called "Swamp Pinks," wild azaleas. Both thrive in acidic soil. Hindsight is always 20/20.

Understanding pH

Soil pH is a measure of how acidic or alkaline the soil is. The pH scale runs from 1 to 14, with 7 signifying neutral. Values below 7.0 indicate acidity, and numbers over 7.0 indicate alkalinity.

▲ **A matter of pH.** *Each year Nathan tests and adjusts the soil pH before growing another crop of his specialty, Roy's Calais Flint heirloom corn.*

IDEAL pH RANGES FOR PLANTS

Plant	pH Range	Plant	pH Range	Plant	pH Range
Alpine strawberry	5.0–7.5	Corn	5.5–7.5	Parsley	5.0–7.0
Artichoke	6.5–7.5	Cucumber	5.5–7.0	Parsnip	5.5–7.5
Arugula	6.5–7.5	Dill	5.5–6.7	Pea	6.0–7.5
Asparagus	6.0–8.0	Eggplant	5.5–6.5	Peanut	5.0–6.5
Basil	5.5–6.5	Endive/Escarole	5.8–7.0	Pepper	5.5–7.0
Bean, lima	6.0–7.0	Fennel	6.0–6.7	Potato	4.5–6.0
Bean, pole	6.0–7.5	Garden cress	6.0–7.0	Potato, sweet	5.5–6.0
Beet	6.0–7.5	Garlic	5.5–7.5	Radicchio	6.0–6.7
Broccoli	6.0–7.0	Gourd	6.5–7.5	Radish	6.0–7.0
Broccoli rabe	6.5–7.5	Horseradish	6.0–7.0	Red orach	6.5–7.0
Brussels sprouts	6.0–7.5	Jerusalem artichoke	6.7–7.0	Rhubarb	5.5–7.0
Cabbage	6.0–7.5	Kale	6.0–7.5	Rutabaga	5.5–7.0
Cantaloupe	6.0–7.5	Kohlrabi	6.0–7.5	Sage	6.0–6.7
Carrot	5.5–7.0	Leek	6.0–8.0	Salsify	6.0–7.5
Cauli-broc	5.5–7.5	Lettuce	6.0–7.0	Sorrel	5.5–6.0
Cauliflower	5.5–7.5	Mâche	6.5–7.0	Spinach	6.0–7.5
Celeriac	6.0–7.0	Marjoram	6.0–8.0	Squash, summer	6.0–7.5
Celery	6.0–7.0	Melon	5.5–6.5	Squash, winter	5.5–7.0
Chervil	6.0–6.7	Mizuna	6.5–7.0	Sunflower	6.0–7.5
Chinese cabbage	6.0–7.5	Mustard	6.0–7.5	Swiss chard	6.0–7.5
Chive	6.0–7.0	Okra	6.0–7.5	Tarragon	6.0–7.5
Cilantro/Coriander	6.0–6.7	Onion	6.0–7.0	Tomatillo	6.7–7.3
Claytonia	6.5–7.0	Oregano	6.0–7.0	Tomato	5.5–7.5
Collard	6.5–7.5	Pak choi	6.5–7.0	Turnip	5.5–7.0

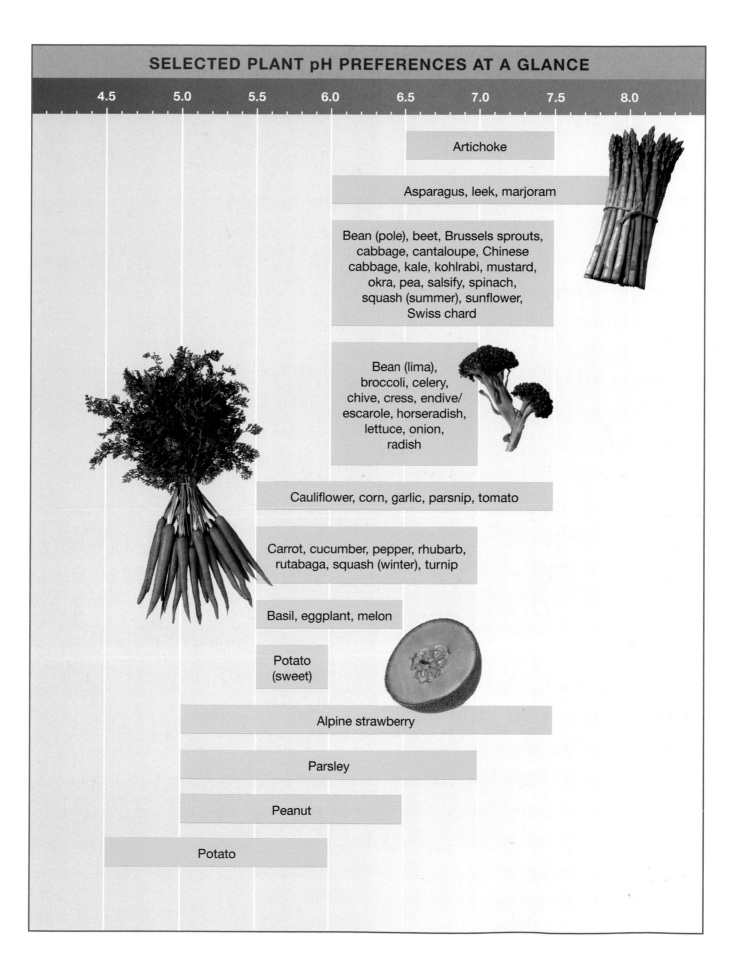

SELECTED PLANT pH PREFERENCES AT A GLANCE

| 4.5 | 5.0 | 5.5 | 6.0 | 6.5 | 7.0 | 7.5 | 8.0 |

Artichoke

Asparagus, leek, marjoram

Bean (pole), beet, Brussels sprouts, cabbage, cantaloupe, Chinese cabbage, kale, kohlrabi, mustard, okra, pea, salsify, spinach, squash (summer), sunflower, Swiss chard

Bean (lima), broccoli, celery, chive, cress, endive/escarole, horseradish, lettuce, onion, radish

Cauliflower, corn, garlic, parsnip, tomato

Carrot, cucumber, pepper, rhubarb, rutabaga, squash (winter), turnip

Basil, eggplant, melon

Potato (sweet)

Alpine strawberry

Parsley

Peanut

Potato

Putting pH Test Results into Action

As the result of a pH test, you'll have a number that indicates how acid or alkaline your soil is. If that number is within 0.5 of the number preferred by the plants you want to grow, you don't have to do anything. If it's more than 0.5 outside your plants' range, though, you'll have to add something to the soil to move its pH into the preferred range.

HOW TO SWEETEN ACID SOILS

The most common way to raise soil pH is to add lime to the soil. Calcitic and dolomitic limestone, as well as wood ashes, all contain lime. Calcitic limestone is primarily calcium, dolomitic limestone is a combination of calcium and magnesium, and wood ash is composed of about one-third calcium with significant amounts of potassium and magnesium. Which amendment you choose depends on whether nutrient soil tests show that your soil is deficient in potassium or magnesium.

As you can see by the chart on the next page, it takes quite a bit more lime-containing additive to raise your pH if you have clay soil or soil with a lot of organic matter.

HOW TO IMPROVE TOO-ALKALINE SOILS

The best long-term solution for improving alkaline soils is to add acidic organic matter such as pine needles, peat moss, leaf mold (particularly

▶ A quartet of pH adjusters. *Clockwise from top left, peat moss, pine needles, wood shavings, and leaf mold will make your soil more acidic.*

oak leaves), or aged sawdust or shavings. This not only reduces pH but also helps improve soil content and structure.

A quicker fix, but one that does not last as long, is to add agricultural sulfur. Like lime, it is best applied in fall, but you can apply it in spring if you do so early. Spread it and fork it in just the way you would add lime.

True Grit

There are many ways to determine if your soil is sandy, silty, or, like the feet of some celebrities, made of clay. Most tests are complicated affairs, but they needn't be. Finding the texture of your soil is literally right at your fingertips: Simply rub a small amount between your fingers. Do this when the soil is moist and comfortably warm. If the soil feels gritty or scratchy, it has a high sand content. Soil that feels smooth, like white flour, is high in silt. Clay soils feel sticky or slippery-smooth, like butter.

TIMING YOUR CORRECTIONS

To correct acidity. Fall is the best time to add lime to your soil to reduce its acidity, but if you find the problem in spring, deal with it in spring. Do so as early as you can, though — and at least three weeks before planting, because it takes a while for the pH to begin to change.

To correct alkalinity. Because organic materials take a while to act, and they tie up nitrogen while decomposing, it's best to add them in fall.

Applying Lime to Make Soil Less Acid

◀ Wear a dust mask whenever you're spreading any dusty soil additive. *Spread the lime or ashes evenly with a scoop or trowel. (Note: It takes about 30 percent more wood ash than ground limestone to raise the pH one unit.) Work lime into the top 6 inches (15 cm) of soil with a garden fork.*

HOW LIME RAISES SOIL pH

Doing a pH test is like taking a census, but instead of counting people it counts two types of charged particles — a positively charged one (acid) and a negatively charged one (base). As long as the positively charged particles outnumber the negatively charged particles, the soil is acidic. The greater the difference, the more acidic the soil. When you add lime to the soil, you're adding lots of the negatively charged particles, which makes the pH go up.

HOW TO CHANGE YOUR SOIL'S pH

Improving Acidic Soils
To raise pH by 1 unit, apply lime at the following rates for every 100 square feet (9.3 m²):

Soil Texture	Calcitic Limestone	Dolomitic Limestone	Wood Ashes
Sandy	2½ lbs. (1.1 kg)	2–3 lbs. (0.9–1.4 kg)	3–4 lbs. (1.4–1.8 kg)
Loam	6½ lbs. (3.0 kg)	6 lbs. (2.7 kg)	8 lbs. (3.6 kg)
Clay	9 lbs. (4.1 kg)	7–8 lbs. (3.2–3.6 kg)	9–10½ lbs. (4.1–4.8 kg)

Improving Alkaline Soils
To lower pH by 1 unit, apply sulfur at the following rates for every 100 square feet (9.3 m²):

Soil Texture	Powdered Sulfur	Aluminum Sulfate	Iron Sulfate
Sandy	1 lb. (0.5 kg)	2½ lbs. (1.1 kg)	3 lbs. (1.4 kg)
Loam	1½ lbs. (0.7 kg)	3 lbs. (1.4 kg)	5–5½ lbs. (2.3–2.5 kg)
Clay	2 lbs. (0.9 kg)	5–6 lbs. (2.3–2.7 kg)	7½ lbs. (3.4 kg)

Nitrogen, Essential for Vigorous Leaves

Nitrogen is among the nutrients that plants need for healthy leaf growth. It is therefore particularly important for plants such as lettuce, spinach, and cabbage, whose leaves are the parts we want. If your plants' leaves are light green or yellow and their growth is stunted, you can suspect that your soil needs more nitrogen. Note: Some plant varieties, especially lettuces, are naturally lighter in color. The fact that your Black-Seeded Simpson lettuce is a lighter green than your Green Star does not indicate a nitrogen deficiency.

WHEN YOUR SOIL NEEDS A NITROGEN BOOST

The best way to achieve and maintain a steady and sufficient supply of nitrogen in your soil is to add compost. If you find that your soil needs a nitrogen boost during the growing season, however, one or more of the following strategies should make a difference.

Green manure. Plants that are grown to maturity and then plowed back into the soil to enrich it are called green manures. Some plants that are particularly high in nitrogen, such as alfalfa, make excellent green manures. Known as nitrogen fixers, these plants take nitrogen from the air in the soil and change it into a form that plants can use. In order to benefit from the nitrogen these plants contain, you must incorporate the entire plant — roots, fruits, leaves, and all — back into the soil. Wait at least two weeks before planting a new crop in the treated bed. This gives the green manure a chance to decompose and release the nitrogen into the soil.

Blood meal and fish emulsion. It may sound like a horror story, but turning plants into vegetable vampires can cure many nitrogen-deficiency problems. Blood meal contains about 12 percent readily available nitrogen. For even faster results, give your plants a foliar feeding of fish emulsion. These remedies work only for a short time and should be followed with more long-lasting treatments. Follow the application advice on the package carefully, especially when using blood meal, since it's very rich in nitrogen. You don't want to overdose.

Nitrogen, Nitrogen, Everywhere . . . and Not a Drop to Eat

A nitrogen deficiency can sometimes occur even when there's plenty of nitrogen in the soil. This problem occurs when nitrogen is temporarily locked up or when soil conditions discourage microbial activity.

Locked-up nitrogen. When fresh organic matter begins to break down in the soil, nitrogen can be temporarily "locked up" and made unavailable to plants. Normally, the microorganisms in the soil break down organic matter slowly, making nitrogen available to plants as they work. Fresh organic matter, however, breaks down very quickly — so quickly that the microorganisms remove available nitrogen from the soil, locking it away from plant roots. For example,

nitrogen can become locked up when raw (unfinished) compost is spread. It's also temporarily unavailable for one or two weeks after a green manure has been turned into the soil. Once the breakdown of the organic matter is complete, the nitrogen is again available to the plants.

Weak microbial activity. Nitrogen is less available when the soil is cold, dry, or wet — all conditions that decrease biological activity in soil. If you test your soil under these conditions, you may get a low nitrogen reading, when in fact a change in weather may show that nitrogen is nearly ideal.

Planting a Green-Manure Crop

1 Prepare the seedbed as you would for any crop, applying slow-release nutrients such as greensand and rock phosphate. Rake it smooth and remove stones and other debris.

HAVING TOO MUCH OF A GOOD THING?

If you have ever grown an absolutely beautiful, big, leafy, dark green tomato plant that bore almost no fruit, you know that it's possible to have too much, as well as too little, nitrogen. All plants — even the leafy greens — can pig out on nitrogen if there is too much of it around, often in the form of too much manure. You should suspect that you've got an overabundance of nitrogen if leafy greens are bitter-tasting or fruiting plants have luxuriant leaves but no blossoms or fruit.

2 Broadcast seeds generously over the area and rake the seeded area thoroughly.

3 When the crop begins to form flower heads, use a common hoe to chop it up and turn it into the bed. Or cut it down with a scythe and cover it with straw or mulch hay.

Slow-Growing Gardens May Lack Phosphorus

A healthy tomato plant should have rich, medium-green leaves. But have you ever seen a tomato plant with purple-green leaves or leaf stems with a reddish purple cast? This strange coloration is an easy-to-detect sign of phosphorus deficiency. Unfortunately, the effects of insufficient phosphorus extend far beyond discolored foliage to touch every part of the plant. Tomatoes with phosphorus deficiency have poor root growth, leading to lower overall growth and poor production of flowers and fruits as well as decreased disease resistance. In many areas phosphorus is the plant nutrient most likely to be deficient or to become deficient in soils. This is so common that it's wise to add phosphorus in the form of rock phosphate whenever you start a new garden. Use about 10 pounds (4.5 kg) per 100 square feet (9.3 m²). To guard against future deficiencies, add rock phosphate to compost piles.

More than Meets the Eye

Don't be misled when you read on a package of rock phosphate that its phosphorus content is only 4 percent (the middle number here: 0-4-0). That 4 percent represents the immediately available phosphorus. The product is actually about 30 percent phosphorus, with more than 25 percent of it in a slow-release form that will become available over time.

▲ **Phosphorus poor.** *If your tomato plants are purplish, you can suspect that your soil lacks phosphorus. A good dose of rock phosphate should correct the problem.*

▲ **Top-notch tomatoes.** *Healthy, delicious-tasting tomatoes result only when they're grown in soil that meets all their nutritional needs.*

Plant Weaklings May Lack Potassium

Some plant nutrients are real showboats. If a plant has pale green leaves and you toss it some nitrogen — wham, the plant greens up in no time. Give phosphorus to your tomato plant with purplish leaves and in a few days it is lush and green again. But potassium is different. You can have a garden full of plants deficient in potassium and you may not notice it. The plants may appear a bit small or thinner than usual but not enough to get your attention. They don't look sick, but they are.

WHAT POTASSIUM DOES FOR PLANTS

Potassium is important to plants in many ways. It helps regulate photosynthesis, moisture content of plant cells, and the stomata, which control carbon dioxide exchange. It even helps move vital nutrients from place to place within the plant. Potassium also aids in the formation of proteins, which directly affects the nutritional value of vegetables. Plants grown in soils deficient in potassium often contain less protein than those grown in potassium-rich soils. Finally, potassium is critical to good soil health. For example, the microorganism responsible for fixing nitrogen in legumes needs a potassium-rich soil to function at its optimum.

FIXING POTASSIUM-POOR SOIL

Despite the subtleties of potassium deficiency, there are some symptoms to look for that may alert you to a lack of potassium in your garden. A plant with potassium deficiency often appears weak and spindly, attracts more pests and disease than usual, and bears small, thin-skinned fruits that often lack good flavor. This is most likely to occur in sandy soils, where the potassium is easily leached by irrigation and rain. Potassium deficiency can be corrected by adding greensand, granite dust, and wood ashes.

Greensand. Yes, it is really green and has the texture of sand. It is also the best source of potassium for the garden. Greensand is mined in places that used to be the bottom of ancient oceans. It contains not only potassium (1 percent immediately available and 6 percent available over time) but also iron, magnesium, calcium, phosphorus, and more than 30 trace elements. Apply greensand directly to new gardens (about 10 pounds per 100 square feet, or 4.5 kg per 9.3 m²) and whenever a soil test indicates a deficiency. Add it to your compost pile to ensure against future deficiencies and improve soil condition.

Wood ashes. These contain about 5 percent potassium in a relatively quick-release form. Because they also raise soil pH, apply wood ashes to your garden only after you test for pH, and do not use them if your soil is already alkaline. Wood ashes can burn sensitive plants, so it's best to add them to the soil when the garden is bare of growing plants — late fall, winter, or early spring.

Granite dust. This is a rock powder that helps restore a potassium balance to the soil in two ways: It provides both a supply of water-soluble potassium that the plant can use immediately and mineral potassium that becomes available over a longer period. Granite dust is about 6 percent potassium; 3 percent is immediately available and 3 percent is available over time. It does not affect pH.

GREENSAND — NUTRIENT ADDITIVE AND SOIL CONDITIONER IN ONE!

In addition to supplying potassium, greensand is also a very good soil conditioner: It loosens clay soils, binds sandy soils, increases water retention, and stimulates biological activity.

Soil Structure: A Delicate Matter

Plants do best in soil that stays loose and thoroughly aerated throughout the growing season. This is because plant roots do not just grow to a certain size and then stop, thereafter simply sucking up nutrients. Given the space, roots continue to grow and grow and grow. Located at the head of the growing root tip, fine root hairs absorb most of the nutrients that nurture the plant. These root hairs generally slough off after only a few days, but new ones appear as the root tip lengthens. This process is most effective when the soil contains root-friendly spaces — spaces large enough to gently direct growing roots around and between soil particles while also channeling the air that plant roots need and the water that carries nutrients to the roots.

Instead of being simply fluffed up, a soil full of long-lasting air spaces has structure. Within a well-structured soil, particles of clay, silt, sand, and organic matter are actually bound together by a waterproof "glue," which is the by-product of the feeding activities of millions of soil organisms. The result is soil crumbs called aggregates. Because they are waterproof, these aggregates remain intact through cycles of wetting and drying, thus preserving the spaces that allow air and water to enter and move about within the soil.

ROTOTILLING: FRIEND OR FOE?

If you're starting with a compacted, heavy clay soil containing little organic matter, rototilling will improve conditions a lot. A tiller is a very efficient way to loosen and aerate severely compacted soil and to chop and mix a large dose of organic matter into it. But if you are starting with soil that has decent structure and adequate amounts of organic matter, rototilling can easily destroy the worm-welcoming environment that already exists. This is because the pulverizing action of the tiller breaks up soil aggregates, disrupts capillaries, and demolishes worm-tunnel networks.

For more than twenty years I rototilled the garden three times a year, twice in fall and once in spring. I did all this tilling because I believed it was the best way to maintain and improve soil, as well as to create

◄ A hairy system. *Delicate plant root systems, like those of this sweet potato, need a soil that provides a friendly environment — one that contains water and air and plenty of room for the root system to develop and take in nutrients. If a soil is to provide for these needs, it must be "full of holes," and it should stay that way throughout the growing season.*

the best conditions for growing plants. I was wrong. It was a painful lesson to learn: Instead of improving the garden, the rototiller gave me more weeds and poorer soil. Here are the three problems tilling creates:

The problem of compaction. Rototilling does loosen and aerate the soil, but it doesn't stay that way. In contrast, the air spaces that form naturally in soil are a result of microorganisms working in the soil. The air spaces formed by rototilling are a result of the tines breaking up that structure. Consequently, although tilled soil is fluffy, its air spaces are fragile. In addition, the tiller destroys soil aggregates, which in turn decreases the water stability of the soil. As the soil settles over the growing season, the air spaces disappear until, long before the growing season is over, most are gone, and the soil is hard and compressed. Tilling creates a catch-22 for the gardener: The more you till, the more you need to till.

The problem of tiller pan. The downward-beating action of the tiller tines compacts the soil at the maximum depth the tiller can reach. This is called tiller pan, a special case of subsoil hardpan. This compacted subsoil layer makes it harder for plant roots, worms, and water to enter.

The problem of inversion. Tilling also brings about wholesale inversion of the soil and the creatures living there. Bacteria that were perfectly suited to certain temperature and moisture levels are suddenly disrupted and put where different temperatures and drier or wetter conditions prevail. Worms, if they aren't killed, are driven away.

IS DOUBLE-DIGGING DOUBLE TROUBLE?

Lest I leave any sacred cows alive, I should point out that a lot of what is true of rototilling is also true of double-digging. Although double-digging doesn't do as much damage to soil aggregates, worm tunnels can't survive the practice. Also, much of the double-dug soil is inverted, displacing soil organisms from the temperature and moisture levels they prefer. Double-dig when it is needed, such as when you're creating a new garden. The rest of the time, though, let the worms do most of the work.

Healthy, well-structured soil

Tiller pan

▲ **Tiller troubles.** *Although rototilling has its place, gardeners should know that it can cause soil to compact, create tiller pan, and destroy beneficial worms and other soil organisms. Note that the untilled soil ahead of the tiller is loose and deeply aerated. Once the blades churn through the bed, they disturb the channels naturally formed by the microorganisms and compact soil into tiller pan under the tiller tines.*

Help Wanted: Structural Workers

Gardeners can do a lot to improve their soils. If the soil is too acidic or not acidic enough, you can add limestone or peat moss to change this. You can add greensand or phosphate rock or other nutrient sources if the soil is deficient in nutrients. But if the soil doesn't have good structure, it's not something you can fix. You have to hire the work out.

WORMING YOUR WAY TO BETTER SOIL

Some of the most important organisms to work your soil into shape are worms. As they munch their way through the soil, worms ingest clay, silt, and sand particles as well as bits of organic matter. These nutrient-rich ingredients are eventually expelled as water-stable granules called castings. The castings make the soil more granular, which helps create soil capillaries and other spaces that improve soil structure while allowing air and moisture to flow freely.

▲ That's the way the cookie crumbles. *Well-structured soil is crumbly, much like the leftovers from a chocolate cake. Soil scientists call these particles of soil aggregates, but I like the term crumbs, because it describes the texture so accurately.*

In addition to these castings, worms also make tunnels that permeate the topsoil, allowing easy and quick access for water and air. These tunnels even penetrate into the subsoil (though to a lesser extent), facilitating deeper root growth and providing additional water-storage space. Soil that has been well worked by worms can take in water four times faster than soil that hasn't. This reduces runoff and prevents water loss through evaporation from puddles that form when soil cannot absorb rainfall quickly enough.

YOU CAN COUNT ON WORMS

Scientists use complicated tests to determine whether soil is healthy. All you really have to do, though, is go out to your garden and count your worms. While worms are by no means the only important inhabitants of the soil, they are the most obvious. If there are many worms in the soil, it's because the soil contains plenty to eat and is a friendly place to live and raise little worms. Worm-friendly soil has lots of organic matter, is well aerated and drained, and has a pH of about 6.0 to 7.0. Because the rest of the soil population has similar needs, the worm population is a mirror of soil life in general. And soil life reflects soil health.

How Worms Affect Soil Structure

- **Castings.** Worms are among the soil-dwelling creatures that form soil particles into aggregates.

- **Channelings.** Worms perforate the soil with a network of tunnels that create spaces where plant roots can grow.

WHEN TO TAKE THE CENSUS

A worm census is most accurate in spring or fall, when soil temperatures are comfortably warm. In summer, when soil temperatures rise above 60°F (16°C) — the comfort zone for garden worms — they move to deeper, cooler levels or die.

LET'S DO THE NUMBERS

Fewer than 10 worms in a 12"×12"×7" (30×30× 17.5cm) soil sample is bad news. The lower the number, the more serious the problem. You'll need more than a quick-and-dirty test to figure out exactly what the problem is, but the soil is probably woefully lacking in organic matter, and organic matter is the breakfast buffet to a worm. Worms do two things very, very well: They eat and they make more worms. Add organic matter to the soil and you supply them with food, and with food nearby, they'll happily make lots more worms.

If you find more than 10 worms, rejoice! Word has gotten around the worm world that your garden is a nice place to live. The more, the merrier; you can't have too many worms. A high score means that the soil is well stocked with organic matter and that the worms and other creatures eating this organic matter are significantly improving soil structure and fertility.

THOUSANDS OF WORKER WORMS
A census of 60 worms means that there are about 24,000 worms at work in a 20'×20' (6×6 m) garden, producing miles of irrigation lines and many pounds of rich castings.

Taking a Worm Census

1 With a spade, remove a block of soil about a foot (30 cm) square and 7 inches (17.5 cm) deep.

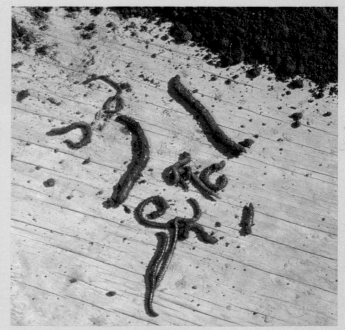

2 Spread the soil on a board and, as you break up the clumps of soil, gently extract and count the worms. Little ones score the same as big ones.

HOSPITALITY 101: MAKING WORMS FEEL WELCOME

Worms have a very simple mission in life: eat and make more worms. The more worms eat, the more worms they make, and the better off your garden will be. Where there is little for worms to eat, there will be few worms. Where there is a lot for worms to eat, there will be lots of worms — as long as the soil temperature, moisture, and pH are acceptable. Also, worms like a peaceful neighborhood. Run the rototiller through the garden too much and the worms will bid your garden goodbye. The best way to ensure conditions conducive to happy worms is to mix plenty of compost into your soil, protect it with organic mulch, and keep the rototiller in the tool shed.

SERVE UP SOME COMPOST AND MULCH

The best food for worms is, providentially, also the best food for garden plants — compost. This is nice to know because it supplies the answer to the question of when to apply compost. This answer is: All the time.

Worms are most content and most productive in loose soil (what agronomists call friable soil) that is moist but not soggy, about 60°F (16°C), with a pH of 6.0 to 7.0, and replete with organic matter. Worms slow down or die when it gets too hot or too cold, especially when that change happens quickly. Organic mulch helps keep soil moist, protects the soil from rapid changes in temperature, and like compost, provides additional, high-quality food for worms.

An automatic moisturizing system. As anyone who has picked up worms knows, they are moist creatures. To survive, they need soil that stays about as moist as they feel when you hold them in your hand. Mulch is an excellent way to retain soil moisture.

A built-in cafeteria. Mulch is food. Worms will eat just about any organic matter suitable for use as a mulch.

▲ **A cozy blanket.** *A covering of mulch can be particularly important as winter approaches. The mulch ensures that freezing temperatures penetrate the soil gradually, allowing worms enough time to move to deeper levels. In unprotected areas, the soil can freeze rapidly, and worms trapped near the surface freeze to death.*

Should I Add Worms to My Garden?

If worms are so important, and there aren't enough in the garden, why not just buy some and solve the problem that way? This sounds like a solution, but many times it isn't.

If there are few worms in your garden, it's probably not because there are few worms in your neighborhood. There are probably plenty of them living beneath the lawn or in the bushes nearby. They aren't in the garden because it doesn't provide them with what they need — moisture, proper temperature, and food. If you import worms, they will leave, for the same reasons that they didn't move in of their own accord.

Beyond Worms: An Introduction to Soil Life

Worms and various other creatures we usually group as "bugs" are the visible part of a living soil, but they occupy just one role in the subterranean ecosystem. If we look at soil under a microscope, we find that there are billions of microscopic creatures living down there, each one contributing to the health of the soil. Since thriving soil is an essential part of a healthy and productive garden, it's important to understand a bit about these creatures and how they can help us become better gardeners.

As scientists have studied soil microorganisms, it's become clear that they are mostly of two types:

Decomposers — These are the organisms, mostly bacteria and fungi, that actually eat organic matter (dead plants and other creatures).

Predators — These are organisms that eat the decomposers. They range from microscopic protozoa and nematodes to quite visible earthworms. The predators incorporate what they need from the bacteria and fungi they eat and excrete the rest in forms that plants can use.

Together, these soil creatures, prey and predator, complete the cycle of life, turning organic matter into plant food.

NITROGEN PRODUCERS NEEDED

Many of the foods that plants need are made available to them by the activities of soil microbes. But among the essential plant nutrients, one is particularly important to plant growth and health — nitrogen. Without it, there can be no chlorophyll. And without chlorophyll, there can be no photosynthesis (see page 130). This is why the foliage and stems of nitrogen-deficient plants turn yellow or light green.

Nitrogen is made available to plants when predator organisms eat decomposer bacteria. Bacteria are actually composed of nitrogen (about one part nitrogen to three parts carbon); because of this, they need to consume large quantities of it. Predators, on the other hand, are only made up of 1 part nitrogen for every 10 parts carbon. When predators consume bacteria, then, they're actually taking in more nitrogen than they need and excrete the excess in a form that is readily available to plants.

In a way, this creates a kind of natural "timed release" fertilizing system for plants. Whenever there is more nitrogen in the soil than plants can use, bacteria and fungi feed on the excess, thereby locking it up in their bodies and preventing it from being leached away. When predators feed on the bacteria and fungi over time, the nitrogen is released. Bacteria and their predators become more active as soil temperature increases. Thus, as the garden season moves from spring to summer and the plants grow and need more food, microbial activity increases and more food for plants is generated.

WHAT'S WRONG WITH CHEMICAL FERTILIZERS?

This process only happens in soil that is alive with a large and varied microbial population. The problem with chemical fertilizers is that they produce a form of salt as a by-product of their decomposition; this creates an environment that's inhospitable for a variety of soil organisms. To see for yourself, just look out your window. If you live in a place where the neighbors use chemical fertilizers, you won't see many robins on their lawn in the spring. (Because their soil doesn't have many worms. And, possibly, because the robins know what's good for them.) The robins will gravitate toward a yard with uncompromised soil, in search of worms. This process is the same for the predators and prey beneath the soil as well, even though you can't see them with the naked eye.

CHAPTER 7

Compost: Fill Your Garden Portfolio with Gardener's Gold

WHENEVER SOMEBODY TELLS ME that I need just one answer for all my questions, I get suspicious. The snake oil that cures all ills doesn't really cure anything; the multipurpose tool does none of its many tasks very well; and the one-size-fits-all garment doesn't really fit anybody.

But then there's compost. Compost sounds too good to be true, but it actually is as good as it sounds.

Compost nourishes both the garden plants and the creatures that live in healthy soil. It makes it easier for soil to receive and retain air and water, while stabilizing soil pH at the level most plants prefer. Compost even helps protect plants against some diseases and pests.

The key to a healthy and healthful garden is fertile, friable soil that is — quite literally — alive. Compost is the magic elixir that brings your soil to life and keeps it alive. It has been called "gardener's gold," and that's no exaggeration. The path to the garden of your dreams leads right through the middle of a compost pile.

Black Gold: The Miracle of Compost

Compost is both partially decomposed organic matter — mostly plants and the manures of plant-eating animals — and the soil-dwelling microbes that do the decomposing. Because it consists primarily of plants in the first place, compost often contains the elements plants need for growth in roughly the proportion they're needed. Gradual decomposition of compost by soil organisms releases these nutrients slowly, at a rate plants can use.

Compost helps the garden in many ways. It:

- **Provides nutrition.** It is a source of all the basic nutrients required for vigorous plant growth.

- **Improves soil structure.** Because it separates soil particles, it improves soil tilth by creating aeration and by nurturing the organisms that build and maintain it, compost brings about the improvement of soil structure.

▲ A truckload of gold. *We use so much compost that we supplement the amount we can create from home and garden waste with a truckload of purchased compost from a local supplier.*

- **Increases the ability of soil to retain water.** Compost holds up to six times its weight in water.

- **Contributes to the health of plants.** Compost may help prevent some plant diseases and promote plant growth by producing growth-stimulating hormones and chemicals.

- **Moderates soil pH.** Most compost has a pH level at which most plants thrive, and it both moderates soil pH and mitigates the effects of less-than-ideal pH levels.

- **Feeds soil organisms.** Most important, compost is a food source for legions of organisms whose activities are essential for plant health and continual soil improvement. Before it becomes food for plants, it is food for countless soil-dwelling organisms whose activities greatly improve soil structure, increase aeration and water retention, and make it easier for roots to grow. Soil bacteria and fungi, protozoa, nematodes, earthworms, and many, many others, large and very small, are all dependent on compost to supply their daily bread. Because each organism prefers a certain kind of food, the more different ingredients you add to your compost pile, the more diverse will be the organisms that feed upon it, and the more beneficial the resulting compost will be.

Good Humus

Humus, the end product of fully decomposed compost, contains humic acid, which makes the essential minerals that are already present in the soil more available to plants. It also stimulates seed germination and plant growth, reduces the need for fertilizers, and encourages better yields.

Compost: Nature's Recycling Method

When you make compost, you're doing what nature does all the time, only a little faster. Compost-making is nothing more than the fine-tuning and acceleration of a process that goes on all around us as bacteria and other soil-dwelling organisms break down organic matter and produce food for new plants. Composting is nature's method of recycling.

For many people, composting is a way to turn otherwise bothersome waste products from their kitchens, yards, and gardens into a valuable resource. But most gardeners soon find that the ordinary stream of household and yard waste isn't enough to produce the amount of compost they need. Although I recycle any organic matter I can from my home and garden, I wouldn't have enough compost if I depended on only that. My garden requires a lot of compost, so I've had to come up with ways to compost more material and design a composting system with my needs in mind.

What to Compost

Just about anything organic can be made into compost, but some things are better for composting than others. You'll end up with more balanced compost, and have it sooner, if you're a little choosy about what goes into it. If you're really particular, you may want to be sure your compost ingredients are organically grown.

- Alfalfa meal and hay
- Algae (pondweeds)
- Apple pomace (from cider making)
- Bean shells and stalks
- Broccoli stalks (but not roots)
- Buckwheat hulls or straw
- Cabbage stalks and leaves (but not roots)
- Citrus rinds
- Clover
- Cocoa hulls
- Coffee grounds
- Corncobs (chopped)
- Cottonseed hulls
- Cowpeas
- Cucumber vines
- Eelgrass
- Eggshells (crushed)
- Farm animal manures
- Flowers
- Fruit peels
- Granite dust
- Grape pomace (from wine making)
- Grass clippings (in thin layers)
- Greensand
- Hay
- Hedge clippings
- Hops (from beer brewing)
- Kelp
- Leaf mold and leaves
- Lettuce and other greens
- Melon vines, leaves, and rinds
- Oat straw
- Peanut hulls
- Pea pods and vines
- Peat moss
- Phosphate rock
- Potash rock
- Potato skins and vines (unless diseased)
- Rhubarb leaves
- Rice hulls
- Shells (ground clam, crab, lobster, mussel, oyster, well buried in the pile)
- Sod
- Soybean straw
- Sphagnum moss
- Sugarcane residue
- Tea leaves
- Vegetable peels, stalks, and foliage
- Vetch
- Weeds
- Wheat straw

Getting the Right Balance

Everything that grows is made up of many different elements. Two of the most important are carbon and nitrogen. Composting occurs fastest and most completely when you use about 30 parts of carbon to 1 part of nitrogen, by weight. Since people don't usually remember which materials supply which of these elements, I like to think in terms of 30 parts "brown" (for the carbon) and 1 part "green" (for the nitrogen).

COMPOST BROWNS: SOURCES OF CARBON

Generally speaking, the browns are the dried-out stems, stalks, and leaves of plants.

- **Straw.** Of the browns that I use, I like straw best. Straw is composed of hollow stalks, which ensures good action in the compost pile. Any sort of straw is good, including oats, barley, wheat, and rye.

- **Hay.** This may contain weed seeds, only some of which may be killed by the heat of composting. I use it anyway if I run short of straw. If you use cow or horse manures, you'll probably end up with some hay, too.

- **Cornstalks and pea and bean vines.** When allowed to wither and dry out, cornstalks, as well as pea and bean vines, are useful browns.

- **Autumn leaves.** Even if they're shredded, leaves tend to mat together and prevent enough air from entering the pile. (A whole other bunch of bacteria — not the ones we want — start working in airless or low-air conditions. You'll know that this has happened if things start to stink.) It is okay to mix some leaves into the straw, but don't make them the main ingredient in your brown layers. Leaves are a valuable addition to garden soil, but rather than composting them, it's better to incorporate them directly into the soil (see page 114).

- **Wood shavings and sawdust.** These decompose much more slowly and have a lower pH than the rest of the pile. I don't usually add these, but because they're used as bedding materials for farm animals, they often end up in the pile if I use animal manures.

DO ACTIVATORS HELP?

To get the composting process going, you need a "starter" population of the microorganisms that will actually do the work. Under most conditions, the best ingredients, called activators, are garden soil and compost. Some activators sold in garden catalogs also contain a big shot of nitrogen, useful in compost piles with too much brown, carbon-rich material.

▲ **A balancing act.** *Try to keep a balance of 30 to 1 between the carbon-rich ("browns") and nitrogen-rich ("greens") materials you add to your compost pile.*

- **Pine needles.** These also break down slowly and are very acidic. I use these materials as mulches for acid-loving plants like blueberries but not in the compost pile.

COMPOST GREENS: SOURCES OF NITROGEN

Important "greens" include just about any fresh or slightly wilted plant matter. Grass clippings and kitchen scraps are obvious examples, but all nonpoisonous weeds (before they go to seed) are also good additions to the pile. Seaweed, especially kelp, is a very good green because it is likely to contain trace minerals. Plant residues from the garden can go into the compost pile as long as they are not diseased and have not gone to seed.

If you can find a nearby source, pondweeds, apple or grape pomace, and bird feathers can go in the pile as nitrogen-rich greens. (Some nitrogen-rich compost materials, such as these weeds, pomace, and feathers, as well as manures and alfalfa hay, aren't actually green but still belong in the "green" category.)

WHAT NOT TO COMPOST

Diseased plants. Don't compost any part of a diseased plant. Some plant parts, like the roots of any cabbage family member, are likely enough to harbor soilborne diseases that they shouldn't be composted at all. Some plant diseases can survive in even the hottest hot piles, and many more will survive if the pile doesn't get hot enough and stay hot long enough. Play it safe and keep diseases out of the compost. If you burn the diseased plants, the ashes are safe for the garden.

Weeds gone to seed. Most weeds are okay, but if they've gone to seed, don't add them to a cold pile. Avoid pieces or whole roots of weeds, like witchgrass, that propagate themselves from roots.

Ashes. Coal ashes can be toxic to plants, so don't use them. Wood ashes are a source of considerable

disagreement. They raise pH, and I may not want to change the pH of either the compost or the particular bed to which it will be added. Instead of using wood ashes in the compost pile, I add them directly to the garden if I need to adjust the pH of the soil.

Some kinds of manure. Don't use manures of cats and dogs in the compost pile. Manures of animals other than herbivores may contain diseases or parasites that are harmful to people. Also avoid using manures from industrial feedlots, which are likely to contain antibiotic-resistant strains of E. coli.

Some lawn clippings. Some people use herbicides on their lawns. If you use grass clippings from these lawns in your compost, you'll end up applying herbicides to your garden. If you collect grass clippings from your neighbors or from a lawn-care service, make sure the clippings have no herbicides.

Meat and dairy products. Most experts suggest that these be omitted. The problem isn't that animal products won't compost; they will. (Whole cows can be composted, leaving only the bones.) But meat and diary products can attract animals that may make a big mess of your compost pile while searching for a meal.

Creating More Greens

If you want to make a lot of compost, it may be difficult to come up with enough greens. One solution is to grow some. If there is extra space in your garden, plant a crop of buckwheat, annual alfalfa, cowpeas, or field peas. These plants are often referred to as green manures. Instead of tilling in these plants, as you normally do with green manures (see page 49), mow or pull them and add them to the compost pile. Or plant perennial alfalfa in an otherwise unused garden space; you may get as many as three harvests a year from a good stand.

Getting Your Compost Pile Started

Composting methods, and the compost piles that result, can be identified as either "hot" or "cold." As is often the case with such neat divisions, the reality is a bit more complex. All composting gives off some heat, the by-product of bacteria digesting organic material. The heat generated by bacteria that prefer temperatures at about 55°F (13°C) gradually raises the temperature to a level where different bacteria are more comfortable, between 70° and 90°F (21° and 32°C) — which is about the limit for a cold pile. These bacteria, in turn, may raise the temperature still further, beyond their own comfort range, and create conditions for yet another bunch of bacteria whose feeding activities may raise temperatures as high as 160°F (71°C). This kind of pile is a hot pile. You get a cold or hot pile depending upon how you build and maintain it.

QUICK AND SURE: HOT COMPOSTING

A hot compost pile is the best way to produce large amounts of compost fairly rapidly. It has the further advantage of killing many of the pathogenic organisms and weed seeds that may be present in the composted materials. A hot pile works best if it is made up all at one time and then allowed to compost completely without further additions of material. Because of this, it's best to build hot piles when it is easiest to come by the materials, particularly the greens. I have a lot of green matter in late spring, when I mow around the garden and along the driveway. There are a lot of greens at harvest, but not necessarily enough for a pile; I therefore plan a green-manure harvest at the same time.

SLOW BUT STEADY: COLD COMPOSTING

Cold compost piles take longer and do not destroy pathogens or weed seeds, but they can be built over a period of time. They are ideal for recycling small, steady streams of organic matter. Bacteria that prefer either cool or moderate temperatures do all the work in cold piles, which usually don't heat up beyond 90°F (32°C).

Once the cold pile is constructed, you can take some time off and let nature do the rest of the work. Monitor the moisture level, and add water if necessary. After a few months, turn the pile, bringing material from the middle out to the edges. Rewater if necessary and fluff the material well. It will take a year or more to get finished compost, but you can use it sooner as a topdressing or mulch, or you can mix it into the soil in fall.

WHERE TO PUT COMPOST PILES

Permanent piles. Any place fairly near the garden with good drainage can be the site for a compost pile or piles. Before you put any composting material in place, loosen the soil where you intend to build your compost pile so worms can get in. If possible, make more than one compost setup. Put a cold pile near the kitchen to handle the small but constant stream of kitchen and garden wastes. In addition, build a hot-pile setup wherever is convenient for you.

In-garden compost piles. If there's enough room, you can put your compost pile right in the garden. Make the compost pile a part of the crop rotation and put it in a different spot each year. Any compost left behind enriches the garden, and any nutrients that leach out of the compost settle in the soil. Additionally, worms can help a lot with the later stages of compost development, and if things are going as they ought in your garden, you should have plenty of worms in the beds.

Composting Hardware: Bins and Tools

All our kitchen scraps end up in one of these plastic compost bins. When one is full, I let it sit for a year and start using the other one. The black color helps to maintain a temperature higher than the ambient air. Compost bins aren't necessary, but they are desirable. An unrestrained pile can be messy, and it can get a lot messier if animals get into it. A good bin also makes the process easier and more fun.

Size. Hot compost requires a bin at least 3' × 3' × 3' (0.9 × 0.9 × 0.9 m). A smaller pile won't heat up enough. A pile larger than 4 feet (1.23 m) on a side will need additional ventilation in the center. Bins for cold piles can be smaller but should be large enough to handle the volume of kitchen waste you anticipate.

Shape. Most bins are square or rectangular, though some are round. They can be made of wood, wire, wood and wire, plastic, cement blocks, straw bales, or metal. I like a bin to be enclosed on all sides to give the pile support all the way around. I also like easy access to one side when turning the pile or removing finished compost, and I prefer not to have to take the whole bin apart to get this access.

▲ **All shapes and sizes.** *It doesn't really matter what your compost bin looks like, as long as it's sturdy and well built.*

Here are four very different composting bins; they all work. Choose the one that meets your needs and fits your budget.

A COLD COMPOSTER FOR A SMALL KITCHEN GARDEN

You'll find quite a variety of polyethylene composters at garden centers and from mail-order suppliers. The square bin shown in the photograph is made by Gardener's Supply; the round one is called The Earth Machine. Both have a fitted top that keeps out rain and animals. Both are of marginal size for hot composting, but are good bins to put near the kitchen to receive garden trimmings and kitchen waste for a cold pile. (Keep some straw and leaves in a container nearby so that you can add browns from time to time to keep the carbon-nitrogen ratio in balance.) It is handy to have two of these bins: One can be filling while the other is composting.

WOODEN COMPOST BIN

For our major composting we use bins that are made of white cedar, a naturally rot-resistant wood. The wood isn't treated with any chemicals, and it lasts for years. While white cedar is one of the best woods to use for compost bins, other good choices are redwood, tamarack, or even oak.

Our bins are a good size for hot compost making and well-enough braced so they needn't be fixed to the ground. Portability is a nice feature, if you'd like to place your compost bin in the garden and move it from spot to spot over the years. The angled slots on the front hold the wooden slats and allow the lower slats to be removed while the upper ones remain in place. This feature makes loading, re-piling, and unloading easy.

A trio of these wooden bins makes a nice compost factory. Compost can be turned from one bin into the next. Then a new pile goes in the first bin.

A FREE-CYCLED COMPOST BIN

Wood pallets, often still in very good condition, are frequently available for the taking at lumberyards, hardware stores, or garden centers. They make excellent compost bins. Join four of them with wires or screw at the corners. (If you have enough pallets, use one for the bottom of the bin to provide for air movement up through the compost pile.)

With 10 pallets, you can make a nifty three-bin composting system.

STRAW BALE HOT BIN

If you've got an inexpensive source of old straw bales, this is a good, functional compost bin. It isn't the prettiest thing, but it does make good compost, which is what matters most. The straw bales will hold together longer if the baling is plastic or wire; if not, tie new twine around them once a year. After a few years, the bales will decompose, and you can add them to the compost pile and create a new bin. Arrange the bales in much the same way as for the straw bale cold frame pictured on page 62. As your compost grows, simply pile on additional straw bales.

COMPOST VENTILATING SYSTEM
To ventilate a large compost pile, insert a 4-foot-long (1.2 m) piece of perforated plastic drainage pipe as soon as the pile is deep enough to support it. Continue to build the pile up around the pipe.

▲ The path to success. *Our compost bins are conveniently located, along with our greenhouse, right in the middle of the garden. Here, they're not only easy to fill and access, but they remind us that they really are the key to our success.*

▲ Free is better. *This compost bin cost me the gas to go after the pallets and a few pennies' worth of electric fence wire. It works just as well as a purchased bin costing over $100.*

Tools for Compost-Making

Although compost-making is a natural and simple process, a few tools can make the operation go more smoothly.

- **Compost thermometer** with a 20-inch (50 cm) probe. Taking the temperature of your hot compost pile tells you whether it's behaving correctly, when to turn the pile, and when the compost is finishing.

▲ Compost thermometer

- **Six-tine manure fork.** The tines of this fork are slim and pointed, more like the tines of a pitchfork than those of a garden fork. They enter the pile easily. This is the best tool for making, turning, and aerating the pile.

- **Watering can or hose.** Add water as you build the pile. The whole pile needs to be moist but not soggy.

- **Shredder.** This expensive tool is optional. Materials like cornstalks and tomato plants will be easier to handle and compost a lot faster if chopped. Instead of an expensive shredder, you can use a machete and a chopping block for this task; it just takes more time and energy.

▲ Six-tine manure fork

- **Lawn mower.** You can shred leaves and other composting materials by running over them with a lawn mower a few times, then raking up the clippings and tossing them on the pile. (If you have a bagger, you can skip the raking; just empty the bag into a garden cart or right into a bin for making leaf mold.) The smaller the material is, the faster it will compost, provided it doesn't pack down and exclude air. To avoid this, if you're using finely chopped material, make your green layer thin.

▲ **A one-step wonder.** *My battery-powered electric mower cuts the grass and picks up, chops and bags the leaves . . . all without using any gasoline.*

If You Build It, You'll Get Compost

Hot and cold piles are built the same way, but the recipe for a hot pile is a little more exact. Also, a cold pile is created gradually, as materials become available, whereas a hot pile is built all at once. A cold pile that isn't quite perfect just takes longer to break down, but an improperly made hot pile may not heat up at all, or it may not stay hot long enough to produce the best compost.

Ideally, all the ingredients in a compost pile should be mixed together. In practice, layering works fine, provided the layers aren't too thick. "Too thick" depends on what makes up the layer, so here are some guidelines that apply to both hot and cold piles.

GARDEN LASAGNA

Start with a layer of straw about 3 inches (7.5 cm) deep. Add 1 to 6 inches (2.5 to 15 cm) of green material. The looser the material, the thicker the layer you can add without risking compaction and loss of air. For instance, you can safely add pea or bean vines in a thick layer (6 inches [15 cm]). Mowings from green-manure crops, weeds, and hay (either green or dry) can be piled about 3 inches (7.5 cm) deep. Grass clippings and kitchen scraps will mat together and exclude air if they're piled more than an inch or so deep. There's a bit more art here than there is science. Just keep this rule in mind: Leave room for air to circulate throughout the pile.

On top of each green layer, sprinkle about ½ inch (13 mm) of soil (no more). If you're using manure, this is where it should go. This time, use no more than an inch (2.5 cm) and mix it with soil. The bioactivator for the pile, soil contains the organisms that will break down the organic material into more soil. Unless the soil is seriously deficient in organic matter, and therefore in biological activity, ½ inch (13 mm) should be enough. If you're in doubt, add some compost as a starter.

Add another straw layer and keep building, "lasagna-fashion," until the pile is about 4 feet (1.2 m) high. The pile will settle, and it needs to be at least 3 feet (0.9 m) high after settling to heat up properly.

How Much Compost Should I Make?

In cool climates you'll want to spread compost at least an inch (2.5 cm) deep on every bed, with some available for sidedressing during the season.

If you live in a warm region, you'll need even more compost. The warmer your climate, the more quickly soil organisms will digest compost, because there's more biological activity as soil temperatures rise and the activity goes on for more of the year. In the warmest regions, you may need 2 or even 3 inches (5 to 7.5 cm) of compost a year for each bed.

▶ **More is better.** *The greater the variety of wastes going into the compost pile, the more kinds of soil microbes will be eating there and the better the compost will be.*

Four Easy Steps to Hot Composting

1 Make succeeding layers of straw, green material, and soil lasagna-fashion as described on page 150 until the pile is about 4 feet (1.2 m) high. As you spread on the layers, fluff them to allow spaces for air to circulate through the pile.

2 Compost needs moisture just as it needs air. Your goal should be to get a mixture that feels something like a squeezed-out sponge, damp to the touch but definitely not soggy. Add water to the brown layer, which is the driest, as you build the pile.

3 When you've finished making the pile, cover it. This reduces evaporation from the top of the pile and also prevents accidental overwatering from rain. You can cover it with a nylon-reinforced tarp, as shown, or use black plastic, which absorbs sunlight and adds warmth to the pile. White plastic reflects sunlight and can keep the compost pile too cool.

4 You'll get better results with a hot compost pile if you check it and tend it regularly. Using a compost thermometer, preferably one with a long probe, take the temperature of the pile daily. If everything is going as it should, the pile should reach 140° to 160°F (60° to 71°C) within a few days. Whenever the temperature starts a steady drop, turn the pile. With each turning, moisten the pile if necessary, fluff it for aeration, and move the material from the outside into the center.

Don't Leave Out the Leaves

Leaves, particularly oak leaves, are very good for garden soil. They contain micronutrients drawn from the depths of the earth. Unfortunately, in a compost pile they mat together and promote the growth of anaerobic bacteria, the smelly ones we don't want (see The Good Guys vs. the Bad Guys, below).

A better way to add leaves into the garden is to work them directly into the soil. You can do this by first putting them through a shredder or running over them a few times with a power mower and then using a three-tine cultivator to mix them into the soil. You can also till them in, but I prefer the gentler method (see page 114).

LEAF MOLD

Another way to get the benefits from leaves is to make leaf mold. The end product of leaves decomposed in a moist environment primarily by fungi, leaf mold is the rich-looking, crumbly material that lies beneath the layer of recognizable leaves on the floor of a deciduous forest. It is very good for plants, particularly carrots and members of the cabbage family.

Making leaf mold is very easy. Wait for the leaves to fall from the trees and then simply make a leaf pile. If the leaves aren't wet, water them down. Then, just like the cold compost pile, let them sit. It takes a bit longer to make leaf mold than compost — about two or three years — but it's worth the wait. Just turn the pile once a year to give the fungi that are doing all the work a breath of fresh air.

As is the case with compost piles, a bin keeps things neater. A circular bin 3 to 5 feet (0.9 to 1.5 m) in diameter made of heavy-gauge wire fencing works well. You can also make a serviceable bin from a length of snow fence. Just form it into a circle and secure with wire. A few large rocks or concrete blocks placed around the base of the bin will help to keep it from bulging.

▲ **Fall roundup.** *Use fencing to make a movable bin for leaves. In two or three years you will have leaf mold, one of the best soil amendments, especially for carrots and cabbage family members.*

The Good Guys vs. the Bad Guys

Aerobic bacteria need oxygen; anaerobic bacteria don't. Both kinds of bacteria act upon and break down organic compounds, but the former are a lot more helpful if what you want is a plentiful supply of compost. Aerobic bacteria work much faster, and they do a more thorough job. The end products of their work are basic plant nutrients in a form readily available to plants. Anaerobic bacteria are slow, and they leave the job only partly done. Their end products leave many nutrients still locked in compounds and unavailable to plants or even toxic to them. Finally, as if to let us know that they really aren't being much help to us, anaerobic bacteria create a monstrous stink.

TROUBLESHOOTING COMPOST TROUBLES

Symptom	Possible Cause	Solution
Unpleasant odor	■ Lacks air, because of compaction	■ Aerate.
	■ Lacks air, because of overwatering	■ Add browns, which will absorb moisture, and aerate.
	■ With ammonia smell, too much nitrogen	■ Add browns and aerate.
	■ Lacks nitrogen	■ Add greens like grass clippings, fresh manure, or blood meal.
	■ Too wet	■ Add straw or other browns and turn pile.
Pile doesn't heat up	■ Lacks moisture	■ Poke holes in pile so you can water well inside.
	■ Needs turning	■ Use manure fork to bring materials from the outside to the center of the pile.
	■ May be finished	■ If it's dark, crumbly, and earthy smelling, you have finished compost.
Hot pile cools off	■ Needs turning	■ Use manure fork to bring materials from the outside to the center of the pile.
Pile is damp and warm only in the center	■ Too small	■ Gather more materials and rebuild a larger pile.
	■ Not enough nitrogen	■ Add a nitrogen source, such as manure or fresh grass clippings.
Animals get into pile	■ Meats and/or dairy products attract them	■ Avoid adding meats and dairy products. Throw a loose covering, such as a piece of chicken wire or fencing, over the pile.
Some material doesn't break down	■ Lacks nitrogen and/or moisture	■ Add water. Cover pile and water whenever it feels dry. Add nitrogen source, such as manure or fresh grass clippings.
	■ Needs mixing	■ Turn pile, breaking up any whole or matted material and mixing it in.
	■ Pieces too large or woody	■ In the future, chop coarse material before adding it to pile. For now, sift compost to remove large pieces.

When You Can't Make Your Own Compost

Not very long ago, the only way to get compost was to make it. Now, with organic vegetables featured in supermarkets and organic gardening gaining popularity, compost has become big business and is commercially produced out of everything from autumn leaves to animal manures to residue from breweries.

If you are just starting to garden, or just starting to make compost, buy some of the commercial stuff to get your garden off to a good start. Don't skimp. Compost is crucial to a healthy, productive garden, and any money spent now will come back to you in many ways, many times over, especially when it comes time to harvest.

If you have a large garden, or if your soil test indicates the need for a hefty initial dose of organic matter, consider buying compost by the cubic yard (meter) rather than by the bag. I am fortunate to live only 25 miles (40 km) from a commercial composting operation. I can buy about 1,200 pounds (545 kg) for what 200 pounds (91 kg) would cost in bags. Even if you have to pay someone else for hauling, you will likely come out way ahead.

COMPOST CREDENTIALS

Not all of what passes for compost belongs in the garden. Buy the compost you use to grow vegetables as carefully as you would buy vegetables. So far, there are no universally accepted standards for judging compost quality and no certification organizations to monitor compost production. Until there are widely accepted standards for compost certification, a well-known brand with a good reputation is your best guarantee of quality.

Buying compost, no matter how good it is, is just a temporary solution. The best way to get the compost you need is to make it yourself. Making your own is certainly cheaper than purchasing compost. Most of the ingredients are things you presently throw away. Even more important, if you make your own compost, you know what's going into it. You grow your own food so you'll be sure it is safe and nutritious, and "growing" your own compost ensures that it, too, will be safe and nutritious.

▲ Look at the label. *You'll have the best chance of getting high-quality compost if you buy a well-known brand with a good local reputation among gardeners and farmers.*

Composted Sludge: Okay to Use?

Composted sewage sludge is the by-product of municipal sewage treatment plants. Because municipal sewage usually includes chemical waste from factories and cleaning plants, as well as toxic household cleaning products, the resulting sludge may be contaminated with heavy metals, which are not good for plants or people. I don't like taking chances with my food or family, so I don't use or recommend compost made from sewage sludge.

What to Look For in Store-Bought Compost

If you make your own compost, you know what's in it and you know how it was made. If you're buying compost, you may or may not know either. There are not, so far, any widely accepted standards for compost. You may have to make your choices based on what you can infer about the compost based on how it looks, smells, and feels.

WHAT DOES IT LOOK LIKE?

To start with, the compost you're evaluating shouldn't look like its source material. You shouldn't be able to identify plants or plant parts, and there shouldn't be identifiable chunks of bark or twigs. Good compost will have a dark color, and will be loose and uniform in texture.

WHAT DOES IT SMELL LIKE?

Your nose knows. The aroma of good compost is akin to that of good earth or of the duff on a forest floor. It shouldn't be offensive in any way — not musty or stale or rotten; it shouldn't smell of manure.

WHAT'S IT MADE OF?

Good compost is made from a diversity of source materials — leaves, poultry feathers, animal and bird manures, grass clippings, yard waste, food scraps, fish, spoiled hay, sawdust. The more varied the ingredients in compost, the more varied will be the kinds of soil microbes that create and make up the finished product, and the better the compost will be.

WHAT'S IT NOT MADE OF?

There are some things that don't belong in compost but sometimes get in anyway. (See Composted Sludge: Okay to Use?, page 154) Some herbicides and pesticides that might be on lawn clippings or food waste break down in compost piles and become harmless. But some don't. Clopyralid, a popular herbicide used on lawns, retains its ability to kill broad-leaved plants even after composting. And very little can kill all the broad-leaved plants in your garden. If you buy compost containing lawn clippings, make sure it has been tested and is guaranteed not to contain herbicides.

ASK AROUND

As organic gardening becomes more popular, more and more gardeners are using compost. Where do your neighbors or local organic growers get their compost?

◀ **Dark and crumbly.** *High-quality compost will look and feel like dark, rich soil.*

CHAPTER 8

Bugs, Slugs, and Things That Go Chomp in the Night

AT VARIOUS TIMES IN THE GARDENING YEAR, we gardeners find ourselves competing with other creatures for the bounty of the garden. How might we go about weighting that competition in our favor, ensuring that most of the harvest ends up on the dining table instead of on the menu of some garden marauder? Paradoxically, we can best ensure that garden pests will rarely be a serious problem by creating a garden teeming with all sorts of bugs, some large enough to be visible and others microscopic. Some of those bugs are pests; they're dining on some parts of some of the garden plants some of the time. But many of those bugs are dining on the plant-eating bugs. And still others are pollinating, ensuring that fruiting plants do bear fruit. Among the smaller "bugs" — bacteria, fungi, and other microscopic creatures — the same is true. This chapter is mostly about creating a garden environment where creatures that protect plants and help them to grow outnumber and help to control the creatures that eat plants or disturb their growing; it's about creating an ecologically balanced garden.

Controlling Pests the Natural Way

Garden-dwelling insects are pests to the extent that their taste in food is similar to ours. Fortunately, however, it is often the case that insect gourmets don't have exactly the same preferences we do. Insect pests often prefer sickly plants to robust ones, stressed plants to ones whose growth has been free of interruption, and malnourished plants to ones that have all the nutrients they need. Like many predators in nature, garden pests tend to attack the easiest prey. They'll even bypass healthy, vigorous plants to attack the stressed ones. Stresses include extreme fluctuations in soil or air temperature, too little or too much water, interruptions in the supply of any nutrient, compacted soil, and improper soil pH. Anything you can do to improve growing conditions for a plant makes the plant less likely to be attacked by pests and disease and better able to recover when any pest attacks do occur.

A plant overcome by pests or diseases is very likely a plant in less than optimal health. The pests or diseases are not the real problem; they're the symptoms of the real problem — plants that aren't growing as well as they should. Growing healthy plants in fertile soil with enough water and sunlight is the first step toward having a garden where pests are really not much of a problem. The pests and diseases are letting us know that something is not right in the garden.

A PEST-CONTROL STRATEGY

- Grow healthy plants in healthy soil
- Prevent the predator from getting to the prey
- Make the garden a haven for predators
- Solve the problem as gently as you can

Garden Health Checklist

- Put your garden where there's enough sunlight, especially in the morning, and adequate air circulation, to dry the dew quickly. Diseases do better in a damp environment.

- Build and maintain a living soil, full of the microbes that help plants to grow and protect them against diseases.

- Rotate crops so that disease-causing organisms that live in the soil won't find their host crop when spring arrives.

- Plant varieties that resist whatever diseases are likely to occur in your gardening neighborhood.

- Intercrop whenever possible.

- To keep diseases from spreading, don't work in the garden when plants are wet.

- Keep at least a ½-inch (1.25 cm) layer of compost on growing beds all the time. Compost not only ensures a steady flow of balanced nutrients to the plants but also has been shown to inhibit many plant diseases. (See pages 141–145.)

- Make sure plants have enough water. By the time it begins to look droopy, a plant is already stressed, and a stressed plant is an open invitation to pests and diseases. (See page 83.)

- Use mulches and row covers to maintain soil and air temperatures within the plant's preferred range. (See pages 68–71.)

Don't Just Do Something, Stand There

When you see damaged plants in the garden, it's good to remember that the appearance of pests does not always indicate a pest *problem*. Even if it is, it's not always something we have to deal with. It's natural for some pests to be in the garden all the time; our goal as gardeners is to react to those pests only when necessary and only to the extent necessary.

Not all pest damage is significant damage. Holes in the leaves of a mature tomato or bean plant, even quite numerous and substantial holes, bother the gardener a whole lot more than they bother the tomato plant. In nature, there's always some insect damage; that's the way it has been for eons, and plants are designed to cope.

▲ Before. *These bean plants have lost well over half of their leaf area to earwigs.*

▲ After. *Not only have the plants survived, they've thrived and produced a good crop of shell beans for freezing.*

▲ Before. *The leaves of this young broccoli plant are peppered with holes made by flea beetles. I was sure the plants would not survive to produce a crop.*

▲ After. *This is the same broccoli plant some weeks later, sporting a large, well-formed and delicious head.*

◄ Deadly larvae. *Colorado potato beetles are not, in themselves, a pest problem, but the larvae hatching from their eggs will be.*

Grow Healthy Plants in Healthy Soil

This is not to say that healthy plants will never suffer damage from pests, but given the choice, most pests most of the time will choose a plant weakened by stress of some kind, or lacking in some nutrient, or growing in less than optimal conditions. Plants grown in depleted, compacted soil and fed a limited diet of chemical fertilizers are sitting ducks for pests. A gardener's first line of defense against pests is to garden so that vegetable plants have the best possible conditions for rapid, uninterrupted growth.

A garden full of healthy plants getting all they need is a garden where pests and diseases are not very likely to be problematic. Start with deep, wide beds filled with soil rich in organic matter — preferably compost — and the right amounts of all the nutrients the various plants require, add enough water and sunlight, and protect the plants from extremes of hot or cold. You've already solved most of your potential pest problems and made the rest easier to solve.

AVOID STRESS

A plant that's less than fully well is a plant more vulnerable to pests and diseases. Anything that interferes with plant growth — anything from too-long germination to not enough water later in life — is a stress and weakens the plant to some extent. Plants vary a lot in their abilities to cope with stress, but they're all better off if we gardeners can protect them in the first place.

Squashes, both summer and winter, don't transplant well: direct seed them, using hot caps or row covers to protect against cold weather, or start them indoors in large (at least 4 inches [10 cm]) pots and transplant very, very carefully before they become pot-bound.

Basil and cauliflower don't like cool (below 40°F [4°C]) nights. Don't plant or transplant them until night temperatures are above 40°F (4°C). If there's a cool night anyway, protect the plants with row covers or hot caps. Corn won't germinate well or quickly until the soil temperature is at least 60°F (16°C). Carrots won't germinate well and young onions won't grow well unless their soil is continually moist.

FERTILIZE WISELY

When you fertilize your plants, you may not realize that fertilizer does more than provide nutrition to the plants. Fertilizing can also make your pest problems worse . . . or better. Plants grown in soils too rich in nitrogen, for instance, are more attractive to pests like aphids, mites, and whiteflies. On the other hand, plants grown in soils rich in phosphorus and potassium are less attractive to wireworms.

Get the pH Right

By keeping the pH of the soil at the optimum value for the plants you grow, many pest and disease problems can be greatly reduced or eliminated. The proper soil pH allows the plant access to the nutrients it needs, which keeps it from being stressed and in turn reduces pest problems. Cabbage-family crops grown in soil where the pH is at least 7.0 are less susceptible to club root. If your potatoes have scab, try growing them in a more acid soil.

Prevent the Predator from Getting to the Prey

Once a pest is living on or in a vegetable plant, there may be many more or less acceptable ways to prevent or minimize harm to the plant, but things are a whole lot simpler if you can keep the pest from getting to the plant in the first place. What follows are various ways to keep pest and plant from getting together.

TRICKS OF TIMING

You can keep pests away from garden plants by making sure they're not in the same place together. Or you can let them be in the same place but not at the same time.

In search of the earliest harvest in the neighborhood, many gardeners plant each vegetable as soon as they can in spring. Unfortunately, those early crops are often attacked by legions of pests that are lying in wait for the first meals of the new year. Your plants will have fewer pests if their life cycles are out of phase with the life cycles of the creatures that prey upon them. For example, if you wait until the peonies flower to plant cabbage family crops, you'll have fewer problems with cabbage worms. There are many

▲ **Well timed.** *Sometimes all it takes to outwit pests is to plant a crop out of sync with their life cycle. For example, planting potatoes later than usual may help avoid problems with Colorado potato beetles.*

more flea beetles in the spring and early summer than there are in the "dog days" of July and August. Broccoli planted or transplanted in July isn't as likely to be overwhelmed by these leaf-nibbling critters as is broccoli set out in early spring. A neighbor of ours never plants potatoes until the Fourth of July. And he never has a problem with Colorado potato beetles. By the time his potato sprouts emerge, the overwintering beetles have long since emerged, found no food, and gone on to someone else's garden.

COMPANION PLANTING FOR PEST CONTROL

There is some spotty, mostly anecdotal, evidence than certain plants, mostly those in the wide-ranging and strong-smelling onion family, repel certain pests, or at least make it harder for them to smell out their favorite meals. There may be something of value here; many gardeners think so. Take what's written here and elsewhere with a grain of salt, and try some experiments. It's not likely to hurt anything and may do some good.

- Onions, garlic, and other members of the onion family are universally despised by pesky bugs, probably because the onion group is stinky. Almost all other garden plants will be less bothered by insects if they live among onions.

- Garlic offends Japanese beetles, vegetable weevils, and spider mites.

- Celery is reputed to deter the white moth that begets the green caterpillar that eats cabbage, broccoli, and other cabbage family crops.

- Beans and potatoes live nearby to mutual benefit, not interplanted, but in adjacent beds. The beans may repel Colorado potato beetles; the potatoes may reciprocate by driving away Mexican bean beetles.

DETER PESTS WITH HERBS AND FLOWERS

If you're going to make life miserable for pests and diseases, you might as well enjoy it, so say it with flowers and herbs. Many plants give off volatile chemicals that are attractive to the pests that feed on them. If you plant stronger-scented plants among your vegetable crops, you may be able to disguise or hide the crops' attractive scent so that the pests are confused and never find dinner. For example, onions, chives, and garlic can block ants, aphids, and flea beetles. Marigolds are useful against aphids, Colorado potato beetles, and whiteflies. And rosemary deters carrot flies and cabbage moths. At the same time that these aromatic herbs and flowers confuse insect pests, many of them also attract beneficial insects.

SOW CONFUSION WITH INTERPLANTING

Plant-eating bugs just love the way most gardens are laid out. All the carrots go here, all the tomatoes there, and all the onions together somewhere else. The technical term for this is monoculture. That sort of a garden layout is giving your garden's pests one-stop shopping — a mini-mall for munching bugs that start at one end and eat an entire row.

Breaking up the pattern makes it harder on the pests and easier on the garden and the gardener. The greater the distance any bug has to cross from one snack to the next, the greater the chance that the bug itself will become a snack for some other predator.

◄ The defensive lineup. *Thyme (A) repels cabbage moths, sage (B) is offensive to both cabbage moths and carrot flies, nasturtium (C) discourages squash bugs and whiteflies, and borage (D) repels tomato hornworms.*

CAMOUFLAGE OUTFITS

You can take confusion to a higher level by actually scattering different crops in the same bed. Planting in this fashion intermingles the odors of the plants, so pests have a more difficult time finding lunch, while increasing cover used by insect predators. Diverse planting often increases the number of beneficial insects while decreasing the number of pests.

ROTATING YOUR GARDEN

Rotating plants from one part of the garden to another after each crop cycle keeps you one step ahead of the pests and diseases. It works best for pests that don't move around much, such as those that live primarily in the soil as well as those that don't survive very long without a suitable place to dine.

Avoid planting any crop in the same place two years in a row. To pests, rotating crops is a little like their favorite restaurant moving but not leaving a forwarding address. All of your plants will benefit by having a fresh supply of the nutrients they require, and insect pests will be discouraged from depending on the availability of the plants they prefer. Here's how it works:

If your eggplant is attacked by fusarium wilt, that is not only a problem for the current growing season. It

Don't Let the Cure Be Worse than the Disease

Mint is reputed to discourage cabbage moths and ants, and horseradish, bean beetles. But both mint and horseradish are hardy perennials that, left uncontrolled, will quickly spread all over your garden and become pests in themselves. If you use mint and horseradish in the garden, plant them in large clay pots set in the appropriate beds of vegetable plants.

▲ **Moth be gone.** *Tuck pots of mint in the cabbage patch to deter cabbage moths.*

▲ **All mixed up.** *Planting a number of different vegetables in the same bed diffuses the plants' attractive odors, making it harder for pests to find their favorite food. As a bonus, interplanted beds are also more resistant to drought than conventionally planted gardens.*

affects future ones as well, because the fusarium fungus can survive in the soil for more than one year. If you plant eggplant in the same spot in the garden the next season, it doesn't take a rocket scientist to guess the outcome. The solution is to play hide-and-seek with your vegetables. If you don't want your eggplant attacked by a pest, move it to a spot where the pest won't find it.

COHOSTS: PAIRINGS TO AVOID

Some insect pests have a taste for several different plants. If you plant them near one another you'll be providing a buffet just as appetizing and easy to access as a monoculture. Here are a few plantings to avoid:

- **Corn and tomatoes.** If found in an ear of corn, it's called a corn earworm; if found in a tomato, it's called a tomato fruitworm. It's the same beast. Keep some distance between the corn patch and the tomatoes.

- **Potatoes, tomatoes, peppers, and eggplant.** Although it is called Colorado potato beetle, this pest will feed on any plant related to potatoes, such as tomatoes, peppers, or eggplant. It actually prefers eggplant to potatoes.

- **Cucumbers, squash, melons, and pumpkins.** Pickleworms, which bore into fruits and stems, probably prefer cucumbers but will not turn down a nice melon, squash, or pumpkin either.

An Ounce of Prevention: Row Covers

Keeping plant predators from their prey is what row covers are all about. Available in various weights, these polypropylene blankets lie atop a row or bed — either supported by hoops or lying right on the plants — and prevent insect pests from attacking the plants beneath. They let in most of the light, air, and rain but block wind and insects. The heavier versions provide some protection against cold or frost as well. Weight the row cover edges with lumber scraps or plastic bags filled with sand or soil. Or just cover the edges with soil. Some row covers have built-in hoops; they're easier to set up, and you don't need to weight the edges.

For pest control, apply row covers right after planting, either supporting them with hoops or laying them loosely right over the soil. The lighter-weight covers will not impede plant growth and will be lifted by the plants as they grow. If you are protecting a crop that needs pollination from insects, such as squash, remove the covers when blossoms appear. A couple of hours a day should be enough.

▲ **Extra security.** *Built-in hoops keep the row cover edges secure when the wind blows.*

▲ **For small beds.** *A pop-up row cover is a good way to protect seedlings. It's simple to set up and easy to fold and store when the gardening season is over.*

Make the Garden a Haven for Predators

Insect pests will seldom do significant damage in the garden when their numbers are kept in check by other creatures whose diet includes insect pests. Many of these predatory creatures — especially insects — can be purchased from garden supply catalogs, but you're better off setting things up so that these pest controllers and others that you can't buy feel at home in and around your garden. That way, potential pest problems may never grow into real pest problems. And if pest problems do occur, the solvers are already there, waiting to spring into action.

Some garden plants attract beneficial insects. For example, morning glory vines attract ladybugs and hoverflies, while goldenrod beckons ladybugs, assassin bugs, and parasitic wasps. Many gardeners plant a "predator garden" near the vegetable garden to serve as habitat for beneficial insects and beneficial animals like birds, toads, and newts. Such a garden can be as simple as planting some grasses, perennial alfalfa, goldenrod, or hairy vetch in front of a row of fruit-bearing shrubs. If your property is small, locate your perennial garden near the vegetable garden so it can serve the same purpose. Intersperse a few fruiting shrubs, such as swamp holly or cranberry bush, as well. The flowers and grasses can harbor many beneficial insects, while the shrubs are home to birds that think garden pests are great hors d'oeuvres.

▲ **Bug muncher.** *This newt is just one of the many helpers you can attract to your garden to manage plant-eating pests.*

Finally, don't forget the flowers and herbs. The flowers attract pollinating insects, and the aromatic herbs, such as dill and thyme, attract beneficial insects that prey on pests. See Beneficial Insects to Attract to Your Garden on the next two pages.

A TOAD BY ANY OTHER NAME IS STILL A PRINCE

Is it toads or frogs that, when kissed, change into handsome princes? It doesn't really matter. Toads are welcome in my garden just as they are. They probably eat more bugs as toads than they would as princes anyway.

Toads are beneficial in any kind of garden, but they're especially helpful if slugs and cutworms haunt your garden. Toads seem to love these garden pests, and toads are most active at night, when slugs and cutworms come out. Toads also eat gypsy moth larvae, sowbugs, armyworms, and various beetles — up to 15,000 noxious garden pests a year. And all they ask for this work is room and board.

Home Sweet Bug Home

Some seed mixes attract and sustain beneficial insect populations. One of these mixes is called Good Bug Blend and is available from a few suppliers. What seeds are in the mix changes from company to company, but most contain a blend of clovers, plus alfalfa, alyssium, carrot, celery seeds, daikon, dill, and nasturtium.

Beneficial Insects to Attract to Your Garden

Assassin bug

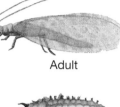

These ½-inch-long (13 mm) insects look like miniature robot monsters from some science fiction movie. What they lack in beauty, however, they more than make up for in appetite for pests.

Green lacewing

This is a real Jekyll-and-Hyde bug. In its adult phase, the green lacewing eats only pollen and nectar, as befits its delicate appearance. But in larval form, this is the famous "aphid lion,"

Adult

Larva

a creature that devours soft-bodied insects such as aphids, scale, thrips, mealybugs, spider mites, whiteflies, the nymphs of leafhoppers, and the eggs of many caterpillars. Green lacewings can be purchased as eggs, larvae, or adults. You can also attract them with special bug foods or by interplanting flowers to provide nectar to feed adult lacewings.

Hoverfly

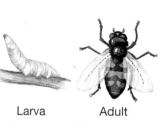

These master flyers are able to zip around, hover, and even fly backwards; they have

Larva

Adult

all the agility of miniature helicopters or humming-birds and are just as much fun to watch. Adults feed on nectar and deposit eggs on the leaves of plants that attract various pests. The eggs hatch into ugly little maggotlike larvae that feed on aphids and other small, succulent bugs.

Ladybug

Also known as lady beetles, ladybugs are colorful, small, and cute. How can you not like a bug that looks like a little Volkswagen? But aphids don't think ladybugs are cute. Neither do asparagus beetles, Colorado potato beetle larvae, chinch bugs, bean thrips, mites, nor numerous other soft-bodied insects. Each adult ladybug can consume about 5,000 aphids in its lifetime. Even the black-and-orange alligator-shaped larvae eat 50 or 60 aphids a day.

You can buy ladybugs in lots of ¼ pint (118 ml) (about 2,300 adults) to 1 gallon (3.8 L) (72,000, give or take a few), but unless you have a very, very large garden and an overwhelming aphid problem, that is not the best way to go. If you bring in too many predators at once, they'll wipe out all the prey, and then they'll leave because there's nothing left to eat. When the next hatch of pests appears, there's nobody there to eat them.

LADYBUG LARVAE

Everything the adult ladybug is by way of cute, the larva is not. It is aptly described as dark, flightless, and alligator-like with orange spots. If you

don't know that this apparition is really your friend, you will be sure that it is one of the bad guys and be tempted to dispatch it forthwith. Don't!

Ladybug larva

A better plan is to attract and maintain a population of adult ladybugs, which eat nectar as well as insect pests, by providing their favorite flowering plants, like goldenrod, yarrow, and morning glory. Having some ladybugs around all the time leads to an ecological balance in which there are always some prey insects available and always some predator insects to keep the pest population from getting large enough to inflict serious crop damage.

Minute pirate bug

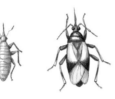

Nymph   Adult

As the name suggests, these are very small, as are their prey — mites, aphids, thrips, and tiny caterpillars. They work in the garden but are particularly effective in a greenhouse because they like the high temperatures and humidity.

Praying mantid

Possibly best known of the beneficial insects, praying mantids are also the most overrated. Given their size, they don't eat much, and when they're eating, they'd just as soon munch good insects as bad ones. To a mantid, if it moves, it's food. Honeybees are just as tasty as bean beetles.

Spined soldier bug

This bug likes to harpoon its prey, which includes hornworms, potato and bean beetles, and cabbage worms. It then injects a paralyzing venom and sucks the victim's body fluids. With that as a modus operandi, it is somehow appropriate that this creature is a member of the stinkbug family.

Trichogramma wasp

This is the best known of a group of parasitic wasps. The adult wasps feed on nectar, but they lay their eggs within the eggs of garden pests like corn earworms, cutworms, cabbage worms, and various borers. The newborn wasp starts life by feasting on the embryo of the host.

▲ Good morning. *In our garden, morning glories like Grandpa Ott's attract ladybugs and offer a reason for gardeners to stop and contemplate in the early morning mist.*

Any garden offers food aplenty for toads, but they won't take full advantage of the "board" unless they can also find a "room" in or very near the garden. Toads need a cool, moist, ventilated, and fairly dark place to hide away from sun, predators, and disturbances like lawn mowers. If you provide that hiding place, you'll have toads. They are creatures of habit and will return to the same place each night and even year after year.

A toad house can be as simple as a board or a flat rock propped at an angle over some loose soil in a little-traveled spot in the garden. A clay flowerpot, upside-down and propped with a stone to allow access, or with a gap broken out of the rim, will also make a fine toad house. They'll also live beneath thick, moist organic mulches like straw or hay.

IT'S FOR THE BIRDS . . . AND BATS

Above the earth and garden plants is the open sky. And if you're fortunate, that sky will be a flyway for birds. In early spring here in the North, when most other migratory birds are still enjoying southern vacations, the phoebes are already at work snatching insects from the air or soil surface itself. A few weeks after the phoebes' return, the tree swallows come back, followed by the barn swallows, and if we're lucky, bluebirds. At night there are bats. All of these creatures live around the garden throughout the summer, eating insects that eat the garden, as well as those that eat me as I tend the garden, spoiling the fun of being there.

The phoebe likes a place to perch while watching for prey, and nests in a nearby open shed, as does the barn swallow. Tree swallows and bluebirds like birdhouses. If you live where purple martins are found, attract them with a communal house. Hummingbirds, which eat insects as well as nectar, like to perch in tree or shrub branches along the edge of the garden. The birds don't require large trees and shrubs, but they prefer their resting places to be densely branched.

▲ House for rent. *Birds can be some of the most useful tenants of your garden. Do all you can to entice them to stay around.*

▲ Room and board provided. *We found a quiet corner of the garden to tuck away this little toad house, consisting of a flat rock propped over a couple of rock "walls."*

Solve the Problem Gently

If I do have a pest problem that really is a pest problem, one I haven't been able to prevent or avoid and can't afford to ignore, my job is to solve that pest problem without creating a worse problem in the process. I want to deal with the pests in ways that don't harm other creatures that live in or around the garden or in the soil.

There's no nice way to say it: The time has come for killing. It's down to a very basic choice, the veggie or the bug. I'm going to have to kill some bugs, and I need to do that in a way that doesn't involve killing — or even hurting — any of the other creatures upon whose existence my garden's health and success ultimately depend.

PETER PIPER PICKED A PECK OF PESTS

If I've got to kill some pests, there isn't a way with less collateral damage than this: One by one, pick them or knock them from the plant and into a tin can of water mixed with a little dishwashing soap to break the surface tension. This technique works for Japanese beetles, Colorado potato beetles, cabbage caterpillars, and squash beetles. The best hunting time is early morning, when the bugs are logy and tend to fall right off the plant and into the water.

Squash bug eggs

Handpick troublesome pests. A 15-minute early morning tour of the potato patch is all it takes to keep Colorado potato beetles under control by handpicking. Whenever I find an adult Colorado potato or a squash bug, I check the undersides of all the plant leaves, looking for the bright orange eggs of the former and the golden brown eggs of the

▲ A soapy death. *Handpick caterpillars by knocking them gently from the plant into a can of water with a bit of dish detergent added. The detergent breaks the surface tension of the water, so that the caterpillars readily sink beneath the suds.*

▲ Just rewards. *Our daughter, Lindsey, earned the money to buy these ducks by handpicking Colorado potato beetles from a neighbor's garden.*

latter. And I crush them or put eggs, leaves and all, into the soapy water.

Unless there are an awful lot of them, you can control the adult Colorado potato beetles solely by regular handpicking. If you have young children in the family (or the neighborhood), try offering a beetle bounty. Our daughter, Lindsey, at four, learned to count so she could keep track of her beetle earnings. A couple of years later she picked 450 beetles at a neighbor's garden at ½ cent each to earn the purchase price of three ducklings.

BIOLOGICAL CONTROLS

Some very tiny — actually microscopic — creatures can infect and disrupt the feeding of caterpillars and some other larval insects.

- *Bacillus thuringiensis* (Bt). Sold under many brand names, Bt is a bacterium that, when ingested by various caterpillars, including cabbage worms, hornworms, corn borers, and the like, paralyzes the gut, giving the insect a fatal case of indigestion. Specialized strains of Bt are effective for specific pests, including Colorado potato beetles.

- **Milky spore.** Milky spore disease is a biological control of Japanese beetles caused by the bacteria *Bacillus popillae* and *Bacillus lentimorbus.* Apply it over grassy areas such as lawns, where adult beetles lay eggs and larval grubs feed on the roots of grasses. The grubs will ingest the bacteria and die within two or three weeks. The white spores that fill the grub's body will then reenter the soil, waiting for more grubs to come along. It can take two or three years for milky spore to become established in a treated area.

- **Beneficial nematodes.** The nematodes we usually hear about are the bad guys that mess with vegetable roots. But not all nematodes are garden enemies. The ones sold for insect control feed on soft-bodied, soil-dwelling pests such as wireworms and root maggots. They are not interested in earthworms or plant roots. These are so tiny that you apply them to the garden by suspending them in water and using a spray attachment on your hose.

Nothing's Perfect

Bt is a safe, reliable tool for controlling pests in the garden, but it isn't perfect. In addition to controlling pests, it can also be harmful to the larvae of certain butterflies, including swallowtails and monarchs.

- **Swallowtail caterpillars,** also called parsleyworms, can often be found nibbling on parsley, dill, celery, cilantro, parsnips, and carrots. Parsleyworms are

Swallowtail caterpillars

pale green, accented with stripes of black and yellow. Before spraying Bt in the garden, handpick the parsleyworms and relocate them to a place away from the garden, such as a patch of wild carrot, also known as Queen Anne's lace.

- **Monarch caterpillars** prefer to hang around milkweed, which is their favorite food, and don't usually wander into the garden. When applying Bt, take care not to spray plants adjacent to the garden.

Monarch butterfly

NATURAL PESTICIDES THAT ARE RELATIVELY KIND TO NATURE

We can't get away from the fact that the pesticides we apply to our crops are poisons, whether they come from a chemistry lab or, like pyrethrum, from a daisy. In fact, many natural pesticides, including pyrethrum, rotenone, and sabadilla, are just as nasty as their synthetic brethren. But some botanical pesticides appear to do their work with few drawbacks: Garlic spray and hot pepper wax repel pests; insecticidal soap and neem usually kill pests without injuring other life-forms. When applying these or any pesticides to your garden, be sure to read and follow label directions carefully.

- **Garlic spray.** Strictly speaking, this is supposed to *repel* rather than kill. But it may very well repel insects other than the target ones, so we'll talk about it here rather than with other "invisible fences" discussed above. Garlic repels a wide range of pests, including aphids, spider mites, and whiteflies. Simply spray on plants *before* pests appear and the garlic spray does the rest. (The italicized words are the key to this method; garlic spray won't chase the bugs away once they've started feasting.) You'll notice a garlicky odor when you first spray it, but once dry, the smell disappears. Garlic spray does not affect the flavor of vegetables, and it's environmentally safe and biodegradable.

- **Hot pepper wax.** Like garlic spray, this is supposed to work as a repellent, rather than a poison. Its ability to irritate, though, suggests that its effects may be more than just repellent. A blend of food-grade paraffin wax, herbs, and capsaicin (the active ingredient in hot peppers), hot pepper wax is derived from cayenne peppers. Many garden pests, including aphids and whiteflies, don't like spicy things and avoid plants sprayed with hot pepper wax. In addition to repelling pests, hot pepper wax also helps protect plants from dry or windy weather. The plants don't absorb the spray, so it doesn't alter the flavor of the vegetables. Simply wash the vegetables under warm running water to remove any remaining wax before preparing. Capsaicin can irritate your skin and eyes.

- **Insecticidal soap.** If you'd like your pest problems to just dry up and blow away, use insecticidal soap. As its name implies, insecticidal soap is a biodegradable soap used to control pests. Its most common active ingredient, potassium salts of fatty acids, is derived from plants. When sprayed on a pest, the soap damages cell membranes, making them more permeable. Vital cellular fluids then leak from the cells and the pest dies of desiccation.

▲ **It (mostly) leaves them be.** *Neem won't harm or discourage beneficial organisms such as butterflies, spiders, earthworms, or ladybugs, but it may harm bees.*

THE FACTS ON INSECTICIDAL SOAPS

- Not harmful to most beneficials
- Low impact on mammals, birds, aquatic organisms, and other wildlife
- Damaging to predatory mites and some insects, such as hoverflies, in their larval stage

This is most effective on soft-bodied pests, such as aphids, and must stay in contact with the pest for as long as possible to work well. It's less effective when mixed in water containing high amounts of minerals such as iron or calcium. Apply it in the early morning or late afternoon, when it takes the longest to dry.

- **Neem.** This is derived from the seeds of the neem tree, which is found in southern Africa, India, Australia, and southeast Asia. The active ingredient, azadirachtin, blocks the progression of the insect pest's life cycle. Although it sometimes takes days to kill the pest, neem has another trick up its sleeve: azadirachtin also acts as an appetite suppressant. One or two nibbles on a treated plant and the pest stops feeding.

Applied as a spray, neem is a relatively safe pesticide that apparently has little or no effect on beneficials such as butterflies, spiders, earthworms, and ladybugs, though there is some evidence to indicate that it can poison bees, so don't use it when bees are visiting the plant you want to protect, and try not to get any on or near flowers. In addition, the evidence we now have shows it has little impact on birds, aquatic organisms (including fish and mammals), or other wildlife. You may also find neem oil insecticidal soap, which combines the two products.

There's No Such Thing as a Pesticide

Most of the things we are taught to think of as pesticides are much more than that; they are insecticides, in that they are capable of killing many more kinds of insects than those listed on the label as target species. Many of them are actually better described as biocides, in that they kill life-forms in addition to insects. A poison sprayed on potato plants to kill Colorado potato beetles will also kill the ladybugs that were there eating aphids and other soft-bodied, sap-sucking insects. Birds and toads, feeding upon dead or dying poisoned insects, may, in their turn, die. Poisons that linger on the plant can kill bees and butterflies and numerous other insects that pollinate our crops. Poisons that drip on the ground can kill worms and other soil-dwelling creatures that help plants to grow.

Even a relatively carefully aimed killer like Bt (a bacterium discussed in Biological Controls, page 170) isn't totally without potential collateral damage. Although the target is supposed to be the caterpillars that munch on cabbage family crops or on tomatoes or corn kernels, any caterpillar will do as a target. For example, if some Bt manages to land on the food source for larvae of the black swallowtail (any carrot family plant, like carrots or parsley) or the monarch butterfly (milkweed), the result will be just as deadly for those caterpillars as it is for the green creatures that we sometimes find in our broccoli.

Poisons derived from plants, like pyrethrins (from a daisylike chrysanthemum native to Kenya), rotenone (from a tropical plant of the Derris family), or neem (extracted from the seed of the tropical neem tree), are less dangerous to gardeners and to the garden's ecology than chemically synthesized poisons. They break down quickly and don't build up in the food chain or remain active in the soil. However, all of them, especially the very potent rotenone, but even including the relatively benign neem, do affect some beneficial insects and can, by killing too many of the target insects, deplete natural predator populations and cause what are called "secondary pest outbreaks."

PEST CONTROLS AT A GLANCE*

Pest	Control
Aphid	Yellow sticky traps, water spray, green lacewings, ladybugs, garlic spray, hot pepper wax, insecticidal soap, neem, neem oil soap
Armyworm	*Bacillus thuringiensis* var. *berliner* (Btb), beneficial nematodes, spined soldier bugs
Asparagus beetle	Green lacewings, ladybugs, praying mantids, neem
Bean beetle	Handpicking, beneficial nematodes, green lacewings, ladybugs, praying mantids, spined soldier bugs, neem
Broccoli worm (cabbage worm)	*Bacillus thuringiensis* var. *berliner* (Btb), green lacewings, ladybugs, praying mantids, spined soldier bugs, trichogramma wasps, garlic spray, neem oil soap
Cabbage looper	Yellow sticky traps, *Bacillus thuringiensis* var. *berliner* (Btb), green lacewings, ladybugs, praying mantids, spined soldier bugs, trichogramma wasps, beneficial nematodes, neem oil soap
Cabbage root maggot	Beneficial nematodes
Colorado potato maggot	Handpicking, *Bacillus thuringiensis* var. *san diego* (Btsd), beneficial nematodes, green lacewings, ladybugs, praying mantids, spined soldier bugs, neem
Corn earworm	Beneficial nematodes, green lacewings, ladybugs, praying mantids, trichogramma wasps, garlic spray, neem
Cucumber beetle	Beneficial nematodes, green lacewings, ladybugs, praying mantids, neem oil soap
Diamondback	*Bacillus thuringiensis* var. *kurstaki* (Btk), *Bacillus thuringiensis* var. *berliner* (Btb), trichogramma wasps, garlic spray
Earworm	*Bacillus thuringiensis* var. *berliner* (Btb)
European corn borer	Beneficial nematodes, *Bacillus thuringiensis* var. *kurstaki* (Btk), green lacewings, ladybugs, praying mantids, trichogramma wasps
Flea beetle	Beneficial nematodes, neem oil soap
Fruitworm	*Bacillus thuringiensis* var. *berliner* (Btb)
Hornworm	Handpicking, *Bacillus thuringiensis* var. *berliner* (Btb), spined soldier bugs, neem oil soap
Japanese beetle	Handpicking, diatomaceous earth, beneficial nematodes, milky spore (*Bacillus popillae*), neem, neem oil soap
Leafhopper	Insecticidal soap, neem, neem oil soap
Leaf miner	Yellow sticky traps, beneficial nematodes, green lacewings, ladybugs, praying mantids, neem
Mite	Green lacewings, ladybugs, minute pirate bugs, neem, neem oil soap, water spray
Mosquito	*Bacillus thuringiensis* var. *israeliensis* (Bti)
Root maggot	Beneficial nematodes, insecticidal soap, water spray
Slug/snail	Copper tape or foil barrier, diatomaceous earth, slug and snail traps, sawdust, wood ashes
Squash bug	Praying mantids, garlic spray
Squash vine borer	Beneficial nematodes, garlic spray
Striped blister beetle	Diatomaceous earth, beneficial nematodes
Thrip	Glue sticky traps, yellow sticky traps, diatomaceous earth, green lacewings, ladybugs, minute pirate bugs, praying mantids, garlic spray, insecticidal soap, neem
Tomato fruitworm	Beneficial nematodes, green lacewings, ladybugs, trichogramma wasps
Tomato pinworm	Beneficial nematodes, green lacewings, ladybugs, trichogramma wasps
Whitefly	Yellow sticky traps, green lacewings, ladybugs, praying mantids, garlic spray, insecticidal soap, neem, neem oil soap

The stronger biological insecticides, rotenone, sabadilla, and pyrethrum, are not listed here, although they are considered acceptable for organic growing. I neither use nor recommend these poisons because of their effects on life-forms other than the target pests.

DISEASE CONTROLS AT A GLANCE

Disease	Control
Anthracnose	Plant resistant varieties; rotate crops annually; spray foliage with aerated compost tea*; avoid getting foliage wet when watering. *Don't use compost tea made the traditional way, by soaking compost in water; this anaerobic environment promotes the growth of undesirable microbes.
Aster yellows	Cover plants with row covers; remove infected plants and nearby weeds; plant resistant varieties.
Bacterial blight	Apply neem oil; plant resistant varieties; remove severely infected plants; add organic matter to soil.
Bacterial wilt	Cover plants with row covers; rotate crops annually; remove infected plants.
Black leg	Rotate crops annually.
Blossom-end rot	Keep soil at proper pH for crop; mulch around plants; avoid high-nitrogen fertilizers; add organic matter to soil.
Catfacing and cracking	Mulch around plantings.
Clubroot	Keep soil pH above 7.0; solarize soil; rotate crops annually; add organic matter to soil.
Curly top	Cover plants with floating row covers; remove infected plants.
Damping-off	Sow seeds in sterilized medium containing sphagnum peat moss; avoid overwatering; water with aerated compost tea.
Downy mildew	Apply neem oil; rotate all crops annually; eliminate weeds; spray foliage with aerated compost tea.
Early blight	Apply neem oil; plant potato-leaved tomatoes and other resistant varieties; spray foliage with aerated compost tea; use row covers to exclude flea beetles.
Fusarium wilt	Solarize soil; rotate crops annually; plant resistant varieties; add organic matter to soil.
Gray mold (*Botrytis*)	Apply neem oil; space plants farther apart; spray plants with aerated compost tea.
Late blight	Apply neem oil or plant certified seed; spray foliage with aerated compost tea.
Leaf blight	Apply neem oil.
Leaf spot	Apply neem oil; spray foliage with aerated compost tea.
Powdery mildew	Apply neem oil; spray with chamomile tea or baking soda.
Root-knot nematode	Plant French marigolds; add chitin to soil; add organic matter to soil; solarize soil; plant resistant varieties.
Root rot	Remove infected plants; avoid overwatering; rotate crops annually; solarize soil; add organic matter to soil; water plants with aerated compost tea.
Rust	Apply neem oil; spray foliage with aerated compost tea.
Southern blight	Add organic matter to soil; drench plants with aerated compost tea.
Sunscald	Avoid leaf drop from moisture stress or leaf diseases.
Tobacco mosaic virus	Plant resistant varieties; remove infected plants.
Verticillium wilt	Rotate plants annually; plant resistant varieties; add organic matter to soil.

A Gallery of Garden Rogues

Even a well-tended garden will harbor some pests, and every so often those pests will become numerous enough and cause enough damage to require a response. Before you take action, however, you'll need to know what sort of creature you're dealing with. The insects below are the pests you're most likely to encounter. For more help identifying and dealing with pests, contact your local Cooperative Extension Office.

Aphids

PLANTS AFFECTED: Just about everything

DESCRIPTION: Aphids are small (a bit larger than pinhead size when mature) and shaped like little pears. Like pears, they come in various colors, most often green, the better to blend with the leaves they feed upon. Aphids prefer to feed on young, soft plant tissue; they cluster on buds, small stems, and the undersides of young leaves, sucking sap and causing the leaves to become deformed and growth to be stunted. During the warmer months, aphids reproduce asexually, with females giving birth to live young. This means that an aphid population can grow from "a few" to "too many" in a big hurry. As the population increases on a plant, winged aphids appear and then fly off to infest other plants.

CONTROL: Step one — avoid the problem. Use yellow sticky traps; encourage lacewings and ladybugs. Make the host plant distasteful by applying garlic spray or hot pepper wax spray. (This works only if the repellent is on the plant before the aphids appear; it doesn't seem to chase them away once they have settled in.) You can also use a water spray to control aphids. You need enough force to knock off the aphids but not enough to damage the plants. This works best on young plants still in pots; turn the pot right over and spray the undersides of the

leaves, where the aphids congregate. Get all of them, or you'll have a new infestation in just a little while.

As a last resort, use poison, starting with the least potent. (Try to find a spray bottle with a reversible nozzle, so you can coat the undersides of the leaves.) If things get really dicey, especially in the greenhouse or cold frame, I just remove and dispose of the affected plants. Sometimes it's better to cut my losses and just try to prevent the problem from spreading.

Armyworms

Moth

Larva

PLANTS AFFECTED: Bean, beet, cabbage, corn, cucumber, lettuce, pea, peanut, pepper, spinach, and tomato

DESCRIPTION: Armyworms are 1- to 2-inch-long (2.5 to 5 cm) caterpillars that range from greenish blue to brownish, usually with prominent stripes down their sides. They feed at night or on cloudy days, chewing ragged holes in leaves and fruit. Armyworms are a persistent problem in warm climates, where they can cause damage most of the year. In cool regions, infestations most often occur in fall.

CONTROL: Beneficial nematodes and spined soldier bugs are good long-term solutions. For more immediate control, handpick or spray with Btb (*Bacillus thuringiensis* var. *berliner*).

Asparagus Beetles

PLANTS AFFECTED: Asparagus

DESCRIPTION: Asparagus beetles are small, about the size of a ladybug, and come in many colors, from blue and black to brown and russet. They begin feeding on asparagus as soon as the spears begin to emerge in the spring. They lay dark-colored eggs on the spears, from which blackish larvae emerge. Both larvae and adults feed on the spears and, later in the season, the ferny leaves. CONTROL: Handpick both larvae and adults. Predators include ladybugs, lacewings, praying mantids, and spined soldier bugs. You can get fast control by spraying plants with neem.

Cabbage Worms and Cabbage Loopers

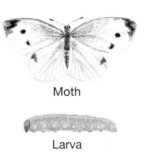

Moth

Larva

PLANTS AFFECTED: Cabbage family crops

DESCRIPTION: Although cabbage worms and cabbage loopers are different pests, they usually occur together in the garden. Cabbage worms are medium green, 1-inch-long (2.5 cm) caterpillars, marked with subtle yellowish stripes along their sides and covered with short fuzzy hairs. The adults are antique white butterflies with two or three black dots on each upper wing.

Cabbage loopers acquired their name because they arch, or loop, their backs as they move along. These green caterpillars have faint whitish stripes along their sides. The adults are grayish night-flying moths with a silver chevron on each wing.

Both cabbage worms and cabbage loopers are serious pests to many cabbage family crops. Leaves develop ragged-shaped holes, and cabbage and broccoli heads become a hideaway.

CONTROL: By far the best solution here is row covers. There won't be any nasty little caterpillars if the pretty little flutterbys can't lay eggs on the plant in the first place. If you don't use row covers, you can try handpicking, but I've found that neither easy nor particularly effective because the "worms" are soft, especially the young, small ones. Natural predators include lacewings, ladybugs, praying mantids,

spined soldier bugs, and trichogramma wasps, but they don't keep the brassicas in my garden pest-free. Yellow sticky traps are effective, especially for loopers. For immediate control apply Btb (*Bacillus thuringiensis* var. *berliner*) or neem oil soap. (I prefer not to use even these relatively benign controls, so if I've failed to follow my own good advice about row covers, I just live with the problem. I've got some holes in the outer leaves of the cabbages, and I'm very careful to check the broccoli before cooking it, but in neither case have I lost a crop nor been terribly inconvenienced.)

Colorado Potato Beetles

PLANTS AFFECTED: Eggplant, pepper, potato, and tomato

DESCRIPTION: These fingernail-sized beetles have dome-shaped shells brightly decorated with black and yellow stripes. The adults lay clusters of orange eggs on the undersides of the leaves. The eggs then hatch, revealing ugly larvae that look like dull reddish orange blobs with black legs and heads. The adults and their repulsive children both eat holes in potato leaves. A large number of them can harm the plant, but it is fairly easy to make sure that there are never enough of them to do much damage.

CONTROL: First thing in the morning, as soon as the potato shoots have poked though the soil, I check daily for adult beetles. (They have wintered in the soil and emerge as soon as there is something eat.) Whenever I find a beetle, I check the undersides of all the leaves on that plant for eggs. Beetles and eggs I crush or drop in a can of soapy water. Most of the time that's enough to prevent a large hatching of larvae later in the season. If there are some larvae, they too end up in the soapy drink. That's all I've ever had to do. If you don't handpick or don't do it carefully enough, you end up with lots of eaters.

Beneficial nematodes, praying mantids, lacewings, spined soldier bugs, and ladybugs all eat various stages of the pest and may help keep the population small enough. Mulching after the final hilling or growing potatoes under mulch instead of hilling is reputed to suppress Colorado potato beetles. If all else fails, spray with Btsd (*Bacillus thuringiensis* var. *san diego*) or neem.

Corn Earworms

Moth

PLANTS AFFECTED: Bean, corn, pea, pepper, potato, squash, and tomato

DESCRIPTION: Earworms, also called fruitworms,

Larva

are about 1-inch-long (2.5 cm) caterpillars that can range in color from green to brown to yellowish tan, with dark stripes down their sides. The pale tan adult moths lay single, cream-colored eggs on leaves or corn silk in spring. On corn, the earworm consumes the silk before eating its way into the developing ear. After a month, it drops to the soil to pupate. On other crops, earworms feed on stems, leaves, and fruits.

CONTROL: Introduce or attract beneficial insects, including spined soldier bugs, lacewings, and trichogramma wasps. Spray with Btb (*Bacillus thuringiensis* var. *berliner*) in spring, when young are hatching.

Cucumber Beetles

PLANTS AFFECTED: Cucumber, melon, potato, squash, and other plants

DESCRIPTION: Cucumber beetles come spotted and striped. Each is about ¼ inch (6 mm) long with shiny yellow wing covers decorated with either 11 black spots or 3 black stripes. Larvae are thin whitish grubs with brown or black heads.

CONTROL: Adult beetles emerge in spring and lay eggs on soil near plants. After hatching, the larvae enter the ground to feed on roots. Apply beneficial

nematodes in spring to attack larvae in the soil. Try a handheld, battery-powered vacuum cleaner to suck the beetles up. Adults can be controlled by spraying plants with neem oil soap as needed. Introduce green lacewings, praying mantids, and ladybugs, all of which feed on cucumber beetles.

European Corn Borers

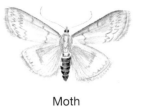

Moth

PLANTS AFFECTED: Bean, corn, and tomato family plants

DESCRIPTION: European corn borers are about the same size as corn earworms, but they are lighter colored, usually tan to antique white, with brown

Larva

spots on each body segment. Another way to tell the two apart is by counting how many worms are in each ear of corn. There is usually only one corn earworm in each ear, while as many as three to five European corn borers can occupy a single ear. European corn borers are most numerous in cool climates during warm summers.

CONTROL: Spray Btk (*Bacillus thuringiensis* var. *kurstaki*) a week or so after you notice the white eggs clinging to corn leaves. Natural predators include lacewings, ladybugs, praying mantids, and trichogramma wasps.

Flea Beetles

PLANTS AFFECTED: Just about everything, but especially tomato, cabbage, and beet family plants

DESCRIPTION: Flea beetles are the pinhead-sized dark brown to black beetles that jump away, just like fleas, when threatened. Though small, these little pests can quickly pepper leaves full of tiny holes so affected foliage looks more like a screen door than a leaf. They also spread plant diseases as they bounce around the garden.

CONTROL: Use row covers as soon as seeds are planted or seedlings transplanted. Spray plants with neem oil soap. Apply beneficial nematodes for long-term control.

Leaf Miners

PLANTS AFFECTED: Leafy greens

DESCRIPTION: Leaf miner is a term that refers to the larvae of a collection of moths, beetles, and flies. The leaf miner that affects vegetables is a small grayish yellow fly. The flies lay tiny white eggs from which small green maggots emerge. The maggots chew tunnels in the leaves for a few weeks, and then they drop down to the ground to pupate. In about three weeks, the adult fly emerges to begin the cycle all over again.

CONTROL: Grow crops beneath floating row covers. Remove infested leaves as they appear. Natural predators include lacewings, ladybugs, and praying mantids. For long-term control, treat the area with beneficial nematodes. You can also use yellow sticky traps to catch adult flies or spray plants with neem.

Mexican Bean Beetles

PLANTS AFFECTED: Bean

DESCRIPTION: Mexican bean beetles look similar to ladybugs in size and shape. They have a coppery-tan back sprinkled with black dots; the young adults have no spots. Mexican bean beetles have huge appetites and feed on bean leaves and fruit, leaving skeletonized foliage and nibbled pods. Eggs are yellowish and appear on the undersides of bean leaves. Larvae, which also feed on bean plants, are light-colored with a spiny appearance.

CONTROL: Handpick or apply beneficial nematodes. Natural predators include lacewings, ladybugs, praying mantids, and spined soldier bugs. For fast control, spray plants with neem.

Mites

PLANTS AFFECTED: Just about everything

DESCRIPTION: Mites are very, very small relatives of spiders. Some, like the predatory mites that feed on thrips and nasty mites, are good. Those that feed on the sap of many species of vegetables and ornamentals are bad. Plants infested with mites often have pale-colored leaves or foliage covered with yellowish specks. Mites are most often found on the undersides of leaves and clinging to soft young stems, leaves, and buds. To see if mites are infesting a plant, use a hand lens or place a sheet of white paper beneath the leaves. Gently tap the top of the leaf and examine the paper for any tiny moving specks.

CONTROL: Natural predators include lacewings, ladybugs, minute pirate bugs, and predatory mites. Deliver a water spray using a mist nozzle head placed an inch or two (2.5 to 5 cm) from the plant. For quick control, try applying the botanical insecticide neem or neem oil soap.

Slugs and Snails

Slug

Snail

PLANTS AFFECTED: Just about everything

DESCRIPTION: If you're going to be a pest, you might as well be slimy — it fits the job description. Slugs and snails are slimy. They feed on the soft tissues of a number of vegetables and flowers, leaving raspy, rough-edged holes and slime trails to mark their passing. Like vampires, they usually work at night or on cloudy days.

CONTROL: If you can't sleep at night, grab the flashlight and go slug and snail hunting. After dark, they are easy to handpick and drop in a can of soapy water. Other methods include setting boards, stones, or overturned pots as traps in the garden. Check them in the morning, pick off any slimy visitors, and drop them in a can of soapy water. Apply an unbroken line of wood ashes, diatomaceous earth, or sawdust around susceptible plants. Tack copper foil to the sides of supported raised beds or stick copper strips vertically in the soil. The copper gives the slug or snail an electrical shock, which discourages further travel.

Squash Bugs

PLANTS AFFECTED: Cucumber, gourd, melon, pumpkin, and squash

DESCRIPTION: Squash bugs are from ½ to 1 inch long (1.25 to 2.5 cm), black to gray, with a back as flat as an aircraft carrier. They pierce the outside skin of plants and suck out the juices, leaving infested plants dotted with yellow or brown spots. In severe cases the plants are pale green to yellowish and stunted, with few fruit.

CONTROL: Plant resistant varieties when possible. Many winter squash, including butternuts and Hubbards, are resistant, while other squash, such as pattypan, are more susceptible. Sprays of insecticidal soap help. Apply garlic spray regularly, starting early in the season. Rotate plants annually.

Squash Vine Borers

PLANTS AFFECTED: Cucumber, melon, pumpkin, and squash

DESCRIPTION: Squash vine borers are the plump, 1-inch-long (2.5 cm) larvae of a winged moth with two

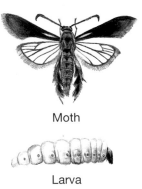

Moth

Larva

black and two transparent wings. The adults lay eggs on plants in early summer. On hatching, the larvae tunnel into the stem, where they feed. Squash vine borers weaken the plants and can damage them so much that the vines wilt and die.

CONTROL: Apply beneficial nematodes for long-term control. To repel moths from plants, regularly treat leaves and vines with garlic spray. Grow young plants under floating row covers to exclude moths from plants. Grow resistant varieties.

Tomato Hornworms

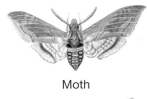

Moth

Larva

PLANTS AFFECTED: Tomato

DESCRIPTION: As much as 4 inches (10 cm) long and as thick as your pinky finger, hornworms are pale to medium green with chalky white streaks across the body. Small eyelike spots decorate their sides; their backsides sport a red or black spiky tail. They can devour most of a tomato plant in a day or two. Adults are large (4 to 5 inches [10 to 12.5 cm]), brownish gray moths with orange spots on the abdomen. Eggs are tiny greenish yellow balls on the undersides of tomato leaves.

CONTROL: Spray small ones with Btb (*Bacillus thuringiensis* var. *berliner*) or neem oil soap. When they're larger, handpick and drop them into a can of soapy water. If you find a hornworm wearing clusters of small white eggs on its back, it's best to leave it be. The eggs belong to a small braconid wasp that parasitizes and destroys the worm.

Whiteflies

PLANTS AFFECTED: Cucumber, potato, and tomato

DESCRIPTION: Whiteflies are small — a little larger than a pinhead — with tiny snow-white wings. Walking through a severely infested garden is like strolling through a snow globe with specks of white swirling around. Whiteflies suck the sap from plants and usually gather on the undersides of leaves or near soft, succulent growth.

CONTROL: Natural predators include lacewings, ladybugs, and praying mantids. Use yellow sticky traps near target plants to capture adults. Spray with neem, insecticidal soap, or neem oil soap for immediate control. Use garlic spray to repel whiteflies from plants.

Common Diseases and Balanced Solutions

Over decades of gardening and visiting gardens I've noticed that some gardens are plagued year after year with many different diseases treated with many different remedies and other gardens are rarely troubled by disease. The latter are usually better set up to grow plants than they are to grow disease-causing organisms — they have healthy, well-drained soil that's teeming with life. In a sense, this whole book is about preventing plant diseases, because it is about creating a garden environment where diseases don't stand much of a chance.

But if you've got a disease problem right now, that's just good advice for next year! Maybe you haven't yet gotten your garden soil as healthy as you'd like it to be. Or maybe, in spite of all you do to prevent it, you still end up with a disease problem serious enough to affect your harvest. If that's your situation, here are some relatively benign ways to cope.

Anthracnose

PLANTS AFFECTED: Many, including bean, cucumber, eggplant, lettuce, melon, pea, pepper, potato, radish, rhubarb, spinach, tomato, and turnip

DESCRIPTION: "Out, damn'd spot! out, I say!" is a quote from Shakespeare's *Macbeth*, but it could easily have been uttered by any gardener with vegetables infected with anthracnose. This disease produces small spots on leaves, stems, and fruit. The spots, which vary from light tan to brown, grow in size and subsequently cause the plant to die back.

CONTROL: Spray plants with aerated compost tea. Rotate crops annually and use resistant varieties.

Bacterial Blight

PLANTS AFFECTED: Bean, cabbage, and pea

DESCRIPTION: In cabbage family plants, early infection results in stunting, with one side of the plant often larger than the other. Mature plants often lose older leaves. On pea and bean plants, dark or light green spots appear on leaves. As the disease progresses, the spots dry out, becoming bronze or brown. The disease, which is most common in humid areas, can also infect flowers, pods, and stems.

CONTROL: Use resistant varieties when possible. Remove and destroy severely infected plants. Spray plants with minor infections with neem oil.

Bacterial Wilts

PLANTS AFFECTED: A broad range, including carrot, cucumber, eggplant, some melons, peanut, pepper, potato, pumpkin, rhubarb, squash, sweet potato, and tomato

DESCRIPTION: Bacterial diseases are often characterized as slimy and smelly, which is an apt description for bacterial wilts. Infected plants often have a brown, soft lesion on the stem, which enlarges until the plant is girdled. The plant then rapidly wilts, sometimes briefly recovering during the night. The stems develop brown streaks before dissolving into a brown jelly.

CONTROL: One type of bacterial wilt lives in the gut of cucumber beetles, while another overwinters in the soil, where it can survive for over five years. Cover plants with row covers to protect from cucumber beetles. Rotate crops on a four- or five-year cycle. Destroy infected plants as soon as you notice them.

Blossom-End Rot

PLANTS AFFECTED: Pepper, squash, tomato, and watermelon

DESCRIPTION: Blossom-end rot is not caused by an organism but by environmental conditions, including soils deficient in calcium and long periods of wet weather followed by dry. It begins with the appearance of a dark, watery spot at the blossom end of the fruit. The spot slowly enlarges, sometimes engulfing most of the fruit. Small fruits may quickly drop from the plant, while larger fruits often persist.

CONTROL: Test soil before growing season begins. If your soil needs calcium and the pH is also low, add limestone. If pH is not excessively acidic, add gypsum. Mulch plantings to maintain even moisture. Avoid excessive fertilizing.

Clubroot

PLANTS AFFECTED:

Broccoli, Brussels sprout, cabbage, cauliflower, Chinese cabbage, kale, kohlrabi, mustard, radish, rutabaga, and turnip

DESCRIPTION: Clubroot is a disease that infects vegetables of the cabbage family. The disease is caused by a funguslike organism that destroys the plant's root system, producing swollen, lumpy roots and wilted, yellowish leaves. If you allow the roots and plants to rot, disease spores are released into the soil, where they can be spread to other locations by dirty shoes and tools or even manure from animals grazing on infected plants.

CONTROL: Remove infected plants as soon as you notice them. Enrich the soil with compost instead of manure, plant resistant varieties when available, and raise soil pH to at least 7.2.

Cracking

PLANTS AFFECTED: Celery, rhubarb, and tomato

DESCRIPTION: In tomato, the fruit splits longitudinally, while in celery and rhubarb, the leaf stem splits. Cracking in tomato is caused by a quick change in soil moisture, usually from dry to wet. In celery and rhubarb, cracking is caused by a deficiency of the trace element boron.

CONTROL: Mulch tomatoes to help regulate soil moisture levels; water during dry periods. Harvest ripe fruit promptly. Test soil before the growing season begins, and add amendments as needed.

Curly Top

PLANTS AFFECTED: A wide range, including bean, beet, cabbage family crops, carrot, celery, cucumber, eggplant, melon, pumpkin, spinach, squash, Swiss chard, and tomato

DESCRIPTION: Curly top is a viral disease. It's most prevalent west of the Rocky Mountains, but it can appear anywhere. Symptoms include an upward curling of leaves accompanied by a thick, leathery appearance. Beans buck this trend by having their leaves bend downward. This disease affects so many plants that often more than one crop in the garden is infected. It is spread by leafhoppers.

CONTROL: Cover plants with row covers. Remove infected plants promptly. Keep weeds in and around garden under control.

Damping-Off

PLANTS AFFECTED: All

DESCRIPTION: Damping-off is a disease that most often infects seedlings. It's caused by many different fungi. There are two forms of the disease: preemergent, where the seedling rots before

it emerges from the soil, and post-emergent, where the stem and roots rot after they emerge from the soil. Manage both forms the same way.

CONTROL: Discard seedlings with damping-off and disinfect the containers. To prevent the disease, sow seeds in clean, sterilized containers and sterilized or pasteurized seed-starting mixture. Water with aerated compost tea, but avoid overwatering. If germinating seeds are in a covered container, remove the cover as soon as plants emerge. If you sow outdoors, avoid spacing seeds too close together. If possible, avoid sowing when the weather is expected to be warm and humid.

Downy Mildew

PLANTS AFFECTED: A wide range of plants, including those of the sunflower, cabbage, pea, onion, beet, and carrot families

DESCRIPTION: Downy mildew is a fungal disease that thrives during times of cool, humid nights with heavy dew, and warm days. Symptoms first appear as spots on leaves, followed by a fluffy, often violet, mold over the spot; the mold grows on both sides of the leaf. Other fungi then invade the plant, causing extensive rot.

CONTROL: Spray foliage with neem oil or aerated compost tea before symptoms appear. Plant resistant or tolerant varieties where available. For example, red onions seem more resistant than other onions. Remove weeds, as they may harbor the disease, and rotate plants annually.

Early and Late Blight

PLANTS AFFECTED: A variety of plants

DESCRIPTION: Although these diseases affect similar plants, they're caused by very different fungi. Early blight most often appears before the first fruits have ripened. It produces brown, circular spots on leaves, each spot marked with concentric rings. Plants are most often infected during periods of warm, humid weather.

Late blight, which can attack seedlings or mature plants, sounds like a tardy sibling of early blight, but it isn't. It's called late blight because it most often appears during spells of warm, wet weather — conditions that most often occur late in the growing season. Late blight is the disease that caused the great potato famine in Ireland in 1845. The scientific name of the fungus that causes the disease translates as "plant destroyer." The disease first appears as dark spots on the leaves, which often have a strong, offensive odor. Eventually the plants rot and collapse.

CONTROL: To control early blight, spray plants with neem oil or aerated compost tea. Avoid damaging plants when cultivating, remove weeds regularly, plant resistant varieties, and use row covers to exclude flea beetles that can spread the disease.

To control late blight, spray plants with neem oil or aerated compost tea at the first sign of the disease. To prevent the disease, rotate crops annually and plant certified seed.

Fusarium and Verticillium Wilts

Verticillium wilt

PLANTS AFFECTED: Many crops, including bean, cucumber, dill, melon, pumpkin, squash, sweet potato, and tomato

DESCRIPTION: In many plants, the leaves turn yellow and then brown as the disease advances up the stem. Stems can turn brown and split.

CONTROL: Remove and destroy infected plants. Before the growing season begins, solarize soil and add additional organic matter. Rotate plants annually, and plant resistant varieties.

Gray Mold (*Botrytis*)

PLANTS AFFECTED: Just about everything

DESCRIPTION: Gray mold is one of those diseases that seem to pop up here and there throughout the growing season. It can infect seedlings as well as mature plants, and it even attacks fruit and flowers. The most common symptom is the appearance of an airy gray mold above a brown, water-soaked, rotten area on stems, leaves, flowers, or fruit. Gray mold can be lethal to seedlings but is largely just a nuisance on larger plants.

CONTROL: The best way to control gray mold is sanitation. Keep seed-starting supplies clean, provide plants with good air circulation through proper spacing, and remove dead leaves and flowers from the garden promptly. Spray plants with neem oil or aerated compost tea.

Powdery Mildew

PLANTS AFFECTED: A broad range of plants, including those of the squash and pea families

DESCRIPTION: Powdery mildew is a very common disease that coats leaves, buds, and flowers with a powdery white coating. Powdery mildew weakens plants, deforming young leaves and flowers and reducing yields. The disease is most often a problem late in the growing season and during periods of hot, humid weather.

CONTROL: Keep susceptible ornamental plants, such as phlox and bee balm, away from vegetable plantings. Spray plants with neem oil or baking soda spray. Chamomile tea spray also works well but should not be sprayed on plants in direct sunlight.

Root-Knot Nematodes

PLANTS AFFECTED: A broad range of vegetable, ornamental, and other plants

DESCRIPTION: Root-knot nematodes are tiny worms that parasitize the roots of plants. They draw food from the plant, damage or destroy the roots, open wounds where disease organisms can enter, and ultimately kill the plant. Other types of parasitic nematodes attack potato tubers (potato rot nematodes); onion bulbs (stem and bulb nematodes); and celery, bean, corn, and pepper (awl nematodes). Vegetables infested with root-knot nematodes are often stunted and sickly, with roots covered with small galls that cannot be broken off. In contrast, you can easily break the beneficial nodules on legumes from the roots. Root-knot nematodes were once considered a problem only in warm climates, but it's now recognized that they can become a problem just about anywhere.

CONTROL: An attractive and effective way of managing nematodes is to grow marigolds (*Tagetes* spp.) in infested soil. You can attain subtle effects by growing marigolds near susceptible plants, but for the best control, grow marigolds as a cover crop and turn them into the soil as soon as the plants begin to flower. This treatment is usually effective for about one year.

Other solutions include soil additives, such as chitin, a natural substance found in the shells of some shellfish, to encourage nematode predators, and organic matter, as well as solarizing infested soil and planting resistant varieties.

Root Rot

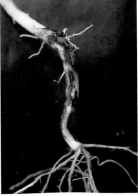

PLANTS AFFECTED: Just about everything

DESCRIPTION: Many organisms cause root rot, but the majority have similar symptoms and controls.

Root rot typically results in a wilting of the plant along with a yellowing of lower leaves. The wilting can be very gradual or rapid, and it occurs in moist or wet soil. The roots are brown to black, often soft and easily broken, and sometimes smell foul. Root rots most often occur during wet, cool weather.

CONTROL: Remove infected plants as soon as you notice them. Water plants with aerated compost tea before symptoms appear. Before the growing season begins, solarize the soil and add more organic matter. Rotate crops annually and avoid overwatering plants.

Rust

PLANTS AFFECTED: Many plants, including asparagus, bean, beet, carrot, corn, onion, pea, peanut, spinach, sunflower, and Swiss chard

DESCRIPTION: You'll most often see rusts late in the season during periods of wet weather. The fungi infect foliage, producing red, yellow, or orange dots, usually on the underside of the leaf. On onions and asparagus, the tips of the foliage become brownish red. Rust infection can range from being a nuisance that blemishes leaves to a virulent disease that destroys crops.

CONTROL: You can control rust to some extent by spraying plants with neem oil or aerated compost tea before symptoms appear. Plant resistant cultivars, but be forewarned that some previously resistant varieties, such as Martha Washington asparagus, are not resistant to newly emerged strains of rust.

Southern Blight

PLANTS AFFECTED: Just about everything

DESCRIPTION: Southern blight begins as a web of white to pinkish fungal growth that appears at the base of the stem at the soil line. As the stem is attacked, the leaves turn yellow and drop.

CONTROL: Remove infected plants and surrounding 6 inches (15 cm) of soil. Add compost or other organic matter before the growing season begins. Water plants regularly with aerated compost tea before symptoms appear.

Tobacco Mosaic Virus

PLANTS AFFECTED: Pepper and tomato family

DESCRIPTION: Infected plants have yellow to pale green leaves, often smaller than normal, mottled, and deformed. Plants are often stunted, and yields are reduced or negligible.

CONTROL: Tobacco mosaic is transmitted by contact — by touching an infected plant and then handling a healthy one. Remove infected plants as symptoms appear, disinfecting hands and tools before working near plants again. Plant resistant varieties when available. If you smoke, wash your hands before handling tomato plants. Keep smokers out of your tomato garden and greenhouse.

Big-Time Pests: Guess Who's Coming to Dinner?

Everything that's true for little garden pests does not apply here. Big pests like rabbits, raccoons, woodchucks, and chipmunks will eat well-nourished and well-grown plants no matter how carefully you weed and water them. And they can do more damage in a night than a horde of tiny munchers can do in a month of Sundays.

Raccoons can destroy your corn patch; rabbits or woodchucks have a liking for anything green and tender; and dogs, cats, wild turkeys, and skunks can just make a mess of things. There's only one way to deal with these critters: Keep them out of the garden in the first place.

FENCING OUT SMALL CRITTERS

A 3-foot-tall (90 cm) chicken-wire fence will often keep small animals — hares, rabbits and woodchucks — out of the garden. Set the posts no farther than 8 feet (2.4 m) apart (to keep the fencing taut), and bury the base of the fencing at least 1 foot (30 cm) deep (to stop animals from burrowing under it). That may not be enough; both rabbits and woodchucks are very good burrowers. I use a two-strand electric fence similar to the raccoon fence described below.

Raccoons are smarter than ground squirrels, woodchucks, and rabbits. In fact, in my experience, they're smarter than just about any other garden pest. A raccoon will climb over a mesh or chicken-wire fence in the blink of an eye. Sometimes a line of electric fencing strung atop the fenceposts will deter the less

KEEP THE SALAD BAR A SECRET

It's best to erect fences before any animal damage occurs. If they develop a taste for your garden, deer, woodchucks, and rabbits have much greater motivation to get inside to the salad bar.

ambitious ones. I've kept the coons out of the corn for three decades using a two-wire electric fence, with the bottom wire about 5 inches (12.5 cm) from the soil and another about 12 inches (30 cm) high.

▲ Radical raccoon repeller. *Raccoons are determined, and they can do a lot of damage in a short period of time. I've managed to keep them away from our corn with two strands of electric fence, 5 inches (12.5 cm) and 12 inches (30 cm) high.*

DEALING WITH DEER

A deer is an appetite with four legs and a big white tail. It takes a whole lot of flea beetles to do much damage to a cabbage plant, and a dozen or more Colorado potato beetles are needed to lay serious siege to a potato plant. But in just one night a single deer can decimate your pea vines, munch the tops off all your carrots and beets, or wipe out your whole Brussels sprouts harvest.

Deer can jump. Big time. Given a decent running start, an adult deer can clear an 8-foot (2.5 m) fence with a bit of room to spare. A good deer fence of woven wire may need to be 10 feet (3 m) tall if the deer in your neighborhood are sufficiently athletic. You can get by with less if you top a fence of lesser height with a wire or two from which are hung aluminum pie plates or something else flashy and noisy.

▲ **A deer-proof garden.** *You'll need very tall fencing to keep out high-leaping deer. This deer fence at Shepherd's Garden Seeds, in Litchfield, Connecticut, is 8 feet (2.4 m) tall.*

Variation on a Theme

A neighbor who protects his nursery stock with an electric fence puts in this extra step to make sure the deer know the fence is there and what it's all about. Dab some peanut butter (creamy is better than chunky) on the electric strand (before you turn on the electricity). When deer come to investigate the peanut butter, they get a harmless but memorable shock, bound away, and — one hopes — the garden goes unscathed.

Or you can try what has worked for me for the past quarter century, an electric fence about nose-high to a deer (3 feet [0.9 m] or so). The deer could jump that fence easily, but (so far) haven't. Erect the fence before there is anything in the garden worth eating. (Exception: When a hard frost has killed off most everything green, including most of what deer can find outside the garden, desperation sets in, and deer will jump the fence and eat whatever is left in the garden — Brussels sprouts, kale, even corn stalks buried in the compost pile. To save the kale and Brussels sprouts, I put up a 6-foot (1.8 m) chicken-wire fence around and fairly close to the plants.

Be Careful What You Catch

Humane trapping is a much kinder way to handle problem animals than many traditional alternatives, but it can have a downside too. Although I've caught corn-stealing raccoons this way, I've also caught a cat and a skunk in traps meant for raccoons. The cat was quite unhappy and loudly conveyed what I'm pretty sure were cat profanities when I let it go. But a cat is a cat and profanities were the extent of its arsenal. The skunk was a different story. The first two times I tried to let it go, I failed. Each time I set the trap door open and made my own escape, the skunk panicked, tripped the trigger, and recaptured itself. I finally managed to prop the door open with a flowerpot, and the skunk crept from the trap and disappeared into the woods. At the time, I thought the skunk's cramped quarters in the trap protected me from its own version of chemical repellent. I have since learned that such is not necessarily the case, making this form of pest control potentially quite memorable. I was just lucky.

Repellents: The Smell of Success

There is a story about a gentleman sitting on a bench in Central Park, tossing confetti. "Why," he is asked, "are you throwing confetti?" "To repel tigers," he replies. "But there are no tigers in Central Park," he is told. A knowing smile crosses the man's face. "I know. Works pretty well, doesn't it?"

Repellents are relied on by some and laughed off by others. Garden catalogs feature repellents — everything from garlic, rotten eggs, castor oil, and soap to fox and bobcat scent and coyote urine. I haven't needed to use these (my fence hasn't failed me yet), but here are the options, in case you'd like to try them.

NATURAL REPELLENTS

Repellents protect something tasty (the garden) with something that is offensive but harmless (the repellent). The marketplace is a grab bag of repellents. Some smell bad. In fact, some smell so bad they repel you as well as the pests from the garden.

- **Garlic and hot pepper products.** Some repellents use garlic and hot peppers to repel both insects and larger animals. One commercial spray smells like a combination of rotten eggs, hot peppers, and garlic. But it's not for use on edibles, so spray it around the garden edge, not on plants.

- **Plastic clips.** These devices contain a very concentrated garlic oil. The clips may be either pushed into the soil near the target plants or hung around the edge of the garden.

- **Hair.** Ask at your barbershop or beauty parlor for the clippings they sweep up each day, and spread the hair around the edge of the garden or near susceptible plants.

- **Blood meal.** Sprinkle blood meal right on plants, and be sure to renew it after each rain.

- **Soap.** Tie bars of deodorant soap to stakes and place them among the target plants.

SCARECROWS

Scarecrows have been used to repel pests as long as there have been gardens. A scarecrow is likely to be more effective if it doesn't just hang around. Some have active parts that move or make noise that really does confound the nuisances. You can make a minimalist scarecrow by hanging aluminum pie plates or strips of shiny foil from fencing and branches. Or you can purchase big balloons decorated with huge eyes that float in the wind.

Sprinkler scarecrows. You'll even find that some mail-order sources carry a high-tech scarecrow with a built-in brain, in the form of a heat-and-motion sensor. If motion is detected, it shoots a spray of water at the intruder. Remember to turn this one off before you go into the garden, or you'll be the target!

ELECTRONIC REPELLENTS

Some electronic devices rely on sound waves to keep pests away from an area. Small models have different frequency settings to repel insects, mice, squirrels, and even spiders. Larger units are used to repel dogs, cats, skunks, raccoons, and other animals.

WHEN ASKING NICELY DOESN'T WORK

Some animals, through sheer persistence, cross the boundary between being a nuisance and being intolerable. If you can't keep them out, and you can't chase them away, try humane trapping. Humane traps, that capture animals without injuring them, come in many sizes, ranging from mouse size to dog size. They are easy to use and maintain and can be purchased from many garden centers, mail-order catalogs, and hardware stores.

PART THREE

PLANT DIRECTORY
Index of Vegetables and Herbs

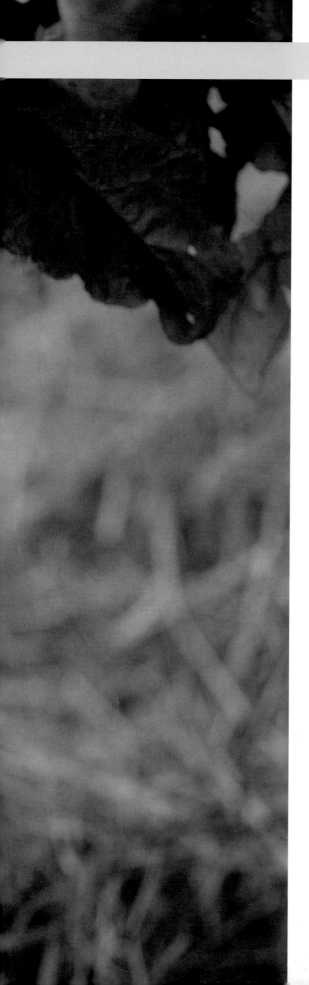

Getting to Know What You Grow

U NTIL NOW WE'VE BEEN BUILDING the stage upon which the yearly garden pageant unfolds, painting the backdrops and setting the scenes. Now it's time to introduce the players and set them off on the great spectacle that becomes your own Garden of Eden. This is where you meet the players on the garden stage and learn their strengths, weaknesses, needs and foibles, and how each reacts (or refuses to react) with the other players. Where to plant, what to plant, with what, when, and how. Here they are — the players, great and small, in your yearly garden drama.

Amaranth

This summer-tolerant green is often called *vegetable amaranth* to distinguish it from the similarly named but different grain amaranth, and in the Caribbean it goes by the name *calaloo*. Unlike most salad greens, this one thrives in hot weather, so if you grow amaranth — or tetragonia, Malabar spinach, orach, or purslane, for that matter — you can keep the salads coming all summer long. In addition to tasting somewhat spinachlike, amaranth is healthful: lots of protein, vitamins, minerals and dietary fiber.

SOWING AND GROWING

Amaranth is not a fussy plant. Anywhere you can grow lettuce or any other green will suit it just fine. Aim for good fertility without too much nitrogen. Sow thinly (12 to 15 seeds per foot ⅛ to ¼ inch [3 to 6 mm] deep in warm (70°F [21°C]) soil. Thin to 6 inches (15 cm) apart. Remove terminal buds to encourage branching.

HARVEST

Pick individual leaves as needed.

BEST VARIETY

Red-leaf vegetable amaranth. Medium-green leaves with burgundy-red overlay.

▲ **Heat-lovin' greens.** *Amaranth delivers salad makings even in the dog days of August, when lettuce and spinach have long since bolted.*

Sow & Grow

Amaranth (*Amaranthus tricolor*)
Amaranth family (Amaranthaceae)

SOWING

Seed depth: ⅛–¼" (3–6 mm)
Germination soil temperature: 70–75°F (21–24°C)
Days to germination: 8–10
Sow outdoors: When soil temperature is 70–75°F (21–24°C)

GROWING

pH range: 6.0–7.0
Growing soil temperature: 70°F (21°C) and above
Spacing in beds: 6" between plants; 12–18" (30–45 cm) between rows
Water: Moderate
Light: Full sun
Nutrient requirements: Moderate
Rotation considerations: None
Seed longevity: Several years

Artichoke

Artichokes come mighty close to being an edible flower; the part we eat is the bud of what could become — if we let it — a quite impressive thistle-like bloom. Mediterranean natives, artichokes are accustomed to warm and sunny climates without very deep freezing temperatures in winter. In their native habitat they're perennials that begin to bear during their second year. But in North America, artichokes don't grow well outside of California if grown the way they like to grow. Until recently, to grow them successfully, gardeners have needed to pull off a bit of horticultural sleight-of-hand to grow them as annuals. In just the past few years, however, plant breeders have made this approach unnecessary by developing a variety ('Imperial Star') that grows easily and well as an annual.

THE SITE

Artichokes are big, hungry plants that do best when they grow rapidly. Plant them in well-drained, fertile soil with plenty of compost or rotted manure.

SOWING

Artichokes are a bit fussy to grow from seed; if a nearby nursery sells plants, that's the easier way to go, and the way I choose for the few artichokes I grow as special culinary treats. If you grow your own plants, sow the seeds indoors in a starting mix in flats or pots and keep the temperature at 70 to 80°F (21 to 27°C); the seedlings should appear in about 12 days. Transplant into 4-inch (10 cm) pots as soon as the first set of true leaves appears, reducing temperatures to 60 to 70°F (16 to 21°C) during the day and 50 to 60°F (10 to 16°C) at night.

GROWING

When all danger of frost is past, but early enough so the plants will get about a dozen nights of sub-50°F (10°C) temperatures, transplant to the garden about

▲ **This bud's for me.** *A nice, tight artichoke bud, just ready for harvest.*

Sow & Grow

Artichokes (*Cynara scolymus*)
Sunflower family (Compositae)

SOWING

Seed depth: ¼" (6 mm)
Germination soil temperature: 70–80°F (21–27°C)
Days to germination: 10–14
Sow indoors: Late winter to early spring — 8 weeks before last frost
Sow outdoors: Not recommended

GROWING

pH range: 6.5–8.0
Growing soil temperature: 60–75° (16–24°C)
Spacing in beds: 24" (60 cm)
Watering: Heavy
Light: 8 hours or more per day
Nutrient requirements: N=high; P=high; K=high
Rotation considerations: Avoid following Jerusalem artichoke or sunflower
Seed longevity: 5 years

2 feet (60 cm) apart or to a large, self-watering container (one plant per container). In warm regions, the plants are ready for the garden when they are about six weeks old. Protect with a row cover for a week or two.

- **Watering.** Water evenly throughout the growing season.

- **Fertilizing.** Big, deep-rooted and heavy feeders, artichokes need a soil enriched with plenty of compost or well-rotted manure. Feed once a month with an organic liquid fertilizer such as fish emulsion or aerated compost tea.

How You Grow It Depends on *Where* You Grow It

Where winter temperatures never go below about 14°F (–10°C; USDA Zones 8–11), artichokes can be grown as perennials, the way nature intended. During their first year, the plants make leaves but no buds (the edible portion of the plant). The second year, they produce buds in late summer and fall. In areas with warm, dry climates, such as the southwestern United States, buds may form all year long but are of best quality in spring. Bud production can go on for three to five years.

In colder regions (USDA Zones 7 to 4), either grow Imperial Star or follow these instructions to get your artichokes in one growing season:

Beginning when artichoke plants are six weeks old, keep seedlings below 50°F (10°C) but above 35°F (2°C) for at least 250 continuous hours (about 10½ days). Since it is difficult to prevent times when temperatures rise above 50°F (10°C), give the plants the cold treatment for an even longer period: from four to six weeks. Put the plants in a cold frame about six weeks before the last frost. Keep the frame open during the day for cooling and closed at night for frost protection.

When all danger of frost is past and the soil temperature is above 60°F (16°C), set plants about 2 feet (60 cm) apart in the bed.

HARVEST AND STORAGE

A mature artichoke bud, ready for the dinner table, is firm, tight, and a nice even green color. If it begins to open, the tenderness quickly deteriorates. The first bud to mature is the top, or terminal, bud, followed over the next few days by the lateral, or secondary, buds. The terminal bud is often a bit larger than the lateral ones.

Using a sharp knife, cut the buds at the base. Harvest during cool, moist weather for best flavor. The buds can be refrigerated for up to two weeks.

WINTER CARE

In warm regions (USDA Zone 8 and warmer): After harvest in late fall, cut the plants at or just beneath ground level and cover with an organic mulch.

In cool areas (USDA Zones 6 and 7): Cut the plants to about 12 inches (30 cm) from the ground and mound a light organic mulch, such as oat straw, over the stumps. Cover everything with an inverted bushel basket. Mulch some more and, if practical, drape with a rainproof cover. Good mulching can bring plants through some winters even in regions as cold as Zone 5.

VARIETIES

Green Globe. This has been the standard variety to grow as a perennial in the West and other warm regions.

Purple Italian Globe. Another warm-region favorite, this one sports pretty purple heads.

Imperial Star. This is the variety to grow as an annual in cooler areas, though it sometimes won't have time to mature in Zone 4.

A BLUE RIBBON CONTAINER PLANT
In the cooler parts of the country, like where I live, even Imperial Star sometimes doesn't have time to ripen its crop of buds. But grown in a large, self-watering container, an artichoke is a sure bet even in chilly Zone 4. A few years ago, our family won the coveted Judges' Choice award at the Tunbridge World's Fair with a container-grown artichoke plant bearing nine buds.

Arugula

One of many salad greens long popular in Europe, arugula — also known as roquette or rocket — adds a delightful nip to salads. Some describe it as peppery, some, as tangy or just nutty. Preferring cool weather, arugula is frost hardy enough that it will bear right through winter in a cold frame or unheated greenhouse. The plant is small, with a compact root system, so it is easy to grow in containers or in a flat on a sunny windowsill.

THE SITE

Arugula is neither fussy nor hard to grow. Any well-drained, fairly fertile spot will do, as will a window box filled with a compost-based container mix.

SOWING AND GROWING

Prepare the seedbed by working some finished compost into the top 3 inches (8 cm) of soil. Plant seeds outdoors in spring as soon as the soil can be worked. Make additional plantings every three weeks as long as the cool weather lasts. For winter harvest, sow seeds in midfall.

HARVEST

You'll be able to harvest leaves when they're about 2 to 3 inches (5 to 7.5 cm) long, two or three weeks after the plants germinate. Cut individual leaves or whole plants. The leaves are best when young, but they retain good flavor until the plant starts to bolt. The flowers are also edible, so let some plants blossom, gather the flowers, and toss them in among the greens of your salad.

VARIETIES

Astro. Compared to most varieties, Astro is ready to harvest a few days earlier and has a milder flavor.

Rocket. Another early variety, Rocket bears tender leaves with a spicy, peppery flavor.

Sylvetta. (*Diplotaxis tenuifolia*) Also known as wild arugula, Sylvetta is smaller, slower-growing, and more pungently flavored. Its edible flowers are yellow rather than white. Sylvetta is often used in mesclun mixes.

▲ A little nip in your salad bowl. *Tangy is the best way to describe this easy-to-grow specialty.*

Sow & Grow

Arugula (*Eruca sativa*)
Cabbage family (Cruciferae)

SOWING

Seed depth: ¼" (6 mm)
Germination soil temperature: 40–55°F (4–13°C)
Days to germination: 5–7
Sow indoors: Late fall through early spring
Sow outdoors: As soon as soil can be worked

GROWING

pH range: 6.0–7.0
Growing soil temperature: 50–65°F (10–18°C)
Spacing in beds: In rows, 1" (2.5 cm); in beds, 6" (15 cm); thin progressively to 6" (15 cm)
Watering: Moderate and even; light in cold frame
Light: Full sun to partial shade
Nutrient requirements: N=low; P=low; K=low
Rotation considerations: Avoid following cabbage family crops
Seed longevity: 5 years

Asparagus

Like the king who wanted just a bit of butter for his bread, asparagus is not really very fussy. There is some serious work involved to get an asparagus patch off to a good start, but after it's established, this delicacy is a pretty easy keeper. Just give it a good place to grow, enough food and water, and keep the weeds at bay. Every spring for years to come you'll have food fit for a king.

THE SITE

Asparagus is a perennial that can bear for 15 years or more, so choose the site for its bed carefully. It's going to be there for a long time. Although it can tolerate some shade, asparagus is most productive when it's sited in full sun. There's not a lot of surface area on its delicate fernlike foliage for photosynthesis, so it needs all the sun it can get.

Asparagus beds at the edge of the garden are continually invaded by weeds, especially witchgrass and other sneaky sorts that creep in underground. After losing the weed battle with a couple of asparagus beds at the edge of the garden, I now have them right in the middle of the garden, a long way from possible invaders.

The soil should be fertile, well-drained, and on the sweet side, with a pH of at least 7.0. Add lime or wood ashes if necessary and loosen the soil to a depth of 16 inches or so. Work in plenty of compost or well-aged, weed-free manure, as well as some greensand and rock phosphate.

If you can fit it into your gardening schedule, prepare the asparagus bed in the late summer or fall to be ready for planting the following spring. That gives any lime, wood ashes, or rock powders a chance to start working. If you prepare the bed in late summer, you also may have time to plant a nitrogen-fixing green manure crop like buckwheat; asparagus has a pretty good appetite for nitrogen.

▲ **Sweet spring treats.** *For the best flavor, you've got to grow your own, because asparagus quickly loses its flavor after it's been cut.*

Sow & Grow

Asparagus (*Asparagus officinalis*)
Onion family (Liliaceae)

SOWING/PLANTING

Seed depth: ¾"
Germination soil temperature: 75–80°F (24–27°C)
Days to germination: 10–12
Sow indoors: 3 months before the last frost
Sow outdoors: After danger of frost is past

GROWING

pH range: 6.5–7.5
Growing soil temperature: 60–70°F (16–24°C)
Spacing in beds: 18" (45 cm)
Watering: Heavy
Light: 8 hours or more per day for best yield; will tolerate 4–8 hours
Nutrient requirements: N=high; P=moderate; K=moderate
Rotation considerations: Avoid following onion family crops

Planting Asparagus Crowns

1 Dig a hole about 12 inches (30 cm) deep for open-pollinated varieties such as Martha Washington, and 6 inches (15 cm) deep for Jersey hybrids such as Jersey Knight and Jersey King. Add about 1 inch (2.5 cm) of compost to the bottom of the hole. Place plants 18 inches (45 cm) apart. Don't crowd them; asparagus likes plenty of room.

2 Place the one-year-old crowns in the bottom of the hole, and spread the roots out evenly. Cover the crowns with 2 inches (5 cm) of soil. As the ferns grow during the summer, gradually fill the hole with soil, adding no more than 2 to 3 inches (5 to 7.5 cm) at a time, until the hole is filled. At the end, mound the soil a bit to prevent puddling.

SOWING

Starting asparagus from seed has a few disadvantages and one very big advantage. Starting from seed is more work, and you have to wait an extra year for your first harvest. (The crowns you buy are already one year old.) And some of the most popular varieties are not available as seeds. The advantage? Seeds are much less expensive; a whole packet of them costs less than two crowns.

Plant asparagus seeds indoors two to three months before the last frost, ¾-inch (2 cm) deep in 4-inch (10 cm) pots filled with germination mix. Germinate at 75 to 80°F (24 to 27°C) during the day; lower the temperature to 65°F (18°C) at night. It may take as long as three weeks for seedlings to emerge. Fertilize only moderately.

After danger of frost is past, transplant hardened-off seedlings into a W-shaped trench about 6 to 8 inches (15 to 20 cm) deep, with the center point of the W about 2 inches (5 cm) high. Locate the seedling at that center point to keep the roots from being saturated by a heavy rain.

PLANTING

Although asparagus can be grown from seed, most gardeners (including me) start with one-year-old crowns. You can plant the crowns in either a trench or a hole, the depth of either depending on the variety you've chosen. Heirloom, open pollinated varieties (Martha Washington and Mary Washington) need about

GETTING THE ACIDITY RIGHT

Test your soil before you plant asparagus; it does best in a slightly alkaline soil (pH of 7 or higher), a higher pH than you generally want in the rest of the garden. Dig any amendments deeply into the soil.

12 inches. The newer, all-male varieties of the so-called Jersey Series are content being planted just 5 or 6 inches (12.5–15 cm) deep.

In most regions, you should plant asparagus crowns in early spring, at about the time daffodils bloom. In very warm areas, such as the southwestern United States, plant in the fall or winter.

GROWING

Fertilizing. As vegetables go, asparagus has a pretty big appetite. Because they are perennials, the plants need to produce enough energy to survive the winter, feed us, and then produce new ferns. It may be possible to overfeed asparagus, but it isn't easy. To ensure a steady supply of nutrients for the plants and keep soil organisms busy loosening and aerating the soil, apply a thick (3- to 5-inch; 7.5–12.5 cm) layer of compost or well-rotted manure to the bed after you're done harvesting the spears and again in the fall, after you've cut back the dead ferns.

▲ **Weed no more.** *A thick straw mulch around asparagus plants holds down weeds and helps keep soil moist and cool.*

Weed control. If asparagus has to share nutrients with weeds, its vigor is affected and its yield and longevity are ultimately reduced. Around midsummer, apply a straw mulch to help with weed control as well as to moderate the soil temperature and conserve moisture. Create a buffer zone between the bed and garden edge by using an opaque mulch, such as layers of newspaper or cardboard covered with straw, to discourage invading grasses.

For asparagus, any competitor is a weed. This includes the asparagus seedlings that sprout from those red berries produced by open-pollinated varieties. Hoe them out, being careful not to damage the roots of the parent plants. Or you can avoid the pretty red berries entirely by growing all-male varieties such as Jersey Giant.

"Weeds" also include any potential companion plants. No matter what anybody says about good companions for asparagus, I don't want any competition here. The asparagus bed is for asparagus, period.

HARVEST

You can harvest fresh asparagus from the garden the second spring after planting (the third if you're starting from seeds). The first harvest should be light, no more than two or three spears per plant over a period of about two weeks. Each following spring, harvest spears that are more than ⅜ inch (1 cm) in diameter and 6 to 8 inches (15 to 20 cm) tall. Let the skinny spears grow into ferns. Stop harvesting when most of the emerging spears are small and the tips become loose and open; this will happen at about the time you start harvesting peas. A typical harvest lasts from four to eight weeks.

There are two schools of thought on how to harvest: Cut the spear at or just below the soil with a knife; or, my preference, bend the spear until it breaks, which leaves a bit of it still above the soil.

STORING

You've got to be kidding. You don't *store* asparagus, you *eat* asparagus . . . immediately after cooking, or sooner, if you count the half-dozen spears munched raw, right in the garden.

If you must store asparagus, either immerse the newly harvested spears in a tub of cold water or stand the bunch in a shallow container filled with 1 to 2 inches

▲ **Nip them in the bud.** *Loose tips, like the one on the left, mean stringy asparagus. Choose stalks like the one on the right with its nice, tight buds. Check your asparagus every day during the harvest season, so you don't miss the perfect picks.*

▲ **Bend or cut?** *I prefer the bend-and-break method of harvesting asparagus because only the most tender, flavorful portion of the spear remains in my hand. If you cut the stalk with a knife, on the other hand, you get any tough parts as well.*

(2.5 to 5 cm) of cold water for a few minutes. Drain and refrigerate in plastic storage bags. It stays fresh for about a week. Storage temperature is important for asparagus; for best results, it must be just above 32°F (0°C). Asparagus does freeze well, but I prefer to eat it fresh.

PREPARING FOR WINTER

The thick growth of asparagus ferns, or brush, that covers the bed in late summer and early fall turns brown and brittle at the end of the growing season. In early to midfall, cut back this brush and add it to the compost pile. Test the soil and add amendments to restore soil fertility and maintain a pH of about 7.0. Next, spread compost or rotted manure at least 3 inches (7.5 cm) thick over the bed. Finish with a mulch of straw about 6 inches (15 cm) deep. This both protects the asparagus crowns from winter damage and allows soil organisms to continue improving the soil in both fall and spring.

VARIETIES

Open-pollinated types have both male and female plants, the latter of which produce the red berries that become the "weeds" you need to rogue out each spring.

Martha Washington and **Mary Washington**. These old-fashioned, open-pollinated cultivars reliably produce large crops.

Eat Now, Pay Later

Unlike other garden vegetables, which reward us only after we work all summer long to tend and nurture them, asparagus gives us the reward first. From the plant's perspective, however, the important part is still to come: It must grow lush and hardy ferns to make lots of food to store in the roots for the following spring. But we've already had what we want from the plant, and all too often we neglect it during what, for it, is a critically important time. Be fair to your asparagus: Keep it well weeded, fertilized, and watered throughout the growing season.

Purple Passion*. Purple spears that turn green when cooked and have 20 percent more sugar than green asparagus; will overwinter to Zone 3.

Rutgers hybrids (Jersey Giant, Jersey Knight***, and Jersey Supreme)**. These all-male varieties produce huge crops of thick, tender spears; very disease resistant; all will overwinter to Zone 3.

UC 17*. High yields and exceptional flavor, about 70 percent male seedlings; overwinters to Zone 6.

* Available as seeds.

Beans, Bush

If, for you, "beans" has meant green or yellow snap beans and little more, you're in for a consciousness-expanding treat. Beans in one or another form are a large part of our garden. And with good reason: beans are good food and tasty in a variety of ways. Most beans have pretty much the same cultural needs, but the same or similar processes lead to myriad culinary outcomes. Snap beans — long ones, short ones, green, yellow, even purple or speckled. Shell beans, with yet another batch of colors, shapes, sizes, and tastes. And dry beans: even more colors, shapes, sizes, and tastes. All beans are high in protein, vitamin B, and minerals including iron, calcium, phosphorus, and potassium, are cholesterol-free, and as a general rule, are very easy to grow. That's a combination hard to beat.

BUSH BEANS

Bush beans, whether they are snap, shell, or dry beans, grow on compact bushes rather than vines. They have similar needs regardless of whether they reach the table as young "snap" beans, as somewhat older "shell" beans, or as fully mature "dry" beans. Some bean varieties, can, in fact, be used in some or all of the above growth stages.

▲ Bush beans galore. *Beans like this 'Black Valentine' are among the easiest vegetables to grow and harvest.*

Sow & Grow

Bush Beans (*Phaseolus vulgaris, P. limensis, Vicia faba*)
Pea family (Leguminosae)

SOWING

Seed depth: 1" (2.5 cm)
Germination soil temperature: 75–85°F (24–29°C)
  NOTE: Fava (55–75°F) (13–24°C) have different germination temperatures
Days to germination: 7–10
Sow indoors: Not recommended
Sow outdoors: When soil temperature reaches 60°F (16°C)

GROWING

pH range: 6.5–7.5
Growing soil temperature: 60–65°F (16–18°C)
Spacing in beds: 4" (10 cm) between plants, in rows across the bed 8" (20 cm) apart
Watering: Low at planting, medium at flowering, heavy through harvest
Light: Full sun
Nutrient requirements: N=low; P=moderate; K=moderate
Rotation considerations: Avoid following other legumes; not before or after onion family crops
Seed longevity: 3 years

THE SITE

Beans like a well-drained soil, moderately fertile, with a pH around 6.5, but definitely above 6.0. They do best in full sun and are less susceptible to mildew if there's some gentle air movement through the garden. If you can, avoid planting bush beans where other legumes have grown in the previous three years. (This isn't always easy to do if you grow many legumes; just do the best you can.)

SOWING

For most bush bean varieties, starting them too early is not doing them a favor. Cold soil slows down germination, makes the seedlings more susceptible to disease, and can damage the plants so much they never produce a good harvest. Most bush beans won't germinate at all until average daytime soil temperature is at least 60°F (16°C), and best germination occurs between 70°F (21°C) and 90°F (32°C). The seedbed should be moist, but not wet, and raked smooth so the seeds have good contact with the soil. Plant seeds with the "eye" down.

GROWING

Watering. During the 7- to 10-day germination period, make sure the soil is always moist. After germination, monitor soil moisture during dry spells and water well if the first inch or so becomes dry. Avoid overhead watering, which wets the leaves and fosters disease.

Fertilizing. Beans, along with peas, alfalfa, and some other plants, belong to a group called legumes. Legumes are special because they get much of their nitrogen through a partnership with *Rhizobia* bacteria, instead of relying on supplies in the soil. But it takes a little time after germination for the bacteria to become established on the roots of each plant, so for a few weeks beans need to get their nitrogen from the soil like other plants.

Fertilize with a liquid organic fertilizer, such as fish emulsion, at planting time and again at two and four weeks if the leaves are not deep green in color. (Pale greens or yellow indicate a need for nitrogen.)

Note: To avoid spreading disease, don't work in the bean patch while the leaves are wet.

Succession success. Bush snap beans often bear for longer than they ought: After the first few harvests,

▲ **Bean there.** *Sow several plantings of beans about 10 days apart, to ensure a continuous harvest. Plant bean seeds with the eye down, so they can see where they have bean.*

Give Your Beans a Bacterial Boost

Beans and other legumes supply much of their own nitrogen needs through their relationship with certain bacteria that live in their roots. They do a better job at this and produce heavier crops if the seeds are inoculated with *Rhizobia* bacteria before sowing, especially if you're still in the process of building up the organic content of your soil. If the soil you're planting in has been regularly enriched with compost, inoculating seeds with *Rhizobia* shouldn't be necessary.

To inoculate your beans, simply put the black powder containing the bacteria (available in most seed catalogs) in a bag with the seeds. Shake the bag until the seeds are coated, and then sow them. Keep in mind that different beans need different inoculants. Beans need one; peas and lentils, another; and soybeans, yet another. Be sure you're using the right one.

taste starts to go downhill. Instead of sowing one big crop, make several small plantings about 10 days apart. As soon as the next crop starts, pull the old plants and compost them, beans and all. You'll have a continuous harvest of tender, fresh beans over most of the garden season, and the harvest quality will be better. As a bonus, you get some fresh green material for the compost pile.

A BEAN FOR ALL SEASONS

Snap beans. These are the familiar "green beans," (also available in deep purple and in yellow ("wax beans"). They used to be called "string beans" until plant breeders got rid of the strings. Also included here are French "filet" beans (*haricots verts*) and Italian flat-pod beans. They're all eaten, pod and seeds, when they're young and tender.

Shell beans. When the seeds of some beans begin to swell, but are not completely mature and ready for drying, they make delicious eating shelled, fresh from the pod, and they freeze well.

Dry beans. These are harvested when the beans are fully mature, the plant itself dead and dry. They're among the best of storage crops and filled with nutritional benefits. Dried beans are a valuable staple for cold-weather soups, stews, and casseroles.

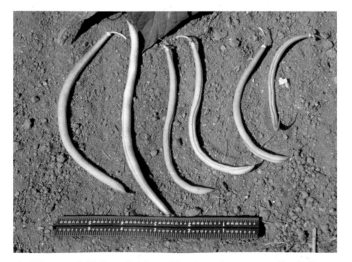

▲ **Slim and fit for picking.** *The two beans on the left are too large and will be tough. The two in the middle are at their peak, but those on the right are too young and will therefore lack flavor.*

HARVESTING SNAP BEANS

The easiest time to mess up a snap bean crop is right at the end. Snap beans taste their very best for a fairly short part of their growth: too young, and the flavor hasn't developed yet; too old, and they're not as tender or sweet. As beans mature, they grow longer and bigger around. Length at prime harvest time most often varies by variety; diameter, though, varies with ripeness.

Green (and purple) beans and wax beans. Pick these when the pods are ¼ to ⅜-inch (6 to 10 mm) in diameter, about the thickness of a pencil.

French, or filet, beans. Considered by many to be the tastiest bush beans, French beans should be harvested when they're very slender, about ⅛ inch (3 mm) in diameter. Beans allowed to grow larger quickly get tough and stringy. At times of peak harvest, this can mean picking filet beans about every other day.

Snap Bean Varieties

Black Valentine. This heirloom variety is noted for heavy yields and good flavor, freezes well, and is well adapted to cool temperatures.

Bush Blue Lake. This is the bush variety of the renowned Blue Lake pole bean. Bush beans can't match the best pole beans for flavor, but this comes as close as any.

Dragon Langerie. It's hard to know where to categorize this one. It's a yellow bean (with purple tiger stripes), but it's flat rather than round. In spite of its Oriental-sounding name, Dragon Langerie is from Holland. The pods are stringless, crisp, and very juicy — for a very short time; they don't store well or freeze well. Eat them fresh, shortly after harvest.

Indy Gold. Yellow beans with green tips produce a heavy yield and do well in cold, wet weather.

Provider. This bean has been a favorite variety for decades: early, reliable, disease-resistant, and productive in poor soil and adverse conditions; all that plus good taste. As we say up here in Vermont, "You can't beat that with a stick."

Royal Burgundy. This one doesn't start out green; on the bush, the beans are a quite striking purple. But cook 'em up and they turn green, very green.

Royal Burgundy snap beans

Romano beans

Filet Bean Varieties

Isar. A pretty, yellow filet bean, Isar also has good flavor.

Italian, flat-pod, or Romano beans. These aren't strictly snap beans, but they're bush beans eaten in the pod, like snap beans; this seems as good a place as any for them. Pick them when they are 5 to 7 inches (12.5 to 17.5 cm) long, depending on the variety.

Masai. Beans are very good candidates for container growing, and this is the best of the lot. Foot-tall plants produce large yields and good-tasting beans. Masai, unlike other filet beans, holds its flavor and tenderness for as long as a week and therefore needn't be picked every day.

Pension. Pension produces 6 × ¾" (15 x 2 cm) medium green pods with good flavor.

Roma II. This variety consistently produces heavy yields of medium-green, 5" (12.5 cm) pods.

Straight and Narrow. The name says it all: Nice, straight, uniform (and tasty) beans grow on a compact plant. Like Masai, Straight and Narrow is a good choice for container growing.

Masai filet beans

Pennies in the Sand

Collecting colorful beans from the remains of the dry pods (threshing) can be as much fun as finding pennies buried in a sandbox. We usually thresh by hand, on an early winter evening in front of the fireplace. Make sure the beans are thoroughly dry and then store them in airtight jars. If you haven't the time or patience for hand threshing, try either of these methods:

- Take a handful of dried plants and gently bang them on the inside of a clean, dry trash can.

- Stuff the dried plants in a clean feed bag or old pillowcase and tread on it lightly.

HARVESTING SHELL BEANS

Bush shell beans are grown the same as bush snap beans but harvested later, when the pods are swollen with plump, tender seeds. Some varieties, such as Tongue of Fire, can be eaten younger, as snap beans, and others, including Flambeau, can also be used as dry beans. In cool regions, shell beans are a good substitute for lima beans, which grow best in hot weather, something northern gardeners have in short supply.

Shell Bean Varieties
Tongue of Fire. Far and away our favorite shell bean, this is tasty and productive and freezes well.
Note: Large, overmature Kentucky Wonder beans also make very good shell beans.

HARVESTING DRY BEANS

Harvest dry beans when the pods are completely mature and dry. Good air circulation is important so that the pods don't rot before they dry, so allow sufficient space between rows. If you have a run of rainy weather after the leaves have died and the pods have begun to dry, pull the plants and hang them by the roots in an open shed.

Dry Bean Varieties
Andrew Kent, Black Coco, Etna, Jacob's Cattle, Maine Yellow Eye, Midnight Black Turtle, Soldier, Speckled Yellow Eye, Vermont Cranberry

Jacob's Cattle

Calypso

Dutch Bullet

Green Flageolet

Winning at Shell Games: Growing Favas and Limas

Fava beans, also called broad or horse beans, are distant relatives of snap beans. Their pods look like fuzzy limas. These meaty beans have long been a staple of European cuisine, from the Middle East to Italy to northern Europe. In cool regions of North America, fava beans are used as a substitute for lima beans.

Sow fava beans not when you'd plant other beans but when you'd plant peas, "as soon as the soil can be worked." Unlike other beans, favas will germinate well in cool soil. Sow 1 to 2 inches (2.5 to 5 cm) deep and 6 inches (15 cm) apart. Pinching back the top of the plant when the first pods begin to form usually gives more uniform, higher-quality beans. Harvest as soon as the pods are plump, usually when they're about 6 inches (15 cm) long. Don't wait too long; taste takes a nosedive pretty soon after prime harvest time.

VARIETIES

Egyptian. A small-seeded fava bean used in Middle-Eastern cuisine

Windsor. Heirloom variety with 5- to 6-inch (12.5–15 cm) pods containing 3–5 large beans

Caution: Some people are allergic to raw fava beans, so be sure to cook them before consuming.

Lima beans love long stretches of warm weather, a quality that makes them of questionable value for northern gardeners. In warm regions, however, lima beans prosper, yielding delectable, tasty beans that resemble the store-bought kind in name only.

Lima beans need even warmer soil (75°F [24°C]) than other beans for germination, are sensitive to even light frosts, and need warm and dry weather throughout a long growing season. Sow lima beans 1 inch (2.5 cm) deep (slightly deeper in sandy soils) and 3 to 4 inches (7.5 to 10 cm) apart. As with other beans, harvest often to increase yield.

VARIETIES

Bush limas for cool areas: Eastland Baby, Jackson Wonder, and Packers

Bush limas for warm regions: Burpee's Improved Bush Lima, Dixie Butterpea, and Fordhook 242

▲ Regal treats. *Windsor fava beans, ready to eat.*

▲ Sweet anticipation. *Fava bean flowers are gorgeous and have a spicy fragrance.*

Beans, Pole

Flavor is always a debatable point, but most people who grow both bush and pole beans think pole beans are the sweeter, more tender, and better tasting of the two. There is no debate regarding yield. Pole beans produce more pods per plant than bush beans, plus they're much easier to pick.

SOWING AND GROWING

Most of the growing information that applies to bush beans also works for pole beans, with a few exceptions. Because pole beans are vining plants (called indeterminate), they need support to produce the best crops. You can construct a trellis like that described on pages 78–79 or create or purchase obelisk or teepee-style supports like those shown in the photos on these pages.

The vines will climb twine, poles, wire fencing, or netting. For twine or poles, plant seeds in groups of four to six with 16 inches (40 cm) between the groups. For fencing or netting, plant seeds 3 inches (8 cm) apart, with a row on each side of the netting; stagger the rows. Anchor netting or twine to the ground with stakes or loops of heavy wire.

▲ **Beans by the pyramid-full.** *Pole beans continue to grow, flower, and produce pods over a season of six to eight weeks, much longer than bush beans.*

Sow & Grow

Pole Beans (*Phaseolus vulgaris*)
Pea family (Leguminosae)

SOWING

Seed depth: 1" (2.5 cm), 6–8 seeds per hill
Germination soil temperature: At least 60°F (16°C), but better germination at 75–85°F (24–29°C)
Days to germination: 7–10
Sow indoors: Not recommended
Sow outdoors: When soil temperature reaches 60°F (16°C)

GROWING

pH range: 6.5–7.5
Growing soil temperature: 60–65°F (16–18°C)
Spacing in beds: In hills (for poles), 16" (40 cm) apart, 4 plants per hill; in rows (for trellises), 3" (8 cm) apart
Watering: Low at sowing, medium at flowering, heavy through harvest
Light: Full sun for best yield; tolerates light shade
Nutrient requirements: N=low; P=moderate; K=moderate
Rotation considerations: Precede corn; avoid following pea and bush bean
Seed longevity: 3 years

HARVEST AND STORAGE

Pole beans tend to stay tender on the vine longer than bush beans, but regular picking is still required to extend the harvest to its limit. When you have all the beans you need, let the remaining pods mature and use them as shell beans. Pole beans freeze very well, keeping a firmer texture than bush beans.

BEST VARIETIES

Blue Lake. If you could call a bean variety tried-and-true, Blue Lake would be the one. Tender and stringless, these beans stay tasty even when big.

Fortex. Noted for exceptional flavor and easy growing, Fortex's round pods can grow to 11" (28 cm) but may be picked at about 7" (17.5 cm) as "filet beans."

Gold of Bacau. Plants produce very tasty yellow Romano-type, 6–10" (15 to 25 cm) pods.

Kentucky Wonder. Sometimes called Homestead Bean, this old-time favorite goes back to the 1800s and still hits the top of most bean-lovers' Hit Parade; it's consistently very productive and tasty and freezes well. Overmature beans make good shell beans.

▲ Jack never had it this good. *This rustic obelisk makes a sturdy and attractive support for beanstalks.*

▲ From small beginnings. *Sow four to six seeds spaced around each pole.*

▲ Kentucky Wonder beans keep on giving. *Pods too big for eating as snap beans yield a fine harvest of shell beans.*

Beets

Grown for their greens as well as their roots, beets come in many colors and shapes. While it is technically true that those reddish purple things in cans tucked in the back of your cupboard are beets, they aren't the best way to get to know this delicious vegetable. Beets baked in the oven like potatoes, or fresh baby beets and carrots sautéed in butter, are a better introduction to this flavorful, often overlooked vegetable.

THE SITE

Beets prefer a light soil with a pH of between 6.5 and 7.5. If your beets develop scab, keep the pH above 7.0. Enrich the soil with plenty of compost, preferably compost with some seaweed in it. (If you can't manage

▲ **Can't beat this.** *Keep your beets cool by growing them beneath mulches, and try to harvest them when they're no more than 2½ inches (6.3 cm) in diameter. To avoid "bleeding," remove the greens by twisting rather than cutting.*

the seaweed, water after sowing with liquid seaweed fertilizer.) Research at Cornell University has shown that beet roots can grow as much as 3 feet (0.9 m) into the soil; they'll therefore do well in deeply dug, wide raised beds.

SOWING

Each beet "seed" is actually a dried fruit containing a cluster of two to six seeds. Sow these seeds 2 to 4 inches (5 to 10 cm) apart a month or so before the last frost. If you sow beets in midsummer for winter storage, the soil is likely to be warmer than beets prefer. To improve germination, sow seeds at dusk or on a cool, cloudy day. Water well and add a thin dressing of compost to help moderate soil temperatures.

Sow & Grow

Beets (*Beta vulgaris* Crassa Group)
Beet family (Chenopodiaceae)

SOWING

Seed depth: ½" (13 mm)
Germination soil temperature: 75–85°F (24–29°C)
Days to germination: 5
Sow indoors: 5 weeks before last frost
Sow outdoors: 3–4 weeks before last frost

GROWING

pH range: At least 6.0 to as much as 7.5
Growing soil temperature: 65–75°F (18–24°C)
Spacing in beds: For greens, 2" (5 cm); for summer use, 3" (7.5 cm); for storage, 4" (10 cm)
Watering: Moderate and even
Light: Full sun for best yield; tolerates light shade
Nutrient requirements: N=low; P=moderate; K=moderate
Rotation considerations: Avoid following spinach or Swiss chard
Seed longevity: 4 years

◄ Sweet beets go deep. *Pulled from deeply dug, sandy soil, this young beet boasts a taproot of 1 foot (30 cm). Its fine root hairs probed even farther into the soil all around.*

SINGLE SEED OPTION

Thanks to the miracles of plant breeding there is now a hybrid beet with only one embryo per seed. It is called Monetta and produces smooth, deeply colored roots with medium-tall greens.

After seedlings emerge, thin each cluster, leaving the most robust plant. To avoid disturbing the remaining plants, don't pull out the unwanted seedlings; instead, thin by cutting the plants at soil level with scissors. The roots remaining in the soil will feed soil bacteria as they decompose, ultimately feeding the remaining beet plants.

GROWING

Plants that reach harvestable size during hot weather may have poor root color and flavor. Beets grow best in cool conditions and profit from cooling mulches and companion-cropping with plants that shade the soil.

Watering. Even moisture, which allows steady, uninterrupted growth, is important if beets are to reach peak quality. Don't let the soil dry out.

Fertilizing. Too much nitrogen can result in luxuriant tops but poor root development. If your soil is fertile, you probably won't need to fertilize beets, but if the soil isn't yet where you want it, fertilize every three to four weeks with a low-nitrogen, organic fertilizer, high in phosphorus and potassium.

HARVEST

Beets taste best when harvested at about 1½ to 2½ inches (3.8 to 6.3 cm) in diameter. As the roots grow larger, they lose flavor and develop an unappetizing texture. To harvest, pull or dig the roots and remove the tops. Some people cut the greens from the roots, but this can cause bleeding, which reduces the moisture content in the root. To minimize such bleeding, grasp the root in one hand, the greens in the other, and twist off the tops. Place roots in plastic vegetable bags and refrigerate or store in damp sand in the root cellar.

An Exception to Every Rule

Although in general beets grow best in cool weather, an extended cold snap (two or more weeks below 50°F (10°C) that occurs after beet plants have formed a tidy rosette of leaves can force them to bolt, which ruins the quality of the roots. If a long cool period is expected, place a floating row cover over plants to keep daytime temperatures above 50°F (10°C).

VARIETIES

Bull's Blood. Red on the outside, dark red and light red in cross-section; red leaves good in salad or cooked.

Chioggia. Bright red on the outside and striped red and white on the inside.

Detroit Dark Red. An old-time midseason variety that has been popular for decades.

Forono. Five-inch (12.5 cm) long, 2-inch (5 cm) diameter, cylindrical roots; produces uniform slices for cooking or pickling.

Golden Beet. Orange skin with gold flesh.

Red Ace. Considered the best all-around beet; early; good for roots or greens and for baby beets cooked with their greens.

Broccoli

Either you love it or you don't. But even if you don't love broccoli, there are some good reasons to add it to your diet. It contains large amounts of sulforaphane (a compound that can prevent some types of cancer), antioxidants that help protect the body from other diseases, and plenty of vitamins A, B, and C, plus potassium, phosphorus, calcium, and iron. All these goodies are even more concentrated in broccoli sprouts that are easy to grow on a kitchen countertop. Maybe Popeye would have been better off with broccoli?

THE SITE

Broccoli is a hungry and thirsty plant; it needs fertile, friable soil with good moisture-holding capacity. It also needs a lot of nitrogen, so work in 3 or more inches (8-plus cm) of compost or well-aged manure and some leaf mold. (Or add some chopped leaves to the soil the previous fall.) If you don't add greensand and rock phosphate to your compost, add both to your soil for this and other cabbage-family crops. Broccoli prefers full sun and a pH of 6.5 to 7.5.

SOWING

For an early summer harvest, sow broccoli seeds indoors about four to six weeks before the last spring frost. Seeds will germinate in about six days at 75°F (24°C). Once plants show true leaves, fertilize with an organic fertilizer such as fish emulsion at half strength. For a second, or fall, crop, direct-seed in late spring in cool regions and summer in warm areas.

Don't start broccoli too early or too late. If you plant too early, you'll end up with large, root-bound transplants that may produce tiny broccoli heads, or "buttons." Long exposure to cold weather can also produce buttoning. On the other hand, if your summers are very warm, don't plant broccoli too late; in hot weather, it may bolt before the heads are fully formed.

▲ **Hale and hearty.** *Broccoli is delicious and versatile, with health benefits as well.*

Sow & Grow

Broccoli (*Brassica oleracea* Italica Group),
 (*B. rapa* Ruvo Group)
Cabbage family (Cruciferae)

SOWING

Seed depth: ¼" (6 mm)
Germination soil temperature: 68–85°F
 (18–29°C), ideal 77°F (25°C)
Days to germination: 4–7
Sow indoors: 6–8 weeks before last frost
Sow outdoors: Early summer for fall crop

GROWING

pH range: 6.5–7.5
Growing soil temperature: 60–65°F (16–18°C)
Spacing in beds: 16" (40 cm), staggered
 pattern, 3 rows to a wide (36"; 0.9 m) bed
Watering: Moderate and even
Light: Full sun for best yield; tolerates partial
 shade
Nutrient requirements: N=moderate to high;
 P=high; K=high
Rotation considerations: Avoid following
 with cabbage family crops
Seed longevity: 3 years

GROWING

Broccoli transplants well, but be careful not to disturb the roots. Transplant when seedlings are about 3 inches (7.5 cm) tall, and set plants 1 inch (2.5 cm) deeper than they grew in the pots. Plant in a staggered pattern 16 inches (40 cm) apart, with 12 inches (30 cm) between rows. Three rows can fit in a 36-inch-wide (0.9 m) bed.

FERTILIZING

If you've added enough organic matter and fertilizer to the soil, you probably won't need to fertilize more during the year unless you see signs of deficiency (slow growth, pale green or yellowish leaves, purplish leaf stems). If needed, fertilize with fish emulsion or another complete, fast-acting liquid fertilizer.

Bug Off

Flea beetles are the bane of brassicas. They can kill small, young, and tender plants and set back even fairly large ones by cutting down the leaf surface area available for photosynthesis. There are various "approved for organic growing" poisons of differing potencies that may or may not kill off enough beetles to minimize injury to the plant, but all of them bring along more or less serious collateral damage: They can kill more than just the target organisms and therefore disrupt the garden and soil ecologies. And even the more potent poisons don't always work.

Row covers *do* work. Put them on as soon as you sow the seeds or set out the transplants. Leave them there until the plants are big and tough and the flea beetle population is in its seasonal decline; if you leave the row covers there all summer, you'll avoid the other brassica banes, cabbage caterpillars and root maggots.

If flea beetles are a major problem in your area, plant later in the season for fall harvest. The flea beetle population declines later in the summer and the young broccoli are barely troubled. We find that we don't eat a lot of early broccoli anyway; there's so much else to eat during the summer.

Cabbage caterpillars, as their name implies, eat cabbage, but they're at least as happy to munch on broccoli. The damage they do is seldom serious, but their ability to hide in the midst of a broccoli head can lead to some gross surprises at the dinner table. You can try your hand at handpicking — I've found it neither fun nor particularly effective. You can use *Bt* to kill them. But if you drape the plants with lightweight row covers, the cute butterflies that lay the eggs that become the caterpillars won't get the chance to lay the eggs. I either use the covers or just live with the problem, being very, very careful to search for caterpillars before cooking broccoli.

▲ A stitch in time. *This row cover, supported by wire hoops, will protect broccoli from flea beetles.*

HARVEST

The part of the broccoli plant we gardeners want is actually a large cluster of flower buds that would, if we permitted it, become myriad small, yellow blooms. Harvest when the bud cluster, or head, is dark green and fully formed, with tight buds and no hint of yellow. Cut the head with a sharp knife. More, smaller heads will soon form as side shoots, a process that can continue until hard frost finally kills the plant. The more you harvest, the more you get. The plant will stop sending out new shoots if some of them finally get to the flower stage. Some varieties are better than others at this game; I like to pick the ones that produce lots of shoots for a long time.

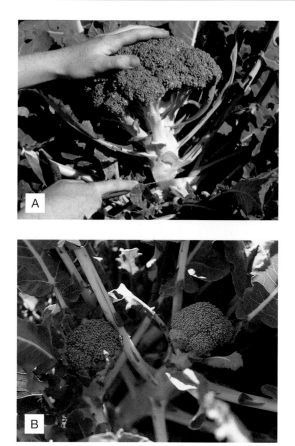

▶ Cut-and-come-again broccoli. *After the main head has been harvested (A), broccoli continues to produce side shoots (B) for several more weeks.*

Romanesco Broccoli

Is it really broccoli? In some seed catalogs you'll find it with other broccolis. Sometimes it's off with cauliflowers — and it looks like neither of them. It looks, in fact, like no other vegetable: The head is a spiral of spirals, clusters of pointed pinnacles. For all its otherworldly beauty (or oddity, depending on the eye of the beholder) it's tasty and nutritious raw or cooked.

THE SITE

Romanesco plants are big and hungry. They need deep, fertile soil enriched with plenty of compost or well-rotted manure (6 inches; 15 cm, or more).

If grown in less than super-fertile soil, these plants can be a disappointment, with small and poorly formed whorls.

SOWING

Start seeds indoors six to eight weeks before the last frost. Germinate at 70°F (21°C) and grow at 60°F (16°C). Harden off gradually and transplant to the garden after the danger of frost is past. Plant at least 18 inches (45 cm) apart.

GROWING

As long as they have enough to eat, these are not fussy plants. If flea beetles are a problem in your garden, use row covers until the plants are big enough to tolerate some damage.

HARVEST

Cut the heads before the curd (bud clusters) becomes loose.

VARIETIES

Arcadia. Mid- to late-season. Big heads and good cold tolerance.

Belstar. Grows well in many conditions, including warm winters; good side shoot production.

Nutribud. Open pollinated and especially high in glutamine (a protein building block that is thought to be a healing nutrient); good side shoot production.

Packman. Early, with good side shoot production; may button if transplanted too early in the spring (buttoning is not a problem if the plant is direct-seeded).

Small Miracle and **Munchkin.** Compact plants suitable for small spaces or containers.

Waltham. An old favorite; late season with good side shoot production.

All in the Family: Broccoli Rabe

Broccoli rabe and broccoli are related, and their flavors are akin, but you wouldn't confuse the two if you saw them side by side. Broccoli looks like, well, broccoli, while broccoli rabe (also known as "raab," "rape" or "rapini") has thin, leafy shoots topped by small, loose clusters of buds. Other differences become manifest in the garden (broccoli rabe matures sooner) and at the table (you eat leaves, stems, and buds of broccoli rabe, and its flavor has a bit more zip to it).

THE SITE

As for regular broccoli, choose a site in full sun with fertile soil and a neutral pH (6.5 to 7.5) into which you've worked plenty of compost (3 or 4 inches; 8 to 10 cm).

SOWING

You can start broccoli rabe indoors, but it grows fast and can tolerate a bit of frost, so it makes sense to plant it directly in the garden a couple of weeks after you'd plant peas. Succession plantings 7 to 10  days apart or small plantings of varieties that mature at different times will yield a continuous harvest. Sow the tiny seeds ½-inch (13 mm) deep and as close as you can get to a couple of inches apart. If you're planting short rows across a bed, space the rows apart at 6 inches (15 cm). Water well with a fine spray and keep the soil moist until seedlings emerge in three to five days.

GROWING

Thin the plants to about 6 inches (15 cm) when they are about 3 inches (8 cm) tall. Monitor soil moisture and water deeply if the top inch of soil is dry. If the soil dries out too much, broccoli rabe turns bitter.

HARVEST

The window of opportunity is small here: Harvest about the top half of the plant after it "bolts" (sends up stalks and bud clusters) but before the flower buds have a chance to open. Cut at the point where the tender part of the stem meets the tough part. The whole show here will take just a day. You snooze, you lose the best flavor. When you harvest this way, taking a large part of the plant, use it all — buds, stems and leaves. With some varieties, you can harvest just the bud clusters for a continuous harvest. Flavor is best if you use broccoli rabe right away, but it will store in the refrigerator in a plastic bag for a week or so.

VARIETIES

Quarantina. Very early; a small plant suitable for small spaces and containers

Sel Fasano. Big leaves on short stems; produces side shoots after the main stalk is harvested

Spring Rabe. Late, large and slow to bolt

Zamboni. An heirloom variety good in salads or sautéed vegetable mixes

Brussels Sprouts

If you grow Brussels sprouts, you'll be eating fresh vegetables after most of the harvest is only a memory; they're one of the hardiest vegetables in the garden. They not only survive fall frost and light snowfalls, they thrive — the cold treatment actually makes them taste better. This is one of the few vegetables that give cool-region gardeners an edge over their warm-region counterparts.

Sow & Grow

Brussels sprouts (*Brassica oleracea* Gemmifera Group)

Cabbage family (Cruciferae)

SOWING

Seed depth: ¼" (6 mm)

Germination soil temperature: 75–85°F (24–29°C)

Days to germination: 5–8

Sow indoors: 4–6 weeks before last frost

Sow outdoors: At least 4 months before the first fall frost

GROWING

pH range: 6.0–6.8

Growing soil temperature: 60–65°F (16–18°C)

Spacing in beds: 16–18" (40–45 cm), depending on type; staggered pattern, 3 rows to a wide bed (36"; 0.9 m)

Watering: Moderate and even

Light: Full sun for best yield; tolerates light shade

Nutrient requirements: N=moderate; P=high; K=high

Rotation considerations: Avoid following cabbage family crops

Seed longevity: 4 years

Seeds per ounce: 8,500 (283 seeds per g)

▲ **Losing your marbles?** *Get an early start on your Brussels sprouts harvest by picking the first, marble-sized buds that form at the bottom of the plant. You'll be able to continue to harvest this vegetable long after the rest of the garden has been put away.*

THE SITE

Brussels sprouts are tall plants reaching from 2 to 3 feet (0.6 to 0.9 m), with thick stems and heavy bud production. Their root system, however, is close to the soil surface and, though dense, not very far-reaching. These qualities mean Brussels sprouts require a rich, fertile soil and even moisture to grow their best.

Prepare the bed in fall by working in plenty of compost or well-rotted manure and autumn leaves. In spring, test the soil for nutrients and to be sure the pH is between 6.0 and 6.8. If you're getting the bed ready in spring, add compost and any fertilizers your soil test indicates and loosen the soil with a broadfork or garden fork. Work the compost and fertilizer in well with a three-tine cultivator or a potato fork and smooth the soil with a rake. When transplanting, add some compost or well-rotted manure to the planting hole.

SOWING

Even the shortest-season Brussels sprouts take a long time to grow (about 100 days), so start the plants indoors or in a cold frame about a month before the last frost date. Seeds will germinate in about a week at 75 to 80°F (24 to 27°C). Transplant when seedlings are from four to six weeks old. If your growing season is about four months long, Brussels sprouts can be direct-sown.

In warm regions, such as the U.S. Gulf Coast, direct-sow from mid-October to Christmas for harvest in spring. Sprouts grown in warm regions are often more open and less flavorful than those grown in cool areas.

GROWING

Brussels sprouts grow best in cool, evenly moist soil. Apply an organic mulch, such as straw, to moderate soil temperature during the warm months. Maintain a layer of compost on the bed under the mulch to supply nutrients and encourage the activity of worms. In areas exposed to persistent winds, plants may need staking. Insert stakes when transplants are planted to avoid damaging the roots of established plants.

You can stimulate the growth of sprouts by pinching out the growing tip — a rosette of small leaves at the top of the plant — about four weeks before you expect the first hard frost.

Fertilizing. These are big plants and heavy feeders. Fertilize every three to four weeks from transplanting to late summer with an organic fertilizer such as fish emulsion.

HARVEST

Although the buds improve in flavor after a frost or two, harvest whenever some buds are firm, between "aggies" and "shooter" marbles in size (½ to 1 inch; 13 to 25 mm). Break off the leaf stem below the bud and either snap off or cut the bud.

If there are still sprouts left when night temperatures are near 25°F (−4°C), cut the whole plant, strip the leaves, and hang it in the root cellar; the sprouts will be good for another three weeks.

VARIETIES

Bubbles. Tolerant of warm weather and resistant to powdery mildew.

Diablo. Fairly long season (110 days); good production of uniform, medium-sized sprouts.

Oliver. Relatively short season (90 days); a good choice for northern climes.

Roodnerf. Considered the only really good-tasting open pollinated variety.

▲ Topping off. *About a month before you expect a hard freeze, top the plant by pinching out the growing tip. This directs all the plant's energy into maturing the remaining sprouts.*

▲ The cold shoulder. *After the rest of the garden is buried in snow, you can still harvest Brussels sprouts, all the sweeter thanks to a bit of "cold treatment."*

Cabbage

Cabbage is one of the few green (or red) leaf vegetables that you can store for most of the winter in the root cellar, and even longer in the form of sauerkraut. Before we started growing salad greens in a solar greenhouse and in cold frames, we grew more cabbage than we do now. We still grow some green and some red cabbage for storage; it makes a nice coleslaw in deep winter, and it's tasty sautéed with onions. And we grow some savoy cabbage for salad greens after the lettuce and spinach have petered out in the heat of summer.

▲ C is for Cabbage.

Cabbage is easy to grow and delicious to eat either raw or cooked. An excellent source of vitamin C, it's useful in dishes from many ethnic traditions. Here, we have a solid head (top) and a savoy (bottom).

Sow & Grow

Cabbage (*Brassica oleracea* Capitata Group)
Cabbage family (Cruciferae)

SOWING

Seed depth: ¼" (6 mm)
Germination soil temperature: 75–85°F (24–29°C)
Days to germination: 5
Sow indoors: 4–6 weeks before last frost
Sow outdoors: 10–12 weeks before first frost for fall crop

GROWING

pH range: 6.0–7.5 (7.2–7.5 to inhibit clubroot)
Growing soil temperature: 60–65°F (16–18°C)
Spacing in beds: Early varieties, 12" (30 cm); late varieties, 18" (45 cm)
Watering: Heavy from planting to head formation, then moderate
Light: Full sun for best yield; tolerates light shade
Nutrient requirements: N=high; P=high; K=high
Rotation considerations: Avoid following cabbage family crops
Seed longevity: 4 years

THE SITE

Cabbage needs a rich, fertile soil with a pH of 6.0 to 7.5, with the optimum about 6.5. Add wood ashes (see page 133) if the pH is below 6.5 and your soil test shows a need for potassium. If your garden plan allows it, plant cabbage-family crops where a nitrogen-fixing green manure grew the previous year. Cabbage does best in full sun, especially in cool regions and other areas with short growing seasons. In warmer climates, cabbage tolerates light shade.

SOWING

Sow cabbage seeds for early crops in flats in early to midspring; sow late varieties in midspring. Germinate with soil temperature of at least 75°F (24°C). Once seedlings emerge, lower temperatures to about 60°F (16°C). When the plants have a few true leaves, transplant directly from the starting flat to a 3-inch (7.5 cm) pot. Transplant early-maturing varieties in early to mid-spring, spacing plants 12 inches (30 cm) apart; transplant fall varieties in early summer, spaced 18 inches (45 cm) apart. Be careful not to disturb the rootball.

You can also direct-sow both early- and late-season cabbage, thereby avoiding the possibility of damaging the roots during transplanting. If you use this option, make sure that weeds don't crowd the seedlings, and use floating row covers to discourage flea beetles.

GROWING

Fertilizing. All cabbages are heavy feeders and need ample, even supplies of most nutrients, including nitrogen, potassium, phosphorus, and boron.

Mulching. Cabbage has a shallow, dense root system, with many feeder roots very close to the surface. The roots are easily damaged by everything from cultivation to fluctuations in soil moisture to high soil temperatures. Mulch with straw or seed-free hay to control weeds, maintain soil moisture, and moderate soil temperature.

Weeding. Early competition from weeds slows growth, particularly of direct-seeded plants, but cabbage roots are easily damaged by cultivation, so use your hoe carefully or weed by hand. If a weed is big enough or close enough to the cabbage plant to cause damage when pulled, clip the weed with scissors. Avoid hoeing or working in the cabbage patch early in the morning, when leaves are full of moisture and brittle. Once heads begin to form, put the hoe away and do any weeding by hand.

HARVEST AND STORAGE

Early cabbage. Early varieties do not store well and should be harvested for use any time after the head reaches the size of a softball. The heads can grow larger, but they are most tender and tasty at this early stage, and the plant will often produce another head or heads, with the total harvest adding up to more than a single mature head would yield.

Late cabbage. Rather than cutting late crops grown for storage, pull them from the ground, roots and all. Remove the large leaves and all but a few wrapper leaves. Take care not to bruise the heads, as this will shorten their storage life. Late-season cabbage can

Splitting Headaches

Cabbages have a tendency to split and bolt. In general, any stress that disrupts growth after head formation can cause a head to split. These stresses include fluctuations in soil moisture and heads that have grown too large. There are a couple of ways to slow growth and thus prevent splitting:

- Wait until just after the heads firm up, and then twist the plants to break some roots (A).

- Plunge the blade of a spade into the soil on one side of the plant (B).

- Space the plants more closely together. For early varieties, space plants 8 to 12 inches (20 to 30 cm) apart; space late types 12 to 16 inches (30 to 40 cm) apart. Heads will be smaller, but they will also have better flavor and be less likely to split.

- Plant a variety that is more resistant to splitting than others. Some good choices include Primax, Columbia, Dynamo, and Super Red 80.

tolerate some frosty nights before harvest. You have several different options for storing late cabbage:

- Cut off the roots and any loose or damaged leaves and place heads on shelves in the root cellar.

- Prepare as above and wrap in newspaper; store as above.

- Hang by the roots in the root cellar.

- Leave the roots on and lean the plants against the root cellar wall, covering the roots with damp sand. If you use this method, you'll receive a little bonus when you get around to using the cabbage. After you have cut the head from the root, plant the root in a pot filled with damp sand and put it in a sunny window. You'll soon be harvesting small cabbage leaves for salads, right in the middle of winter.

Two Heads Are Better than One

To extend your early-cabbage harvest, try making one plant produce more than one head. When a cabbage head is ready to harvest, carefully cut it from the stalk just below the head, leaving a stump. Cut a cross pattern into the stalk, making the slice about ¼ inch (6 mm) deep. In a little while, up to four small heads will begin to appear. Harvest when the heads are about the size of baseballs.

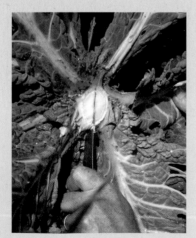

In general, green cabbage doesn't store as well as red. Scanbo is a nice exception to this rule. Until we discovered Scanbo, our green cabbages never kept as well as the reds. Now it's a toss-up. I can't report on the storage quality of savoy cabbages: we like their taste so much in late-fall salads that the savoys are always gone before we get around to storing them.

BEST VARIETIES

Early-Season Green
Dynamo. Disease and split resistant and an All-America winner.
Primax. Open pollinated; good taste and split resistant.
Tendersweet. Disease and split resistant, with a sweet flavor to boot.

Late-Season Green
Scanbo. Disease resistant and stores very well.
Storage No. 4. Tasty, crisp leaves; stores very well; and handles weather and fertility stress.

Red
Des Vertus. Open pollinated, French; mild, juicy, semisweet.
Ruby Perfection. Mid–late, stores very well.
Samantha. Small, pointy-headed and tasty.

Savoy
Savoy King. Good flavor, split resistant, and an All-America winner.
Super Red 80. Early, split resistant, with an excellent flavor.

Cardoon

A close relative of the artichoke, cardoon is popular in Italy and much of Europe. Like an artichoke, cardoon produces buds and eventually large, thistlelike flowers, but it is the tasty leaf stalks we're after here. They're used in soups, stews, and salads or served alone.

THE SITE

Although it is a perennial in its native climes, and can be grown that way in Zones 7 and up, cardoon is usually grown as an annual, like its artichoke cousins. Growing to nearly 4 feet tall when mature, this is a big plant. It needs a rich, fertile, well-drained soil with plenty of compost, as well as full sun and a steady supply of water. It grows very well in a large self-watering container.

SOWING

Start indoors in late winter (late January or early February, here in Vermont). Sow three or four seeds ¼ inch (6 mm) deep in 4-inch (10 cm) pots; keep the temperature in the 70–75°F (21–24C) range and keep the soil moist throughout the germination phase of two to three weeks. When the first true leaves appear, thin to the best plant and reduce the temperature to 60–70°F (16–21°C). Harden off and transplant to the garden when danger of frost is past.

GROWING

If your soil is rich and fertile, you can probably grow cardoons without extra fertilizer, but if fertility isn't quite as you'd like it to be yet, feed the plants once a month with an organic liquid fertilizer such as fish emulsion. Monitor soil moisture and water deeply during dry periods. Too little water will make the stems pithy. Some gardeners recommend blanching cardoon by wrapping the plant in newspaper and tying with twine. I haven't found that the unblanched product needs any improvement.

HARVEST AND USE

Harvest individual leaves or wait and harvest the whole plant before frost. The leaves and the green growth on the stalks are bitter; remove them and give the stalks a good scrubbing with a vegetable brush. Strip away the biggest of the celery-like fibrous strands and cut in 2- to 3-inch (5 to 8 cm) pieces, discarding any pithy ones. Boil in lightly salted water for 15 to 20 minutes or until the pieces can be pierced easily with a fork.

▲ **Tastes like artichoke.** *This artichoke relative is grown for its leaf stems rather than its flower buds.*

Sow & Grow

Cardoon (*Cynara cardunculus*)
Sunflower family (Compositae)

SOWING

Seed depth: ¼" (6 mm)
Germination soil temperature: 70–80°F (21–27°C)
Days to germination: 7–10
Sow indoors: Late winter to early spring, 8 weeks before the last frost
Sow outdoors: Not recommended

GROWING

pH range: 6.5–8.0
Growing soil temperature: 60–75°F (16–24°C)
Spacing in beds: 24" (60 cm)
Watering: Heavy and even
Light: Full sun, at least 8 hours a day
Nutrient requirements: N=high; P=high; K=high
Rotation considerations: Avoid following Jerusalem artichoke, artichoke, or sunflower
Seed longevity: 5 years.

Carrots

If you are just now making the transition to deeply worked, raised garden beds, use the first of your beds for carrots. The differences in size, shape, flavor, and yield per square foot between row-crop and wide, raised, deep bed–crop carrots are — putting it mildly — dramatic. Like the carrot on the stick that keeps the horse walking forward, the beautiful carrots you pull from your first raised bed will encourage you to grow all your vegetables this way.

THE SITE

Prepare and enrich the bed the previous fall by forking in a layer of fallen leaves. If you're preparing the bed in spring, mix in a generous amount of compost a few weeks before seeding. Rake and smooth the bed carefully so there will be good contact between the moist soil and the tiny carrot seeds.

SOWING

Carrots can germinate in a week with a soil temperature at about 75°F (24°C). The colder the soil, the longer the germination period. If it gets much below 45°F (7°C), germination may not happen at all. Plan to sow carrots about the time you sow pole beans or transplant tomatoes. The other key to good carrot germination is moisture. Carrot seeds won't germinate in dry soil. If

▲ A 24-karat vegetable. *When carrots are stored, they often lose their moisture and sweetness. What better reason to grow your own? Once you've experienced the pleasure of pulling those slender beauties from the earth, you're sure to be hooked on homegrown carrots.*

you need to, water the carrot patch every day until the seedlings emerge.

Carrot seeds are tiny and devilishly hard to space evenly. Over the years gardeners have come up with a number of solutions to this problem. I've tried many of them but haven't been really happy with any of the results. The easiest way to sow carrots is to broadcast

---

Sow & Grow

Carrots (*Daucus carota* var. *sativus*)

Carrot family (Umbelliferae)

SOWING

Seed depth: ¼–½" (6–13 mm)
Germination soil temperature: 75°F (24°C)
Days to germination: 6
Sow indoors: Not recommended
Sow outdoors: Early spring to midsummer

GROWING

pH range: 5.5–6.5, but best above 6.0
Growing soil temperature: 60–70°F (16–21°C)
Spacing in beds: 2" (5 cm) apart in rows 6–8" (15–20 cm) apart, 3 rows to a 30" (0.75 m) bed, 4 rows to a 36" (0.9 m) bed
Watering: Moderate
Light: Full sun for best yield; tolerates light shade
Nutrient requirements: N=moderate; P=low; K=low
Rotation considerations: Avoid rotating with celery, dill, fennel, parsley, or parsnip
Seed longevity: 3 years

them over the bed. This method takes only seconds to accomplish, but the eventual thinning of seedlings can take hours. I've also tried mixing the seeds with dry coffee grounds or vermiculite before sowing. That was an improvement, but I still found the spacing somewhat irregular.

Pelleted seeds are easy to handle and space but the pellet material adds another layer the germinating seeds must push through before reaching daylight. Seed tapes look like a good idea but are too expensive for my liking. After experimenting with many ways to sow carrot seed, I've resorted to patiently sowing them one or two at a time as shown in the photo at right. It takes time, but it takes less time than thinning later on.

GROWING

No matter how carefully I space the seeds, carrots always seem to need some thinning. Carrots can grow very close together and still produce excellent crops, but if they grow too close together they'll be stunted, very slender, or deformed. If the seedlings are really close together, don't pull the extra ones; you'll probably damage the ones left behind. Cut off the extras with floral scissors. If the spacing is pretty good and you can pull extra plants without damaging the ones you want to keep, postpone thinning until the carrot seedlings are a couple of inches long and beginning to look like carrots. At that point, they'll also have begun to taste like carrots, so you can get some pay for your labors.

Carrots prefer their roots to be cool and their tops to be warm. When the soil temperature rises above 70°F (21°C) carrots will be small and bland tasting. When the warmer days of early summer arrive, mulch the carrot patch with grass clippings to moderate the soil temperature. Repeat as needed throughout the growing season.

HARVEST AND STORAGE

In loose soil, you can harvest carrots by pulling them from the ground by their tops, but if the tops break, loosen the soil first with a garden fork or broadfork. Clip the foliage about an inch (2.5 cm) from the root. Cull any damaged or misshapen roots and refrigerate them for immediate use; they won't store well. Layer storage carrots in damp sand or sawdust in a bin, box, or plastic pail in the root cellar.

▲ Practice makes perfect. *With a little practice, you can sow the seeds ½ inch (13 mm) apart by rolling them, a half dozen or so at a time, between your thumb and first finger, so that one (or sometimes two) emerges at a time.*

▲ Easy does it. *Thinning carrots, like sowing them, is best accomplished on days when patience can rule your actions. Thin with floral shears to no less than 2 inches (5 cm) between plants.*

▲ Hidden treasure. *Carrots grown in deeply dug beds will be larger, more shapely, and more flavorful than you can imagine.*

▲ Long life. *Carrots store best if you cut off the greens, leaving about 1 inch (2.5 cm) of stem.*

Give Your Carrots a Head Start

Because of their small size, carrot seeds produce tiny seedlings that do not have the strength to push through crusted soil. Help them out by:

- **Covering the seed lightly.** Use very fine soil or finely sifted compost.

- **Interplanting them with radishes.** The radishes will emerge first and break up crusted surface soil.

- **Keeping the soil moist throughout the germination period.** This keeps the soil from crusting.

ONE FOR NOW, ONE FOR LATER

Plant a quick-maturing variety for summer eating as soon as you like, but postpone the winter storage crop until the soil warms up, about the time you plant tomatoes (or even later, especially if earwigs feast on your early plantings).

▲ **A carrot of another color.** *"Roses are red, and violets are blue."* And carrots are orange? Nope. Not all the time. Carrots are white, yellow, and also purple (on the outside, at least; they're orange on the inside).

VARIETIES

Baby or Mini. These tasty, small carrots with a range of shapes are best used fresh. This type is a bit of a catchall category, since, if it's little, it can go here. Some popular varieties include Amsdor, Minicore, Parmex, and Thumbelina.

Chantenay. All-purpose carrots with a broad shoulder, stocky build, and blunt tip, Chantenays keep their shape better in stony or heavy soils than other carrots. Some varieties are Chantenay Imperial, Chantenay Red-Cored, and Chantenay Royal.

Danvers. These good all-around carrots are similar in shape to Chantenay but longer. Their flavor is good, but they lack the sweetness of Nantes. Some good varieties include Danvers Half-Long and Danvers Red-Cored.

Nantes. A longtime favorite of home gardeners, these sweet, crisp, full-flavored carrots are easily recognized by their cylindrical, sausage shape and blunt tip. Some excellent Nantes varieties include Bolero, Mokum, Napoli, Nelson, Sweetness II, and Scarlet Nantes.

Imperator. This is the long, tapering supermarket carrot. Easy to harvest and ship (which means little to gardeners), Imperators have less overall flavor and crispness than many other types. Some of the best varieties in this group, including Artist and Nevis, are actually hybrids with Nantes types.

Specialty

Crème de Lite. The pale yellow color makes these carrots stand out.

Parmex. Small, early, round carrots, Parmex grows well in shallow soils and in containers. Space seeds ½ inch (13 mm) apart and harvest at 1½-inch (4 cm) diameter.

Purple Haze. With sweet flavor and dark purple skin with an orange interior, these have 7- to 8-inch (18 to 20 cm) roots.

White Satin. With sweet flavor and crispness, White Satin is adaptable to difficult growing conditions.

Cauliflower

Cauliflower has long had a reputation for being a vegetable prima donna. It is the easiest of the cabbage family vegetables to stress, and when it stresses, it bolts. Cauliflower can be set back by cool temperatures in spring, by hot weather in summer, or by dry conditions at any time. And to top everything off, it's the most sensitive of the cabbage family to frost. It's worth all the extra fussing, though; nothing can quite match cauliflower with a nice cheddar cheese sauce.

THE SITE

Cauliflower requires a pH of at least 6.5, but it grows best and is most likely to be free of root diseases in a nearly neutral or slightly sweet soil (6.8–7.2 pH). Like its cabbage-family cousins, cauliflower needs fertile, compost-enriched soil with good moisture-holding ability.

SOWING

Start plants indoors where you can provide a germination temperature of 70°F (21°C) or more and early growth temperatures of at least 60°F (16°C). Start in flats a month before the last frost date so the seedlings will be no more than four to five weeks old when they go into the garden. Move the seedlings from flats to 2-inch (5 cm) growing cells as soon as they can be handled. Moderate but even moisture is critical at this time.

You can direct-sow seeds in midspring for early crops or in early summer for fall crops.

▲ **Flower power.** *Harvested at its prime, cauliflower has a sweet, nutty flavor, delicious raw or lightly steamed.*

DON'T JUMP THE GUN WITH CAULIFLOWER

Time your sowing so that plants are no older than five weeks when it's safe to put them in the garden. Transplants older than this are too easily stressed by transplant shock. Older plants may also "check," which means they become root-bound and stop growing. These plants often produce only "buttons," little heads that never grow to be big heads.

Sow & Grow

Cauliflower (*Brassica oleracea* Botrytis Group)
Cabbage family (Cruciferae)

SOWING

Seed depth: ¼–½" (6–13 mm)
Germination soil temperature: 80°F (27°C)
Days to germination: 6
Sow indoors: 4–6 weeks before last frost
Sow outdoors: From last frost to late spring

GROWING

pH range: 6.5–7.5
Growing soil temperature: 60–70°F (16–21°C)
Spacing in beds: 15" (37.5 cm) staggered pattern, 3 rows to a bed
Watering: Moderate and even
Light: Best yields in full sun; tolerates light shade
Nutrient requirements: N=high; P=high; K=high
Rotation considerations: Precede with nitrogen-fixing cover crop; avoid following cabbage family crops
Seed longevity: 4 years

GROWING

Transplant four-week-old seedlings to the garden in spring about the time of the last frost after hardening outdoors for at least a week. Transplant carefully; don't disturb or damage the roots.

Watering and fertilizing. Keep plants evenly watered throughout the entire growing period. Cauliflower is a heavy feeder and may need additional feedings with fish emulsion or liquid kelp fertilizers.

Blanching. Blanching, a technique used for white varieties, limits the amount of light that contacts the developing head. The result is cauliflower with a nice, white color, improved flavor, and none of the unappealing yellow color and ricey texture that sometimes develops during hot weather. Even self-blanching varieties have the best flavor and color if blanched. It's time to blanch when the head is about 2 or 3 inches (5 or 7.5 cm) wide. Fold some of the leaves over the head and secure them together at the top with rubber bands or twine. Good news! Purple, green, and orange varieties don't need to be blanched.

Pest protection. Like all their cabbage-family cousins, cauliflower plants, especially young ones, are adored by flea beetles. The best defense is row covers applied as soon as the seeds or transplants are in the ground.

HARVEST AND STORAGE

After tying leaves for blanching, check heads daily for maturity. In warm weather, harvest heads about four days after tying; in cool weather, harvest in about 10 days. Don't wait longer than these recommended times to harvest, as the head may rot.

Cauliflower is ready for harvest when the head is tight and fairly regular, and the curd has not begun to separate, a condition called riciness. Purple types have a more irregular head and should be harvested when the curd looks like a tight bunch of broccoli.

You can store cauliflower in the root cellar or the refrigerator for about a month, but it tastes much better if used soon after harvest. Cauliflower freezes well.

BEST VARIETIES

The following white-curd varieties are bred for resistance to heat and cold stress.

Amazing. Self-blanching.

Fremont. Self-blanching.

Snow Crown. Tolerates frost to 25°F (−7°C).

Panther. Lime-green heads; best for fall harvest.

Violet Queen. Cauliflower-like leaves and a purple, broccoli-like head that turns green when cooked.

▲ Cheddar. *This variety is early, high in vitamin A, and has a beautiful orange color that intensifies when cooked.*

▲ Graffiti. *Unlike Violet Queen, Graffiti produces a true cauliflower head; it loses some of its color when cooked but retains its purple cast.*

Celery

Celery has the reputation of being fussy, but it isn't really. It's just different. And once you take account of the differences, it's not difficult to grow. Celery is a big plant with a lot of stalk and leaf, as well as a very dense and compact root system. It can't grow quickly or well unless there is plenty of water and food within easy reach.

THE SITE

The key to good celery? Warmth and moisture during germination; food and moisture thereafter. Celery's root system is dense but not very far-reaching; food and water need to be nearby and plentiful. That calls for fertile soil with good moisture-holding ability. Work in plenty of compost or well-rotted manure and some complete organic fertilizer. Celery does best in full sun but can tolerate partial shade.

SOWING

Start celery indoors 10 to 12 weeks before the last frost date in a small starting flat. (A tofu container works fine.) Sow seeds on top of a compost-based potting mixture and lightly cover with finely granulated potting mix. Celery seeds need light to germinate; don't cover seeds too deeply. Moisten, cover with clear plastic (a plastic bag works just fine), and place in a warm area with indirect light. For best germination, keep

▲ **Celebrating celery.** *It's easy to overlook this familiar vegetable, but as long as you give it fertile conditions, it will reward you with a crisp, sweet harvest for many months.*

temperatures between 65 and 75°F (18 and 24°C). Germination may be erratic, but seedlings should begin to appear in about one week.

When the plants are up, remove the plastic cover and move the container into a warm, sunny place. Be sure to keep the soil moist. Transplant to 2-inch (5 cm) growing cells when there are two true leaves.

Sow & Grow

Celery (*Apium graveolens* var. *dulce*)
Carrot family (Umbelliferae)

SOWING

Seed depth: Just cover
Germination soil temperature: 70°F (21°C)
Days to germination: 7
Sow indoors: 10 weeks before last frost
Sow outdoors: Not recommended

GROWING

pH range: 6.0–7.0
Growing soil temperature: 60–70°F (16–21°C)
Spacing in beds: 8" (20 cm), 3 rows to a bed
Watering: Heavy and even
Light: Best yields in full sun; tolerates light shade
Nutrient requirements: N=high; P=high; K=high
Rotation considerations: Avoid following lettuce or cabbage
Seed longevity: 3 years

GROWING

Plant outdoors only after day temperatures stay consistently above 55°F (13°C) and night temperatures above 40°F (4°C). Warm the soil with plastic mulch for a week before planting, and cover plants with floating row covers for about a month after planting. Celery exposed to temperatures below 55°F (13°C) for 10 days considers that it has had winter, that it is two years old, and (being a biennial) it is therefore ready to make seeds. With that in mind, it bolts.

Fertilizing. The key to growing good celery is organic matter. Celery has a small root system and grows best in soil rich in organic matter. Before planting, add plenty of compost or rotted manure to the bed. Add some compost to the planting hole when transplanting, and sidedress with compost and liquid fish and seaweed fertilizer during the growing season.

Weeding and watering. Because the roots are very near the surface, keep the patch weeded, but don't cultivate deeply. Check soil moisture regularly and water as needed, but don't let the soil get soggy. Mulch will help keep the soil surface moist.

HARVEST AND STORAGE

Begin harvesting stalks from the outside of the plants whenever they are big enough to suit you. You can harvest whole plants by cutting them at the soil line. Harvest plants when you want to; even small ones taste good. Celery can survive light frost if covered.

For best flavor and longest storage, water celery the day before harvest. It will keep in the refrigerator for a couple of weeks or longer in the root cellar. It also freezes well — just cut it up and put it in a pint-sized freezer container. In the middle of winter, dump it into a vegetable soup and let it simmer.

If you're growing celery in a self-watering container, just bring it indoors when frost threatens. You'll have fresh celery long into the winter. Stems will start to get porous in spring when it prepares to send up a seed stalk.

VARIETIES

Conquistador. An early variety, tolerant of temperature and moisture stress as well as average soil fertility.

Ventura. An early, disease-tolerant variety with an upright habit, strong stalks, and a tender, sweet heart.

All in the Family: Celeriac

Celeriac (*Apium graveolens* var. *rapaceum*) is a close relative of celery, though not as fussy; it's grown for its root rather than its stalks. Grow it following the same procedures as you do for celery, but you needn't be quite so careful about moisture and soil fertility.

After the first few light frosts in fall, loosen the soil around each plant with a garden fork and lift it free. Cut the tops an inch or two (2.5 to 5 cm) above the root and store in the root cellar.

During the winter, plant a celeriac root in a large clay pot in damp sand. Place it in a sunny window at room temperature and keep the sand moist. In a little while you'll have small celerylike stalks and greens for fresh winter salad.

Chinese Cabbage

This Asian cousin of domestic cabbages combines a mild cabbage flavor with the look and texture of romaine lettuce. Open-head types have a loose, lettucey look, while closed-head, or napa, types have outer leaves that wrap over the top of the slightly tighter head. Whatever shape your Chinese cabbage takes, all types taste good either raw or cooked, with a mild, slightly pungent, spicy flavor.

THE SITE

Although Oriental in origin, this is still a cabbage and has cabbage needs: fertile soil and steady, even moisture. A good shot of compost ensures both.

SOWING

In warm regions, sow two seeds each in 4-inch (10 cm) pots in late winter; in cooler areas, sow seeds in mid-spring. After seedlings emerge, thin with floral shears to one plant per pot. I like to thin after the first true leaves appear to be sure the seedling I choose is the stronger of the two.

Summer crops. Set plants in the garden about four weeks after true leaves appear and night temperatures are consistently above 50°F (10°C). Don't be impatient and move this plant into the garden too early, as a week or more of nights when the temperature drops below 50°F (10°C) can trigger the plant to bolt a few weeks later. Chinese cabbage is sensitive to transplanting, so set plants in the garden very carefully so roots are not damaged.

Fall crops. Direct-seed about two months before the first frost. Open-head, lettucelike types are good for all harvests. Plant as a successor crop to peas or early beans.

GROWING

Like many plants in the cabbage family, Chinese cabbage has a delicate and fairly shallow root system that grows quite close to the surface. To grow the best Chinese cabbage, follow these guidelines:

▲ **Beautiful and tasty.** *It looks a bit like romaine lettuce, and the texture is a bit like savoy cabbage, but there's a bit more tangy zip here than in either of them.*

Sow & Grow

Chinese cabbage (*Brassica rapa* Pekinensis Group)
Cabbage family (Cruciferae)

SOWING

Seed depth: ¼–½" (6–13 mm)
Germination soil temperature: 75–80°F (24–27°C)
Days to germination: 7
Sow indoors: 4–6 weeks before last frost
Sow outdoors: 10–12 weeks before first frost for fall crop

GROWING

pH range: 6.0–7.0
Growing soil temperature: 60–70°F (16–21°C)
Spacing in beds: 12–18" (30–45 cm), depending on type
Watering: Moderate and even
Light: Full sun
Nutrient requirements: N=high; P=high; K=high
Rotation considerations: Avoid rotating with cabbage family crops
Seed longevity: 3 years

General care. Water evenly from transplant to harvest, cultivate lightly and carefully, mulch during warm weather, and keep weeds under control, especially when the plants are young.

Fertilizing. Chinese cabbage can grow large and has a big appetite for soil nutrients, particularly nitrogen. Mix in plenty of compost at planting.

HARVEST AND STORAGE

As with cabbage, Chinese cabbage can be harvested as soon as the plants are large enough to use. Once it's mature, harvest promptly, or it'll likely bolt. Cut the entire plant at the base and remove the outer, or wrapper, leaves. Freshly harvested heads of spring and fall crops will keep for about a week in the refrigerator.

Chinese cabbage keeps for several weeks in the root cellar, providing tender, tasty greens long after the garden has been put to bed for the year.

To store, wrap the cabbage in newspaper and place it on a shelf in the root cellar or other cool spot. Fall crops tend to store better than spring crops.

VARIETIES

Michihli Tall Type
Greenwich. Tall (14"; 35.5 cm) narrow heads, bolt resistant.

Napa Type
Blues. For early spring planting, pungent flavor.
Bilko. Large heads, bolt and disease resistant.

All in the Family: Pak Choi

Pak choi, pac choi, or bok choy . . . however you spell it, it's the same vegetable, perfect for stir-fry and other Asian dishes. It's easy to grow as either a spring or a fall crop, maturing in a month and a half or so. Some varieties are harvested early as microgreens. Pak choi is also a good container crop.

SOWING AND GROWING

Any friable, reasonably fertile soil with good moisture retention in full sun will do for pak choi. This cabbage-family crop doesn't tolerate heat well; plant in spring for an early summer harvest or in late summer for fall harvest. It can be direct-sown, after the last frost in spring or in late summer. Plant three seeds ¼- to ½-inch (6 to 13 mm) deep every 12 inches (30 cm) and thin to the best plant with scissors. I prefer to start pak choi indoors, two weeks before the last frost or in late summer for a fall crop. Plant three seeds in 2-inch (5 cm) cells or pots and thin to the best plant. Transplant outdoors after danger of frost is past; pak choi exposed to frost may bolt later on.

Flea beetles like this plant just as much as they do its cabbage-family cousins. Use row covers as soon as you plant or transplant pak choi.

VARIETIES

Chinese Pak Choi. About 15 inches (37.5 cm) tall, this variety is very easy to grow and has excellent flavor. Its leaf stems are pale green and hold wide, thick, shiny leaves.

Choy Sum. Harvest when yellow buds form on the tender, bright green flowering stalks, leaving three or four leaves on the plant for successive cuttings.

Joi Choi. Displaying icy white leaf stems with dark green leaves, Joy Choi tolerates heat and cold, grows quickly, and is slow to bolt.

Mei Qing Choi. This dwarf, or baby, pak choi has pastel green leaves and pale greenish white leaf bases. It tolerates heat and cold well and is slow to bolt.

Red Choi. This variety is useful at many growth stages — micro mix, baby, and full size. The young leaves are green with maroon veins; the mature ones, dark maroon on top and green underneath.

Claytonia

Claytonia, a North American native also called miner's lettuce, isn't the best-known salad green, but it deserves to be; it's tasty and very easy to grow as well as being very cold tolerant. It's another in that wonderful group of cool-weather, frost-hardy greens that can supply salads all winter from a cold frame or unheated greenhouse.

▲ **Cool-weather beauty.** *Easy to grow, frost hardy, and uniquely attractive and tasty to boot, claytonia is a good green to get acquainted with.*

Sow & Grow

Claytonia (*Montia perfoliata*)
Purslane family (Portulacaceae)

SOWING

Seed depth: ¼" (6 mm)
Germination soil temperature: 50–55°F (10–13°C)
Days to germination: 7–10
Sow indoors: Late fall to late winter for indoor growing
Sow outdoors: 4 weeks before last frost

GROWING

pH range: 6.5–7.0
Growing soil temperature: 50–65°F (10–18°C)
Spacing in beds: Plant seeds 2–3" (5–7.5 cm) apart in rows that are 8" (20 cm) apart; thin to 4–6" (10–15 cm)
Watering: Moderate and even; light when grown in a cold frame over winter
Light: Full sun to partial shade
Nutrient requirements: N=low; P=low; K=low
Rotation considerations: Avoid following with radicchio, endive, escarole, or artichoke
Seed longevity: 5 years

A WORD TO THE WISE

Those pretty little flowers are the precursors of seeds. Claytonia will, if you let it, pass from the flower to the seed stage and very quickly begin planting itself here and there all over the garden. It will, in a word, become a weed.

THE SITE

Claytonia not only tolerates cold, it needs it. Grow it in a cold frame, poly tunnel, or solar greenhouse. It's not fussy; just give it moderately fertile soil to grow in.

SOWING AND GROWING

Claytonia is related to the dainty wildflower called spring beauty, which is fitting, because claytonia is as decorative as it is tasty. Claytonia is easy to grow and continues to grow vigorously even during the colder months. Like other cool-weather greens, it languishes in the heat of summer. Before planting, work at least an inch (2.5 cm) of compost into the seedbed.

In cool climates, sow seeds in the garden every three weeks from early spring to midspring, and then begin to sow again in late summer to midfall. For winter greens, put the mid-fall sowing in a cold frame or unheated greenhouse.

In warmer climates, sow in the garden in late fall and successively every three weeks until early winter for winter and early-spring crops.

HARVEST

Begin harvesting as soon as leaves are of edible size. If you cut the leaves and stems as needed, the plant will continue to grow and produce. If you fall behind on harvesting, claytonia will produce little white flowers near the tops of the plants. In some vegetables this is a sign to discard the plant. Not with claytonia. The blossoms are edible and make a nice addition to salads.

Corn

A satisfying ear of sweet corn shouldn't taste like sugar — it should taste like sweet corn. It seems that every year the seed catalogs feature a new variety of sweet corn supposedly sweeter than last year's sweetest. I'm not a fan of supersweet corn. The main virtue of these varieties is commercial: Their sugar is slow to convert to starch after harvest, so they can mimic fresh sweet corn even after a long trip to the supermarket.

If there's not enough sweet in your homegrown sweet corn, the problem is more likely how you're growing it than what you're growing. Provide your sweet corn with good growing conditions and you'll be rewarded with corn that is both sweet and full-flavored.

THE SITE

Begin preparing the corn bed in fall. Apply at least an inch (2.5 cm) of compost or rotted manure and work it into the soil with a garden fork. To encourage worm activity, mulch the bed before a hard freeze. If you can, plant corn in beds where you grew a nitrogen-fixing cover crop the previous fall.

SOWING

In spring, remove the mulch to let the soil begin heating, and apply some finished compost. Cover the corn beds with black or IRT plastic at least a week before sowing and monitor soil temperature with a soil

▲ **Summer rewards.** *To grow sweet corn like this, give it a spot in the sun, plenty of compost or well-rotted manure, and even, steady moisture.*

thermometer. Don't plant sweet corn until soil temperatures are consistently at least 60°F (16°C); it won't germinate. (Note: So-called "treated" seeds will germinate at 55°F [13°C]. I don't use or recommend treated

---

Sow & Grow

Sweet Corn (*Zea mays*)
Grass family (Poaceae)

SOWING

Seed depth: 1" (2.5 cm)
Germination soil temperature: 80°F (27°C)
Days to germination: 4
Sow indoors: Not recommended
Sow outdoors: 1 week after last frost

GROWING

pH range: 6.0–7.0
Growing soil temperature: 65–75°F (18–24°C)
Spacing in beds: 8" (20 cm)
Watering: Moderate early; heavy from flowering to harvest
Light: Full sun
Nutrient requirements: N=high; P=high; K=high
Rotation considerations: Precede with a nitrogen-fixing crop
Seed longevity: 1–2 years

seeds because the "treatment" is a fungicide. I don't want to kill fungi in my soil because many of them help plants to grow.)

Sow the seeds 1 inch (2.5 cm) deep and 8 inches (20 cm) apart, down the center of a 30-inch (75 cm) bed. To ensure good pollination, plant each variety in blocks of four short rows rather than a single long row. Sow new blocks every two weeks for successive harvests throughout the season.

After sowing, keep the soil moist and install a fabric floating row cover supported by hoops to maintain soil temperature and protect seedlings against frost and crows. Remove the cover when night temperatures are consistently above 60°F (16°C).

KEEP THOSE SWEETS APART

If you grow any of the supersweet varieties, isolate them from normal sugary or sugar-enhanced types to prevent cross-pollination. You can do this either by keeping the plantings at least 25 feet (7.5 m) apart or by sowing the seeds of one at least 10 days after you sow the seeds of the other, so that they flower at different times.

GROWING

Corn is a heavy feeder — a really heavy feeder — particularly of nitrogen. Yet, for a plant of its large size, corn does not have a very deep or extensive root system. This means that corn needs deeply tilled, fertile soil with readily available nutrients. This allows the plant to produce roots that compensate in density for what they lack in range.

Like other plants with relatively shallow roots, corn is sensitive to fluctuations in soil moisture, which stress the plants. Regular and shallow (about 1½ inches; 3.8 cm) cultivation controls weeds while making nutrients available. Water regularly and fertilize every two weeks with a complete organic fertilizer, such as fish emulsion.

HARVEST

How to pick. It's easy to know when to pick a tomato, but knowing when to harvest corn is a little trickier. Examine the silk at the top of the ear. A ripe ear of corn has a small amount of pliant, greenish silk near the top of the husk, with dry, brownish silk at the ends. The brownish silk should come away from the green silk with a gentle tug. The ear should feel full beneath the husk. Feel the ear through the husk and make your guess about the state of ripeness before you husk it; you'll gradually train your sense of ripeness.

▲ **Sunken treasure.** *In dry areas, plant corn in groups of four, slightly below the level of the bed. The "bowl" that is created will collect every drop of precious water from rain or irrigation.*

▲ **A moisture lifeline.** *Drip irrigation laid between the rows of corn gets the right amount of moisture right to the roots.*

Standing Up to the Wind

Thanks to corn's shallow roots and tall stature, good, stiff wind can lay your whole crop flat. Sometimes, lifting each stalk carefully and packing soil around the roots will fix the problem. Sometimes it takes a bit more. After righting the corn as above, drive some stout stakes into the ground at the corners of the corn bed every 8 feet (2.5 m) or so. Connect the stakes with garden twine about two feet off the ground.

▶ **Fenced in.** *This temporary support will hold the corn upright and allow the ears to ripen. If you experience windstorms regularly, put up the support system before the accident happens.*

When to pick. Very soon after picking, the sugar in corn begins turning to starch. Some people like to pick their dinner corn a few minutes before it gets dropped into the cooking pot. These folks believe the faster an ear of corn moves from the garden to your plate, the sweeter it will taste. It makes sense. But corn actually has its highest sugar content in the early morning, not just before the evening meal. The old-timers I've known pick their corn early in the morning, before it's warmed by the sun, and refrigerate it in the husk until supper. I've tried both ways and ended up siding with the old-timers: I pick corn first thing in the morning.

SWEET CORN VARIETIES

There are many, many excellent varieties of sweet corn. The trick to selecting the best ones is to bypass the super-sweet hype and focus on flavor, ears per stalk, number of rows per ear and, one more time — flavor. Ask your neighbors. Get the names of good varieties you find at farmers' markets. Here are a few of my favorites.

Yellow
Sugar Buns. Our favorite yellow, its only weakness is a need for warm soil at planting. Wait until soil temperature is above 60°F (16°C).

▲ **Is it ripe yet?** *Feel the husk to see if it seems full and rounded, and look for greenish, pliant silk turned drier and brown at the very ends. Then pick the ear and see how well you've guessed.*

Roy's Calais Flint

Bicolor

Luscious. With large ears and good taste, Luscious needs a soil temperature of at least 55°F (13°C) at planting.

Montauk. A later variety with exceptional taste, this is one of our favorites.

White

Silver Queen. Big ears with sweet and tender kernels, this variety requires a minimum soil temperature of 55°F (13°C).

Standard (open pollinated)

Double Standard. The first bicolor open-pollinated sweet corn, Double Standard germinates in cool soil and has excellent traditional corn taste. (That may not be what you're used to or like. Try it before you change over the whole corn patch.)

FIELD CORN VARIETIES

Field corn is a term that lumps dent, flint, and flour corn into one category. The names are unimaginative but accurate:

- Dent corn has a dent in each kernel when dry.

- Flint corn has rock-hard kernels. Both flint and dent corn can be used to make cornmeal.

- Flour corn makes the best-quality corn flour. Many of the varieties are also very colorful.

To harvest field corn, allow the husks to dry completely while the ear is on the plant. Unlike most other corns, you can harvest field corn after a few frosts. Husk the ears and bring them to a cool, dry, well-ventilated space to finish drying. Store kernels on the cob or shuck them and store in covered glass containers.

Abenaki Calais Flint. (Also known as Roy's Calais Flint) An heirloom variety that germinates well in cool soil and produced good crops even in short growing seasons.

Hopi Blue Flour. Makes a beautiful blue flour, which, in turn, makes a fine cornbread.

Painted Mountain. Earliest maturing dry corn; kernels are gold, orange, red, purple, and everything in between; can be ground for flour, parched, boiled for hominy, or even eaten fresh.

POPCORN

Popcorn, like field corn and ornamental corn, has a higher starch content than sweet corn, but the growing requirements for all of these are the same as for sweet corn. The difference is in the harvesting.

Popcorn has been a part of the American diet for millennia. Native Americans have grown it for thousands of years, and the Pilgrims feasted on it hundreds of years before it became a movie theater staple. Yet many people's experience with popcorn is still limited to the snack aisle of the supermarket.

Popcorn comes in many varieties, from red and blue to white and yellow. Popcorn takes longer to mature than sweet corn, so choose a variety that has enough time to develop in a typical growing season in your area.

VARIETIES

Robust. Gourmet-quality tender popcorn with golden yellow kernels.

Ruby Red. Burgundy red kernels, decorative and tasty.

Shaman's Blue. Pretty bluish red kernels.

Tom Thumb. A New England heirloom, yellow kernels, early, with short stalks.

Popcorn That Really Pops

It's not popcorn if it doesn't pop, and it won't pop unless it is properly cured. For a kernel to pop, it must have just the right amount of moisture inside it.

It all starts with the harvest. Wait until the kernels are completely mature — plump, hard and glossy. Spread the husked ears in a dry, airy (and mouse-free) place for several weeks. Then start "test popping" some kernels every few days until you get a batch that "really pops." Shell out the ears and store the kernels in airtight jars. You can shell the ears by gripping them with two hands and twisting in opposite directions. Wear stout leather gloves. (If you've never done it, this is how we pop popcorn: Cover the bottom of an oiled, covered saucepan with kernels and place on the stove over medium heat, constantly shaking the pan. When the popping stops, you're done. In a good popping, most of the kernels explode fully.)

Fending Off Corn Thieves

Raccoons and crows cause more problems for corn growers than either insect pests or disease.

Raccoons. I have kept the raccoons out (so far!) with a two-strand electric fence, the lower strand at 5 inches (12.5 cm), the upper at about 12 inches (30 cm). Install the fence at least a week before the corn is ripe. The raccoons seem to consider corn ready to harvest about two days before I do.

Birds. Crows and other grain-eating birds can do a lot of damage to the corn patch, digging up the seed or pulling up seedlings. A favorite deterrent, the scarecrow, gets its name for good reason. If you use a scarecrow, dress it in light, flowing clothes that will move in the wind and decorate it with strips of aluminum foil. Another popular scare tactic is a big, brightly colored balloon or beach ball painted with large eye spots. Whichever you choose, change its location every few days, so the birds don't get used to its being in one place.

▲ **Live wire.** *Two strands of electric fence wire along a corn row is a good deterrent for raccoons.*

Cress

Curly cress, Presto cress, Persian cress (all variations of *Lepidium sativum*), and Upland cress (*Barbarea verna*) all have a peppery tang that livens up salads, sandwiches, and vegetable dishes. And all are easy to grow.

SOWING AND GROWING

If the meek are destined to inherit the Earth, then cress will inherit the garden. This stuff will grow just about anywhere. You can grow cress indoors in a flat or flowerpot for sprouts any time of year. Just fill a flat with moist seed-starter mix or soil, sprinkle the seeds evenly, and lightly cover with a little vermiculite or seed-starting mix. The seedlings will emerge in as little as two days and can be harvested anytime after the first true leaves begin to appear, usually within 10 days.

To grow outdoors, broadcast seeds in bands about 3 inches (7.5 cm) wide down the bed. Space bands about 4 inches (10 cm) apart. Sow every two weeks from early spring until the weather warms. Resume sowing when cool weather arrives in late summer or fall. Sow every two weeks until mid- to late fall. In warmer areas, sowing can continue through most of the winter months.

▲ Greens for your windowsill. *Cress grown in containers provides a taste of spring all winter long.*

HARVEST

When plants are 2 to 3 inches (5 to 7.5 cm) tall, harvest by cutting them at the soil line with sharp scissors. Under ideal conditions, cress can be harvested in two to three weeks from sowing. If plants get too large, or if the weather warms, the leaves will develop an unappetizing bitterness. With cress, harvesting young pleases the tongue.

Sow & Grow

Garden Cress (*Lepidium sativum*)
Cabbage family (Cruciferae)

SOWING

Seed depth: Cover lightly
Germination soil temperature: 55–75°F (13–24°C)
Days to germination: 2–6
Sow indoors: Anytime
Sow outdoors: Every 2 weeks from early to midspring, then every 2 weeks from late summer to midfall

GROWING

pH range: 6.0–6.7
Growing soil temperature: 50–75°F (10–24°C)
Spacing in beds: 1–2" (2.5–5 cm)
Watering: Moderate
Light: Full sun, but will tolerate partial shade
Nutrient requirements: N=low; P=low; K=low
Rotation considerations: Do not precede or follow cabbage family crops
Seed longevity: 5 years

Cucumber

Cucumbers like to climb on things. They can't help themselves; it's in their nature. Last year, I had one wander out of its assigned space and 4 feet (1.2 m) over to a tomato trellis, which it climbed. Breeders have tried to mute this propensity by developing bush cucumbers. But even the caged bird sings, and inside every cucumber (whether bush type or vine) remains the desire to climb. The cucumber knows what it's doing; the wise gardener lets the cucumber make the rules. Trellis-grown cucumbers are straighter, more uniform in shape, and less likely to rot or be eaten by slugs or other pests. They are also less likely to become overripe because they've been overlooked. You don't have to grow cucumbers on a trellis, but you'll get more and better-quality fruits if you do, and you'll use less garden space.

▲ **It's easy being green.** *Cucumbers mature rapidly, and if you keep the vines picked, you'll be able to harvest them over a long season.*

Sow & Grow

Cucumber (*Cucumis sativus*)
Cucumber family (Cucurbitaceae)

SOWING

Seed depth: ½–1" (13–25 mm)
Germination soil temperature: 80–95°F (27–35°C)
Days to germination: 3–4
Sow indoors: 3 weeks before last frost
Sow outdoors: After last frost

GROWING

pH range: 6.0–7.0
Growing soil temperature: 70–80°F (21–27°C)
Spacing in beds: Trellised, 18" (45 cm); on the ground, 36" (90 cm)
Watering: Moderate until flowering; heavy from flowering to harvest
Light: Full sun
Nutrient requirements: N=moderate; P=high; K=high
Rotation considerations: Avoid rotating with other gourd family crops
Seed longevity: 5 years

THE SITE

Although they're not as big as squash or pumpkins, cucumbers use a lot of soil nutrients just the same. You'll get higher yield and better-tasting fruits if you apply an inch (2.5 cm) of compost to the bed before planting and work it into the top few inches of soil.

SOWING

In cool regions, start the plants indoors rather than direct sowing. Cucumbers do not like to be transplanted, however, so handle them carefully when you put them into the ground. Sow three seeds to a 4-inch (10 cm) pot, three to four weeks before your transplant date. Keep the soil moist and temperatures above 70°F (21°C) during the day and 60°F (16°C) at night. When the first set of true leaves appears, thin to one plant per pot by cutting the extras with scissors. Transplant after danger of frost is past and the soil has warmed to about 70°F (21°C). Set out the plants on a cloudy day or in the evening, being very careful not to disturb the roots.

You can direct-seed cucumbers if the soil is at least 70°F (21°C) and promises to stay that way during the germination period. Use row covers or hot caps to keep the soil warm.

▶ **Bigger isn't better.**
The two fruits on the right are much tastier, crisper, and less seedy than the overmature one on the left. (That said, I've argued with old-timers who insist that no cucumber is ever too ripe to make good pickle relish.)

▲ **Growing up.** *You'll get cleaner, straighter cucumbers if you support them on a trellis.*

BITTER MEDICINE

If cucumber beetles afflict your crops, grow bitter-free varieties. Standard cucumber plants produce a bitter compound in their skins that apparently attracts cucumber beetles. Bitter-free varieties, such as Aria, Jazzer, Holland, Poona Kheera, and Lemon, are less attractive to the insects.

Poona Kheera cucumbers

GROWING

Cucumbers are a genuine warm-season crop, very sensitive to frost at both ends of the growing season and demanding warmth from germination to harvest. But cucumbers also mature quickly, so they'll usually bear fruit in even the shortest of summers.

If your soil is in good shape, you shouldn't need to fertilize cucumbers; keep watch for slow growth or yellow leaves. If you find them, feed with a liquid fertilizer that has a good shot of nitrogen.

Thirsty cucumber plants grow bitter fruits. Monitor soil moisture and water as necessary.

Cucumber vines can climb pea netting and other trellises used for climbing garden crops (see pages 76–77). Or you can build an A-frame trellis like that at the left, and cover it with netting or chicken wire to support the cukes.

Keep cucumber beetles away with row covers or handpick the little buggers first thing in the morning while they're still sluggish.

HARVEST AND STORAGE

Harvest cucumbers whenever they are large enough to use; the little ones generally taste better than the big ones. Check the vines daily; the fruits grow quickly. Harvest big fruits while the whole cucumber is still dark green. Yellowing at the blossom end indicates an overripe fruit that is past its prime. Cucumbers store well in a refrigerator and very well as pickles.

VARIETIES

Diva. 2002 All-America winner noted for exceptional taste; smooth, thin, no-peel skin; best tasting when picked at pickle size; resistant to mildews and scab.
Genuine. Early, tasty, and easy to grow.
Little Leaf. Sets fruit without pollination (can grow covered all season); compact plant with good production; excellent for pickling as well as fresh eating.
Marketmore 76. An old-favorite slicing cucumber popular since 1970; handles weather stress well.
Poona Kheera. From India, 4- to 5" (10–12 cm) fruits shaped like a potato, ripen from ivory to yellow to russet brown; crisp, sweet, juicy and bitter-free at all stages; vigorous, disease resistant, and heavy yielding.

Dandelion

Although it looks and tastes a lot like the ubiquitous (and edible) "weed" that crowds out grass in showcase lawns, this plant, commonly known as Italian dandelion, is not a true dandelion, but a chicory. It grows more upright and faster than the common dandelion and has a deeper green color. If it is allowed to make flowers, they'll be blue, rather than yellow. The young greens are good in salads; mature greens are tasty braised with bacon bits and served with a little vinegar.

▲ **Good greens.** *Italian dandelion greens give salads a bit of a bite.*

THE SITE

Any spot in the garden that will grow lettuce will grow Italian dandelions. That means friable, well-drained soil enriched with good compost. Dandelions can tolerate some shade but grow fastest in full sun; they're tolerant of cold temperatures and light frosts.

SOWING AND GROWING

Either start indoors and transplant or direct seed. Dandelions can tolerate light frost. Space about 6 inches (15 cm) apart if you want to harvest mature plants; closer, if you want young leaves for a salad mix.

HARVEST

For salad greens, harvest about four to five weeks after emergence. For cooked greens, harvest when the leaves are about 10 inches (25 cm) long.

VARIETIES

Clio. A new variety noted for its uniformity and tenderness.

Red Rib. Bright red stem with a dark green leaf.

Sow & Grow

Dandelion (Italian) (*Cichorium intybus*)
Sunflower family (Compositae)

SOWING

Seed depth: ¼" (6 mm)
Germination soil temperature: 40–60°F (4–16°C)
Days to germination: 7–14
Sow indoors: 3–4 weeks before transplanting
Sow outdoors: As soon as the ground can be worked

GROWING

pH range: 6.5–7.0
Soil temperature: 55–65°F (13–18°C)
Spacing in beds: 6" (15 cm)
Watering: Moderate
Light: Full sun to partial shade
Nutrient requirements: N=high; P=high; K=high
Rotation consideration: Avoid following lettuce, radicchio, endive, escarole, artichoke, or cardoon
Seed longevity: 1 year

Edamame

A rose by any other name might smell as sweet, but would edamame (literally, "beans on a bush") be anywhere near so exotic if called just "soybean, vegetable type"? That's all edamame is — a lowly soybean eaten while still young and green. But once you've tried this flavorful and healthful bean, you'll want to grace it with its fancy name to separate it forever from its ubiquitous and frumpy kinfolk. Edamame soybeans come to us from Japan by way of China, where they have been a dietary staple since the eleventh century BCE. They're full of protein and an excellent source of vitamins A, C, and E, calcium, phosphorus, and dietary fiber.

▲ **Beans on a bush.** *Like most legumes, edamame beans grow well in average soil.*

THE SITE

Edamame is not terribly fussy: A well-drained, fertile soil that stays moist will do just fine. Full sun is best, preferably with some gentle air movement to keep the foliage dry. Try to plant it where no legumes have grown for the past three years.

SOWING

Like many other beans, edamame does not germinate well in cool soil. Wait until the soil temperature reaches 65°F (18°C). As long as the soil is fertile, plants can grow well spaced as closely as 3 to 4 inches (8 to 10 cm) apart, three rows to a 30-inch-wide (75 cm) bed. Plant the seeds about an inch (25 mm) deep in moist soil raked smooth, so there's good contact between seed and soil.

GROWING

Like other legumes, soybeans get most of the nitrogen they need with the help of soil-dwelling bacteria that infect the plant roots and capture atmospheric nitrogen for the plant in exchange for nutrients the plant provides. This process takes some time (and warm soil) to get going; in the meantime, soybeans, like the rest of their legume cousins, get their nitrogen directly from the soil.

Sow & Grow

Edamame (*Glycine max*)
Legume family (Leguminosae)

SOWING

Seed depth: 1" (2.5 cm)
Germination soil temperature: 60–90°F (16–32 °C) (optimum 85°F; 29°C)
Days to germination: 7–10
Sow outdoors: When it's time to plant sweet corn (soil temperature at least 60°F; 13°C)

GROWING

pH range: 6.5–7.5
Growing soil temperature: 60–65°F (16–18°C)
Spacing in beds: 4" (10 cm) apart, in rows 8–10" (20–25 cm) apart
Watering: Even and moderate, especially during flowering
Light: Full sun
Nutrient requirements: N=low; P=moderate; K=moderate
Rotation considerations: Avoid following any legume (pea, bean)

If the soil is sufficiently fertile, there will be enough nitrogen to supply the plant. But building soil fertility takes a few years, so you may need to apply some liquid organic fertilizer such as fish emulsion at planting time and again two and four weeks later. Watch leaf color as the plants grow: Pale green or yellow leaves indicate a need for nitrogen.

Soybeans like steady moisture. Monitor soil moisture during dry spells and water deeply if the soil is dry more than an inch or so down. Use a watering wand to keep the water off the foliage; wet foliage may foster disease.

So far, I've only had one pest interfering with edamame, but that pest was a big one — a woodchuck — and did a lot of damage. I kept the soybeans from further damage with a two-strand electric fence like the one I use to protect the corn from raccoons: One strand is about 5 inches (12.5 cm) from the ground; the second is 12 inches (30 cm).

HARVEST AND PREPARATION

Harvesting as Edamame, or Green Soybeans

Two things to pay attention to here: Edamame beans tend to ripen all at once, and they're at their sweetest and most tender for just a few days. Once the pods begin to form, check daily. When the pods are plump and the beans inside are almost touching, cut the whole plant at soil level, leaving the roots — with their nodules and *Rhizobia* bacteria — in the soil. (Compost the plants or chop them up and work them into the soil.) Evening harvest is reputed to yield the best flavor. The pods should still be deep green in color, with no yellowing. Strip the pods from the plants and prepare by steaming or by boiling for five minutes in salty water. At that point, the traditional way to consume edamame is to squeeze the pod and pop the beans right into your mouth, followed by a sip of cold beer. Or shell them out as you would peas; they're ready then for either eating or freezing.

Harvesting as Dry Soybeans

Like any soybean, edamame can be harvested dry and used as one would any dry soybean or saved for next year's seed. When the pods are dry and almost all the leaves are gone, pull the plants and finish the drying under cover. Thresh by putting the dry plants into a large bag and treading on it. You can also thresh with a flail or, if you've got the patience, by shelling the pods one by one. (I find it a restful process on an autumn evening, with music in the air.)

Note: If you garden where the growing season is short, you may not be able to get soybeans to the dry bean stage. And after you've tried eating edamame fresh, you may not want to.

VARIETIES

Beer Friend. As the name suggests, this is the edamame most likely to be snacked upon with a cold beer. 87 days to maturity.

Envy. This is the choice for northern growers, with a maturity time (to the fresh shell stage) of 75 days. Plants are about 2 feet (0.6 m) tall.

Sayamusume. If you have a warmer climate and consequent longer growing season, this variety has a reputation for exceptional taste. 92 days to maturity.

▲ **Nothing beats these beans.** *Edamame (also called butterbeans) are often cooked in the shell, lightly salted, and eaten warm out of hand. Delicious!*

Eggplant

For northern gardeners, eggplant is a fussy, fussy plant. We like it once it's on the dinner plate, but in the garden it can drive you batty. Most of the gardeners in my neck of the woods have given up trying to grow it — though some just go on trying through sheer cussedness. If you garden in a warm climate, you no doubt know what makes this plant happy. Eggplant's most pressing need is for warmth, and the weather must remain warm throughout the plant's growth cycle. If you live in a climate with hot summers, the plant is more forgiving than in regions with short, cool growing seasons. In cooler regions, you'll have to resort to some tricks in order to have success. (Trick #1: Grow eggplants in containers. We seldom have success with eggplant in the garden and always succeed in containers.)

▲ Putting your eggs in one basket. *Eggplants come in a surprising variety of sizes, shapes, and colors, from tiny-fruited kinds like Rosa Bianca, to large pear-shaped kinds like Galine, to skinny cucumber-like varieties like Orient Express.*

THE SITE

Start with a place in full sun, preferably with a southern exposure, where the pH is about 6.0, the soil is friable, and drainage is good. (Eggplant does not like wet feet.) Add plenty of compost or well-rotted manure. Warm the soil with black plastic or IRT two weeks before transplanting.

Or don't bother with the garden at all: Grow eggplants in medium to large (30 to 40 quarts [29 to 38 L] of soil) containers, preferably the self-watering kind. This is the only way I can grow eggplants here in Vermont.

SOWING

Start eggplant indoors eight weeks before your transplanting date. Time the sowing so you'll transplant when you can count on the following conditions: soil temperature of at least 70°F (21°C); daytime air temperature consistently above 70°F (21°C); night air temperature not below 60°F (16°C).

Sow & Grow

Eggplant (*Solanum melongena*)
Tomato family (Solanaceae)

SOWING

Seed depth: ¼" (6 mm)
Germination soil temperature: 85°F (29°C)
Days to germination: 7
Sow indoors: 4–6 weeks before last frost
Sow outdoors: Not recommended

GROWING

pH range: 5.5–7.0
Growing soil temperature: 80–90°F (27–32°C)
Spacing in beds: 18" (45 cm) staggered pattern
Watering: Heavy
Light: Full sun
Nutrient requirements: N=moderate; P=high; K=high
Rotation considerations: Follow bean or pea
Seed longevity: 4 years

Eggplant is very sensitive to transplant shock, so instead of sowing seed in flats, start the plants in 4-inch (10 cm) pots right away, two or three seeds to a pot. Germinate with bottom heat and try to maintain a soil temperature of at least 80°F (27°C) until the seedlings emerge and 70°F (21°C) thereafter. (You'll probably need a heat mat to maintain the germination temperature.) Thin to one plant per pot by cutting the extras with scissors. Grow under lights if you have them. As the plants grow indoors, prepare their outdoor planting bed by warming it with plastic mulch.

Harden off the seedlings for a week before transplanting by decreasing the air temperature to 60°F (16°C) and cutting back on water. Outdoors, cut slits in the plastic mulch and transplant carefully to avoid root damage.

GROWING

Once the plants are in the garden, use floating row covers to provide steady heat.

Flea beetles, aphids, and Colorado potato beetles all love eggplant. (The latter may actually prefer eggplants to potatoes.) The best defense against these pests is the very same row cover you're using to keep the eggplants warm. Eggplants don't need to be pollinated by insects, so you can leave the row covers on from transplant to harvest. About a month before the first frost, snip off any remaining blossoms to encourage the existing fruits to ripen.

THERE'S A LOT AT STAKE
Although many varieties of eggplant grow into bushy plants about 2 to 3 feet (60 to 90 cm) tall and need no staking, some, including many of the thin-fruited Asian types, do best if grown on a trellis or stake and pruned like indeterminate tomatoes (see page 313).

HARVEST

Harvest fruits anytime after they've reached half their mature size. The smaller fruits taste better, and you'll get a bigger total yield because keeping the plants picked stimulates further production. Eggplant stems are brittle, so cut the fruits from the plants with shears, leaving some stem attached. Eat soon; eggplant doesn't store well.

BEST VARIETIES

Asian Bride. Long, skinny, and pale white, this variety has a subtle flavor and an unusually creamy texture.

Bambino. This variety produces charming early, little 1½-inch (3.8 cm) fruits, as you can imagine from the name.

Diva. A traditional purple eggplant, Diva has thin skin and a mild flavor.

Fairy Tale. Compact Fairy Tale has high yields of 2- to 4-inch-long (5 to 10 cm) fruits with purple and white stripes and excellent flavor.

Galine. Galine is high-yielding even in the North and produces glossy black fruit.

Kermit. Small green and white fruits the size of a hen's egg are typical of Kermit's eggplant.

Little Fingers. With lots of stout little purple fruits that resemble fingers, this eggplant tastes wonderful. Harvest when fruit is small for best flavor.

Machiaw. This eggplant looks like a blushing cucumber, with long, thin fruit brushed with rosy purple skin. It tastes good and yields very well.

Neon. Bright neon purple skin covers the tender, tasty flesh of Neon. Its yields are good, and it's strikingly attractive to boot.

Orient Express. With early, long, slender, glossy, black fruits, this variety handles both cool and hot conditions well.

Rosa Bianca. Another attractive variety, Rosa Bianca has skin in shades of rose, lavender, and white that change throughout the season. Its flesh is sweet and mild.

ENDIVE & ESCAROLE • ENDIVE & ESCAROLE • ENDIVE & ESCAROLE

Endive & Escarole

Endive and escarole are different forms of the same plant. Endive has curly or crinkly-edged leaves and a sharp, somewhat bitter taste. Escarole is hardier with flat, somewhat thicker leaves and a milder flavor.

▲ **Besting the bitters.** *Endive and escarole both become bitter in warm weather. Grow them in spring or fall, and harvest them young in hot weather.*

Sow & Grow

Endive and Escarole (*Cichorium endivia*)
Sunflower family (Compositae)

SOWING

Seed depth: ¼" (6 mm)
Germination soil temperature: 60–65°F (16–18°C)
Days to germination: 5–7
Sow indoors: 8 weeks before last frost
Sow outdoors: Stagger every 2 weeks from spring to early summer and from late summer to fall

GROWING

pH range: 5.5–7.0
Growing soil temperature: 45–65°F (7–18°C)
Spacing in beds: 12" (30 cm) is usually recommended, but endive will self-blanch (and be more tender) if spaced at 8–10" (20–25 cm)
Watering: Moderate; light to none when grown in cold frame over winter
Light: Full sun to partial shade
Nutrient requirements: N=moderate; P=moderate; K=moderate
Rotation considerations: Avoid following radicchio
Seed longevity: 4–6 years

SOWING AND GROWING

For spring planting, sow endive and escarole about 8 to 10 inches (20 to 25 cm) apart as soon as the soil can be worked. Sow successive plantings every three to four weeks until the weather warms. For the winter garden, sow seeds about two months before the first frost in fall. Plants grown in fall and subjected to a few light frosts have a richer, less bitter flavor than spring-grown plants.

Water plants evenly and regularly to keep leaves green and growing. If the ground freezes in winter, withhold water unless the top of the soil dries out (then water only very lightly). Plants grown in soil with lots of organic matter, such as compost, usually need no supplemental fertilizing. In poorer soils, apply a solution of fish emulsion or seaweed once a month.

HARVESTING AND STORING

Harvesting can begin as soon as the outer leaves are of usable size. Gather the leaves as needed, or cut the whole plant at soil level. The leaves are best eaten fresh. In Europe, many gardeners harvest the roots after the first light frost, pot them up in buckets of moist sand, and bring them into the root cellar for forcing.

VARIETIES

Endive
Neos. Dark green, very frilly leaves indicate Neos' high nutrition level.
Rhodos. A French Heirloom variety, Rhodos has pale green leaves with a mild taste.

Escarole
Coral. An early-maturing escarole that produces a thick head of broad leaves, Coral is slow to bolt and well-flavored.
Sinco. A very tasty escarole, Sinco has crisp, full-flavored leaves.
Taglio. This variety matures early and is nicely flavored. It is tolerant of many conditions, from hot to cold and wet to dry.

Endive & Escarole 243

Fennel

There are two fennels, both biennials grown as annuals. One is called leaf fennel and is grown for its anise-flavored leaves, used in salads, coleslaw, and dressing, and its stems, used like celery. The other is called bulb fennel; it also has edible leaves and stems but is grown primarily for the bulb that forms just above the soil. In mild areas where they can overwinter, both kinds will produce pretty yellow flowers in their second year, followed by seeds that are used in baking and for teas and tinctures.

THE SITE

Fennel likes fertile, well-drained soil that's a bit on the sweet side. It also prefers consistent moisture.

SOWING AND GROWING

Leaf and bulb fennels are both grown the same way. Start the seeds indoors about a month before last frost or direct sow in midspring to early summer, spacing the plants about a foot apart. If you start the seeds indoors, transplant carefully so as to avoid disturbing the roots; fennel responds to such disturbance by bolting. Fennel doesn't get along well with other plants and is best grown in a separate bed, so it doesn't perturb nearby vegetables. It also self-sows, so deadhead regularly. It usually requires no fertilizing but needs even, light watering for best growth, especially during dry times. Mulch around the base of the plant to conserve soil moisture and to blanch the bulb to make it more tender.

HARVEST

Harvest fennel leaves and stalks whenever you need them, but don't trim bulb fennel too heavily or you'll stunt the bulb growth.

Harvest bulb fennel when the bulb is about 4 inches (10 cm) across and firm to the touch. Collect the entire plant. The leaves can be used like sweet fennel and the stems like celery. Plan on using the stalks and bulb within a day or so of harvest for best flavor.

▲ Lovely licorice. *Fennel is grown both for its anise-flavored leaves and its crunchy bulb.*

VARIETIES

Bulb
Orion. Big and high-yielding.
Perfection. Good for cool climates; resists bolting.

Leaf
Bronze Fennel. Sweet flavor and bronze foliage.
Grosfruchtiger. Abundant foliage and sweet flavor.

Sow & Grow

Fennel (*Foeniculum vulgare*)
Carrot family (Umbelliferae)

SOWING

Seed depth: ¼" (6 mm)
Germination soil temperature: 65–75°F (18–24°C)
Days to germination: 7–14
Sow indoors: 4 weeks before last frost
Sow outdoors: Midspring through early summer

GROWING

pH range: 6.0–7.0
Growing soil temperature: 65–80°F (18–27°C)
Spacing in beds: 12" (30 cm)
Watering: Moderate
Light: Full sun
Nutrient requirements: N=moderate; P=low; K=low
Rotation considerations: Avoid rotating with members of the carrot family
Seed longevity: 3 to 4 years

Garlic

Much of what our family eats starts with a clove or three of garlic. Given what it costs at the grocery store, it is a good thing that garlic is pretty easy to grow: plant it in fertile soil, keep the weeds at bay, and garlic will do the rest by itself.

THE SITE

Like its onion-family cousins, garlic needs a fertile, friable, and well-drained soil enriched with plenty of compost; its root system reaches neither far nor deep, so it needs to have plenty of food and water nearby. Garlic is happy with a soil pH of about 6.5, right where most garden vegetables like it.

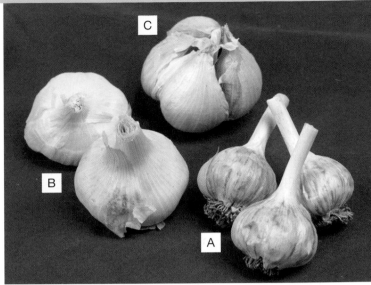

▲ **A garlic trio.** *You can choose among three kinds of garlic for your garden: (A) Stiff-neck (or hardneck) garlic has a single ring of cloves enclosing a stiff, central stem. It is the most winter-hardy. (B) Soft-neck garlic is the kind generally sold in supermarkets; it's somewhat less hardy than stiff-neck and has a stronger taste. Its soft neck allows this variety to be braided. (C) Elephant garlic produces a few very large cloves with a pleasing, mild flavor. Closely related to leeks, elephant garlic is less hardy than true garlic. You plant and tend all three kinds of garlic the same way, but there are some differences when the time comes for harvest and storage.*

Sow & Grow

Garlic (*Allium sativum*)
Onion family (Liliaceae)

SOWING/PLANTING

Clove depth: 2" (5 cm), with pointed end up
Germination soil temperature: 55°F (13°C)
Plant outdoors: Late summer to fall

GROWING

pH range: 6.0–7.0
Growing soil temperature: 55–75°F (13–24°C)
Spacing in beds: 6" (15 cm)
Watering: Low
Light: Best yields in full sun; tolerates light shade
Nutrient requirements: N=moderate; P=moderate; K=moderate
Rotation considerations: Should not follow any onion family or cabbage family crops

---

SPRINGING FOR SEED GARLIC

The seed garlic you buy will look about like what you'll see in the grocery store, and it may be more expensive, but it's a better bet. Grocery store garlic may have been treated so it won't sprout, making it keep longer, but pretty much ruining it for reproducing more garlic.

PLANTING

Plant garlic cloves in the fall, about a month or so before the soil freezes. In cool climates this can be as early as midautumn; in warm regions, early winter. For your first planting, buy cloves from a local garden center or mail-order catalog. (In future years, you can use some of your harvest for the next year's crop.) Use only the larger cloves, which will produce larger bulbs, and eat the smaller ones or plant them for a harvest of green garlic in early summer. Push the cloves into the earth, 6 inches (15 cm) apart, blunt end first, about 2 inches deep. I plant three rows to a 30-inch-wide (75 cm) bed, but if your soil is fertile enough, you may be able to plant four or even five rows about 6 inches (15 cm) apart.

After planting but before the ground freezes, mulch with a thick layer of straw or leaves to protect the bulbs from freezing or heaving out of the ground; mulch also encourages worms, which help keep the soil friable.

GROWING

In spring, when the daffodil leaves are a few inches out of the ground, remove the mulch and spread some compost on the bed. The bright green leaves may already be showing, and if they aren't, they will pop out shortly. Many gardeners leave the mulch off the beds at this point; I don't. I put it back and leave it there until harvest, to help the soil stay moist and to encourage earthworm activity. Alternatively, apply an inch or so of compost to the garlic bed just before you mulch in the fall, then just leave the mulch in place. (Keep watch in the spring; some of the garlic leaves may need some help coming through the mulch.)

Changing a Good Thing

Garlic is an adaptable plant that actually changes to fit the growing conditions of your garden. To customize garlic to your garden, start by purchasing and planting a variety recommended for your area. After harvesting and curing, select the largest cloves for replanting. Do this every season and the garlic will slowly adapt to the climate of your garden.

HARVESTING AND STORING

It's time to harvest garlic in late summer when the bottom two or three leaves have turned yellow (stiff-neck) or the tops fall over (soft-neck and elephant). Loosen the soil with a garden fork or broadfork and pull the bulbs. Cure as shown on page 247.

VARIETIES

Stiff-Neck
German Extra Hardy. East to grow and winters very well. White outer wrapper.

Russian Red. Hardy, somewhat smaller than German Extra Hardy. Purple-striped wrapper.

Soft-Neck
New York White. Strong flavored. Good for braiding. Not as hardy as stiff-neck varieties.

Elephant
Elephant. Very big cloves with a milder taste than other varieties. Apply a heavy winter mulch in northern areas.

▲ **We're ready!** *Garlic is ready to harvest when the bottom two or three leaves have turned yellow.*

◀ Nip the buds. *Stiff-neck garlic sends up a stalk, called a scape, from the center of the bulb. As it grows, it curls into a circle and ends with a bulbous, pointed seedpod. If you leave the scapes in place, the garlic bulbs won't grow as big. Cut them off with floral scissors and eat them. They are delicious roasted, sautéed, stir-fried, or pickled and are quite expensive at upscale markets.*

There's More than One Way to Skin a Garlic

For most of the time I've grown garlic, I've cured it straight out of the garden. And I've been mostly pleased with the results. But it takes a lot of time to get all the dirt off the dried bulbs, and sometimes, if the drying conditions are less than ideal, the bulbs get moldy. One recent summer that was particularly wet and rainy, a couple of gardener friends suggested the following variation. It's easier, the bulbs are clean and white, and curing is faster because there is less to dry. Cured bulbs remain fresh for between five and eight months.

1 Harvest the garlic by prying up the entire plant with a garden fork or shovel. Gently remove most of the soil clinging to the bulb.

2 Identify the two leaves that form the outer two layers of "skin" on the garlic bulb.

3 Peel the leaves back and break them off at the roots.

4 Cure the plants in full sun for 2 to 3 weeks, until the leaves, stems, and roots are thoroughly dry. Cover with a tarp at night and when it rains.

5 Trim the roots, cut the stems to about 1 inch long, and store in a mesh bag in a cool (about 40°F [4°C]), dry place.

Horseradish

Some people claim to grow horseradish, but this vegetable is so easy it really grows itself. Rather than growing from seeds, this perennial develops from pieces of roots called root cuttings. You just plant the cuttings and stand back. The first season, let the plants grow and develop strong roots. Harvest the following fall after the first hard frost.

THE SITE

Let me share with you one of my Great Garden Goofs: I planted horseradish in the garden. So what's the problem? The problem is that the horseradish has decided to colonize the whole garden; I've been trying for two years to root it out and still haven't stopped the invasion. (Every broken piece of root I leave behind becomes a new plant. Horseradish makes the Hydra look like a household pet by comparison.) Were I to have the chance to do it over again, I'd give horseradish its very own plot a good ways from the garden, or grow it in a pot.

▲ Ready for the borscht. *Horseradish is easy to prepare; just grind it up and mix it with a little vinegar.*

PLANTING AND GROWING

In spring, add a bit of compost or well-rotted manure to the spot where you plan to grow horseradish. Loosen the soil with a fork to a depth of about a foot (30 cm) as you mix in the compost or manure. After raking the bed smooth, dig a furrow about 6 inches (15 cm) deep. Set horseradish root cuttings along the side of the trench so that buds are toward the soil surface. Cover roots with about 2 inches (5 cm) of soil and water well.

The shoots should appear in about a week or two. After the first few leaves have completely unfolded, fertilize once a year with some well-rotted manure. Don't overdo it; horseradish doesn't need much help to grow quite vigorously. Water during long dry spells.

HARVEST AND STORAGE

After the first hard frost, loosen the soil around the plants with a garden fork. Lift the plants gently from the soil with the fork, trim off the tops, and brush the roots with a clean scrub brush to remove most of the soil. Remove some of the side shoots to replant. Store roots in the root cellar like carrots or in plastic vegetable bags in the refrigerator. Roots remain fresh for about three months. To prepare horseradish, all you do is grind it up or grate it. Stand back! The smell is enough to knock you on your ear. Mix the grated horseradish with a little vinegar and store it in a tightly sealed jar, in the refrigerator.

Sow & Grow

Horseradish (*Armoracia rusticana*)
Cabbage family (Cruciferae)

SOWING/PLANTING

Root cutting depth: 4" (10 cm)
Soil temperature: 40–60°F (4–16°C)
Days to germination: Not applicable
Sow indoors: Not applicable
Plant outdoors: Early spring

GROWING

pH range: 5.5–7.5
Soil temperature: 50–70°F (10–21°C)
Spacing in beds: 12–18" (30–45 cm)
Watering: Low to moderate
Light: Shade to full sun
Nutrient requirements: N=low; P=low; K=low

Jerusalem Artichokes

Also known as sunchokes, Jerusalem artichokes are members of the sunflower family and produce potato-like tubers that are edible either raw or cooked.

THE SITE

Like horseradish and mint, these perennials will take over whatever garden space they're allotted, so give them a territory of their own a decent distance from the vegetable garden. Any sunny spot with moderately fertile soil will do, even if it's too wet or too dry for most garden plants. These are tall plants (6 feet [1.8 m]), so don't plant them where they'll shade the garden.

PLANTING AND GROWING

Jerusalem artichokes grow from tubers rather than seeds. Each tuber (a swollen, knotty section of root) contains eyes, much like a potato's. To prepare for planting, cut the tubers into sections with at least two eyes per section. Don't let the tubers dry out; if you can't plant them right away, store them in the crisper drawer of the refrigerator.

Dig a trench about 4 inches (10 cm) deep and sprinkle in an inch or two (2.5 to 5 cm) of compost. Set the tubers onto the compost, spacing them 12 to 18 inches (30 to 45 cm) apart. Cover and water well. Once shoots appear a week or two after planting, the plants need little care. (Note: Tubers for seed are normally shipped in the fall, right after they are harvested. Either plant them when they arrive and mulch for winter protection or store them in the refrigerator until spring.)

HARVESTING AND STORING

Although you can gather tubers anytime from late summer to early winter, they taste best after a few hard frosts. After the plants have turned brown, cut back the stalks and loosen the ground with a fork. Use the fork to sift through the soil, gathering only as many tubers as you will use in the next couple of weeks; they're best

▲ **Above and below.** *Jerusalem artichokes produce small yellow sunflowers to lighten the spirit as well as flavorful tubers that make dinner a feast.*

Sow & Grow

Jerusalem artichokes (*Helianthus tuberosus*)
Sunflower family (Compositae)

SOWING/PLANTING

Tuber depth: 4" (10 cm)
Soil temperature: 50–60°F (10–16°C)
Days to germination: 7–14
Sow indoors: Not applicable
Plant outdoors: Fall, or after last frost in spring

GROWING

pH range: 6.0–6.7
Soil temperature: 60–70°F (16–21°C)
Spacing in beds: 12–18" (30–45 cm)
Watering: Moderate to heavy
Light: Full sun
Nutrient requirements: N=moderate; P=moderate; K=moderate
Rotation considerations: Do not follow any member of the sunflower family
Seed longevity: Not applicable

eaten fresh but can be frozen or stored in a refrigerator or root cellar as long as the tubers are kept moist.

Mulch the bed with a thick layer of straw to keep the soil from freezing. Jerusalem artichokes can be harvested all winter. Whatever is left in the ground will come up in spring and provide next year's crop.

Kale

Kale is like a really good friend — there for you when everything else in the garden (and in life) has failed you. It's easy to grow, healthful, and hardy enough to harvest from under the snow. It even survives most winters without protection. It's a salad when there's nothing else fresh and green in the larder, and it adds flavor and zest to winter stir-fries and soups.

THE SITE

Create a good site for kale by working in some chopped leaves or leaf mold the previous fall or planting a nitrogen-fixing green manure crop. Kale tastes best when it grows fast, so enrich the soil with compost at least a month before sowing. Full sun is best, but kale can tolerate partial shade.

SOWING AND GROWING

About three months before the first fall frost, plant three seeds ¼ to ½ inch (6 to 13 mm) deep every 16 to 18 inches (40 to 45 cm), two rows to a 30-inch-wide (75 cm) bed. Thin to the strongest plant in each cluster. (Or grow from purchased transplants.) Keep the weeds at bay and the soil moist. Kale pretty much takes care of itself. For better-flavored leaves and less frost damage, stop watering after the first frost.

▲ **Almost perfect.** *Kale has just about everything — good looks, good flavor, and high vitamin and mineral content. Plus it's superhardy and rarely bothered by bugs.*

Like other members of the cabbage family, kale is a favorite of flea beetles, but fortunately, it isn't Number One on the Hit Parade. Also, flea beetles aren't around much when kale is young, so in fall this is usually a problem in theory rather than in practice. If you do have flea beetle problems, grow kale under row covers until the plants are big and tough enough to avoid damage.

Sow & Grow

Kale (*Brassica oleracea* Acephala Group)
Cabbage family (Cruciferae)

SOWING

Seed depth: ¼–½" (13 mm)
Germination soil temperature: 45–95°F (7–35°C)
Days to germination: 5–7
Sow indoors: 6 weeks before last frost
Sow outdoors: In cool climates, late spring or early summer; in warm climates, early spring; and for overwintering, late summer or early fall

GROWING

pH range: 6.0–7.0
Growing soil temperature: 60–65°F (16–18°C)
Spacing in beds: 16" (40 cm), staggered
Watering: Heavy during growing season, light after first frost
Light: Best yields in full sun, but tolerates partial shade
Nutrient requirements: N=moderate; P=moderate; K=moderate
Rotation considerations: Avoid following cabbage family crops
Seed longevity: 4 years

Deer also like kale, especially in the fall and early winter when everything else on the deer menu is frost-killed. The electric fence that kept the deer out of the garden all summer is no help here. If you have deer in the neighborhood, surround your kale patch with a woven wire fence at least 6 feet (1.8 m) high.

HARVEST AND STORAGE

The flavor of kale improves after the leaves are nipped by frost, but you can begin to harvest individual leaves as soon as they are large enough to toss in a salad. To avoid tearing the stems, use scissors or a sharp knife to gather the leaves. Harvest entire plants by cutting the stems about an inch (2.5 cm) above the ground.

Leaves stored in the refrigerator in a vegetable storage bag keep for two weeks to about a month. Kale freezes well. Stuff the leaves in a large freezer bag and crumble them — still frozen — into soups toward the end of the cooking process.

VARIETIES

Note: Low-growing varieties, such as Winterbor, are more frost-hardy than tall ones, such as Lacinato.

Even' Star Smooth. Open pollinated, produces well in cold weather.

Red Russian. Purple stems, flat, tooth-edged grey-green leaves with purple veining; good for salads and stir-fry; stores better if you dunk the leaves in cold water before refrigerating.

Toscano. Lacinato type, also known as dinosaur kale, with dark green leaves that don't curl but are heavily savoyed; tolerates heat and cold, but not as hardy as Winterbor.

Winterbor. Very hardy, with curled, ruffly, and deep blue-green leaves; regrows well for additional harvest and is suitable for container growing; our favorite kale.

Winterbor

Toscano

Kohlrabi

Kohlrabi is a member in good standing of the cabbage family, but you sure couldn't tell that by looking at it; it more resembles an alien spacecraft than it does a vegetable. It is a vegetable, though, and it's good to eat — very good, in fact. The edible part is a swollen portion of the stem just above the soil. Kohlrabi stores well in the root cellar and can be eaten raw (grated in coleslaw or salad), pickled, or cooked (in soups or stews, or as a baked side dish).

THE SITE

If it is to be tender and tasty, kohlrabi must grow fast and without interruption. To do that, it needs rich, evenly moist soil and cool temperatures. Kohlrabi thrives on plenty of compost and benefits from leaf mold as a sidedressing.

SOWING AND GROWING

Start seeds indoors if you like, but best results come from direct sowing. If you're growing kohlrabi as a late-season crop, start the plants elsewhere and transplant them as a succession crop when there's space available.

Once kohlrabi is off and growing, just make sure the soil stays moist. If your soil is well amended and compost-rich, you shouldn't need to fertilize. If you're still bringing your soil up to snuff, fertilize with a complete organic fertilizer, such as fish emulsion, every two to three weeks. As the stems begin to swell, add a layer of compost or well-rotted manure to the rows.

HARVEST AND STORAGE

To use fresh. Begin harvesting when stems are about 2 inches (5 cm) in diameter. Pull the entire plant and trim the leaves and roots. Plants can be stored in the refrigerator for a month or two.

For winter storage. Harvest 3- to 4-inch (7.5 to 10 cm) stems after a few frosts. Trim the leaves and store in a root cellar for about three months. In Zone 6 and farther south, kohlrabi can stay right in the garden through fall and be harvested as needed. If a cold snap is forecast, mulch plants with straw.

▲ **Beauty is only skin deep.** *It may look funny, but it sure tastes good — a bit like broccoli.*

Sow & Grow

Kohlrabi (*Brassica oleracea* Gongylodes Group)
Cabbage family (Cruciferae)

SOWING

Seed depth: ¼–½" (6–13 mm)
Soil temperature: 50–70°F (10–21°C)
Days to germination: 5–7
Sow indoors: Not recommended
Sow outdoors: In cool climates, from 1 month before the last frost for spring crops and early summer for fall crops; in warm climates, in late winter for spring crops and fall for early winter crops

GROWING

pH range: 6.0–7.0
Soil temperature: 50–65°F (10–18°C)
Spacing in beds: 6–8" (15–20 cm), staggered pattern, 4 rows to a wide bed
Watering: Moderate and even
Light: Best yield in full sun; tolerates light shade
Nutrient requirements: N=moderate; P=moderate; K=moderate
Rotation considerations: Avoid following cabbage family crops
Seed longevity: 3 years

Leeks

A bowl of leek and potato soup on a chilly fall evening is all the reason I need to grow leeks. They are gentle on the digestive system and they taste good, in addition to being easy to grow and frost hardy. Leeks also stay fresh all winter long under a thick blanket of mulch.

THE SITE

Like their onion-family cousins, leeks grow best in fertile, friable, and well-drained soil enriched with compost or well-aged manure. Full sun is best; there isn't a whole lot of leaf surface for photosynthesis. Soil pH should be between 6.0 and 7.5.

Sow & Grow

Leeks (*Allium ampeloprasum* Porrum Group)
Onion family (Liliaceae)

SOWING

Seed depth: ¼" (6 mm)
Soil temperature: 75°F (24°C)
Days to germination: 5–7
Sow indoors: 4 weeks before last frost
Sow outdoors: Not recommended

GROWING

pH range: 6.0–7.5
Soil temperature: 60°F (16°C)
Spacing in beds: 6" (15 cm) in rows, 3 rows to a bed
Watering: Moderate
Light: Full sun gives best yields, but tolerates partial shade
Nutrient requirements: N=moderate; P=moderate; K=moderate
Rotation considerations: Avoid following onion, shallot, garlic, chive
Seed longevity: 2 years

▲ **The short and long of it.** *You can choose between short- and long-season leeks. Short-seasons have a thinner stem and don't keep as well as the hardier long-season types. I grow only long-season varieties like these, with their thick, cylindrical stems carrying a fan of dark green leaves.*

SOWING AND GROWING

Start long-season leeks indoors in late winter. Sow seeds in flats, and when the seedlings are about 2 inches (5 cm) tall, transplant them to individual growing cells. Fertilize once every two weeks with fish emulsion.

When they're ready for transplanting to the garden, about a week after the last frost, the plants should be as big around as a pencil and 6 to 12 inches (15 to 30 cm) tall. Don't worry if they're bigger than that. With leeks, bigger transplants mean bigger yields.

Alternatively, you can purchase started plants. Leek plants are often available at nurseries and from seed catalogs. That's the route I take for the dozen or so plants I grow each year.

I've tried two ways of planting leeks and had good results with both. The goal here is to produce plants with a long, white midsection (the edible portion of the plant). Method 1: Make a long, skinny hole about 4 or 5 inches (10 to 12.5 cm) deep with a dowel or pencil and drop in a leek seedling. Use the dowel or pencil to nudge the soil firmly around the leek. Method 2: Set the transplants as shown in the photos on page 254.

Transplanting Leek Seedlings

1 Remove the leek seedlings from the growing flat, gently teasing the roots apart with your fingers.

2 Trim the roots to about 2 inches (5 cm).

3 Use a hoe to dig a trench about 8 inches (20 cm) deep. Set the leeks in the trench, spacing them about 6 inches (15 cm) apart. Fill the trench with soil and press it firmly but gently in place.

4 Mulch the planting with grass clippings.

5 As the leeks grow, hill the soil up around their base. This traditional technique bleaches, and sweetens, the stems.

Water the transplants well and maintain soil moisture throughout the growing season to keep the stems tender. A mulch of grass clippings will help.

HARVEST AND STORAGE

Harvest short-season leeks during the summer and long-season varieties from late summer through winter. To harvest, loosen the soil gently with a garden fork and pull the plants from the ground. Leeks don't store very long — about a week in the refrigerator — so harvest only as much as you need. In early fall, but before the first hard freeze, mulch the bed with a thick layer of straw. This will keep the soil workable through most of winter, allowing you to harvest fresh leeks from the garden anytime a craving for leek and potato soup strikes.

VARIETIES

Bandit. This long-growing leek is very winter-hardy. (120 days)

King Richard. The classic leek, popular since its introduction in 1978, it boasts both long stems and early maturity. (75 days)

Lettuce

There are a whole lot of very different-looking and surprisingly different-tasting plants sitting under the lettuce umbrella. You can choose from among hundreds of different varieties of lettuce in a wide range of shapes, colors, and forms. Leaf lettuces, oak leaf lettuces, summer crisps, icebergs, romaine, butterheads, and Bibbs, green ones of all different shades, red ones, red and green ones. And you can harvest them as microgreens, baby greens, half-grown, or full-grown. The choices are pretty much endless, as are the differences in texture and taste. Whatever kind you grow, the secret to the sweetest lettuce is the same: Keep it growing fast.

THE SITE

If you want all the taste that the many lettuces can offer, grow them in fertile soil enriched with your best compost, provide continual moisture and, in the heat of summer, a bit of shade to keep the temperatures down and forestall bolting.

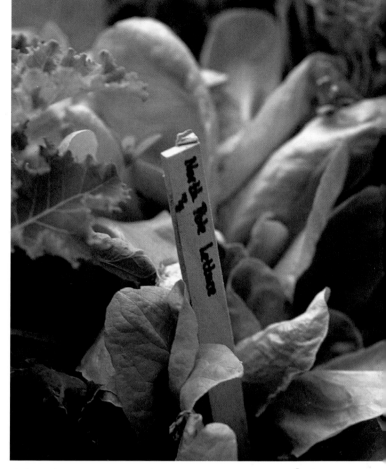

▲ **Lovely lettuce.** *This North Pole leaf lettuce flourished in our unheated greenhouse over winter, surviving outside temperatures of –20°F (–29°C).*

Sow & Grow

Lettuce (*Lactuca sativa*)
Sunflower family (Compositae)

SOWING

Seed depth: ¼–½" (6–13 mm)
Soil temperature: 40–60°F (4–16°C); germination rates decline above 68°F (20°C)
Days to germination: 7–14
Sow indoors: 4 weeks before transplanting
Sow outdoors: When soil can be worked

GROWING

pH range: 6.5–7.0
Soil temperature: 55–65°F (13–18°C)
Spacing in beds: Leaf lettuce for continuous harvest, ½" (1.3 cm) in bands; leaf lettuce to form heads, 8" (20 cm); summer crisp types, 8–12" (20–30 cm); iceberg, 8–12" (20–30 cm); romaine (cos), 10" (25 cm); butterhead, 8–10" (20–25 cm); Bibb, 6–8" (15–20 cm)
Watering: Light to moderate
Light: Full sun for best yields, but will tolerate partial shade
Nutrient requirements: N=high; P=high; K=high
Rotation considerations: Avoid following radicchio, endive, escarole, or artichoke
Seed longevity: 1 year

SOWING

All lettuces are easy to grow and have similar needs — with some important differences. Lettuces that form a head, including romaines, need more space than leaf types. Some types, particularly romaine lettuces, tolerate warm weather better and are less likely to bolt.

You can start lettuce indoors, or in a cold frame, or direct-sow it. If you start plants indoors or in a cold frame, sow seeds about four weeks before setting out. In cool climates, direct-sow seeds beginning in early spring and continuing through late summer. In mild climates, sow seeds from fall through early spring.

Lettuce seeds need light to germinate. Sow them on top of the soil and cover very lightly with soil. Keep the seedbed evenly moist. Lettuce germinates and grows best in cool weather. Although it's tolerant of light frosts, provide protection, such as a floating row cover, if temperatures dip below 30°F (−1°C). In warm soil (above about 75°F [24°C]), the seeds become temporarily dormant.

Succession Success

Lettuce is a good crop for succession planting. To have a continuous supply of lettuce over the season, make successive plantings every 10 days to two weeks. As the weather warms, grow varieties that tolerate hot weather and resist bolting, such as crisphead varieties.

GROWING

The key to tender and tasty lettuce is rapid growth, but lettuce has a relatively shallow, compact root system that doesn't absorb nutrients and moisture from the soil very efficiently, which can slow growth. To encourage fast growth, add plenty of finished compost before planting. If your soil is less than fully fertile, fertilize at planting time with liquid fish or fish-and-seaweed fertilizer. Don't overdo the nitrogen, though; a surplus can cause a bitter taste.

Lettuce doesn't require a lot of water, but it needs water consistently. Lack of moisture causes plant growth to stop, which can also produce a slightly bitter flavor in the leaves. In warm weather, lettuce likes a little shade, which you can provide by growing it under shade cloth or next to taller companion plants.

HARVEST

Lettuce goes from seeds to salad in about a month in many regions and only a little longer in others. Once it has grown to the size you prefer, there are three ways you can harvest the bounty.

Harvest as microgreens. Many lettuces, particularly leaf lettuces, are grown to be harvested as microgreens for salads when the leaves are only 2 to 3 inches (5 to 8 cm) long. Cut the whole plant just above the soil.

Gather outer leaves. With all except iceberg types, start gathering the outer leaves as soon as they're big enough for the salad bowl. The harvest is over when a central stem starts to form. This signals that the plant is getting ready to bolt, and the leaves will start to have a bitter taste.

Cut-and-come-again. Cut leaf lettuces about an inch (2.5 cm) above the soil as soon as most of the leaves are salad-sized. The plant will continue to grow and provide a second and sometimes a third harvest.

Harvest the entire plant. This method can be used for any type of lettuce. Wait until the plant is mature, but still young and tender, and harvest the whole thing.

◀ Getting bigheaded. *Given the space, butterhead lettuce forms a graceful, impressive head.*

VARIETIES

There are so many lettuces out there that even a fairly extensive list like this gives you only the merest peek at what is possible in the lettuce patch; Peter Rabbit would be in ecstasy. Here are just a few that we have tried and liked and a few recommendations from our neighbors, too.

Leaf Lettuce

In four to six weeks, leaf lettuce forms a loose rosette of tender, sweet-tasting leaves. No lettuces are easier to grow than these.

Black Seeded Simpson. Very early, a popular heirloom.

Cracoviensis. A twisting rosette head with purple accenting and buttery-flavored leaves; an excellent lettuce.

Esmerelda. Soft green leaves; one of my favorites.

Les Oreilles du Diable ("Devil's Ears"). An heirloom deer-tongue variety with good color and excellent taste.

Merlot. Known as a "cutting lettuce," best used very young for baby greens in salad mixes.

Red Sails. Deep burgundy over green; slow-bolting.

Red Salad Bowl. Compact rosettes with frilly leaves and a bronze-red color; buttery flavor.

Salad Bowl. Best in cool weather and has good frost tolerance.

Romaine (Cos)

Romaine lettuce has oblong leaves that form fairly loose, upright, conical heads. The leaves have a crisp, slightly tart flavor and come in shades of green and red.

Brune d'Hiver. An old-time French romaine with extremely good frost tolerance.

Freckles. Also known as Trout Back and *Forellenschlus*; an heirloom romaine with butterhead taste, dark green leaves freckled with dark red splotches; good from baby greens through maturity.

Red Rosie. Bright red, good both as a baby lettuce or full-grown.

Rouge d'Hiver. An old-time French lettuce; red, with very good frost tolerance (but very little heat tolerance).

Winter Density. A French romaine that looks like tall buttercrunch; very good frost tolerance.

Butterhead and Bibb

Characterized by broad rosettes of tender, wavy leaves, this type of lettuce has a delicate flavor and creamy texture.

Buttercrunch. One of the classics; easy to grow, crisp and sweet; hearts self-blanch.

Deer Tongue. Heirloom, slow-bolting; good for baby leaf harvest.

Focea. Small, dense heads, early maturity; excellent taste.

Tom Thumb. My favorite lettuce; one head is just right for an individual salad.

Summer Crisp. A blend of some of the best features of leaf and head types, this variety boasts a loose head of large, crisp leaves with good flavor.

Cherokee. Dark red, slow-bolting.

Loma. Frilly, dense, early small heads with excellent flavor and a good "crunch."

▲ **A leaf at a time.** *Enjoy a continuous harvest of large outer leaves until the bitter center core develops.*

▲ **A second chance.** *If you cut leaf lettuce 1 inch (2.5 cm) above the soil, it will regrow one or two more heads.*

Black Seeded Simpson

Loma

Les Oreilles du Diable ("Devil's Ears")

Tom Thumb

Cracoviensis

Merlot

Nevada

Focea

Red Rosie

Esmerelda

Mottistone. New introduction: the first speckled summer crisp.

Nevada. Dark green leaves; good spring or summer.

Crisphead (also known as Iceberg)

As close as you can get to "store lettuce" but better tasting.

Crispino. Glossy green, early; firm heads, juicy and mild flavor.

Red Iceberg. Compact, burgundy red, medium-sized heads with good flavor.

Lettuce Mixes

Many seed catalogs now offer lettuce mixes, blends of many colors and textures that look and taste good together and grow at about the same rate; they're usually harvested at three to six weeks for salad mixes. We sometimes plant a mix and then transplant out the most colorful varieties to grow to maturity, eating the rest as baby greens. Many lettuce varieties are part of mesclun mixes. (See Mesclun below.)

Mesclun: A Salad in a Packet

Mesclun isn't one particular vegetable — it's a whole salad of mixed greens. More and more seed catalogs offer mesclun mixes, which include seeds for a variety of lettuces and European salad greens that both grow well together and taste good together. There are brassica mixes, spicy greens mixes, braising mixes, spicy or mild salad mixes. Add some mystery to your garden by trying out several kinds. Or make your own mix.

The site. Grow mesclun anywhere you'd grow lettuces, spinach, or other salad greens. That includes window boxes, flats, or any other sort of container. Self-watering containers are ideal because they make it easy to maintain the right soil moisture level. Fertile soil means fast growth, and fast growth means tender, tasty greens. Don't forget the compost.

Sowing and growing. Before sowing, shake the seed packet well to mix up the seeds. Either space seeds about ½ inch (13 mm) apart in rows or broadcast them in a thin band. Cover seeds with about ⅛ (3 mm) inch of fine soil. Moisten the soil and be sure to keep it moist until the seeds have germinated. Keep the soil moist until harvest.

Mixes containing cabbage-family plants may attract flea beetles. Lettuces and spinach may attract aphids. Use row covers to deter pests.

Harvest. Harvest in "cut-and-come-again" fashion at about three weeks by cutting the plants with scissors ½ inch (13 mm) above the soil. Most of the plants will regrow.

Mâche

Also known by the colorful names of lamb's lettuce, field salad, and corn salad, none of which give a hint about the major virtue of this nutty-flavored salad green: It is extraordinarily hardy, easily able to survive winter temperatures of −20°F (−29°C). Plant mâche, and you'll have fresh salad makings in the darkest and coldest depths of winter.

THE SITE

Cold. That's not just what mâche can survive, it's what mâche likes. Grow it in the early spring and in the fall, right into and through winter. Mâche can stand the cold, but it may not survive wind, freezing rain, and snow, so either grow it in a cold frame or solar greenhouse from the get-go or plan on sheltering it with a cold frame or mini hoop house when the weather gets nasty. Mâche has a dense and fairly shallow root system and can be grown in a shallow container or a flat.

SOWING AND GROWING

When you plant depends on when you want to harvest. For late-spring harvest, plant in early spring; for fall and winter harvest, plant in early to midfall, the same time you'd plant spinach for winter harvest. Sow seeds an inch (2.5 cm) apart in rows 4 inches (10 cm) apart. Mâche does not germinate well in warm soil and takes about 10 to 14 days to emerge.

HARVEST

Cut the heads right at soil level when they are 2 to 4 inches (5 to 10 cm) across. Smaller is a bit tastier and tenderer. Don't leave the 4-inchers (10 cm) in hopes of more growth; that's as big as mâche gets.

VARIETIES

Verte de Cambrai. Small-leaved variety with exceptional frost tolerance.
Vit. Succulent, firm, with dark green leaves.

▲ Into the mâche pit! *This is one hardy green; it's a good choice for growing in a cold frame through the winter.*

Sow & Grow

Mâche/Corn Salad (*Valerianella locusta*)
Valerian family (Valerianaceae)

SOWING

Seed depth: ¼–½" (6–13 mm)
Germination soil temperature: 50–70°F (10–21°C)
Days to germination: 10–14
Sow indoors: Not recommended
Sow outdoors: Spring, as soon as the soil temperature is at least 50°F (10°C)

GROWING

pH range: 6.5–7.0
Growing soil temperature: 60°F (16°C)
Spacing in beds: 1" (2.5cm)
Watering: Moderate
Light: Full sun or partial shade
Nutrient requirements: N = moderate; P = moderate; K = moderate
Seed longevity: 5 years

Melons

Melons are fairly easy to grow as long as you're growing them where they can get what they want — nice, even heat and plenty of sun. Even if you live in the North, you can usually get a decent crop most years if you stick to short-season varieties bred especially for cool weather areas, but you'd best hope nonetheless for a sunny and warm summer. I grow melons only in the solar greenhouse; it's a good way to use that space in the summer.

THE SITE

Melons are heat lovers. They really need more heat than they can get in northern regions, but they can grow there with some help from plastic mulch and row covers. Melons are also a bit particular about pH, intolerant of anything below 6.0 and preferring 6.5 to 7.0.

At the same time you start the seeds indoors, work plenty of compost and some seaweed or rotted manure into their bed and then cover the soil with a sheet of IRT plastic to get it good and warm.

SOWING

Start melons indoors in a seed-starting mix, three weeks before the last frost date. Sow three seeds each in 3-inch (7.5 cm) pots. Germinate at a steady 80° to 90°F (27 to 32°C). Once the seedlings appear, lower the temperature to 75°F (24°C) for about a week until the first true leaves begin to emerge. Thin to one plant per pot with scissors. Lower the temperature to 65° to 70°F (18 to 21°C) and reduce watering for another week to harden the seedlings.

INSIDE OR OUT?

In warm climates you can direct-sow melons, but it's probably a better bet to start them indoors. Melons like very warm soil when they're germinating but cooler soil once they start growing. It's easier to give them that if they start life indoors.

▲ **Passport to summer.** *A galia-type melon, this Passport melon has sweet green flesh — a darker green near the rind fading to white-green at the center. Because it's an early melon, it's a good one to grow in cool-summer regions.*

Sow & Grow

Melons (*Cucumis melo* and *Citrullus lanatus*)
Cucumber family (Cucurbitaceae)

SOWING

Seed depth: ½" (13 mm)
Soil temperature: 80–90°F (27–32°C)
Days to germination: 3–5
Sow indoors: 3 weeks before last frost
Sow outdoors: When soil reaches 70°F (21°C) and after last frost

GROWING

pH range: 6.0–7.0 (6.0 is the absolute minimum; production drops below this)
Soil temperature: 70–85°F (21–29°C)
Spacing in beds: 16" (40 cm)
Watering: Moderate and even from germination to hardening off; low for 1 week prior to transplanting; moderate again from transplanting until fruit is full-sized; low or none during ripening of fruit
Light: Full sun
Nutrient requirements: N=low; P=high; K=high
Rotation considerations: Avoid following cucumber, pumpkin, and summer and winter squash
Seed longevity: 4–5 years

GROWING

Make sure the soil temperature is at least 70°F (21°C) before transplanting. Plant 16 inches (40 cm) apart, one row in the middle of a narrow (30-inch [76 cm]) bed. To avoid transplant shock, be very careful not to disturb the roots while planting. In cooler regions, melons need every day of the growing season to ripen fruit and cannot afford any setbacks. After planting, cover the beds with floating row covers to increase warmth and exclude pests. Remove the row covers when the plants begin to bloom.

Melons are sensitive to drought throughout the season but especially from transplanting to fruit set. To get fruits of the proper size, water evenly but not too much; melons don't taste as good if they've had too much water. Check soil moisture frequently. If new leaves are more yellow than older ones, fertilize with diluted fish emulsion or other liquid fertilizer.

HARVEST

It's pretty easy to tell when most vegetables are ripe, but melons offer a bit more of a challenge. It helps to know that all the fruits on any individual melon plant will ripen over a short period of time. If one melon is ripe, the remaining melons won't be far behind.

Most melons. With the exception of watermelons and French charentais, melons are ripe when the rind changes from gray-green to yellow-buff. The fruit is still firm, but gentle thumb pressure easily separates the stem from the vine.

Charentais melons. When the leaf nearest the fruit fades from green to pale yellow, you'll know they're ripe. Harvest charentais melons by cutting the stem (which is still firmly attached to the fruit) with scissors or shears.

VARIETIES

Charentais. Medium-sized fruit with a grayish green rind and bright orange, aromatic, and sweet flesh, charentais melons are very popular in Europe, especially France, and are becoming increasingly available in North America. Varieties include Alienor, Charmel, Honey Girl hybrid charentais, and Savor.

Galias. Medium to large fruits with greenish rinds covered with beige netting, galia melons boast translucent green flesh with a rich, sweet, and spicy flavor. Varieties include Galia Perfume Melon and Passport.

Honeydews. Medium melons with smooth yellowish white rinds; flesh ranges from icy white, through shades of green to orange depending on the variety. Honeydews are very sweet. Varieties include Earlidew, Honey Ice, and Hon-I-Dew.

Crenshaws. Similar to honeydews, crenshaws produce medium to large fruits with a yellowish rind. The flesh is usually pale green, but some varieties have an orange tone. Varieties include Burpee Early Hybrid, Early Crenshaw, and Honeyshaw.

Muskmelons. Medium to large, often ribbed, fruits have rinds covered with tan netting. The flesh is sunset orange, juicy, and sweet. Muskmelons are the most popular garden-grown melon. Varieties include Alaska, Ambrosia, Burpee Hybrid, Earligold, Earlysweet, Honey Bun Hybrid, and Sweet'n Early.

A Cantaloupe by Another Name

As common as this melon is, in some places what is called a cantaloupe is really something else entirely. In North America muskmelons are often called cantaloupes, but the two are really very different. A cantaloupe has a hard, warty rind, while a muskmelon, like the one pictured here, has a soft rind covered with netting.

Mizuna

In seed catalogs, you'll sometimes find mizuna hidden away among Asian greens, specialty greens, or mesclun ingredients. It deserves a place of its own. It's among the few greens that can tolerate cold and frost and is therefore a good candidate for growing in a cold frame or solar greenhouse over the winter. It can be eaten in salads and stir-fries.

THE SITE

Any fertile spot where you'd grow greens will do. As usual, add some compost. Mizuna is also a good container plant.

SOWING AND GROWING

Sow the seeds in early spring or in the fall for winter harvest. Plant about an inch (2.5 cm) apart, thinning (and eating) the young plants to achieve a 10-inch (25 cm) spacing. Alternatively, for early harvest as salad mix, sow in 2-inch-wide (5 cm) bands.

Mizuna is a brassica, second cousin to cabbage, broccoli, and the rest of that crowd. That means flea beetles, and flea beetles mean row covers should be laid down right after the seeds are in the ground.

HARVEST

Harvest young plants as microgreens. Or wait a while to harvest larger (3 to 4 inches high [8 to 10 cm]) but still tender plants. Or let the plants get even bigger and harvest individual leaves.

VARIETIES

Kyona Mizuna. Japanese origin, produces rosettes of thin, white stalks with deeply cut, fringed leaves; mild flavor, good in salads; regrows after cutting.

Purple Mizuna. Green leaves with purple margins when young; purple tinged all over when mature; bolt resistant.

▲ A super salad green. *In its more-mature stages, mizuna is great in stir-fries, too.*

Sow & Grow

Mizuna (*Brassica rapa* var. *juncea*)
Cabbage family (Cruciferae)

SOWING

Seed depth: ¼–½" (6–13 mm)
Germination soil temperature: 75–85°F (24–29°C)
Days to germination: 5
Sow indoors: 2–3 weeks before transplanting
Sow outdoors: Early spring to midsummer; in the South, plant in fall for late fall/early winter harvest

GROWING

pH range: 6.0 to 7.5
Spacing in beds: 8–10" (20–25 cm)
Watering: Average
Light: Full sun
Nutrients: N=high; P=moderate; K=moderate
Rotation: Do not follow or precede cabbage family crops
Seed longevity: 2 years

Mustard

Probably the plural, mustards, would be more accurate here, for there are lots of different mustards of many colors and flavors ranging from pungently sweet to downright hot. Depending on variety and age, mustard greens may find a place at the table as microgreens, garnishes, major or minor salad ingredients, or elements of a stir-fry. Mustard seeds also make good sprouts.

THE SITE

Mustards like fertile, friable soil with a good amount of compost mixed in. Check to be sure that phosphorus is in adequate supply.

SOWING AND GROWING

Prepare the soil as you would for cabbage, a near relative, adding compost or well-rotted manure and working it in well. Mustard is tolerant of some cold and can be sown a few weeks before the last frost. You can start plants indoors if you'd like, but direct-sown crops seem to establish themselves faster and grow more vigorously. Sow seeds in early spring with succession planting every three weeks until the weather warms. Resume planting in the fall. The plants grow quickly, with most types ready to harvest about a month and a half from sowing, earlier if you're after microgreens. If slow growth indicates the need for fertilizer, use fish or fish and seaweed liquid.

HARVEST

Begin gathering individual leaves after the plant has formed a rosette of leaves, usually when the plants are about 3 to 4 inches (7.5 to 10 cm) tall. You can cut entire plants any time after they reach about 4 to 6 inches (10 to 15 cm) tall. If you cut an inch (2.5 cm) or so above the soil line, the plants will regrow, but the resulting leaves are of poorer quality, often having a bitter taste.

VARIETIES

Golden Streaks. Deeply serrated, golden green leaves; mild, sweet mustard flavor, good in salads, steamed, or in a stir-fry.

▲ Cutting the mustard. *Like other greens, mustard tastes best when grown in cool weather.*

Sow & Grow
Mustard (*Brassica juncea*)
Cabbage family (Cruciferae)

SOWING
Seed depth: ¼" (6 mm)
Germination soil temperature: 65–70°F (18–21°C)
Days to germination: 4–6
Sow indoors: 2 weeks before last frost
Sow outdoors: Every 3 weeks from spring to summer for early crop, and from late summer to early fall for fall crop

GROWING
pH range: 5.5–7.0
Growing soil temperature: 50–70°F (10–21°C)
Spacing in beds: 6–15" (15–37.5 cm)
Watering: Moderate
Light: Full sun to partial shade
Nutrient requirements: N=high; P=moderate; K=moderate
Rotation considerations: Do not follow or precede cabbage family crops
Seed longevity: 4 years

Green Wave. Upright growth habit, bolt-resistant; spicy when raw, milder cooked.

Osaka Purple. Mild flavor, medium green leaves with purple-red veins; good raw or cooked.

Red Mustard. Slow bolting, long harvest period, good as a microgreen or full-sized.

Okra

Okra is a pretty plant, with red-centered, pale yellow flowers. But its beauty is much more than skin deep. In the South, where preparing and consuming the pods is an art, okra can be boiled, cooked slowly with tomatoes and spices, or dipped in batter, breaded, and fried. I have grown okra here in the North, but it's a lot easier to grow farther south where it gets the kind of heat it loves.

THE SITE

Pick a spot in full sun that will warm quickly in the spring. Okra likes a nice, light soil with plenty of compost or rotted manure. Don't plant okra where tomatoes, peppers, eggplants, or potatoes have grown recently.

SOWING AND GROWING

In cool climates or for early crops in warm regions, warm the soil with black plastic for about three to four

▲ **Okra is more than okay.** *Wherever you garden, from Zone 4 to Zone 11, easy-to-grow okra can add delicious variety to your garden and dinner plate.*

weeks before transplanting okra. At the same time, sow seeds indoors in individual 4-inch (10 cm) pots. Plant three seeds to a pot and thin to the best plant. Germinate at 80 to 90°F (27 to 32°C). After all danger of frost has passed, the soil is warm, and air temperatures are consistently above 60°F (16°C), set plants 1 foot (30 cm) apart, being careful not to disturb the roots. It won't hurt to mix a shovelful of compost in the planting hole. In warm climates, you can also direct-sow okra. In any case, use whatever is needed to keep okra growing steadily even if the weather is uncooperative — row covers, grow tunnels, or hot caps. Water during dry periods and fertilize once a month with a natural fertilizer such as fish emulsion or seaweed.

HARVESTING AND STORING

Some folks harvest okra pods when they are 3 inches (8 cm) long, but the pods are probably most flavorful and tender if gathered when 2 inches (5 cm) long. Keep the pods picked or production will stop.

BEST VARIETIES

In recent years, dwarf, spineless, and early-maturing varieties have brought okra to short-season gardens where it couldn't be grown before.

Burgundy. Four feet (1.2 m) tall with very attractive, deep wine-colored stems and pods, as pretty on the plate as in the garden; pods are equally tender picked large or small.

Cajun Delight. High-yielding and early, making it the natural choice for cool-season gardeners.

Sow & Grow

Okra (*Abelmoschus esculentus*)
Mallow family (Malvaceae)

SOWING

Seed depth: ¾" (19 mm)
Germination soil temperature: 80–95°F (27–35°C)
Days to germination: 5–14
Sow indoors: 5 weeks before last frost
Sow outdoors: After last frost (only in warm climates)

GROWING

pH range: 6.0–8.0
Growing soil temperature: 70–90°F (21–32°C)
Spacing in beds: 12" (30 cm)
Watering: Low
Light: Full sun
Nutrient requirements: N=moderate; P=moderate; K=moderate
Rotation considerations: Do not precede or follow tomato family crops
Seed longevity: 2 years

Onions

It's been said that you can't kill an onion. That's an exaggeration, but onions are pretty tough. The first time I bought onion plants through the mail was a real eye-opener; those plants looked dead on arrival. I didn't think they had any chance of survival, let alone to become respectable onions. They did survive; in fact, they thrived and produced as good a crop of onions as I'd ever grown. But, tough as they are, onions do benefit from a bit of extra care when they're young. They'll probably survive regardless, but they'll be excellent instead of simply good if you make sure their soil is always moist for their first two weeks of growth. And keep the weeds at bay. Onions have small root systems close to the soil surface; they don't compete well for water and food.

THE SITE

Onions are picky about certain things, and the soil they call home is one of them. They prefer fertile, loose, friable soil that is well drained with lots of organic matter. Sandy loams are just about ideal. Before planting, turn in good amounts of compost or well-rotted, weed-free manure, no matter what kind of soil you have.

SOWING AND PLANTING

You can grow onions from seeds sown indoors, direct-seed them in the garden, grow them from purchased plants, or grow them from sets. There are more varieties available as seed or plants than as sets, and onions grown from seed or plants store better than those grown from sets.

Growing onions from seeds indoors. Onion plants grow very slowly and need a good head start on the growing season. At least 8 to 10 weeks before the last frost date, sow seeds indoors ¼-inch (6 mm) deep, ½-inch (13 mm) apart in flats or four or five seeds per growing cell. Provide bottom heat and keep the soil moist. When the seedlings are tall enough for the tops to droop, give the plants a haircut (see photo on page 266).

Direct-seeding onions. Because direct-seeding involves the least disturbance in the growth cycle,

▲ **A harvest to cry for.** *With good soil preparation but little through-the-season care, onions are a satisfying crop to grow. These Stockton Reds are a beautiful and colorful red onion suitable for northern regions.*

Sow & Grow

Onions (*Allium cepa*)
Onion family (Liliaceae)

SOWING

Seed depth: For transplants, ½" (1.3 cm); for sets, 1" (2.5 cm); for seeds, ¼–½" (6.5–13 mm)
Soil temperature: 65–85°F (18–29°C)
Days to germination: 4–5
Sow indoors: 2 months before last frost
Sow outdoors: Spring

GROWING

pH range: 6.0–7.5
Soil temperature: 55–75°F (13–24°C)
Spacing in beds: 3–4" (7.5–10 cm); 1" (2.5 cm) if grown like scallions
Watering: Medium and even
Light: Full sun for best yield, tolerates light shade
Nutrient requirements: N=moderate; P=moderate; K=moderate
Rotation considerations: Follow squash or lettuce; do not follow any onion family crop or legume
Seed longevity: 1 year

onions grown this way are less susceptible to stress and disease, less likely to bolt, and store better. Many onion varieties take a long time to mature, however, so direct-seeding is not always practical in northern regions.

In spring, when the soil temperature reaches 50°F (10°C), sow one to three seeds per inch (2.5 cm), ¼- to ½-inch (6–13 mm) deep, in rows 4 inches (10 cm) apart. When the seedlings are about 2 inches (5 cm) tall, begin thinning. To produce onions to be used as scallions, thin to 1 inch (2.5 cm) apart. For the best overall yield, thin to 2 inches (5 cm) apart. And for the largest bulbs, thin to 4 inches (10 cm) apart. The thinnings can be tossed into spring salads or transplanted.

Growing onions from purchased plants. Transplant purchased plants (as well as those you started indoors) to the garden four weeks before the last expected frost. For the best yield per square foot, set plants about 3 to 4 inches (7.5 to 10 cm) apart in staggered rows 8 to 10 inches (20 to 25 cm) apart. If purchased plants have long leaves, trim them back by about a third.

Planting onion sets. Commercial growers produce onion sets by sowing seeds very thickly and then growing the plants very close together. These crowded conditions make the plants mature rapidly, while keeping the bulbs small. This is important because by the time you buy the onion set, it is already one year old and ready to flower (bolt), which you don't want it to do.

Plant onion sets so the pointed top is just even with the soil surface, in a staggered spacing about 3 to 4 inches (7.5 to 10 cm) apart, or in rows 6 to 8 inches (15 to 20 cm) apart. If you grow both plants and sets, put them in different parts of the garden; the sets are sometimes more prone to disease. It goes against my intuition that bigger is better, but smaller onion sets are a better choice than large ones; they're less likely to bolt.

GROWING

Onions don't compete well with weeds and are easily damaged by many weeding tools. Use careful, regular, shallow cultivation to nip weeds early while avoiding damaging roots. Pull by hand any weeds growing within an inch or so (2.5 cm) of the onions.

Watering. Their shallow root systems make onions sensitive to fluctuations in soil moisture. Onions don't need a whole lot of water, but they need it all the time.

▲ Give your onions a sunbath. *When the tops have started to flop over, it's time to pull the onions and start drying them in the sun. When it's time to harvest onions, try to anticipate a warm, dry, sunny spell so the bulbs can sun-cure for at least a week. If it rains, move the bulbs to an open shed, porch, or other covered but airy spot.*

▲ Need a trim? *When seedling tops begin to droop, use shears to cut the plants back to about 3 inches (7.5 cm) high. This stimulates additional root growth. Use the clippings in soups or salads.*

▲ Smaller is better. *Small onion sets are less likely to bolt, so look for bulbs about the size of a dime when you choose sets.*

Monitor soil moisture and water whenever the top inch or so (2.5 cm) of soil gets dry. Watering is most crucial in the first week or so after planting, while the roots are developing. During that critical time, you may need to water every few days, or even every day. Mulch to maintain soil moisture and control weeds; I use grass clippings for this.

Fertilizing. Onions don't require large amounts of nutrients, but their root systems are so small and shallow they need to grow in highly fertile soil just to absorb what they do need. Sidedress with compost in late spring. If needed, apply an organic fertilizer such as fish emulsion once a month. Be stingy. Too much nitrogen will produce lots of leaves and small bulbs. As long as the plants are growing well and have dark green leaves, they shouldn't need additional fertilizer.

HARVEST

Onions are ready to harvest when the tops fall over. Just how many tops in the onion patch have to fall over before you begin to harvest depends on where you live. In cool, humid areas, wait until almost all the tops fall over. In cool, dry areas, harvest when about half the tops have fallen over. And in warm regions, begin harvesting when about a quarter to a third of the tops fall over.

Gently pull onions from the ground, clean off dirt and then leave them to cure in the sun for at least a week. If you don't get a week of sunny weather, move the onions to a dry, well-ventilated place to finish curing. When the tops and papery skin on the bulbs are dry and crinkly, remove any dirt and fragmented skin, clip the tops about an inch (2.5 cm) from the bulbs, trim the roots, and store in onion bags in a cool, dry place.

STORAGE

Not all onions store equally well. Sweet onions, such as Walla Walla, should be used within a few weeks of harvest. Storage onions, such as Copra and Prince, keep well for months. Use storage onions grown from sets first, because they don't store as well as the ones grown from seed or plants. Keep stored onions away from apples or tomatoes. These give off ethylene gas, which causes onions to sprout.

All in the Family: Scallions

True scallions are a specialized onion variety that produces a "bulb" no larger, or only a bit larger, than the base of the leaves. In seed catalogs, true scallions are sometimes called bunching or non-bulbing onions. Scallions are used in salads, soups and as a garnish.

GROWING SCALLIONS

Scallions like a friable, well-drained soil and they like even, constant moisture; but they grow neither as big nor as fast as onions, so they don't need especially

fertile soil and aren't likely to need supplemental fertilizing.

Plant the seeds close together (¼ to ½ inch [6 to 13 mm] apart) in rows an inch (2.5 cm) apart, or broadcast in a 3-inch-wide (8 cm) band. Plant in early spring for summer harvest, in late summer for fall and early winter harvest. Scallions are very hardy and may be wintered over in some areas if mulched well.

BEST VARIETIES

Deep Purple. Deep red.

Evergreen Hardy White. The most winter hardy scallion.

Guardsman. White, from England, and ready for harvest in two months.

Nebechan. Traditional Japanese variety with very good flavor.

Red Beard. White, with a red blush near the base.

Note: Ordinary onions that are pulled before the bulb forms are also called scallions, although that's not what they really are. True scallions have a softer, less penetrating flavor than onions, even if the onions are pulled when small.

VARIETIES

Ailsa Craig Exhibition. These onions are very big. The large bulbs can be over 4 inches (10 cm) in diameter, with ice-white flesh and just enough kick to let you know it's an onion. Best if used fresh but can be stored for a few months.

Copra. This variety produces a yellow onion that stores very well.

Desert Sunrise. A short-day variety with deep red skin and a mild, sweet flavor.

Prince. A large, long-term storage onion. Larger than Copra and stores almost as long.

Stockton Red. Medium-sized, deep red bulbs hold flesh that is mild enough for polite fresh eating, while still having real onion flavor; they also store well. Day neutral.

Stuttgarter. Yellow onions available as sets are usually Stuttgarter. They are pungently oniony and store well.

Walla Walla Sweet. A sweet, mild-flavored onion that has been popular for over a century, it bears juicy white flesh that is excellent in fresh recipes. Does not store well.

Yellow Granex. The sweet, mild onion grown in Vidalia, Georgia, Yellow Granex is very juicy but can be peeled with only a hint of a tear. It's an excellent onion for all warm regions, though your crop will probably be slightly more pungent than those grown in Georgia. A "short day" variety suitable only in the South.

▲ Practical and decorative. *If you braid your onion tops before they dry out, they'll store well and be a pleasure to look at as well.*

The Long and the Short of It

Onions are divided into three types, long-day, short-day and day-neutral. Long-day varieties grow well in the North; short-day varieties, in the South. North and South? Call it that the dividing line is about the Oklahoma/Kansas border. Day-neutral varieties will grow anywhere.

Short-day varieties, which need about equal amounts of darkness and light to set bulbs, grow best in southern regions: Yellow Granex, often called Vidalia.

Long-day varieties, which need about 14 hours of light and 10 of darkness, are favored in the North: Ailsa Craig, Borettana, Copra, First Edition, and Walla Walla.

Day-neutral varieties will produce bulbs anywhere in the continental United States: Candy, Stockton Red.

All in the Family: Shallot

The shallot, onion's mild-tasting cousin, looks something like a cross between onion and garlic. On the outside, shallots look sort of like an onion, but they're not. On the inside, they look sort of like garlic, but they're not. A shallot is its own special self. When a recipe calls for shallots, there's nothing else that will really fill the bill. They are costly at the market, but they're easy to grow in the garden, and once you have a big enough harvest to save your own seed stock, they're free.

SOWING AND GROWING

You can grow shallots from sets or, if you have a growing season of at least 100 days, from seeds. Starting with sets is initially more expensive, but easier. To start from seeds, sow indoors 8 to 10 weeks before the last frost date (same as onions) and transplant a bit later than you'd plant peas or direct sow in early spring. Space transplants 2 inches (5 cm) apart. Seeds planted ½ inch (13 mm) apart will produce single shallots; wider spacing will produce clusters. To grow shallots from sets, separate the bulbs into cloves and plant in early spring 6 inches (15 cm) apart, pointed end up, so that ¾ of the clove is buried. In warm climates, plant in the mid- to late fall.

Plant shallots in full sun, in friable, fertile soil enriched with plenty of compost. Keep them well weeded and well watered, and they'll do the rest. Like their onion cousins, they're not likely to be troubled by pests.

HARVEST AND STORAGE

Harvest shallots when the leaves have begun to turn brown and flop over. Cure in the sun as you would onions or garlic and store in a cool, dry place. After the first crop, save your biggest bulbs for planting.

Saffron

Pikant

VARIETIES

Ambition. A large, half-long French variety that stores well. Available as seed.

Saffron. Copper skin with pale yellow flesh; stores very well. Available as seed.

Pikant. French style, mahogany skin and a reddish interior; high yield and stores well. Grown from sets.

Orach

Orach, sometimes called mountain spinach, tastes a bit like spinach. Unlike spinach, though, it can tolerate warm weather without bolting and it comes in different colors — green, red, and gold — each with a subtly different flavor. All that, and it has three times the vitamin C of spinach.

SOWING AND GROWING

Pick a spot with full sun or partial shade and work some compost into the soil.

Sow seeds every two weeks beginning in early spring and continuing until the weather warms. Orach tolerates warm weather but tastes best when temperatures are cool. Pinch back the tips to increase leaf production and discourage bolting.

HARVEST

Begin harvesting leaves at 1 to 2 inches (2.5 to 5 cm) long for salads or at 2 to 4 inches (5 to 10 cm) long for steaming or stir-fry. You can gather the leaves individually until the plants begin to flower, or cut the entire plant at the soil line when it's about 6 inches (15 cm) tall. The leaves are tender and mild flavored, a good addition to summer salads when most other greens have bolted and become bitter.

VARIETIES

Gold orach, such as Aureus, bears yellowish gold leaves with a softer flavor than either red or green orach.

Green orach, such as Green Spires, produces attractive green foliage with a balanced, slightly sweet flavor.

Red orach, including Rubra and Purple Savoyed, produces dark, wine-red leaves with a rich spinach-like taste.

▲ **Seeing red.** *Colorful in the garden and in the bowl, red orach is an excellent addition to your salad garden.*

Sow & Grow

Orach (*Atriplex hortensis*)
Goosefoot family (Chenopodiaceae)

SOWING

Seed depth: ½" (13 mm)
Germination soil temperature: 50–65°F (10–18°C)
Days to germination: 7–14
Sow indoors: 3 weeks before last frost
Sow outdoors: After soil reaches germination temperature

GROWING

pH range: 6.5–7.5
Growing soil temperature: 50–75°F (10–24°C)
Spacing in beds: 2" (5 cm); thin to 6" (15 cm)
Watering: Moderate
Light: Full sun to partial shade
Nutrient requirements: N=moderate; P=moderate; K=moderate
Rotation considerations: Do not follow or precede beet, spinach, or Swiss chard
Seed longevity: 5 years

Parsnips

Some people invest in the stock market; I invest in parsnips. This pale cousin of the carrot is like a bank certificate of deposit. I deposit some seeds and labor during the warm months, and my investment matures early the next spring, when my vegetable reserves are at their yearly low. An early-April meal of parsnips fresh from the still-slumbering garden renews my energy and restores my faith that summer is just ahead.

THE SITE

Parsnips like a deeply dug, friable soil, but too much nitrogen fertilizer or recently added manure makes the roots fork and become hairy.

SOWING AND GROWING

Parsnips can take even longer to germinate than carrots (about two to three weeks). Plant seeds ½ inch (1.3 cm) deep and 1 inch (2.5 cm) apart in rows 4 to 6 inches (10 to 15 cm) apart across a bed. Keep the soil evenly moist during the germination period. If your soil tends to form a crust, cover the seeds with sifted compost rather than soil; the seedlings are not strong enough to break through a crust.

When the parsnips are 4 to 6 inches (10 to 15 cm) high, thin them to 3 to 4 inches (7.5 to 10 cm) apart, apply a layer of leaf mold around the plants, and mulch with straw. That's it. Your part is done until harvest next spring. (If you run into a problem with carrot fly maggots, grow parsnips under a row cover until the tops are 3 to 4 inches [8 to 10 cm] tall.)

HARVEST AND STORAGE

You can harvest parsnips at the end of the growing season, but they don't develop their sweet, almost nutty flavor until after they've been through some hard frosts and preferably through a hard winter. Mark the rows so you'll know where the roots are before the foliage appears in the spring; flavor and texture take a nosedive once the tops start to grow. Loosen the soil with a garden fork or broadfork and harvest the whole crop at once. Store in the fridge or root cellar.

▲ Spring tonic. *To me, a true sign of spring is a dish of parsnips, sliced thinly and sautéed in a little butter over a low flame until they're tender.*

Sow & Grow

Parsnips (*Pastinaca sativa*)
Carrot family (Umbelliferae)

SOWING

Seed depth: ½" (13 mm)
Soil temperature: 65–75°F (18–24°C)
Days to germination: 12–14
Sow indoors: Not recommended
Sow outdoors: As soon as soil can be worked

GROWING

pH range: 6.0–7.0
Soil temperature: 60–65°F (16–18°C)
Spacing in beds: 4" (10 cm), in rows 4" apart
Watering: Moderate
Light: Best yields in full sun; tolerates light shade
Nutrient requirements: N=high; P=low; K=low
Rotation considerations: Avoid following carrot, parsley, or celery
Seed longevity: 1 year

VARIETIES

Harris Model. Snowy white flesh, smooth texture, and exceptional flavor.

Lancer. Harris type with uniform roots, disease resistance, and excellent flavor; more resistant to canker than Harris Model.

Peanuts

▲ Surprise! *Peanuts, like potatoes, grow underground, so you don't see your harvest until you dig them up. It's like waiting to open a birthday present.*

Up here in Vermont, we love peanuts, but we can't grow them; peanuts don't like cool climates. But in warm climates these relatives of peas and alfalfa are a standard part of the vegetable garden. You can choose from among four peanut types: Runner, a commercial type; Virginia, which has large kernels; Spanish, which are early maturers and therefore good in cooler climates; and Valencia, with sweet, small kernels. I haven't grown peanuts, so the following is the best advice I've been able to garner from gardeners who have grown them.

SOWING AND GROWING

Before planting, work some compost or well-rotted manure into the soil. Peanuts do best in soils rich in calcium, so add limestone (which also raises pH) or gypsum (which does not raise pH).

Sow seed peanuts in a hole 4 inches (10 cm) deep or in a furrow about 2 inches (5 cm) deep. As the seedlings grow, fill in around the base of the plants with loose soil. About a month after the stems emerge from the soil, blossoms develop near the bottom of the plant. When the petals fall off, the peg (the flower stem and peanut embryo) bends downward and grows into the loose soil. After all the pegs have buried themselves in the soil, mulch around the plants with a layer of straw.

HARVEST

Two months after the plants bloom, test for ripeness by lifting a plant with a garden fork. A ripe peanut will feel firm, with dry, papery outer skin. When peanuts are ripe, lift plants from the ground with a fork and shake off excess soil. Cure plants by laying them on a screen in the sun for two or three days. Next, separate the peanuts from the plants, return the nuts to the screen, and place the screen in a warm, dry location for about three weeks.

Sow & Grow

Peanuts (*Arachis hypogaea*)
Pea family (Leguminosae)

SOWING

Seed depth: 3–4" (7.5–10 cm)
Germination soil temperature: 70°F (21°C)
Days to germination: 7–14
Sow indoors: 3 weeks before last frost, but difficult to transplant
Sow outdoors: After last frost

GROWING

pH range: 6.0–7.0
Growing soil temperature: 70–85°F (21–29°C)
Spacing in beds: 18" (45 cm)
Watering: Heavy until peg enters soil; moderate thereafter
Light: Full sun
Nutrient requirements: N=low; P=moderate; K=moderate
Rotation considerations: Follow root crops such as carrot; avoid following legume crops
Seed longevity: 1–3 years

Peas

Peas are a very, very popular part of the Smith garden. Many of these sweet and tender orbs never make it out of the garden; we eat them raw as a bonus for whoever has drawn pea-picking duty. During pea season, it is rare to have a meal go by without at least one pea-centered dish: new potatoes and peas, peas in the salad, or just a heaping bowl of steamed peas with a dash of salt and a pat of butter. And whatever we don't eat fresh goes in the freezer to brighten meals in the middle of winter.

SOWING

Tradition holds that you plant peas "as soon as the soil can be worked," but actually the colder the soil, the more slowly they germinate: from nine days in 60°F (16°C) soil to 36 days in 40°F (4°C) soil. If you plant peas really early, you will usually get peas sooner, but you may get fewer peas; germination rate is likely to drop if the spring weather is too cold.

Germination isn't the only problem here. Soil-dwelling bacteria, including the ones that capture nitrogen to feed legume-family plants like peas, are not very active in cold soil. If you plant peas early, apply some fish or fish/seaweed liquid fertilizer to tide the plants over until the bacteria become able to supply enough nitrogen. Perhaps a compromise is best: Plant some peas early for an early harvest and plant the main crop a bit later. Don't hold off too long, though, because peas don't bear as well in hot weather. Around here, in northern New England, late-planted peas should be ready by mid-July, the early ones around the Fourth of July. Before I plant, I like to let the soil warm up a little, or use dark plastic mulch to warm the soil, so the seeds spend less time in the ground.

Ask a bunch of gardeners about how far apart to space pea seeds, and you'll hear everything from ½ inch to 4 inches (1.3 to 10 cm). I've had good results with very close spacing, about 1 inch (2.5 cm), staggered in narrow bands on both sides of a trellis.

▲ **Plan in fall for next summer's crop of peas.** *Since peas are one of the first crops to be sown in spring, you'll get the most from your pea crop if you get the soil ready for the spring planting in fall by turning in lots of compost or rotted manure.*

Sow & Grow

Peas (*Pisum sativum, P. s.* var. *macrocarpon*)
Pea family (Leguminosae)

SOWING

Seed depth: 1" (2.5 cm)
Soil temperature: 40–75°F (4–24°C), the optimum is 75°F (24°C)
Days to germination: 14
Sow indoors: Not recommended
Sow outdoors: As soon as soil can be worked; late summer for fall crop

GROWING

pH range: 6.0–7.0
Soil temperature: 60–65°F (16–18°C)
Spacing in beds: 1" (2.5 cm) in a staggered pattern
Watering: Moderate until blossoming, then low
Light: Best yield in full sun; tolerates partial shade
Nutrient requirements: N=low; P=low; K=low
Rotation considerations: Follow with kale
Seed longevity: 3 years

GROWING

You may hear that you needn't fertilize peas because they can get nitrogen right from the air. As with much garden wisdom, this is *almost* correct. The truth is that the bacteria that provide peas with nitrogen don't do this trick at the drop of a hat. It takes a few weeks (and soil warm enough to activate the bacteria) before the plant actually gets any nitrogen from the bacteria. Meanwhile, the plant has to get its nitrogen from the soil like any other plant. To help them along, when seedlings are 2 to 4 inches (5 to 10 cm) tall, fertilize them lightly with fish emulsion or other complete organic fertilizer.

HARVEST

Like corn, peas are delightfully sweet if you pick them at the right time, but they turn starchy if you don't. When you pick, pick everything that's ripe, including what's overripe. If the overripe pods stay on the plant, they send a signal that it's okay to stop producing new pods. Put the passé peas in the compost pile.

"Ripe" varies with the kind of pea you're picking.

Snow peas. Pick snow peas as soon as the pod reaches mature length but before the peas in the pod are very much developed. Check often: The "just-right" stage doesn't last more than a day or so.

Sugar snap peas. These are best when both the pods and the peas are plump and the pods snap like a bean pod. If the pod is stringy, remove the "string" by breaking off the tip and then pulling the string up the inside curve and down the outside.

Shelling peas. For best flavor and texture, pick garden peas when pods have filled out but aren't bulging around the peas. Pick all the large ones you missed earlier. Pods left too long on the vine signal the plant to stop producing more peas. Things can get a bit tricky here, because different varieties look and feel different when they're at their best. With each variety, pick a pod that looks and feels right, pop it open, and do the old taste test right there in the garden. Go on testing until you've got it right. And then do it again for the next variety.

Inoculate…or Not?

The bacteria that form a symbiotic (mutually beneficial) relationship with legumes are present naturally in biologically active soil but in fairly small numbers. It is, therefore, generally recommended that pea growers purchase some of these bacteria (embedded in a black powder) to inoculate the seeds and ensure that enough bacteria are present to do the required nitrogen fixing. That is definitely a good idea in soil that doesn't have much biological activity. But it may not be necessary in biologically active soil. Bacteria multiply very quickly when conditions are right, and legumes are well equipped to attract and feed the specific bacteria they need to work with. If your soil is well-nourished with good compost, you probably don't need the expense and extra work of inoculating seeds. I can't see any difference in my garden between inoculated on non-inoculated plants. Plants have been doing this for longer than we gardeners have, and they have things figured out pretty well.

▲ **Simple and sturdy.** *After trying other ways, I've gone back to growing peas on a chicken-wire trellis.*

Trellising Tricks

Peas are healthier and easier to harvest when they grow on netting, wire mesh, or some sort of a trellis (see pages 76–77). If a vine strays from the netting, just direct it back. If the whole mass bulges out too far, attach some garden twine to one end of the trellis, and then weave the twine in and out of the netting strings. Pull the twine taut, and then tie the twine to the post at the opposite end of the trellis.

I used netting for several years but am back to using chicken wire supported by metal posts, the method favored by the "old-timers" hereabouts. It is not much fun to erect, but the pea vines attach to it more easily and stay attached better.

If you can find enough 4-foot (1.2 m) straight brush an inch (2.5 cm) in diameter at the big end (chokecherry branches are favored around here), you can make brush trellises. Push the pieces about a foot (30 cm) into the soil close enough together so that they form a fence for the vines to climb upon.

▲ **Good wood.** *A brush trellis is effective and free (if you can find enough brush).*

VARIETIES

Shelling Peas

Eclipse. A breakthrough variety, this pea maintains its sweetness for much longer than other peas. Doesn't germinate well in cold soil, so hold off planting until the soil begins to warm.

Feisty. A new variety and a bit of an oddball, it has many tendrils and few leaves, making it easy to harvest and providing a supplemental harvest of pea tendrils, a popular garnish in fancy restaurants. Highly recommended.

Green Arrow. A high-yield variety, Green Arrow produces flavorful peas on 3- to 4-foot-tall (0.9–1.2 m) vines.

Knight. Plants produce plentiful, very early pods on 2½-foot-tall (76 cm) vines.

Lincoln. A reliable heirloom, Lincoln bears long, slender pods filled with sweet peas.

Snow Peas

Some popular varieties include Corgi, with thin, sweet pods that taste great in stir-fries; Norli, with early, very high yields of flavorful, sweet pods; and Oregon Giant, with very large pods around sweet, tiny peas.

Sugar Snap Peas

Thick, succulent, edible pods hold a host of sweet peas. Look for Super Sugar Mel, the best of the sugar peas, with disease resistance, early and heavy yields, and long, sweet pods; and Super Sugar Snap, a tall (6 feet [1.8 m]) variety bearing loads of sweet, tasty peas.

▲ **Mind your peas.** *Picked at just the right time, before the peas in the pod have developed very much, snow peas are tender and sweet, but over-large pods are tough and stringy.*

Peppers

Short and blocky. Long and skinny. Sweet, tart, or hot — anywhere from barely hot to blazing. And all the colors — green (of course), red, yellow, orange, lavender, and white, even chocolate brown. There's a lot more to peppers than just the blocky green fruits most of us associate with the word. And the pepper revue gets better and better as plant breeders introduce new colors, different flavors, and varying degrees of heat. But whatever the form or flavor, peppers need pretty much the same growing conditions and care.

THE SITE

Give peppers a warm and sunny spot where neither peppers nor their kinfolk (tomatoes, eggplant, and potatoes — the nightshade crew) have grown in the past three or four years. In a small garden, that may not be easy; just do the best you can. Peppers need well-drained, fertile soil with adequate phosphorus and calcium and not too much nitrogen.

Peppers are, by the way, very good container plants; you can save garden space and simplify your crop rotation problems by growing peppers in containers.

SOWING

Most of peppers' special needs have something to do with temperature: They are very sensitive to frost at each end of the growing cycle. They like relatively high temperatures for germination and for growth outdoors. But oddly, they produce better with a jolt of cold early in life shortly after they germinate.

TOO MUCH OF A GOOD THING

Like their tomato cousins, peppers can pig out on nitrogen when there's too much of it around. The result is nice, green leafy plants with very little fruit. Give peppers a nice, fertile soil, but don't add extra nitrogen and go a bit light on the rotted manure.

▲ **More than just a pretty face.** *Tasty, colorful, good raw or cooked; peppers are all of that and more: They're a good source of potassium, folic acid, iron, and vitamin B_6 dietary fiber. Green — technically unripe —peppers contain 200 times the recommended amount of vitamin C, red pepper, 300 times, and yellow ones even more than that.*

Sow & Grow

Peppers (*Capsicum annuum*)
Tomato family (Solanaceae)

SOWING

Seed depth: ¼" (6 mm)
Soil temperature: 80–85°F (27–29°C)
Days to germination: 6–8
Sow indoors: 8 weeks before last frost
Sow outdoors: Not recommended

GROWING

pH range: 5.5–7.0 (best results may occur at the acid end of this range)
Soil temperature: 70–85°F (21–29°C)
Spacing in beds: 12" (30 cm)
Watering: Moderate and even
Light: Full sun
Nutrient requirements: N=moderate; P=high; K=high
Rotation considerations: Do not follow or succeed tomato, eggplant, potato
Seed longevity: 2 years

▲ **A bit of a shiver does peppers good.** *After a warm germination period, peppers benefit from about a month in the cold before spending the rest of their pre-garden stage in more moderate temperatures.*

Amp It Up

For increased flower and fruit production, try this: As soon as the first true leaves appear, transplant into 4-inch (10 cm) pots and lower the soil temperature to 70°F (21°C), 60°F (16°C) at night. When the third set of true leaves appears, lower the night temperature to 55°F (13°C) for four weeks. Moving plants from the house to a cold frame will likely accomplish this. At the end of four weeks, grow the plants at 70°F (21°C) day and night until it's time to put them in the garden. **Note:** Plants treated this way should be started two weeks earlier than otherwise.

▲ **Harvest hint.** *Pepper plants are brittle: if you try to twist or break the fruits free of the stem, you may damage the stem. Use a sharp knife instead, or, better yet, floral scissors or pruning shears.*

About eight weeks before the last frost date, fill flats with germination mix, sow the seeds ¼ inch (6 mm) deep and water well. Keep the soil warm, between 80° and 85°F (27–29°C). Warm temperatures are very important for quick germination. Temperatures below 80°F mean slow germination, and slow germination gets the plants off to a poor start.

Because pepper seeds like it warmer than people do, you may need to use a heat mat or find a warm place over a radiator. If you can manage it, grow peppers under grow lights for 16 hours a day. They do best with more light than they get from the late winter sun. Remove any blossoms that appear before transplanting time and a couple of weeks afterward.

GROWING

Peppers love heat, so don't rush them into the garden before the soil is thoroughly warm. "Warm" means soil temperature of 60°F (16°C) and minimum night air temperature of 50°F (10°C). Use plastic mulch (either black or IRT) to warm the soil and floating row covers to warm the plants once you've put them out.

Plant 1 foot (30 cm) apart, depending on mature plant size, or two rows in a 36-inch (90 cm) bed. Peppers like each other's company and grow best when close enough so the leaves of the mature plants are barely touching. As my mother used to say, "Peppers like to hold hands."

Keep the soil evenly moist and remove the row covers when flower buds appear or the air temperature exceeds 85°F (29°C). In my experience, peppers are generally free of disease and insect problems.

HARVEST AND STORAGE

You can harvest peppers when they're green, but they're not completely ripe until they turn red (or whatever other color they're meant to turn). When you harvest is largely a matter of personal preference. Red sweet peppers (bell peppers) are sweeter than green sweet peppers. And red hot peppers are hotter than most green hot peppers. People who prefer green peppers do get a slight advantage over those favoring red: As long as you pick the fruits at the green stage instead of letting them ripen to red, the plant goes right on setting new fruits. Pick when the fruits are red (or yellow, orange or brown) and you'll have sweeter peppers but fewer of them.

Peppers keep in the refrigerator for about two weeks. We like to freeze them for spaghetti sauce or soups by slicing them and putting them in a plastic pint freezer container. It's easy to dry red peppers. Just lay them on a screen or string them and hang them in a dry, airy spot. Dried peppers remain flavorful for about a year when stored in clean glass jars.

VARIETIES

Sweet Peppers
Ace. A bell type and undemanding, Ace produces bountiful, early crops of large, slightly conical fruits.

Bianca. High yielding Bianca peppers start out ivory and then turn red.

Gourmet. This pepper ripens from green to a deep orange, with a sweet taste and thick walls; an easy keeper that adapts well to varied growing conditions.

Hungarian Sweet Banana. Long and thin-walled, this pepper bears yellow to orange, very tasty fruits.

Islander. These colorful peppers have thick flesh and a mild, semisweet taste. They ripen through a stage with violet, yellow, and orange streaks, to all violet and finally to dark red.

Jingle Bells. Producing medium-sized fruits on a compact plant, this is our favorite container pepper.

Purple Beauty. An open-pollinated bell type that's as colorful as a pepper can get, it bears crisp, sweet fruits that start out green, change to purple and then to a deep purple-red.

Sunray. Sunset on a pepper plant! These Dutch-style peppers turn stunning orange when ripe.

Sunrise Orange Bell. Bred for cooler climates, this pepper bears nice, big, blocky, yellow-orange fruits.

Sweet Chocolate. Named for its deep brown skin color but not, alas, for its taste, Sweet Chocolate peppers have a very mild flavor. This variety is more tolerant of cool weather than most varieties and bears reliably large crops.

Specialty and Ethnic Sweet Peppers
Apple. Pimiento type, mild flavor, and juicy, these reach peak flavor just as the fruits turn from green to red.

Italia. Long, shaped like a bull's horn, the Italia starts out green and gradually changes to dark red with a full, sweet flavor. We've found that the plants tend to flop; they need to grow in a cage or be tied to a stake.

Islander

Italia

Apple

Sweet Chocolate

Ace

Hot Peppers

Anaheim. A hot pepper with manners, this variety bears long fruit that is pleasingly mild, with only a suggestion of its hot pepper heritage.

Bulgarian Carrot. Bearing 4-inch (10 cm) long, bright orange fruits, Bulgarian Carrot peppers add warmth to any recipe.

Chilly Chili. A chili in shape and color, but mild in flavor, this variety is a good container plant and very pretty, with simultaneous white, yellow, orange, and red fruits.

Firenza Jalapeño. This is the plant to choose if you want large crops of thick-walled, flavorful hot peppers.

Numex Joe E. Parker. Hot enough to add zip and mild enough to be invited back, Numex Joe E. Parker produces more, and better-tasting, peppers than most hot varieties.

Numex Twilight: A gorgeous chili whose fruits start off purple, then turn yellow, orange, and finally red.

Prairie Fire. Fruits change from chartreuse to cream, then yellow, to orange, and finally to red and have a pungent, fruity flavor. The beautiful plants are excellent candidates for container growing.

Pretty in Purple. Leaves are purple or variegated purple and green. Fruits start out purple and ripen to yellow, orange, and scarlet. Mixed colors are on the plant at the same time; good for containers.

Thai Dragon. One of the best varieties for Asian recipes, Thai Dragon bears lots of 3-inch-long (7.5 cm) peppers that are very hot.

That Warm Feeling Inside

For centuries people knew that not all hot peppers were created equal; some were much hotter than others. Around 1912 Wilbur Scoville discovered a rather complicated way to measure the "heat" of peppers. Today we know the spiciness of a pepper depends on how much capsaicin it contains. Yet in honor of his contributions to pepper lovers, the heat of peppers is still measured in Scoville units. As a point of reference for understanding the following rankings, pure capsaicin is rated at 15,500,000 Scoville units.

Pepper name	Scoville Units
Bell Pepper	0
Anaheim	500–2,500
Jalapeño	2,500–4,500
Serrano	7,000–25,000
Cayenne	30,000–50,000
Thai	70,000–100,000
Habañero	100,000–325,000
Red Savina Habañero	350,000–550,000

Pretty in Purple

Prairie Fire

Potatoes

Commercial growers supply us with so many potatoes that they seem to be everywhere, supermarkets to fast-food restaurants. And they're cheap. With such abundance, why allocate space in the garden for potatoes? That's a no-brainer: Homegrown potatoes, especially fresh-from-the-garden new potatoes, taste way better than store-bought. Plus, you can grow potato varieties commercial producers just don't grow.

THE SITE

Potatoes like to grow in fertile, well-drained soil in full sun. They're not fussy about soil pH; anything from 5.0 to 6.8 will do. Some gardeners recommend a pH around 5 to prevent scab, but others report scab-free potatoes in sweeter soil, provided fertility is high.

PLANTING

Time your potato planting according to where you live:
- **In warm climates,** plant in fall.
- **In warm-temperate areas,** plant in late winter.
- **In cool climates,** plant in early to midspring, about the time dandelions and daffodils bloom.

You'll get off to the best start with certified organic, disease-free seed potatoes you can buy from garden centers or seed catalogs (the latter is more likely to have many varieties). As long as your crop stays free of disease, save some of your own potatoes for seed. If the yield starts to go down, or the foliage doesn't look as healthy as it has in the past, buy some new seed stock.

Some seed potatoes are larger than others. You can plant golf-ball-size tubers directly into the ground without any advance preparation. Cut large tubers into pieces about 1½ inches thick (3.75 cm). Make sure each piece contains at least two "eyes." The eyes should be just beginning to sprout, but not so much that a stem has formed. As a rule of thumb, each piece should weigh between 1½ and 2 ounces (45 and 60 g). To heal the cut potatoes, place them in a well-ventilated area at about 55°F (13°C) for one or two days.

▲ A rainbow of potatoes. *Not too long ago, garden catalogs carried just a couple of potato varieties. Well, things have changed. Today the selection is so diverse that gardeners can even buy a rainbow of potatoes, from yellow to red to blue — and when you get to the end of the rainbow, gold.*

Sow & Grow

Potatoes (*Solanum tuberosum*)
Tomato family (Solanaceae)

SOWING/PLANTING
Tuber depth: 3–4" (7.5–10 cm)
Soil temperature: At least 45°F (7°C)
Plant tubers outdoors: 3 weeks before last frost

GROWING
pH range: 5.0–6.5
Soil temperature: 60–65°F (16–18°C)
Spacing in beds: 12" (30 cm)
Watering: Moderate, particularly during tuber formation, signaled by the appearance of blossoms
Light: Full sun for best yields; tolerates partial shade
Nutrient requirements: N=high; P=high; K=high
Rotation considerations: Do not follow with tomato family crops

Traditional planting method. It's usual to plant potatoes about 1 foot (30 cm) apart in a shallow trench about 3 inches (7.5 cm) deep. When the plants are about a foot (30 cm) tall, "hill" them by drawing soil up around them with a hoe until just the top few inches of the plant poke out from the soil. Some gardeners hill a second time two or three weeks later. Hilling keeps the potatoes from turning green, which happens if the tubers are exposed to sunlight.

Post-hole variation. In well-loosened soil, using a post-hole digger, make a series of foot-deep (30 cm), 4-inch (10 cm) diameter holes down the center of a 30-inch-wide (75 cm) bed. Drop a potato or potato

▲ **Potato prep.** *Cut large tubers into 1½-inch-thick (3.75 cm) pieces, and then let them heal in a cool place for a couple of days.*

▲ **This amounts to a hill of potatoes.** *When the plants are 12 inches (30 cm) tall, hill the soil around them so that just a few inches of the plants show above the soil.*

piece in each hole and cover with about 3 inches (8 cm) of soil. As the plants develop, gradually fill the holes. Filling the holes has the same effect as hilling and prevents greening of the tubers.

Mulch planting variation. Growing potatoes under mulch conserves soil moisture and moderates soil temperature, makes the potatoes easier to harvest, and is less work all around than the traditional method. But straw costs money, so this method is more expensive. Plant in trenches 3 inches (7.5 cm) deep and 1 foot (30 cm) apart. When plants are a few inches tall, apply 1 inch (2.5 cm) of compost topped by a layer of straw so that about a half to two-thirds of each plant is covered. As the plants grow, add more straw, keeping the mulch at least 6 inches (15 cm) deep. Note: Straw mulch also provides a home for beneficial garden denizens like toads, which is a good thing ... and toad predators, like snakes, which you may not experience as a good thing.

GROWING

Potatoes are especially sensitive to changes in soil moisture when they are forming tubers — between the time they flower and two weeks before harvest. Monitor soil moisture and water whenever the soil is dry more than 2 inches (5 cm) down.

Your best defense against potato disease is a good offense — fertile soil. Prevention is the only organic

A Pound of Prevention

Get your crop off to the right start with a couple of simple precautions that should help prevent disease:

- "Seed potatoes" are potatoes grown specifically for planting. To avoid potato diseases, purchase only certified tubers. Avoid planting supermarket potatoes, which can carry disease and are often treated with a chemical to inhibit sprouting.

- Enrich the soil with compost, not manure, which can increase the incidence of potato scab. Potatoes can tolerate a higher pH without forming scab in a well-balanced, fertile soil.

option here; once blight happens, it's too late to do anything about it.

Potato's bug of choice is the Colorado potato beetle, a rather pretty, stubby, round beetle with a big appetite for potato leaves. There are poisons of various kinds and potencies to deal with these creatures in their adult and larval stages; I don't use or recommend any of them. When the adult beetles show up, shortly after the first potato leaves emerge, check each plant daily. Remove and destroy any beetles you find and — most important — whenever you find a beetle, check the undersides of all the leaves on that plant for clusters of bright orange eggs. Crush the eggs, or clip off the entire leaf, eggs and all, and crush or drop into some soapy water. If you get all the eggs, you'll have no voracious larvae to deal with later. Even if you only get most of the eggs, the larval problem will be small and manageable by handpicking.

HARVEST AND STORAGE

You can harvest some tender "new" potatoes a couple of months after planting, either by pulling a plant or by feeling around and snitching one or two from each plant, leaving the rest undisturbed.

Harvest the main crop when the foliage dies back. With a garden fork or broadfork, gently and carefully (lest you pierce a potato) loosen the soil and feel around for the tubers. Harvesting is easier on the hands and better for the potatoes if you let the soil dry out a bit before the harvest.

Leave the potatoes on the ground until the soil on them dries. Brush dry soil gently from the tubers, but don't wash them. Cure for about two weeks at around 55°F (13°C) in humid conditions, and then store at about 40°F (4°C) in a root cellar. Don't store potatoes with apples.

From a Seedy Beginning

Almost all potatoes are grown from other potatoes, but it doesn't have to be that way: A few catalogs do sell potato seed. Sow the seeds indoors about eight weeks before the last frost, and grow as you would tomato seedlings. Harden off the plants and transplant to the garden after there's no danger of frost. Then, grow and harvest as you would potatoes grown from seed potatoes. Advantage? It's sure cheaper: 25 seeds for about $3 instead of $10 a pound for seed potatoes.

VARIETIES

All Blue. (Late) Colorful and flavorful, All Blue bears lots of potatoes, which feature indigo skin and blue and white flesh.

All Red. (Early) A scab-resistent variety, All Red has cranberry red skin and rose-colored flesh.

Catalina. (Late) Buff skin with creamy flesh, Catalina is good for boiling, mashing, roasting, or frying and can be grown in containers.

Gold Rush. (Midseason) One of the best baking potatoes, Gold Rush has a flaky texture and sweet-flavored flesh. Stores well.

Kennebec. (Late) One of the most versatile varieties, with well-formed, yellowish tubers that are very flavorful, Kennebec is disease resistant and stores well.

Red Norland. (Early) Excellent for new potatoes but also stores well. This variety has smooth, red skin and white flesh that is good for baking, boiling, or roasting.

Russian Banana. (Late) Banana-shaped fingerling potatoes with yellowish skin and waxy, light yellow flesh, these have excellent flavor and don't fall apart when boiled.

Yukon Gold. (Early–mid) These vigorous plants produce large, flavorful tubers that have yellow flesh and store well. This is my favorite potato.

Pumpkins

There's a lot of good food wasted when untold thousands of nutritious pumpkins get turned into jack-o-lanterns. Pumpkins make a very good custard; put the custard in a pie shell, and you've got a pumpkin pie. But in olden times the pumpkin menu went well beyond dessert. After all, a pumpkin is a big, orange winter squash, and it can be used as such — baked, steamed, or in soups or stews. And both the blossoms and the seeds are edible, too.

THE SITE

Pumpkins are really a kind of winter squash, and they like pretty much the same growing conditions as the rest of the family. Give these big vines fertile, well-drained soil enriched with lots of compost or well-rotted manure, even moisture, and plenty of room to roam.

SOWING AND GROWING

Like other winter squashes, pumpkins need a long, frost-free growing season; it is difficult to provide them with that in colder climates unless you start them indoors and transplant them after danger of frost is past. But like other winter squashes, pumpkins don't transplant well. What to do?

One option, the way we generally have the best luck with, is to warm the pumpkin patch with black plastic, IRT plastic, or landscape fabric. Either remove the plastic when the soil is warm, or leave it, cut some round holes, and plant the pumpkin seeds. Cover everything with row covers to protect against cold and to deter squash beetles. Remove the row cover for a few hours a day when blossoms appear. You may need to cover pumpkins again in the fall if a hard frost threatens before the fruits are fully ripe.

Alternatively, start the seeds indoors about three weeks before the last frost. If the plants are still young and small when they're transplanted, the roots are less likely to be damaged. (Nonetheless, be very careful.) If frost threatens, protect the plants with row covers or hot caps. Harden off the seedlings for about a week

▲ **Taking the cure.** *After you cut pumpkins from the vine, let them sit in the sun for a week to cure. The skins will harden, and the stems will dry out.*

Sow & Grow

Pumpkin (*Cucurbita pepo*)
Cucumber family (Cucurbitaceae)

SOWING

Seed depth: ½–1" (1.3–2.5 cm)
Germination soil temperature: 70–90°F (21–32°C) (optimum 90°F [32°C])
Days to germination: 6–10
Sow indoors: 3–4 weeks before last frost
Sow outdoors: When soil temperature reaches 70°F (21°C); use row covers or hot caps during cool weather

GROWING

pH range: 5.5–6.5
Soil temperature: 65–75°F (18–24°C)
Spacing in beds: 12–18" (30–45 cm)
Watering: Heavy and even
Light: Full sun
Nutrient requirements: N=high; P=moderate; K=moderate
Rotation considerations: Do not follow squash family members (summer and winter squash, melon, or cucumber)
Seed longevity: 4 years

by reducing water and moving them outdoors for gradually increasing periods of time.

Regardless of the method you choose to get things started, add plenty of compost or well-rotted manure where pumpkins will grow. These are big, big plants growing big fruits; they'll need all the food you can give them.

HARVEST

Pumpkins are ready to harvest when the stem has started to dry and the pumpkin skin has begun to harden. Leave about an inch (2.5 cm) of stem. Handle with care. Don't carry them around by the stem; if it breaks off, the pumpkin won't cure or store well.

If the weather is dry and sunny, pumpkins can be cured in the field in about a week. Cover or move inside if a hard frost threatens. Store at about 55°F (13°C). (Under the bed in a spare room works well.)

VARIETIES

Baby Bear. The 1993 All-America winner is a good pie pumpkin with semi-hulless seeds that are tasty roasted.

Howden. If you're buying a jack-o-lantern pumpkin, it's very likely to be a Howden.

Long Pie. This heirloom pumpkin doesn't look much like a pumpkin. At first glance, it looks like a zucchini that managed to avoid harvest and turned into a monster. It's even green when harvested, so the disguise is pretty convincing. (Long Pie continues to ripen after harvest; it will eventually turn a proper pumpkin orange.) But it is a pumpkin and a tasty one; very vigorous and very productive.

New England Pie. The standard pie pumpkin for years, New England Pie pumpkin bears small, 5-pound (2 kg), nicely shaped fruits with flavorful, smooth, bright orange flesh.

Wee-B-Little. This is a miniature pumpkin with the classic round pumpkin shape, rather than the squashed look of many small pumpkins. The round, 3- to 4-inch (7.5 to 10 cm) diameter fruits are perfect for decorating the holiday table.

Personalized Pumpkins

While pumpkins are still small and the skins are soft, scratch a child's name on one. The name will stay and grow along with the pumpkin. It's a nice surprise at harvest.

Long Pie

Wee-B-Little

Radicchio

Radicchio is a slightly bitter chicory that has been popular as a salad green in Europe for a long time. It hadn't caught on in North America because it was a very fussy and demanding plant. New varieties are easier to grow, and radicchio is gaining a following among salad connoisseurs. Like many slightly bitter foods, it's good for you, adding to your diet iron, magnesium, zinc, and vitamins C, E, and K.

SOWING AND GROWING

You can grow radicchio as a spring crop, but it often matures after the days have grown warm, which makes the leaves somewhat bitter. As a fall and winter crop, however, radicchio is tough to beat. It tolerates cold and frost very well, and if you grow it in a cold frame, you can harvest it throughout the winter in all but the coldest climates.

For fall and winter crops, begin sowing in mid-summer, with succession sowings every 10 to 14 days for a month. For spring crops, direct-sow in the garden as soon as the soil can be worked.

HARVEST AND STORAGE

Unlike the old varieties of radicchio, the new varieties don't need to be cut back before the heads form. Harvest radicchio as soon as the heads are firm. It stays fresh-tasting in the refrigerator for a few days and holds in the garden equally long if the weather is cool.

VARIETIES

Fiero. Elongated, upright growth habit, purple background with white, merging to green, ribbing.

Indigo. Round, softball-sized heads, burgundy with white veining, good flavor.

▲ **The price is right.** *Colorful, tart, and slightly bitter, radicchio is often costly at the market. Grow your own, and you don't have to worry about the price.*

Sow & Grow

Radicchio (*Cichorium intybus*)
Sunflower family (Compositae)

SOWING

Seed depth: ¼" (6 mm)
Germination soil temperature: 60–65°F (16–18°C)
Days to germination: 5–7
Sow indoors: 8 weeks before last frost
Sow outdoors: 2 weeks before last frost and 2 months before first fall frost

GROWING

pH range: 5.5–6.8
Growing soil temperature: 45–65°F (7–18°C)
Spacing in beds: 8–10" (20–25 cm)
Watering: Moderate; light to none over winter
Light: Full sun to partial shade
Nutrient requirements: N=moderate; P=moderate; K=moderate
Rotation considerations: Do not follow escarole or endive
Seed longevity: 5 years

Radishes

If your experience with radishes is limited to small red salad radishes, you're in for a pleasant surprise. All told, there are well over 200 varieties, including French radishes, daikon radishes, and other specialties in a surprising array of colors, including white, purple, black, and even green. Raw, they can be eaten whole, sliced, diced, or grated; or you can cook or pickle them. Most are best eaten fresh, but some can be stored for months in a root cellar. Although growing radishes is very easy, to grow them well you have to grow them fast and harvest them fast.

▲ **Surprise!** *Pulling up the radish variety Easter Egg is as much fun as playing grab bag. Until you harvest this fast-growing, cool-weather crop, you never know which of a rainbow of vibrant colors hides within the moist spring soil.*

Sow & Grow

Radishes (*Raphanus sativus*)

Cabbage family (Cruciferae)

SOWING

Seed depth: ½" (13 mm)

Soil temperature: 45–90°F (7–32°C); the optimum is 85°F (29°C)

Days to germination: 4–12

Sow indoors: Not recommended

Sow outdoors: In cool climates, early spring and fall; in warm climates, winter

GROWING

pH range: 6.0–7.0

Soil temperature: 60–65°F (16–18°C)

Spacing in beds: Small types, 1" (2.5 cm); large (storage), sow 2" (5 cm) apart, thin to 4–6" (10–15 cm)

Watering: Even and moderate to heavy

Light: Best yields in full sun; will tolerate partial shade

Nutrient requirements: N=low; P=low; K=low

Rotation considerations: Precede with a legume cover crop

Seed longevity: 4 years

SOWING AND GROWING

Radishes are particularly sensitive to any interruptions in their growth. Above all, don't allow the soil to dry out. They thrive in cool, moist soil with a lot of organic matter, a pH of about 6.5, and a readily available supply of nutrients. Radishes do nicely where leaves have been worked into the soil the previous fall.

Sow radishes wherever there is an empty space, from early spring until early summer and again in fall. They make useful "row markers" sown among slow-germinating crops like carrots and parsnips. As you harvest the radishes, they leave behind loosened soil and space for other plants to grow.

Flea beetles like radishes. Big time. But the radishes usually do just fine anyway, outgrowing the damage to their leaves and producing nice roots. Row covers applied when the seeds go in the ground will keep flea beetles away and prevent root maggots from spoiling the roots.

Round Black Spanish radish

French Breakfast radish

HARVEST AND STORAGE

Radishes are at their best for a very short time. If they're left in the ground too long, they develop a sharp taste and pithy texture, followed a day or so later by split roots. Harvest the whole crop when it matures, and store the roots in the refrigerator.

VARIETIES

Cherry Belle. The classic radish: red, round, mildly pungent roots that are mature anywhere from ¼–1".

Easter Egg. A multicolor mix of red, purple, and white round radishes, these are a surprise every time you harvest.

French Breakfast. Not likely to be eaten for breakfast in France or anywhere else, but nonetheless this is a fine-tasting radish. Long and cylindrical, rather than round, French Breakfast has a nice radish-red color with a white tip.

Miyashige. With long white roots, this is the classic Asian daikon radish. Sow in late summer for a fall harvest. Miyashige stores and pickles well.

Gotcha! Radishes as a Trap Crop

Like most of the rest of us eaters, insect pests have preferences; they may eat a particular vegetable when that's the only item on the garden menu but ignore it when something more to their liking is available. It is also the case that pests who like one member of a plant family (see page 336) are very likely to enjoy feasting upon other members of the same family. Root maggots that like broccoli roots also like radish roots. Flea beetles adore broccoli and cabbage seedlings, but also kale, turnips, pak choi and . . . radishes. That's the rationale behind planting radishes as a "trap crop," a plant that particular insect pests will attack instead of crops that we gardeners would prefer to leave unmolested. Many gardeners have found radishes to be good trap crop to protect one or more of the many cabbage family plants.

Round Black Spanish. This ancient (sixteenth century) Spanish radish has a black exterior and crisp, hot, white flesh. It's a bit cooler in taste if cooked, either boiled or stir-fried.

Rhubarb

Rhubarb pie, rhubarb pudding, rhubarb syrup or juice, rhubarb jam, or even rhubarb wine. If you have a rhubarb plant or two somewhere in your garden, you can take your pick of these tasty treats. And here's the best part: You can have any of these treats before anything else in the garden is ready to eat. Rhubarb is easy to grow and comes back again every spring.

▲ **It's time for pie!** *To harvest rhubarb, grasp the stem near the base and pull up, giving the stem a twist as you pull. Trim away the base of the stem and the leaves (which are poisonous).*

Sow & Grow

Rhubarb (*Rheum* × *cultorum*)
Buckwheat family (Polygonaceae)

SOWING/PLANTING
Root cutting depth: 1–3" (2.5–7.5 cm)
Soil temperature: 40–60°F (4–16°C)
Plant outdoors: Early spring

GROWING
pH range: 5.5–6.5
Soil temperature: 40–75°F (4–24°C)
Spacing in beds: 24–36" (60–90 cm)
Watering: Moderate and even
Light: Partial shade to full sun
Nutrient requirements: N=low; P=low; K=low
Rotation considerations: Perennial; don't rotate
Seed longevity: Not applicable

THE SITE

Rhubarb likes rich, slightly acid, fertile soil with lots of organic matter. Select a site in sun or light shade and off in a corner of the garden where it can grow without shading or competing with other plants. Rhubarb is a big plant; the bigger of our two is over four feet (1.2 m) in diameter and three feet (0.9 m) high.

PLANTING AND GROWING

Because rhubarb doesn't always come true from seed, it's usually grown from root divisions. Plant in early spring, a few weeks before the last frost. Dig a big, deep hole — at least 2 feet (60 cm) in diameter — and mix a half bushel or so of compost or well-rotted manure into the soil you've removed. If you're planting more than one division, they should be about 3 feet (90 cm) apart. Replace some of the amended soil, making a mound high enough so the crown (where the roots and leaf stalks meet) will be just below the soil surface. Replace the rest of the soil, creating a gentle slope away from the plant.

Water well after planting and keep the soil moist throughout the growing season. Snip off any flower shoots as they appear. Every spring, before the first buds appear, add a goodly serving of compost.

Once established, rhubarb plants grow rapidly and may become crowded, beginning to decline in quality within 5 to 10 years. To rejuvenate the plants, divide them in the fall by slicing through the crown with a sharp spade. Dig up and remove one half of the plant; fill the hole with compost-enriched soil. Plant the other half or pass it on to a neighbor.

HARVESTING AND STORING

Avoid harvesting the first year after planting and take only a few stems the second year. From the third year on, you can harvest just about all you want. Rhubarb is most flavorful in cool spring, but it freezes well.

BEST VARIETIES

Cherry Giant. Likes warmer weather more than most other rhubarbs.

Valentine and Strawberry. Especially vivid red color.

Rutabaga

Many people think a rutabaga is just a big turnip, but turnips and rutabagas are actually different vegetables. The flesh of a turnip is white, while that of a rutabaga is usually yellow. Rutabagas have a rich, mellow taste that goes well with hearty autumn meals.

SOWING AND GROWING

Work compost or leaf mold into soil before sowing to enrich and loosen it. Sow seeds in early summer or, in cool regions, midsummer.

Rutabagas need a good supply of potassium and phosphorus, with slightly lower amounts of nitrogen. To meet these needs, fertilize with aerated compost tea throughout the growing season. Boron deficiency can produce a brown discoloration in the center of the roots. If that occurs, add yet more good quality compost or some agricultural borax.

Protect plants from flea beetles and cabbage root maggots by growing them under floating row covers for the first few weeks.

HARVEST AND STORAGE

After a couple of hard frosts, pull or carefully dig the plants and cut the tops an inch (2.5 cm) from the top of the root. Store in a humid root cellar with the temperature just above freezing or place in a plastic vegetable storage bag and keep in the crisper of the refrigerator. Roots store well for months.

VARIETIES

Gilfeather. A New England heirloom, Gilfeather has a white root crowned with a cap of purple. The flesh is very sweet and mild, with just a slight hint of pungency.

Helenor. Great for storage, Helenor has light orange flesh and a sweet flavor.

Laurentian. This sweet, mild-flavored variety stores very well.

York. Resistant to clubroot, York stores very well and has a smooth, rich flavor.

▲ **Harvest the heartiness of autumn.** *It's usual to dig rutabagas in mid- and late fall, after a few frosts but before the ground freezes. The cool weather helps develop the vegetables' characteristic full flavor.*

Sow & Grow

Rutabaga (*Brassica napus*)
Cabbage family (Cruciferae)

SOWING

Seed depth: ½" (13 mm)
Soil temperature: 60–85°F (16–29°C); the optimum is 85°F (29°C)
Days to germination: 3–5
Sow indoors: Not recommended
Sow outdoors: Early spring

GROWING

pH range: 6.4–7.2
Soil temperature: 60–65°F (16–18°C)
Spacing in beds: 8" (20 cm)
Watering: Moderate
Light: Best in full sun; will tolerate light shade
Nutrient requirements: N=low; P=moderate; K=moderate
Rotation considerations: Good succession crop after onion or scallion
Seed longevity: 4 years

Salsify

Salsify is closely related to parsnip, looks a bit like parsnip, and is grown pretty much like parsnip. But its taste is unique, aptly described as delicious but not comparable to any other vegetable. It's at home in vegetable soups or stews or cooked alone.

THE SITE

The first consideration here is soil depth; salsify grows deeper than any carrot. A deep-dug raised bed is a fine salsify bed. The soil should be friable, well-drained but with good moisture retention, and moderately fertile with a pH between 6.0 and 6.8. Too much nitrogen will cause branching of the root, so go light on the manure.

SOWING AND GROWING

Soak the seeds in warm water overnight to speed germination, which otherwise will take two or three weeks. Plant in early spring to give salsify the four months it

▲ Beauty in the beast. *These salsify roots may not look like much, but they'll taste great in a winter soup or stew.*

needs to mature. Sow thickly to compensate for somewhat sparse germination, about a half inch (13 mm) deep. Keep the soil moist until germination. Thin to about one plant every 4 inches (10 cm). Salsify doesn't like competition, so keep the weeds at bay.

HARVEST

Harvest either in the late fall, after a few frosts, or, for even more intense flavor, mulch the bed and harvest in the early spring, before the greens appear.

VARIETY

Mammoth Sandwich Island. Off-white skin and white flesh.

Sow & Grow

Salsify (*Tragopogon porrifolius*)
Sunflower family (Compositae)

SOWING

Seed depth: ½" (13mm)
Soil temperature: At least 40°F (4°C)
Days to germination: 12–14
Sow indoors: Not recommended
Sow outdoors: Two weeks before last frost date

GROWING

pH range: 6.0–6.8
Soil temperature: 60–65°F (16–18°C)
Spacing in beds: 4"–6" (10–15 cm)
Watering: Moderate
Light: Full sun
Nutrient requirements: N=moderate; P=low; K=low
Rotation considerations: Avoid following scorzonera or sunflower
Seed longevity: 1 year

All in the Family: Scorzonera

Scorzonera (*Scorzonera hispanica*) is a close relative of salsify (*Tragopogon porrifolius*), and, like salsify, is a biennial. Providentially, scorzonera occurs right next to salsify in an alphabetical listing of vegetables and can therefore appear on the same page. The roots are shaped like salsify but are black and have grasslike leaves. Like its relatives, scorzonera grows better and develops its flavor better in cool climates.

Sorrel

Sorrel is a perennial that is also grown as an annual or a biennial. As a perennial or biennial, it's one of the first greens to appear in the spring, a welcome tonic after the long winter. Its sharp, tangy lemon flavor adds zip to salad and to soups or sauces. A new variety has deep maroon veining and stems contrasting with bright green leaves; it is, in a word, spectacular.

THE SITE

Fertile, compost-enriched soil keeps sorrel producing new leaves, and a site in partial shade helps prevent bolting in the heat of summer. If you grow sorrel as a perennial, give it a place off by itself where it won't be disturbed as garden beds are reworked each year.

SOWING AND GROWING

Start indoors and transplant or direct-sow in mid-spring. Plants will produce all year, making a new crop of tender leaves in the fall even after bolting. Remove any seed stalks that appear to forestall bolting. If you want to grow sorrel as a perennial, divide the best plants and replant in the fall.

HARVEST

Cut side leaves until the plants are well established; from then on harvest whole plants right above the crown.

VARIETIES

Red-Veined Sorrel (*Rumex sanguineus*). A real looker!

Sorrel (*Rumex acetosa*). French type, produces greens early in the spring and late in the fall; intense flavor.

▲ **Lemony leaves.** *This young Red-Veined Sorrel is ready to add some zip and color to an early summer salad.*

Sow & Grow

Sorrel (*Rumex* spp.)
Buckwheat family (Polygonaceae)

Seed depth: ¼"
Soil temperature: 50°F (10°C)
Days to germination: 14–21
Sow indoors: Early spring for midspring transplant
Sow outdoors: Midspring

GROWING

pH range: 5.5–7.5
Soil temperature: 70°F (21°C)
Spacing in beds: 8" (20 cm)
Watering: Moderate and even
Light: Full sun or, in warmer climates, partial shade
Nutrient requirements: N=moderate; P=moderate; K=moderate
Rotation considerations: None

Spinach

In the cartoons I watched as a child, Popeye ate a can of spinach and instantly became big-muscled and strong. In the real world, spinach doesn't work quite that fast. But it is good for you, and fresh spinach right from the garden is light years better tasting than anything from a can. One of the first spring garden greens, spinach is high in vitamins and minerals, has excellent flavor either raw or cooked, and is easy to grow. It is also extremely frost tolerant. And who knows? It might be of some help if you have any problems with a neighborhood bully.

▲ **Muscles in a can?** *Spinach is nutritious, and it's versatile in the kitchen, delicious raw in salads, and a basic ingredient in many hot dishes, including lasagna.*

THE SITE

Spinach can handle a wide range of soils as long as they are fairly fertile and moist, but it prefers a pH of at least 6.0; 6.5 to 7.0 is better. Too much nitrogen makes spinach bitter, so go light on the manure.

SOWING

Spinach is frost tolerant and grows best in the cool weather that comes at the beginning and end of the growing season. Direct-sow it in the garden in spring as soon as the ground can be worked, or in the fall, for a late-fall and winter crop. Spinach does not germinate well above 85°F (29°C).

Rather than sowing one large planting, you'll get more and better spinach if you grow a series of small succession plantings every week or 10 days. Stop planting when the warm-weather crops go in — around the last expected frost date — and start again in late summer. Germination is less uniform in warm soil, so sow a bit heavier than in spring. Spinach can survive even very, very cold weather in a greenhouse, in a cold frame, or beneath a floating row cover. In my garden, it has survived –25°F (–32°C) in a solar greenhouse.

GROWING

Spinach grows in a wide variety of soils but does best in fertile soil enriched with compost. In sufficiently fertile soil, it usually doesn't need additional fertilizer. Too much nitrogen gives spinach a sharp, metallic flavor.

Sow & Grow

Spinach (*Spinacia oleracea*)
Beet family (Chenopodiaceae)

SOWING

Seed depth: ½" (13 mm)
Soil temperature: 50–75°F (10–24°C); the optimum is 70°F (21°C)
Days to germination: 7–14
Sow indoors: 3–4 weeks before last frost
Sow outdoors: Early spring

GROWING

pH range: 6.5–7.5
Soil temperature: 60–65°F (16–18°C)
Spacing in beds: 12–18" (30–45 cm)
Watering: Light but even
Light: Full sun to partial shade
Nutrient requirements: N=moderate; P=moderate; K=moderate
Rotation considerations: Benefits all succeeding crops; should not follow legumes
Seed longevity: 3 years

Aphids are sometimes a problem but seldom a problem worth dealing with. I just wash off the aphids before I eat the spinach.

HARVESTING

You can harvest spinach in a variety of ways. Take your pick of any or all:

- Begin snitching individual leaves as soon as they're big enough to use.
- Cut the entire plant at soil level when leaves are large and meaty.
- Cut the entire plant an inch (2.5 cm) above the soil level. The plant remaining will grow another crop of leaves.

In warm weather, spinach bolts; it sends up a central stem that rapidly grows into a flower stalk. When this happens, harvest what you can (the flavor of the leaves may be a bit sharper, but they'll still make a nice spinach pie) and put the rest in the compost pile.

▲ **Keep the harvest coming.** *You'll often get enough spinach for salads by harvesting just the outer leaves (A) and allowing the rest of the plant to continue to develop. You can also cut the plant about 1 inch (2.5 cm) above the soil (B), and the plant will grow another batch of leaves.*

VARIETIES

Smooth Leaf

Bordeaux. Rapid growth, red veins and stems, excellent taste. Bolts early; plant early for an exra-early harvest .

Space. Slowest bolting smooth-leaf spinach.

Savoyed Leaf

Tyee. Very slow to bolt, making it a good spring crop, vigorous and productive.

A Spinach by Any Other Name

If you wish you could have spinach during the hot days of summer, when all the real spinach has bolted, one or the other of these stand-ins might be just what you're yearning for.

Tetragonia (*Tetragonia tetragonioides*), also known as New Zealand spinach, is actually not a spinach at all, but the taste is pretty close. Sow this frost-sensitive plant whenever it's safe to plant tomatoes and peppers. Soak seeds overnight before sowing either in hills, like squash, or spaced about 10 inches (25 cm) apart in rows. Harvest the dark green leaves individually, as needed. You can grow this vigorous, low-growing plant (from 1 to 2 feet tall; 30 to 60 cm) on a trellis or allow it to spread over the bed.

Malabar spinach (*Basella alba*) is another viney plant best grown on a trellis. It takes much longer to mature than New Zealand spinach (110 vs. 55 days) and should therefore be started indoors in the North.

Squash, Summer

Summer squashes are pretty easy to grow. Some would say they're too easy to grow; or, at least, that it's too easy to grow too many of them. The hardest part of growing them is getting yourself to adhere to the First Rule of Summer Squash: Plant no more than ONE of each variety.

THE SITE

If you have the time, prepare the summer squash bed the previous fall by turning in lots of chopped leaves and compost, then cover the bed with a thick mulch of leaves or straw. In spring, remove the mulch and, if you want to get an early harvest, warm the soil with black or IRT plastic. In warm regions, remove the plastic before sowing or transplanting to avoid overheating the soil later in the season.

Any bush-type summer squash, especially ones described as "compact," will grow well in a large, self-watering container.

SOWING

Starting seeds indoors. Summer squashes all grow quickly enough that there's no need to start them indoors to ensure a harvest. But if you just can't wait for that first taste of zucchini or pattypan, start plants indoors three or four weeks before the last frost date. Squash does not transplant well, but if you start plants in 4-inch (10 cm) pots and transplant carefully to avoid disturbing the roots, they'll be okay. Sow three seeds to a pot and thin to one plant by clipping the extras with scissors. Keep temperatures at about 70°F (21°C). Harden off the plants by cutting back on water and gradually lowering the night temperature to about 65°F (18°C) during the week before transplanting.

Direct-seeding. Squash seeds won't germinate in cold soil, so wait until the soil is 70°F (21°C) or warmer, and then sow three seeds to a hill. Space the hills about 18 inches (45 cm) apart. After seedlings have one true leaf, thin to one plant by cutting the others with scissors.

▲ **Squash squad.** *Summer squash comes in a surprising variety of shapes and colors, each with subtly different textures and flavors. In almost every case, summer squash is best when picked young and harvested often.*

Sow & Grow

Summer Squash (*Cucurbita pepo*)
Cucumber family (Cucurbitaceae)

SOWING

Seed depth: ½–1" (1.3–2.5 cm)
Soil temperature: 70–95°F (21–35°C); the optimum is 95°F (35°C)
Days to germination: 6–10
Sow indoors: 3–4 weeks before last frost
Sow outdoors: When soil temperature reaches 70°F (21°C); use row covers during cool weather

GROWING

pH range: 6.0–6.5
Soil temperature: 65–75°F (18–24°C)
Spacing in beds: 12–18" (30–45 cm)
Watering: Heavy and even
Light: Full sun
Nutrient requirements: N=high; P=moderate; K=moderate
Rotation considerations: Avoid following winter squash, pumpkin, cucumber, melon
Seed longevity: 4 years

GROWING

Pretty much the same growing methods work for any of the many types of summer squash. Summer squash is sensitive to cold temperatures and grows best during the long days of summer.

After transplanting indoor-started plants, or when direct-sown seedlings emerge, cover the plants with floating row covers if night temperatures dip below 65°F (18°C). This also keeps insect pests at bay while the plants are young and most vulnerable.

Squash is a heavy feeder, but when grown in soils rich in organic matter, it rarely needs supplemental fertilizing. If leaves are pale or plants lack vigor, fertilize with seaweed or fish emulsion. Too much fertilizer, especially nitrogen, can limit yields.

Although summer squash is reputed to be prey to the same pests that pester winter squash, I have repeatedly grown pest-free summer squash in the same garden with pest-troubled winter squash. To be on the safe side, use row covers until the blossoms appear.

Note: The first few fruits may wither or blacken and fall from the plant. That's not a sign that you've got a pest or disease problem; female flowers sometimes appear before male flowers and therefore don't get pollinated. The "problem" corrects itself as soon as the male flowers appear.

HARVEST

The secret to good-tasting squash is more in the harvesting than in the growing. Pick young. Pick small. And pick often. Here are some tips on picking at the flavor peak.

Zucchini lives life in the fast lane; it grows very quickly. Once fruits appear, visit your zucchini every day or so and pick them when they are about 4 to 5 inches (10 to 12.5 cm) long. Zucchini plants bear for a long time if harvested often, but even with the best of picking, zucchini quality and yields start to decline after a month or so. If you're a real zucchini fan, plan on a couple of succession plantings about a month apart.

Cousa, a specialty zucchini, looks like a compromise between a zucchini and a straightneck squash, with pale greenish yellow skin and the classic summer squash taste. Harvest cousa squash when it's about 3 inches (7.5 cm) long. Keep picking to keep the harvest going.

Yellow summer squash includes both straightneck and crookneck types; they're harvested a little differently. Pick straightnecks at about 4 to 5 inches (10 to 12.5 cm). At this stage, they can be sliced and eaten skin and all. Crooknecks develop a thick skin earlier than straightnecks, so harvest these when they are slightly smaller.

Scallop or pattypan squash are at their best when only 2 to 3 inches (5–7.5 cm) across. If you harvest often, pattypans will keep coming all summer long.

All summer squash keep in the refrigerator for about two weeks and freeze well.

VARIETIES

Zucchini

Costata Romanesco. Fruits are green and marked with lighter-colored ribs. Harvest when fruits are 6 to 10 inches (15 to 25 cm) long. Costata Romanesco makes lots of male blossoms that won't ever become squashes. Pick them, dip them in tempura batter, and fry them.

A Zucchini with Attitude

Most summer squash varieties grow in bush form, but tromboncino (also known as *zucchetta rampicante*), an heirloom zucchini variety from Italy, is a vine — a whole lot of vine. Grow tromboncino on a trellis, and pick the curvy fruits when they are 8 to 12 inches (30 to 37.5 cm) long. They're firm and flavorful, with few seeds. Unlike bush-type zucchini, this plant will produce prolifically for the whole season and is resistant to squash borer.

Italian heirloom zucchini, tromboncino, is named for its trombone shape. This squash can get very long, as pictured here, but it tastes best if harvested a bit younger, at about 8 inches to a foot (20 to 30 cm) long.

Top row: *Costata Romanesco, Benning's Green Tint pattypan, and Seneca Prolific squash*
Bottom row: *Sunburst and Zephyr summer squash*

Eight Ball. With dark green, tasty, nearly ball-shaped fruits, Eight Ball starts to bear earlier than most varieties. A fairly compact size makes it suitable for growing in containers.

Gold Rush. This zucchini looks like a summer squash, with clear, bright yellow skin. Its flavor is very similar to other good zucchini varieties.

Magda. A cousa type squash, Magda has a sweet, nutty flavor. The blocky, pale green, tapered fruits are used for stuffing, stir-fries and pickling.

Spacemaster. As its name indicates, this variety produces lots of fruits on plants that are a little smaller than standard varieties. It's nicely prolific so be sure to pick often; ideal for container growing.

Straightneck

Saffron. This looks and tastes just like a straightneck summer squash should, with rich flavor and clear yellow color. The plants are nicely compact and produce lots of squash.

Zephyr. An eyecatching squash with a pale yellow top and light green bottom, Zephyr produces firm but tender fruits with excellent flavor.

Crookneck

Horn of Plenty. Attractive, delicious fruits grow on these well-behaved, compact, 3-foot-diameter (90 cm) plants. You'll have summer-long production as long as you keep the fruits picked when they're young.

Yellow Crookneck. Buttery-flavored and firm-textured fruits grow on a large plant that bears a bit later than other summer squash.

Pattypan

Benning's Green Tint. Pale green fruits with an excellent nutty flavor grow on a medium-sized plant. This has become our favorite pattypan.

Starship. Great for gardeners with little space, Starship is a compact, space-saving plant that produces green, scallop-shaped fruits.

Sunburst. Prolific and reliable, Sunburst produces clear yellow fruits with a creamy, flavorful flesh that can be diced and tossed into mixed vegetable dishes or sautéed all by itself.

Squash, Winter

Q: "Where does a gorilla sit at the opera?"

A: "Anywhere it wants to."

It's the same with winter squash. Given half a chance, winter squash will take over your whole garden. It is a vine, a very long and vigorous vine that will grow and grow and grow — into and all over any part of the garden it can reach. You can't contain these plants once they get growing. Control them by sowing the seed along the edge of the garden. As the vines grow, direct them outward, away from the rest of the garden. Yeah, it's a bit of extra work, but when the cold days of January roll around and you're eating tasty winter squash, all is forgiven. You'll go ape for this garden gorilla.

THE SITE

Summer squash and winter squash need the same things to grow well — winter squash just needs more of them. Winter squash plants are bigger than their summertime counterparts, and they produce bigger fruits; hence, they need more food (especially nitrogen), more water, and more space.

Before sowing or transplanting, loosen the soil in an area that's at least as deep and as big around as a bushel basket and work in lots of compost or well-rotted manure and some seaweed. (If you can't acquire seaweed, water the seeds or transplants with liquid seaweed fertilizer.) Mark the planting holes with a mound of soil or a stake so you can identify them beneath the plastic cover. Cover a 3-foot-square (90 cm²) area with black or IRT plastic or landscape fabric at least a week before planting. I leave the covering in place all summer for weed control. If you grow a lot of squash, as we do, cover the whole growing area and cut holes for the plants.

SOWING

Winter squash needs three months or more of frost-free growing time, and it's extremely frost sensitive on both ends of the growing cycle. Like summer squash, it does not germinate well in cool soil.

▲ **Winter wonders.** *Squash is healthful, with lots of fiber, vitamin A, and beta-carotene. All that and it's delicious, too. Acorn, buttercup, butternut, delicata, Hubbard, and spaghetti squash all fit into this category.*

Sow & Grow

Winter Squash (*Cucurbita* spp.)
Cucumber family (Cucurbitaceae)

SOWING

Seed depth: ½–1" (1.3–2.5 cm)

Soil temperature: 70–90°F (21–32°C); the optimum is 90°F (32°C)

Days to germination: 6–10

Sow indoors: 3–4 weeks before last frost

Sow outdoors: When soil temperature reaches 70°F (21°C); use row covers during cool weather

GROWING

pH range: 5.5–6.5

Soil temperature: 65–75°F (18–24°C)

Spacing in beds: 12–18" (30–45 cm)

Watering: Heavy and even

Light: Light sun

Nutrient requirements: N=high; P=moderate; K=moderate

Rotation considerations: Not following summer squash, cucumber, and melon

Seed longevity: 4 years

In warm areas, direct-sow once the soil has warmed to about 70°F (21°C) in spring and the danger of frost is past. In cooler regions (generally from Zone 6 north) you can direct-sow if the soil has been pre-warmed with black or IRT plastic and the plants are protected under row covers. Or you can start plants indoors three weeks before the last frost date. Don't start plants earlier than this; older plants often don't transplant well. Sow three seeds per 4-inch (10 cm) pot and thin to one plant by selecting the strongest plant and cutting the extras with scissors. Maintain a temperature of about 70°F (21°C) for germination and growth. Transplant carefully, being sure not to disturb the roots.

GROWING

Use row covers to maintain proper growth temperatures and protect against insect pests when the plants are small, but remove the covers for a few hours a day when blossoms appear. That should be all you need to do until harvest. These are big plants with big fruits; they need water all the time. Monitor soil moisture and water deeply if the soil is dry more than 2 inches (5 cm) down.

▲ Squash likes it hot. *In cool-weather regions, winter squash will perform better if you warm the soil with black or IRT plastic or landscape fabric (which is water permeable) before planting and then leave the plastic in place, not only to maintain soil temperature but also to control weeds. Cut a circle out of the plastic, dig a hole deep enough so that the plant will be at the same height it grew in the pot, and set the transplant in place, being careful not to disturb the plant roots. Firm the soil gently around the plant.*

HARVEST AND STORAGE

In theory, two characteristics signal that winter squashes are ripe:

- The stems begin to shrivel and dry.
- The skin is hard enough so you can't cut it with your thumbnail.

In practice, at least here in Zone 4, I harvest the evening before the first hard frost and hope they're all ripe.

Use pruning shears to cut the fruits from the vine, leaving at least an inch (2.5 cm) of stem. Remember: The stems aren't handles. Because they can't support the weight of the fruit, the stems often break off, and stemless squash doesn't store well.

Winter squash keeps best if it is cured in the sun for 10 days or so to harden the skins before being placed in storage. Dry, warm days are advantageous, but sunshine is what really cures the skins. If there's any chance of frost, cover the squash well or move them into a shed or garage.

Store at 50°F (10°C) where it is moderately dry (about 60 percent humidity). We store our winter squash beneath the bed in the guest room. Eat the acorn, delicata, and spaghetti squash first, since they won't last as long as other varieties. The flavor of both butternut and buttercup improves after a few weeks of storage.

VARIETIES

Acorn

Acorn squash are small, usually about 2 pounds (0.9 kg), ribbed, dark green, and vaguely acorn shaped. They don't need to be cured in the sun and last as long in storage as some other varieties. Like many winter squash, they are best baked.

Jet. Early fruits with good taste on a semi-bush plant.

Tuffy. Thicker, sweeter, and drier flesh than other acorns, with a tough rind; for the best flavor, age for at least two weeks before use.

Buttercup

A buttercup squash looks like a big acorn squash that somebody sat on. The usually dark, blackish green, tough, furrowed rind protects sweet, yellowish orange flesh. Buttercups store well, lasting well into February.

Sunshine

Sweet Dumpling

Burgess (or Burgess Strain). Very popular variety with dark green skin and sweet, rich-flavored flesh.

Sunshine. (Not always listed with buttercups, although they look like buttercups, lacking only the "button" in the bottom.) Spectacular scarlet color, great taste and texture.

Sweet Mama. A hybrid with pleasant-tasting, sweet orange flesh enclosed within a black-green rind; reliably good yields, and excellent storage; our favorite winter squash.

Butternut

Although the shapes vary somewhat, most butternuts are cylindrical with a bulb at the lower end and smooth, tan skin. They keep as well as any winter squash and can last all winter. It takes a few weeks of storage to develop full flavor.

Early Butternut. Medium-size, light tan fruit, mature about 10 days earlier than most varieties; smooth, sweet, orange flesh.

Metro. Resistant to powdery mildew; smaller than Waltham with sweet flesh.

Waltham. The archetypical butternut, small seed cavities and straight necks; sweet flavor best after two months' storage.

Other Squashes

Blue Hubbard. Very large (12 to 15 pounds; 5.4 to 6.8 kg) aqua-blue fruits with sweet, yellow flesh, and a tough, bumpy, furrowed shell.

Red Kuri. Teardrop-shaped "baby Hubbard" (4 to 7 pounds [1.8 to 3.2 kg]) with scarlet skin over smooth-textured flesh; not particularly long storage.

Warted Green Hubbard. A large squash with dark green skin and flavorful yellowish flesh; keeps very well in storage.

Spaghetti. A medium-sized squash with tan skin and yellowish, mildly sweet, nutty-tasting, stringy flesh, sometimes called vegetable spaghetti, because you serve it by scraping out the cooked flesh with a fork, creating spaghetti-like strands. It does look a bit like spaghetti, and although it tastes nothing like pasta, it does go well with spaghetti sauce.

Sweet Dumpling. Small (4-inch [10 cm]) teacup-shaped, ivory background with green stripes; sweet, tender orange flesh; suitable for stuffing.

Delicata. 7 to 9 inches (17.5 to 23 cm) long, 3 inches (8 cm) wide, 1½ to 2 pounds (0.7 to 0.9 kg), cream background with dark green, longitudinal stripes; very sweet, suitable for stuffing or baking; doesn't require curing.

Strawberries

As a general rule, strawberry plants lack self-control. Left to their own devices, they will escape from the neat rows where you planted them and send out runners to make new plants, which will in turn send out yet more runners . . . until, seemingly in a moment when your back was turned to tend some other plants, the whole strawberry bed and the walkways around it are a solid mass of strawberry. But if you can provide the discipline strawberry plants lack, the reward is strawberries with a flavor you'll never find in store-bought fruits.

▲ **Treasure hunt.** *Brush back the leaves, and there they are — bright red Sparkle strawberries perfectly ripe and ready for harvest.*

THE SITE

Strawberries need fertile, well-drained soil enriched with plenty of compost or well-aged and weed-free manure. Keep the bed weeded; strawberry plants do not compete well with weeds, especially perennials and grasses. Full sun is best, but partial shade is okay.

SOWING AND GROWING

You can start some strawberry varieties from seed (the varieties Tarpan and Sarian, for instance), but most are available only as plants, so that's the route most gardeners take. You may be able to get some plants from the runners produced by a neighbor's strawberries — and you may also get any viruses those plants harbor. To avoid the risk, buy virus-free plants from a nursery or seed company.

Plant in early spring, spacing plants 12 to 18 inches (30 to 45 cm) apart down the center of a 30-inch-wide (75 cm) bed or in rows 3 to 4 feet (0.9 to 1.2 m) apart. The middle of the crown should be level with the soil. Keep the soil moist and weed-free. Remove any blossoms during the first year so the plants use all their energy to grow roots and hearty foliage.

In late fall, mulch the plants with straw (yep, that's where the "straw" in "strawberries" comes from). Pull the mulch slightly away from the plants in the spring, but leave it in place to conserve moisture, suppress weeds, and keep the berries clean. If you can keep the weeds at bay and if the plants stay healthy, a strawberry

---

Sow & Grow

Strawberries (*Fragaria* spp.)
Rose family (Rosaceae)

SOWING/PLANTING

Soil temperature: 40–60°F (4–16°C)
Sow indoors: Not applicable
Plant outdoors: In early spring

GROWING

pH range: 6.0– 6.8
Growing soil temperature: 60–80°F (16–27°C)
Spacing in beds: 12–18" (30–45 cm)
Watering: Moderate
Light: Full sun; partial shade okay in warmer climates
Nutrient requirements: N=moderate; P= moderate; K=moderate
Rotation considerations: Avoid following beet, pea, corn, pepper, or tomato

---

bed may remain productive for three to five years. However, you may find that the berries are fewer and smaller as time goes on. I start new beds from runners each year in late summer.

If you choose to keep a strawberry bed after the first productive year, keep the runners confined to the bed and out of the walkways and, once the runners have rooted, remove the old plants.

All in the Family: Alpine Strawberries

Imagine if you could take a big, ripe, garden strawberry, condense it and enhance it, putting all the flavor of the big berry in a little, tiny one. That's pretty close to what you'll get in alpine strawberries (also called *fraises du bois*). The berries are bigger than wild strawberries, though still much smaller than standard varieties, and they're tasty.

THE SITE

Any fertile, well-drained spot will suit alpine strawberries; they like a pH a bit on the acid side (6.0 to 6.8) and can tolerate partial shade. Prepare the bed carefully by working in plenty of compost or weed-free, aged manure, and root out all weeds, especially grasses. Alpine strawberry plants produce few runners, making them good candidates for ornamental plantings in rock gardens or alongside paths. Alpine strawberries are also a very good choice for growing in containers, especially — given their need for continual moisture — self-watering containers. A container with multiple planting spaces is ideal.

SOWING AND GROWING

Alpine strawberries are grown from seed or — if you can find them — started plants. Start the seed indoors in a flat of moist soilless starting mix about 8 weeks before the last frost. Keep the soil temperature between 60 and 75°F (16 to 24°C) and keep it moist for the two to three weeks germination requires. Transplant to 4-inch (10 cm) pots when two sets of leaves have developed. (If you're growing in containers, transplant directly to a container at this point.) Strawberry plants are frost-tolerant, but it's best to avoid hard freezes.

HARVESTING AND STORING

Harvest alpine strawberries when the fruits turn crimson. Although they're much smaller than commercial types, these fruits have a rich, tart strawberry flavor, and they bear from spring to fall. How long they will store is a mystery, as they're always eaten the same day they are picked.

VARIETIES

Among the many fine varieties of alpine strawberries are **Alexandria, Charles V,** and **Pineapple Crush.**

SAVING STRAWBERRY SEED

True alpine strawberries do not produce runners, but it's easy to propagate your own plants from seed. Collect a handful of ripe strawberries and spread them on a sheet of newspaper in a warm, dry, sunny room. When the fruits are dry, work the pieces between your fingers, allowing the seeds to fall onto the newspaper. Dry the seed for another day or two, and then sow in a flat of seed-starter mix. When the seedlings are about ½ inch (1.25 cm) tall, transplant them to individual pots. After they've formed a nice rosette of leaves, you can transplant them into the garden anytime from spring to early fall. If you're not planting them immediately, the seeds can be stored in a paper or glassine envelope until the following spring.

HARVEST

Pick the berries whenever they are fully red but before they turn a very dark red and become a little less glossy. Strawberries freeze well. I hull and slice them into a pint freezer container and add about a tablespoon of sugar.

VARIETIES

Honeoye. Especially good for the Northeast and Midwest; less flavorful in very hot conditions; Zones 3–8.

Seascape. (Day-neutral) Good for the Northeast, summer-to-fall production; Zones 4–8.

Sparkle. An old-time favorite known for its flavor; good for freezing and jam; Zones 3–8.

Temptation. (Everbearing) Early, bred for container growing; medium-sized berries. Harvest as soon as the berries are ripe; they don't keep well on the plant. Few runners.

Tristar. (Everbearing) Bears from spring through fall and in any part of the country.

Starting New Strawberry Plants

As long as your plants appear to be disease-free, you can start new beds from the runners produced by established plants. If you are using runners from your own plants, plant in the fall; this will give the plants time enough to establish good roots, and you'll have a crop the next spring instead of having to wait a year.

1 With pruning shears or scissors, cut the stem that connects the runner to the parent plant.

2 Use a trowel to cut a circle around the runner and gently pry the runner plant from the soil, keeping as much soil as possible around the roots.

3 Dig a 4- to 5-inch-wide hole in the new bed and plant the runner, gently firming the soil around the plant roots.

4 Water well. (Some liquid fish-and-seaweed fertilizer mixed in the water will get things off to a good start.)

A STRAWBERRY FOR ALL SEASONS

Depending on the variety, strawberries can bear in the early summer, or once in the early summer and again later on (everbearing), or pretty much all summer long (day-neutral). Variety descriptions in catalogs will generally tell you which is which. If nothing is said, you can assume that the variety in question is a traditional, early-summer bearer.

Sweet Potatoes

Sweet potatoes are a crop identified with the sunny South, but with a little gentle persuasion and some help from black plastic mulch, this hearty vegetable will provide even cool-climate gardeners with a large, sweet harvest.

PLANTING

Sweet potatoes are grown from rooted cuttings, called slips or draws. You can buy slips or you can make them yourself.

To make sweet potato slips, purchase large, firm sweet potatoes about 30 to 40 days before the last frost. Set the sweet potatoes in sand in a warm, sunny room or greenhouse. Shoots will begin to grow in a day or two.

When the shoots are about 4 to 6 inches (10 to 15 cm) long, gently twist them from the potato. Collect the shoots and put them in a container of water, until they begin to grow roots.

GROWING

When all danger of frost is past, set the slips in the garden in loose, fertile soil that has been amended with compost. Fertilize only if the plants do not appear healthy, as too much nitrogen will diminish yield and produce long, thin roots.

HARVEST AND STORAGE

You can harvest sweet potatoes anytime they reach usable size, usually a period from about 100 to 140 days after planting, depending on the variety. Be sure to harvest sweet potatoes before the first frost. Cold weather can damage the roots. If you can't harvest and a frost is coming, mulch the area heavily with straw before sunset.

To harvest, cut back the vines and lift the roots from the ground with a garden fork. Do this gingerly, as the skins bruise easily. Cure the roots before storage by letting them bask in the sun for a day, and then move them to a shady area that remains at about 80°F (27°C) for 7 to 10 days. They should store well for about six months in a root cellar or similar cool, humid environment.

▲ **A welcome vine.** *Sweet potatoes will be ready for harvest from this prolific vine three to four months after planting, but they do need to be harvested before the first fall frost.*

Sow & Grow

Sweet potatoes (*Ipomoea batatas*)
Morning glory family (Convolvulaceae)

SOWING/PLANTING

Seed depth: Not applicable
Germination soil temperature: Not applicable
Days to germination: Not applicable
Sow indoors: Not applicable
Transplant outdoors: 2 weeks after last frost

GROWING

pH range: 5.5–6.5
Growing soil temperature: 65–90°F (18–32°C)
Spacing in beds: 14–18" (35–45 cm)
Watering: Low
Light: Full sun
Nutrient requirements: N=low; P=low; K=low
Rotation considerations: Avoid following root crops
Seed longevity: Not applicable

VARIETIES

Beauregard. Large, meaty, and smooth-textured, the dark burgundy-purple roots conceal a pumpkin orange flesh; excellent choice for cool climates.

Vardaman. This compact bush variety takes up less space than most varieties and outyields them, too. Roots are large, with deep orange, flavorful flesh.

Swiss Chard

Many years ago, the cartoonist Al Capp conceived a creature called the Schmoo. The Schmoo's mission in life was to become whatever you wanted it to be. I used to think the Schmoo just a fantasy, until I discovered Swiss chard. It's a vegetable garden Schmoo. You want salad? A mess of greens? Some spinach, even though all the spinach has long ago bolted? Asparagus in the middle of August? Or greens either raw or cooked after frost has killed most everything else? And you want all this from a single planting that goes on producing until there's a really hard frost, requiring almost no care along the way? And you'd like all this in bright shiny colors? No problem. You've got it, if you planted Swiss chard.

▲ **A crop of many colors.** *I'd plant Bright Lights Swiss chard just to look at it. Hard to believe it's also good to eat.*

SOWING AND GROWING

How close together you grow Swiss chard plants depends on how you plan to harvest them. If you plan to take the whole plant or to cut it off an inch (2.5 cm) above the soil (it will grow a new set of leaves in this case), space plants about 4 to 5 inches (10–12.5 cm) apart. If you plan to harvest the outer stalks continuously throughout the season, space plants about 8 to 10 inches (20–25 cm) apart to accommodate the larger plants.

If you follow the onetime harvest method, be sure to sow succession plantings throughout summer and early fall. Swiss chard can endure light frosts in spring and tolerate moderate freezes in fall.

Whatever spacing you choose, mulch with a thin layer of compost to ensure sufficient nutrients for the plants.

Sow & Grow

Swiss Chard (*Beta vulgaris* Cicla Group)
Beet family (Chenopodiaceae)

SOWING

Seed depth: ½" (13 mm)
Soil temperature: 50–85°F (10–29°C); the optimum is 85°F (29°C)
Days to germination: 5–7
Sow indoors: 1–2 weeks before last frost
Sow outdoors: After last frost

GROWING

pH range: 6.0–7.0

Soil temperature: Anything above 50°F (10°C); the optimum is 60–65°F (16–18°C)
Spacing in beds: If you harvest entire plant, 4–5" (10–12.5 cm) apart in a staggered pattern; if you harvest outer leaves, 8–10" (20–25 cm) apart in a staggered pattern
Watering: Moderate and even
Light: Best in full sun, tolerates light shade
Nutrient requirements: N=low; P=moderate; K=moderate
Rotation considerations: Avoid following beets, spinach, or orach; benefits following a legume crop
Seed longevity: 4 years

HARVESTING AND STORING

You can begin harvesting the leaves when plants are about 6 to 8 inches (15–20 cm) tall. You have your choice of harvesting methods:

- Harvest the whole plant; the leaves and stems are especially tender.
- Cut the young plants an inch (2.5 cm) above the soil, whereupon they will continue to grow so that you can harvest them again and again.
- Cut stalks from the outside of the plant, leaving the heart, which will continue to grow.

▲ Cutups. *(A) If you cut only the outer stalks, a few Swiss chard plants will offer you a continuous supply of food over several months. (B) You can also cut the entire plant about 1 inch (2.5 cm) above the soil; another plant will grow from the crown to provide you a second harvest.*

BEST VARIETIES

Argentata. A variety popular in Europe, Argentata has crisp leaves and strong, flavorful stems. Excellent.

Bright Lights. Like a display of northern lights in the garden, Bright Lights is a vegetable disguised as a rainbow. The delicious stalks (which taste a bit like asparagus when steamed) come in five colors — white, red, yellow, pink, and orange. The colors fade when cooked, but the flavor does not.

Bright Yellow. The brightest light of Bright Lights has a show of its own. Bright Yellow has lemon yellow stems beneath richly savoyed, dark green leaves. And of course, it is delicious.

Charlotte. A truly stunning variety that is as attractive to look at as it is delicious to eat, Charlotte has large, cherry red stalks and savoyed, dark green leaves.

Fordhook Giant. There are many new and colorful varieties of Swiss chard, but this longtime favorite is the standard they must measure up to. Fordhook Giant is sure to satisfy with its large, meaty stems and thick, tasty leaves.

Charlotte Swiss chard

Tomatillos

Somebody's got to be kidding here. This vegetable comes in its own paper bag? Yep. And what's in the paper bag is a key ingredient in salsa verde and other Mexican dishes. Although it is native to Mexico, this big, viney plant is easy to grow just about anywhere.

▲ **Good taste:** *Tomatillos are essential to authentic Mexican dishes like salsa verde and chili verde as well as being a great addition to spaghetti sauce.*

Sow & Grow

Tomatillos (*Physalis ixocarpa*)
Tomato family (Solanaceae)

SOWING

Seed depth: ¼" (6 mm)
Germination soil temperature: 70–80°F (21–27°C)
Days to germination: 7–14
Sow indoors: 4 weeks before last frost

GROWING

pH range: 6.0–7.0
Growing soil temperature: 60–80°F (16–27°C)
Spacing in beds: 2½' (75 cm)
Watering: Moderate
Light: Full sun
Nutrient requirements: N=low; P=low; K=low
Rotation considerations: Avoid following eggplant, potato, pepper, and tomato; should not follow a legume
Seed longevity: 3 years

All in the Family: Ground Cherry

Like the tomatillo, ground cherry (also known as husk cherry and Cape gooseberry) comes in its own wrapper. What's inside is a bit different, though. Ground cherries are sweet and fruity, suitable for fresh eating or for pies or jams. They can also be dried, frozen, or canned. Grow them as you would tomatillos, but start the seeds about a week or so sooner because they take longer to germinate. At the other end of the season, ground cherries have a bit more tolerance for frost than tomatoes or tomatillos. They're ripe when the fruits are golden and the husks are open. Goldie and Pineapple are good varieties to try.

SOWING AND GROWING

You grow tomatillos in much the same way you grow tomatoes, but they're a bit more sensitive to frost and cold. Start seed indoors in late winter or early spring, and then move the transplants to the garden well after the last frost, about two weeks after you'd set out tomatoes. Set the plants deep in the soil, with only the top few leaves poking aboveground. Tomatillos are rangy plants that can spread more than 4 feet (1.2 m), so give them plenty of room, about 2 to 3 feet (0.6 to 0.9 m) apart. You can support them on tomato cages, but they seem to grow best if allowed to run free. Fertilizing isn't needed.

HARVEST

Harvest usually begins about two months after transplanting. A tomatillo is ripe when the fruit begins to soften and fills out the husk well; at that point, its husk usually splits.

VARIETIES

De Milpa. An heirloom variety from Mexico, stores 2 to 4 weeks at 45°F (7°C).
Purple. Deep purple skin.
Toma Verde. Early and reliable, a good salsa ingredient.

Tomatoes

If there's a meal more delectable than a fresh tomato sandwich for lunch in late summer, I haven't experienced it. And tomato sandwiches are just the beginning. There's also pasta sauce made from rich, ripe-from-the-garden plum tomatoes, flavorful cherry and currant tomatoes tossed in salads, quart after quart of tomato juice, fried green tomatoes, and pickled green tomatoes. Tomatoes have something for everyone, which is probably why they're so popular.

THE SITE

Tomatoes prefer a light, fertile soil with plenty of organic matter but not too much nitrogen; a big helping of rotted manure or an organic fertilizer rich in nitrogen will produce beautiful, leafy plants with very little fruit. Turn some chopped leaves into the soil in fall, or add compost in spring. A couple of weeks before transplanting, cover the growing beds with black or IRT plastic to warm the soil.

In addition to fertile soil, tomatoes need lots of sun. Give yours the best seats in the house, the places with the most hours of unobstructed sunshine. If you don't have space for an inground garden, try growing a few plants in containers. Tomatoes, especially the more compact determinate varieties, grow well in large containers, provided they get enough water.

SOWING

Your tomato garden can start with plants you've grown yourself or with ones purchased from a greenhouse, garden center, or seed catalog.

Germinating seeds. Tomato seedlings are especially susceptible to damping-off, a soilborne disease that kills the plants soon after emergence by constricting the stem just above the soil surface. Use a peat-based, soilless starting mix for your seed flats (a mix including compost is okay, but don't include any garden soil). Five or six weeks before the expected transplanting date, sow seeds ½ inch (1.25 cm) deep and an inch (2.5 cm) or so apart in flats, or two or three to a cell in growing cells. Keep the containers warm (70–90°F

▲ **Queen of the garden.** *If gardeners grow only one vegetable, it's often tomatoes. There's no secret to why this is so: you just haven't tasted a tomato until you've picked a ripe one from the vine and eaten it while it's still warm from the sun.*

Sow & Grow

Tomatoes (*Lycopersicon esculentum*)
Tomato family (Solanaceae)

SOWING

Seed depth: ½" (13 mm)
Soil temperature: 80°F (27°C)
Days to germination: 6–8
Sow indoors: 6–7 weeks before last frost
Plant outdoors: After all danger of frost is past

GROWING

pH range: 5.8–7.0
Soil temperature: 70°F (21°C)
Spacing in beds: 15" (37.5 cm) supported, 24" (60 cm) unsupported determinates; 36" (90 cm) unsupported indeterminates
Watering: Moderate to high during growth, low during harvest
Light: Full sun
Nutrient requirements: N=moderate; P=high; K=high
Rotation considerations: Avoid following potato, pepper, and eggplant, all members of the family that includes tomatoes
Seed longevity: 4 years

[21–32°C]); the optimum is 85°F (29°C). The seeds will germinate at somewhat lower temperatures, but it takes longer. The top of the refrigerator may give just the right amount of heat; if not, use a heat mat. Keep soil moist but not soggy.

Caring for young seedlings. Once the seeds have germinated, move the seedlings to a sunny window-sill or put them under grow lights. If you use a grow light instead of natural light, keep the bulb an inch or two (2.5 to 5 cm) above the plants to keep them from becoming thin and leggy. If your starting mix did not contain compost or fertilizer, feed the seedlings with a complete liquid fertilizer like fish or fish and sea-weed emulsion. If you see a purple color develop in the leaves, it's a sign of phosphorus deficiency. Use a high-phosphorus liquid fertilizer, if necessary. Otherwise, fertilize every two weeks. (You may not need additional fertilizer if your potting mix is composed of 50 percent compost.)

Transplanting seedlings into larger containers. When the first true leaves appear, transplant to 4-inch (10 cm) cells or pots. Plant so that most of the stem is buried. Additional roots will grow from the buried stem section, strengthening the root system. Fertilize with fish emulsion and grow in full sun or under grow lights at 60° to 70°F (16 to 21°C). Water regularly but lightly, just enough to keep the growing medium from drying out.

BUYING TOMATO PLANTS

A good tomato crop begins with vigorous, compact seedlings about six weeks old in 4-inch (10 cm) pots. Many gardeners like to start their own plants, not only because they can ensure the cost and quality but also because many tomato varieties, including some of the best-tasting ones, are not available as started plants. But this is changing as nurseries offer a wider selection including many heirloom varieties, so it's worth checking around to see what's available near you. If you decide to buy plants from a greenhouse or garden center, buy early, buy young, and buy plants that are already growing in 4-inch (10 cm) pots.

Buy early. You'll have the best selection at the garden center if you get there early, and you'll have more control over how the plants are fed, watered, and hardened

▲ **Seedling shopping.** *Your local greenhouse or garden center often carries a wide choice of varieties that will do well in your area. Do your buying early in the season for the best selection.*

Homegrown Tomatoes

There are some advantages to growing your own tomato plants: You're sure of when they were started. (Greenhouse plants are often too old.) You know how they've been cared for. And you get to try varieties not available as started plants. If you have a sunny window, or — better still — grow lights, a bit of patience and some starting flats and pots, you're most likely to end up with the biggest, best, and tastiest tomatoes if you start your own seedlings.

off during their early development. Most of the problems that can lower yield and decrease fruit size happen right at the beginning of a tomato plant's life. If you buy young seedlings, you're over that hump and into smoother cruising.

Buy young. The larger and older a plant is when it goes into the ground, the more likely it is to be stressed and set back. Tomatoes should be transplanted to the garden at roughly the last frost date and should be no more than six to eight weeks old at that time. Try to find out when the seeds were sown. Many nurseries start plants too early for the region's climate. Above all, avoid tall, leggy plants or those with open flowers or fruits.

Buy 4-inch (10 cm) pots. Seedlings grown in anything smaller than a 4-inch (10 cm) pot are likely to be potbound, and a potbound plant is already severely stressed. At this stage in the plant's development, a good root system is much more important than luxuriant top growth. That's why "bargain" plants grown in small cells or six to a flat are not bargains at all. Turn the pot over and check to be sure no roots are beginning to creep out of the drainage hole. If the nursery owner allows it, gently remove the plant from the pot to see that roots have not started to develop around the sides of the rootball.

TRANSPLANTING

The usual advice about when to put tomato seedlings in the garden is "after the last frost date," but that's a little vague, especially because frost is not the only critical variable here; soil temperature and night air temperature are also important. Soil temperature should be at least 55° to 60°F (13 to 16°C), and night air temperatures should not go below 45°F (7°C) unless you protect the plants with row covers. You can guess, or you can measure the temperatures with soil and air thermometers.

Set plants that you plan to support with cages or trellis 15 inches (37.5 cm) apart in a single row down the middle of a 30-inch (76 cm) bed. If you aren't using any kind of supports, allow 2 feet (60 cm) for determinate varieties and 3 feet (90 cm) for indeterminate. Determinate varieties are sensitive to transplant shock, so be very careful not to disturb their roots.

▲ Ready for production. *In cool climates, planting tomatoes in self-watering containers with red plastic mulch increases yields considerably. The tomatoes get all the water and warmth they need to grow and produce well.*

Tomatoes are native to South America, where they get longer and warmer growing seasons than they can get in most of the continental United States. Growing good tomato crops consistently involves setting out well-started plants and then using some tricks to convince them that the growing season is longer and warmer than it really is.

GROWING

Fertilizing. Water newly planted plants with a dilute solution of fish emulsion or other complete liquid organic fertilizer. Because tomatoes can grow quite large, they need plenty of nutrients; unless your soil is very fertile, plan on supplemental feedings every two or three weeks with fish emulsion or another natural fertilizer.

Warming and discouraging insect pests. Row covers help maintain warmth and deter insects, but remove them when blossoms appear or when daytime temperatures reach 85°F (29°C).

Mulching. Studies have shown that tomatoes produce earlier and set more fruit when mulched with red plastic, which both warms the soil and reflects certain wavelengths of sunlight. Red plastic does not suppress weeds as well as black plastic or IRT. I have found that plants do not get enough water through the planting holes in the plastic. Lay down soaker hoses before

◄ Hardening off. *At least two weeks before the plants go into the garden, begin to harden them off by moving them outdoors to a sheltered place, increasing their time outdoors a little every day. If you've been growing them in a cold frame, simply lift the top of the frame, each day increasing the time it's open.*

Transplanting Tomatoes into the Garden

METHOD ONE — DEEP PLANTING

1 Dig a hole at least 6 inches (15 cm) in diameter and deep enough so that only about 4 inches (10 cm) of the plant will be above the soil. You can either clip off any leaves that will be buried or simply leave them in place. I leave the leaves, and new roots grow from the leaf stem as well as from the main stem.

2 Set the plant in the prepared hole. Fill with a mixture of soil and compost. Firm the soil gently around the plant. Water well with diluted seaweed and fish emulsion. This method encourages a deep root system, which benefits tomatoes during prolonged drought and/or hot weather.

METHOD TWO — TRENCHING

This planting method encourages a shallow root system that, grown near the surface, is therefore mostly in warm soil. It works best in cool regions but also makes plants more susceptible to drought and to root damage from cultivation.

Dig a trench 2 or 3 inches (5–7.5 cm) deep and long enough for all but about 4 inches (10 cm) of the plant. Lay the plant in the trench, gently turning the top upward and packing soil against the stem to support it. Cover with a mix of soil and compost, and water well with diluted seaweed and fish emulsion.

applying the plastic mulch and monitor soil moisture regularly.

If you don't use plastic mulch, a thick layer of straw will help keep the soil moist and protect the plants from diseases caused by soil splashing on the leaves during rainstorms. Make sure the soil is well warmed up before you apply the mulch. In cool regions, most gardeners don't use any organic mulch and even avoid companion planting, so that nothing interferes with maximum soil warming. In warm climates, however, things can get too hot even for tomatoes. In these conditions, organic mulch or "living mulch" companion plantings can be a big help.

Pruning. Optional for determinate tomatoes, pruning is highly recommended for indeterminate varieties, particularly if you grow them on a trellis or stake. Don't do any pruning until the plant has been growing in the garden for a week or so. From then on, remove all suckers — the stems that grow between the main stem and the leaf crotches. Pruning directs the growth to a single main stem. Repeat the process once a week.

HARVEST

As the fall frost date approaches, remove the bottom leaves, flowers, and any fruits that will not ripen before the end of the growing season — the small, solid green, hard-as-a-rock ones with no hint of yellow or pink. That helps direct all the plant's energy to ripening the rest of the fruits.

The best tomatoes are vine ripened, but don't leave them on the vine too long. Pick the fruit when the skin of the tomato yields slightly to finger pressure. The shoulder of the fruit is the last part to change color. Some varieties can be completely ripe and still have yellowish shoulders. Often, but not always, ripe tomatoes separate from the plant with slight upward pressure. If they don't come away easily, clip them with scissors to avoid damaging the plant.

You can extend the ripening season through light frosts by draping the plants and their support system with a sheet of clear plastic and closing the ends with clothespins. Before a hard frost, pick any tomatoes that show a light yellowing at the shoulders. Most of them

▲ Seeing red. *Red plastic mulch reflects the red portion of the light spectrum, which leads to earlier and larger tomato harvests. Lay the plastic on the bed in the same way you put down other plastic mulches and cut a circle into the plastic where you can set the plant.*

▲ Don't be a sucker. *Pinch or cut out all the nonflowering stems that grow between the main stem and the leaf crotches (A). If they aren't removed, each sucker will become a new main stem; the resulting plant spreads all over the place, is impossible to trellis, and diverts too much energy to the new growth rather than to setting and ripening fruit on the original main stem. When the plant reaches the top of the support, prune the tip to stop further top growth (B).*

Three Ways to Train Tomatoes

You can just let tomatoes grow the way nature intended — crawling along the ground. But you'll probably get more fruits and lose fewer of them to pests like slugs if you train your plants to some sort of support.

- **Train the vines to a stake.** Tie the main stem loosely to the support with twist-ties, twine, torn strips of fabric, or old nylon stockings (the best). Be sure to set the stake at the same time you plant the tomatoes, to avoid damaging the roots. Determinate varieties, which are smaller plants, can make do with stakes about 3 feet (0.9 m) high, but viney, indeterminate varieties need higher support, at least 4 feet (1.2 m).

- **Grow the plants within cages.** Determinate varieties need cages about 3 feet (0.9 m) high. Indeterminates do better with a taller cage.

- **Support the vines with taut twine suspended from a trellis** (see pages 78–79). This method is the most work, but it results in the biggest yield. Whichever method you choose, train or tie the plants to the support weekly, at the same time you prune them.

◄ **A lot at stake.** *Staking is one traditional method for keeping indeterminate tomatoes under control.*

◄ **Doing the twist.** *Train tomatoes around twine suspended from a trellis and securely staked into the soil.*

will ripen indoors. Don't toss out the green ones; they make delicious green-tomato pickles.

VARIETIES

There are scores of tomato varieties, and more appear in catalogs each spring. All the photos look wonderful, and all the descriptions promise perfection. How to choose? Ask gardeners in your neighborhood what they grow and why. Check local greenhouses and garden centers, and ask questions. That's how we've found our favorites. And always try one or two new varieties each year, if only so you can help other gardeners when they come around asking you what varieties to grow. Here are some of my favorites and some that look like good bets based on catalog descriptions.

Best Varieties of Tomatoes
for Warm Climates

BHN 444. This variety resists Tomato Spotted Wilt Virus, the bane of southern growers, and other tomato diseases. Plants produce large, red, globe-shaped fruit.

Duke. The large red fruit and reliable crops of Duke have made this disease-resistant variety a favorite in warm-region gardens for years.

Floramerica. An award-winning tomato, Floramerica bears large, evenly red fruit and is disease resistant to boot.

Solar Set. Developed at the University of Florida, this variety produces large crops of big red tomatoes in temperatures where other varieties wilt.

Best Varieties of Tomatoes for Cool Climates

Cosmonaut Volkov. This variety has the best of both worlds: superb flavor in an early tomato.

Moskvich. An extra-early variety originally from Siberia, Moskvich produces round, medium-sized, red fruit with full flavor.

Oregon Spring. Gardeners with short seasons will get bountiful crops of large, flavorful fruits in about two months from transplanting Oregon Spring. Flavor is not as good as longer-season varieties, but when summers are short and cool, Oregon Spring tastes a whole lot better than no tomatoes at all. Tolerates cool (though not freezing) temperatures.

Heirloom Tomatoes

Brandywine. This popular heirloom yields large, ribbed fruit noted for its rich, aromatic flavor. A yellow form, aptly called Yellow Brandywine, produces large, though sometimes irregularly shaped, fruit.

Determinate or Not?

Various kinds of tomatoes differ in size, color, disease resistance, and the time they take to ripen, but the most important difference for the gardener is growth habit: Some tomatoes are determinate, some indeterminate.

Determinate plants, better described as bushes than as vines, reach a certain size, flower, set fruit, and then pretty much stop growing. Fruit ripens over a short period of time. You can grow determinate tomatoes without any support at all, allowing them to sprawl along the ground, but they'll do better if you surround them with a low cage-type support. Either way, they don't have to be pruned. Determinate varieties are the better choice for container growing.

Indeterminate plants are true vines. They grow and set fruit continuously, resulting in much larger plants with a higher foliage-to-fruit ratio. As a rule, the bigger the plant, the better the fruit. Although they take more work to grow, the reward is worth the investment. You'll end up with better tasting tomatoes and more of them.

German. German produces very large beefsteak-type tomatoes with a full, rich flavor. The fruits are medium red, with irregular yellow ribs on the shoulders.

Italian Heirloom. Producing large fruit with meaty, thick walls, this tomato bears well, even in conditions where other varieties fail.

Rose. An Amish heirloom, Rose produces large, deep red fruit with high shoulders, good shape, and excellent flavor. I like the taste of Rose, but our growing season isn't always long enough for it.

Standard Varieties

Celebrity. Enjoy medium-sized, deep red, nicely shaped, round fruits with excellent flavor from Celebrity. An old favorite that is disease resistant and very reliable.

Health. This new variety produced loads of flawless, sweet, thick-walled bright red fruits that are high in lycopene.

Jet Star. A fairly old-timey (introduced in 1979) hybrid that produces nice-looking, flavorful, 7- to 8-ounce (0.15 to 0.2 kg) fruits. Good disease resistance. This is our main-crop tomato year after year.

Small-Fruited Tomatoes

Matt's Wild Cherry. With a flavor that rivals larger main-crop varieties, Matt's bears buckets of very small, ruby-red fruit.

▲ **Diversity in tomatoes.** *If you have room, try growing many different kinds of tomatoes. One year certain varieties do better; another year you'll find a different batch more successful. From left to right, in this group are (top row) Amish Paste, Rose, and Brandywine; (second row) Roma, Rutgers, Orange Dust, and Moskvich; (bottom row) three Sungolds and Glacier.*

Italian Heirloom

Oregon Spring

Health

Rose

Sun Gold

German

Sun Gold. These small, juicy fruits with a clear, golden yellow skin are mild-flavored and a nice addition to summer salads. They are the favorite of many of our gardener friends.

Sweet 100 Plus. Easy to grow, Sweet 100 Plus bears more crack-resistant fruit than regular Sweet 100 and produces abundant clusters of small, cherry-sized tomatoes with a sweet tomatoey taste. This is by far our favorite cherry tomato.

Tumbling Tom. This is a great container tomato. The fruits are about an inch (2.5 cm) in diameter and tasty, and there are loads of them.

Paste Tomatoes

Amish Paste. A versatile heirloom variety that can be used for sauce or sliced and eaten fresh.

Milano. An early Italian hybrid, this is disease resistant with large yields of deep red fruit.

Polish Linguica. An heirloom from New York State, this variety produces large, sausage-shaped, and very meaty fruits.

Roma. With nice thick walls and good production, Romas are a favorite for tomato sauces.

Tuscany. These medium-sized, firm red fruits are excellent dried or used in sauce.

Slicing Tomatoes

Big Beef. The large, full-flavored fruits ripen earlier than other large-fruited varieties.

Goliath. As the name implies, these plants provide big, beautifully shaped and flawless fruits.

New Girl. This variety is the latest improvement on Early Girl. It's more disease resistant and better tasting.

Turnips

Turnips, like beets, are grown sometimes for their greens and sometimes for their roots. Either way, they're best tasting when harvested young. The greens make a good addition to salads and are tasty cooked right along with the roots. The roots are good raw, cooked, or pickled.

▲ **Look what turned up!** *Turnips taste best when you harvest them in cool weather. Plant a crop in midsummer and enjoy these sweet root vegetables all fall.*

SOWING AND GROWING

Turnips like friable, fertile soil and can tolerate partial shade. They also like cool weather, so they're an excellent spring crop. Plant them about the same time you would plant peas and expect a harvest in a bit over a month to a month and a half. Sow seeds ¼ to ½ inch (6 to 13 mm) deep and an inch (2.5 cm) apart. Sow short rows about 6 inches (15 cm) apart across the width of a bed. Make succession plantings 10 days apart until early summer. Start planting again in late summer for fall harvest.

Both flea beetles and root maggots enjoy feasting on turnips. Install floating row covers as soon as the seeds go into the ground.

Turnips' large root systems need deep, loose soil with lots of organic matter to grow their best. Given these conditions, they usually don't need supplemental fertilizing and need only a moderate amount of water. To prevent foliar diseases, avoid wetting the tops when watering.

HARVESTING AND STORING

Greens. Begin harvesting turnip greens when the plants are young. (Don't take too many, or root growth will slow down.)

Roots. For best flavor, harvest the roots when they are between 1 inch (2.5 cm) and 3 inches (7.5 cm) in diameter, depending on the variety. Larger turnips develop a strong, unappealing flavor. Store harvested roots in the refrigerator.

VARIETIES

Hakurei. Crisp and tender, round, white roots display dark green tops.

Purple Top White Globe. The most popular garden turnip for many years, this variety produces flavorful roots and tender greens.

Scarlet Queen. The roots have red skin and white flesh with red splashes; the red-stemmed leaves are good in salads.

Sow & Grow

Turnips (*Brassica rapa*)
Cabbage family (Cruciferae)

SOWING

Seed depth: ¼–½" (6–13 mm)
Soil temperature: 50–95°F (10–35°C); the optimum is 85°F (20°C)
Days to germination: 2–5
Sow indoors: Not recommended
Sow outdoors: Early spring to midsummer

GROWING

pH range: 5.5–6.8
Soil temperature: 40–75°F (4–24°C); the optimum is 60°F (16°C)
Spacing in beds: 1" (2.5 cm)
Watering: Moderate
Light: Best in full sun; tolerates light shade
Nutrient requirements: N=low; P=low; K=low
Rotation considerations: Avoid following cabbage family crops
Seed longevity: 4 years
Seeds per ounce: 14,000 (494 seeds per g)

Watermelon

Watermelon is a melon, and it's grown pretty much like any other melon. In the first edition of this book, you'd find watermelons in among the other melons. I never felt quite right about that. When I'm looking for watermelons in a seed catalog, I look under W, not M. And after all, although they are grown the same as other melons, watermelons surely aren't eaten the same. Who ever heard of spitting cantaloupe seeds?

THE SITE

Like all other melons, watermelons are heat-lovers, and they're big, hungry plants that like to roam around. Pick a spot in full sun, preferably with a southern exposure, with room for the vines to grow; work in plenty of compost and — if you can get it — some composted seaweed. (Failing that, water in the transplants with diluted liquid seaweed or seaweed and fish emulsion.) Especially in cooler areas, cover the planting area with black plastic, IRT plastic, or landscape fabric for at least a couple of weeks before you transplant. Soil pH has to be at least 6.0; closer to 7.0 is better.

SOWING

In warm climates you can direct-sow watermelons, but in cooler areas, you'll probably be better off starting them indoors because they germinate best at 80 to 90°F (27 to 32°C). If you direct-sow, wait until all danger of frost is past and soil temperature is at least 70°F (21°C). In the North, starting indoors is the only way to go. Sow in pots at least 2 to 3 inches (5 to 7.5 cm) in diameter to avoid transplanting until the plants go into the garden. Start seeds no more than one month before transplanting outdoors. Older, larger plants are likely to suffer root stress when transplanted. Plant three seeds ¼ inch deep and thin to the best plant after true leaves appear. Keep the temperature between 80 and 90°F (27 to 32°C) until germination and at 75°F (21°C) thereafter. Keep the soil moist and handle the plants gently; they are very easy to damage.

▲ **What a doll!** *A watermelon doesn't have to be red. This Yellow Doll watermelon is even sweeter than the more common reds.*

Sow & Grow

Watermelon (*Citrullus lanatus* var. *lanatus*)
Cucumber family (Cucurbitaceae)

SOWING

Seed depth: ½" (1.3 cm)
Germination soil temperature: 80–90°F (27–32°C)
Days to germination: 3–10
Sow indoors: 3 weeks before last frost
Sow outdoors: After the last frost when soil reaches 70°F (21°C)

GROWING

pH range: 6.0–7.0
Soil temperature: 70–85°F (21–29°C)
Spacing in beds: 18" (45 cm)
Watering: Moderate and even from germination to hardening off; low for a week prior to transplanting; moderate again from transplanting until fruit is full-sized; low while the fruit is ripening
Light: Full sun
Rotation considerations: Avoid following cucumber, pumpkin, and summer and winter squash
Seed longevity: 4–5 years

GROWING

Transplant to the garden after danger of frost is past. Harden seedlings by reducing temperature and water for a week. Transplant carefully to avoid disturbing the roots. Plants should be about 18 inches (45 cm) apart. Water well with diluted fish emulsion.

In cooler areas, cover the growing area with plastic mulch and cut holes for the plants. To keep temperatures warm and steady, the way watermelons like it — and to protect against cucumber beetles — use row covers until female blossoms appear. (The female flowers bulge a bit at the base, where the embryo fruit waits to be fertilized.)

Keep the plants well watered until fruit has set. After that, water only if the soil is very dry and the plants wilt a bit at midday.

If some of the new leaves are pale green, fertilize with fish emulsion.

HARVEST

How do you know when a watermelon is ripe?

- The tendril nearest to the fruit turns from green to brown.
- The underside of the melon, where it sits on the ground, is yellow.
- When you rap it lightly, you hear a low-pitched "thunk" or "thump" instead of a high-pitched "ping." Try a few that aren't ripe to tune your ear to the sound.

VARIETIES

Round Red
Little Baby Flower. Early, small (5½ inches [14 cm], 2–4 lbs. [0.9–1.8 kg]) and sweet.

Moon and Stars. This Amish heirloom takes a long season to ripen, but it is so pretty that we go on trying it even though we don't always get ripe fruit. The rind, rather than being striped, is covered with large (moon) and small (stars) yellow dots. Very sweet flavor.

Sugar Baby. 6–8-inch (15–20 cm) fruits, 8–10 lbs. (3.6–4.5 kg), good flavor.

Oblong Red
Sweet Favorite. The best oblong melon for northern growers; 10–12 lbs. (4.5–5.4 kg) in the North, more farther south; sweet and disease resistant.

Other Colors (all round, or nearly so)
New Orchid. Bright orange flesh and sherbetlike taste.

Peace. Small fruits considered by some to be better than **Yellow Doll.**

Sorbet Swirl. Pastel swirls of red and yellow, sweet and juicy.

Yellow Doll. Yellow flesh and good taste.

Sugar Baby

Moon and Stars

Great Taste and Good Looks

HERBS HAVE THE JOB of turning ordinary meals into something special. A bit of this here and just a pinch of that there, and a pedestrian dinner turns into a feast. Herbs can turn food for the body into sustenance for the spirit. And their special colors and fragrances can bring variety and interest to an otherwise bland garden landscape. They belong in the kitchen, and they belong in the garden, either by themselves or mixed in among the vegetables and the flowers.

Basil

Basil makes the perfect partner for tomatoes, not only in the garden, where its strong scent may confuse predatory insect pests, but also in the kitchen, chopped and sprinkled on thick slices of juicy tomatoes still warm from the sun. Spaghetti sauce isn't the same without basil, and pesto isn't possible. Basil has become such a dietary staple for us that we think of it more as a vegetable than as an herb.

SOWING AND GROWING

A true heat lover, basil is very sensitive even to light frosts and can be permanently set back by temperatures below 50°F (10°C). Because it matures quickly, you can direct-seed it in almost any region. It also transplants well, however, so you can get an earlier harvest if you start plants indoors two or three weeks before the last frost date.

Like many herbs, basil has a naturally low germination rate (about 60 percent). To compensate for this, sow the small seeds 2 to 3 inches (5 to 7.5 cm) apart and cover them with about ⅛ inch (3 mm) of soil. Thin to 4 to 8 inches (10 to 20 cm).

Basil needs warmth and full sunlight but is otherwise undemanding. A light feeder, it's unlikely to need supplemental fertilizing, provided the soil is reasonably fertile. It doesn't need a lot of water, but its roots are shallow, so don't let the soil dry out.

HARVESTING AND STORING

Harvest the flower buds before they open and the leaves any time they are large enough to use. Harvest the whole plant before frost, preferably in the morning.

You can store stems of fresh basil in a glass of water at room temperature. You can also freeze it, either as pesto or whirled in a blender with enough water to make a thick sauce. It's a terrific almost-fresh seasoning for winter soups and stews.

VARIETIES

There are many, including different colors and flavors.
Genovese. Italian type with good bolt resistance and good flavor; good for pesto.

▲ **Pinch me!** *To induce a full, bushy basil plant and increase yield, pinch or snip out the growing tips. The pinchings are also your first harvest. Bon appétit!*

Sow & Grow

Basil (*Ocimum basilicum*)
Mint family (Labiatae)

SOWING

Seed depth: Just cover
Germination soil temperature: 70–85°F (21–29°C)
Days to germination: 5–10
Sow indoors: 4–6 weeks before last frost
Sow outdoors: In warm regions, spring to late summer

GROWING

pH range: 5.5–6.5
Growing soil temperature: 75–85°F (24–29°C)
Spacing in beds: 4–8" (10–20 cm)
Watering: Light and even
Light: Full sun
Nutrient requirements: N=low; P=low; K=low
Rotation considerations: Avoid rotating with marjoram or oregano
Seed longevity: 5 years

Osmin Purple. Dark purple leaves with pale lilac flowers.
Spicy Bush Basil. Small leaves and a spicy taste.
Sweet Thai. Green, 2 inches (5 cm) leaves with purple stems and blooms. Used as a garnish for sweet dishes.

Borage

Borage appears as often in the flower section of seed catalogs as it does in the herb section. It doesn't really make any difference where you classify it, as long as you somehow find a reason to plant some borage in or near your vegetable garden. Borage is reputed to repel tomato pests, and its beautiful blue flowers attract all sorts of pollinating insects. (It is so well-loved by bees that it has been nicknamed "bee bread.") Both the flowers and the young leaves are edible, with a mild cucumber-like flavor.

THE SITE

Borage doesn't need fertile soil, and it's not too demanding about water either. It does need lots of room, though, and it also self-sows. Because of that, it's probably best to keep borage on the fringes of the vegetable garden or give it a spot of its own in a nearby perennial herb or flower garden.

SOWING AND GROWING

Borage is best direct-sown because it has a taproot that makes it very difficult to transplant. You won't need many borage plants; one or two will probably be enough unless you just fall in love with the flowers. Sow in the spring and thin to 12 inches (30 cm) apart. Mature plants will be about 1½ to 2½ feet (45 to 75 cm) tall.

HARVEST

The leaves, which can be used in salads or cooked, are best when young, before their hairy bristles develop. Pick the flowers whenever you need them.

VARIETIES

The classic borage has blue flowers, usually with a few pink ones mixed in. There is also a white variety.

▲ Of borage and bees. *The young leaves and flowers of borage taste like cucumber and are delicious in salads. The flowers are also highly attractive to bees.*

Sow & Grow

Borage (*Borago officinalis*)
Borage family (Boraginaceae)

Seed depth: ¼" (6 mm)
Germination soil temperature: 60–65°F (16–18°C)
Days to germination: 7–14
Sow indoors: 4 weeks before transplanting
Sow outdoors: Spring

GROWING

pH range: 6.0–7.0 is ideal, but will tolerate 4.3–8.5
Growing soil temperature: 55–80°F (13–27°C)
Spacing in beds: 12" (30 cm)
Watering: Moderate
Light: Full sun
Nutrient requirements: N=low; P=low; K=low
Rotation considerations: Avoid following any family member listed above. Note: Borage will self-sow and needn't be rotated.

Chives

Chives are a harbinger of spring. Well before there's anything worth eating in the garden, the long green leaves of chives are there, ready to add a splash of green and a bit of zip to potato salad or potato soup. And soon there will be spicy purple flowers to liven up the monotony of early, all-green salads.

THE SITE

Set plants in soil amended with compost or rotted manure; no other fertilizing is needed. Chives will come back year after year, so pick a spot where they can be undisturbed for a few years.

PLANTING AND GROWING

Grown from seed, chives take about a year before they're large enough to harvest, so most folks purchase started plants. It's usually best to plant in spring. After three years, divide the clump and replant or give away the extras.

HARVEST

In cool climates, chives die back to the ground in winter, but in warm areas, they can remain evergreen throughout the year. You can harvest leaves whenever they're large enough. Use scissors to snip individual leaves or give the entire clump a haircut. The flowers have a more pungent, oniony flavor than the leaves and should be gathered just as they open.

VARIETIES

Fine Chives. The long, very slender leaves on this variety are more attractive than many chive plants.

Purly. This variety has stout, strong leaves that grow quite straight and tall.

Garlic Chives (*Allium tuberosum*) Also known as Chinese leeks, garlic chive, a member of the large onion family, has flat leaves with a mild garlic flavor. Plant the seeds either indoors or out in the spring. Grow about 6 to 8 inches (15 to 20 cm) apart in full sun or partial shade.

▲ **Spring fling.** *Chives are one of the earliest plants to appear in spring, and their freshly snipped stems and flowers are a treat in first-of-the-year salads.*

Sow & Grow

Chives (*Allium schoenoprasum*)
Onion family (Liliaceae)

SOWING

Seed depth: Surface or just cover
Germination soil temperature: 60–65°F (16–18°C)
Days to germination: 7–14
Sow indoors: Spring to transplant to garden; anytime for windowsill growing
Sow outdoors: Spring or fall

GROWING

pH range: 6.1–7.8
Growing soil temperature: 55–70°F (13–21°C)
Spacing in beds: 6–8" (15–20 cm)
Watering: Moderate
Light: Full sun to partial shade
Nutrient requirements: N=moderate; P=moderate; K=moderate
Rotation considerations: None. This is a perennial crop that does not rotate.
Seed longevity: 1–2 years

Cilantro

What you call it depends on why you're growing it. If you want the pungent leaves, it's cilantro. If you want the seeds, it's coriander. The leaves have a place in both Mexican and Asian cooking; the seeds, toasted, in curries.

THE SITE

Cilantro isn't fussy. Pick a spot with well-drained soil amended with some compost or well-rotted manure.

SOWING AND GROWING

Transplanting and dry soil can cause the plants to bolt, so direct-sow the seeds and mulch plantings to keep soil evenly moist. Avoid fertilizing. For a continuous supply of cilantro, make successive sowings every three weeks from spring to late summer.

HARVEST AND STORAGE

Cilantro. Harvest the entire plant when it's about 8 inches (20 cm) tall. Harvest only what you need; cilantro should be used fresh, as it quickly loses much of its potent flavor when dried or frozen or when stored for more than a few days in the refrigerator. You can, though, make a cilantro pesto and freeze that.

 Coriander. Allow the plant to go to seed. The seed heads will turn yellowish, then yellowish brown when ripe. Snip the seed heads, and either dry them in a 200°F (93°C) oven or bunch them together and put them — upside down — in a brown paper bag. Close the bag and place in a warm, dry place. Over the next week or so, as the heads continue to ripen, the seeds will drop to the bottom of the bag, where they can be gathered. Clean the seeds of any sticks or other foreign material and store the seeds in a glass jar.

▲ **What's in a name?** *Whether you call it "cilantro" and use the fresh leaves, or "coriander" and save the spicy seeds, you'll find dozens of ways to enjoy this fast-growing plant.*

Sow & Grow

Cilantro (*Coriandrum sativum*)
Carrot family (Umbelliferae)

SOWING

Seed depth: ¼–½" (6–13 mm)
Germination soil temperature: 55–65°F (13–18°C)
Days to germination: 7–14
Sow indoors: Not recommended; does not transplant well
Sow outdoors: In cool areas, after last frost and every 3 weeks until fall; in warm areas, fall

GROWING

pH range: 6.5–7.5
Growing soil temperature: 50–75°F (10–24°C)
Spacing in beds: 9–12" (22.5–30 cm)
Watering: Moderate
Light: For seeds, full sun; for leaves, light shade
Nutrient requirements: N=low; P=low; K=low
Rotation considerations: Avoid rotating with other carrot family plants
Seed longevity: 5 years
Seeds per ounce: 5,000 (141 seeds per g)

Dill

Dill seed clusters are what make pickles into dill pickles. That would be reason enough to include it in the garden. But pickles are just dill's opening act. Its leaves are essential to many seafood recipes, they go well with potatoes and onions, and they spruce up green beans and many other vegetables. And they're a nice addition to potato salad. No spice rack is full without dill seed. And as if that weren't enough, dill flowers attract many types of beneficial insects to the garden.

THE SITE

Dill isn't very fussy. It does like full sun and well-drained, moderately fertile soil that's a bit on the acid side.

SOWING AND GROWING

Dill is an independent plant that grows best if you leave it alone. It doesn't transplant well, and it grows fast; direct-sowing is the best way to go. As soon as you can work the soil in spring, sprinkle dill seeds on the soil surface, pat them gently into the soil or cover them with fine soil, and water them. Once the plants are 3 inches (7.5 cm) tall, add a layer of mulch to keep weeds down and conserve moisture. That's it.

Dill readily self-sows. When that happens, just let the dill grow where it has chosen to be and do nothing until it's time to harvest.

HARVEST AND STORAGE

Gather the fresh leaves as soon as the plants are large enough to survive without the missing leaves. You can gather the flower umbels for pickles when most of the flowers are open. Harvest seeds when they turn from yellowish to brownish tan. Gather the seed heads and turn them upside down in a brown paper bag, then collect the seeds as they fall to the bottom of the bag.

BEST VARIETIES

Dukat. Slow to bolt, Dukat produces abundant, aromatic dark green leaves noted for rich flavor.
Fernleaf. A dwarf form growing just 18 inches (45 cm) tall, Fernleaf is perfect for containers.

▲ **Another good garden buddy.** *Dill attracts many beneficial insects, including predatory wasps and flies. Interplant it freely in your garden to help keep insect pests under control.*

Sow & Grow

Dill (*Antheum graveolens*)
Carrot family (Umbelliferae)

SOWING

Seed depth: Surface or just cover
Germination soil temperature: 70–85°F (21–29C)
Days to germination: 7–21
Sow indoors: 4–6 weeks before planting out, but transplants poorly
Sow outdoors: In cool regions, every 3–4 weeks from early spring to midsummer; in warm regions, late summer through fall

GROWING

pH range: 5.5–6.5
Growing soil temperature: 60–80°F (16–27°C)
Spacing in beds: 12–15" (30–37.5 cm)
Watering: Heavy
Light: Full sun
Nutrient requirements: N=high; P=high; K=high
Rotation considerations: Follow beet
Seed longevity: 5 years

Hercules. This dill produces very large quantities of ferny foliage.

Marjoram

Marjoram has a milder flavor than its cousin oregano, and it's not at all hardy, keeling over at the least hint of frost. But aside from keeping it safe from freezing temperatures, don't pamper this herb too much; if it lives in rich soil and always has water, marjoram doesn't fully develop its flavor.

THE SITE

The key to good marjoram is plenty of sun; it is, after all, a native of the sunny Mediterranean. Give it a spot in full sun with well-drained, lightly acid, moderately fertile soil.

SOWING AND GROWING

Marjoram is a tender plant that does not grow well in cold weather and has no tolerance for frost. In cool areas, sow seeds indoors a few weeks before the last frost; in warm climates, sow directly in the garden after the last frost. In either situation, expect slow germination. Keep the soil evenly watered, and mulch around the plants with a thin layer of straw. If you buy plants at a nursery, you get to sniff the aroma of various plants and pick the ones you like best; aroma (and flavor) can vary in the plants from the same batch of seeds.

HARVEST AND STORAGE

Begin harvesting leaves when the plants are about 4 to 6 inches (10 to 15 cm) tall and before the flower buds appear. Keep the plant trimmed back to forestall flowering, which brings on a bitter taste in the leaves. Gather individual leaves for immediate use or snip entire stems for drying and storage. You can use the leaves fresh to season vegetable and pasta dishes. Cooking dissipates marjoram's volatile oils; to preserve its flavor add it right at the end of the cooking process. Dry marjoram by hanging the sprigs upside down in a paper bag and store it in jars for later use.

VARIETIES

Marjoram is marjoram, *Origanum majorana*, sometimes called sweet marjoram in seed catalogs.

▲ **Pot up some marjoram.** *Enjoy marjoram fresh all year long, no matter where you live. Grow it in a pot, or, before the first frost of fall, dig up a plant from the garden and transplant it to a pot. Set that pot on a sunny windowsill away from drafts, and you'll have aromatic leaves all winter.*

Sow & Grow

Marjoram (*Origanum majorana*)
Mint family (Labiatae)

SOWING

Seed depth: Just cover
Germination soil temperature: 65–70°F (18–21°C)
Days to germination: 7–21
Sow indoors: 4 weeks before setting out
Sow outdoors: After last frost

GROWING

pH range: 6.5–7.5
Growing soil temperature: 55–80°F (13–27°C)
Spacing in beds: 6–8" (15–20 cm)
Watering: Moderate
Light: Full sun
Nutrient requirements: N=low; P=low; K=low
Rotation considerations: Avoid rotating with oregano and basil
Seed longevity: 1 year

There is also a prostrate marjoram that makes a very nice container plant. And there is a marjoram-like but stronger-flavored oregano cousin, zaatar (*Origanum syriaca*) that is said to combine the flavors of marjoram, thyme, and oregano.

Mint

There are many mints, some stronger-flavored than others, but all pretty potent. A little bit of mint goes a long, long way. Mints are, indeed, so robustly flavored that they are used only sparingly as culinary herbs. (A sprinkling of mint leaves does, though, add a nice sparkle to cooked carrots, and there are many eaters for whom a lamb dinner is incomplete without mint jelly.) Mints do make a nice tea, one that is reputed to calm a queasy stomach.

THE SITE

Make haste with this decision and you may repent, at leisure, for years and years to come. Mint is a member in good standing of the hardy crew I refer to as Garden Huns. Like horseradish and Jerusalem artichokes, mints — whether spearmint, peppermint, apple mint or other — will invade and eventually conquer whatever garden space they are allowed to enter. I am still trying vainly to keep a patch of apple mint from spreading into an adjoining strawberry garden. Either give mint a place of its own far away from the rest of the garden or grow it in a pot. Mint likes high fertility but is reputed to have stronger flavor if it grows in soil that is only moderately fertile. It can tolerate wetter conditions than most other herbs and garden vegetables and does better in partial shade than in full sun.

SOWING AND GROWING

The various mints cross-pollinate with one another and therefore do not breed true-to-type. Seeds are available, but nobody will guarantee what sort of mint they'll produce. It is better to start with plants from a nursery or from a neighbor, so you know exactly what you're getting.

How to grow it? Plant it and stand back. Mint needs little help from us to do just fine. When winter comes, pot some up, and bring it indoors. If you're worried about its Hun-like nature, consider growing it in a container all the time, rather than in the ground.

Mint is not bothered by insects and is reputed to repel them from nearby plants.

▲ Creeping gingerly? *Although variegated ginger mint is attractive and tasty, it's just as aggressive as every other mint-family member. Grow it in a pot or in the ground surrounded by an impenetrable barrier.*

HARVEST AND STORAGE

For storage, harvest stems before flowers appear, dry the leaves on the stems, crumble them off and store in an airtight jar.

VARIETIES

Apple mint. Milder flavor with a hint of apple.
Ginger mint. Beautiful variegated leaves with a gingery taste and smell.
Peppermint. Strong flavor that lends itself well to herbal teas.
Spearmint. This is the mint most people mean when they say "mint."

Sow & Grow

Mint (*Mentha* spp.)
Mint family (Labiatae)

SOWING

Best propagated from root cuttings, runners, or by division.
Plant after danger of frost is past.

GROWING

pH range: 6.0–7.5
Growing soil temperature: 55–80°F (21–29°C)
Spacing in beds: 6" (15 cm) (Mint will spread quickly.)
Watering: Moderate; mint can tolerate wet conditions
Light: Full sun to partial shade
Nutrient requirements: N= low; P= low; K= low
Rotation considerations: Does not apply

Oregano

Oregano is sometimes called wild marjoram, with emphasis on the "wild." Though related to marjoram, oregano has a bolder flavor as well as a hardier constitution — it survives as a perennial in Zone 5 gardens. It adds zest to spaghetti sauce or soups and is essential to many Italian and Greek dishes.

THE SITE

Oregano is the ultimate unfussy crop. It actually tastes better if it has a bit of stress in its life. Plant it in well-drained, moderately fertile soil with a pH of about 7.0. Oregano will grow in a traditional, hole-in-the-bottom container just fine but not in a self-watering container.

SOWING AND GROWING

You can grow oregano from seed, but you probably shouldn't bother; seedlings from the same batch of seed don't all taste the same. I buy plants from a nursery so I can taste-test them and pick the flavor I like best. If you do start from seed, sow it indoors about two months before the last frost. As seedlings grow, select the most fragrant to transplant to the garden and put the rest in the compost bin. Space plants about a foot (30 cm) apart. For the best-flavored foliage, don't pamper oregano. Don't fertilize it, and don't water it unless there's a real drought; just give it a place in the sun and leave it alone.

HARVEST AND STORAGE

You can harvest the leaves as soon as they are large enough to use. Pick individual leaves or snip entire sprigs. Alternatively, shear the plants about 2 inches (5 cm) from the ground just before flowering (flavor goes south if oregano flowers) and again about a month before the first frost. Use the leaves fresh or dry them and store in a jar for later use.

VARIETIES

Some oreganos are so mild they are of little use for seasoning. For the best, spiciest oregano, be sure to grow Greek (also called Italian) oregano.

▲ Early summer haircut. *Shear the plants about 2 inches (5 cm) from the ground just before they flower in early summer. You'll have another harvest at the end of the season.*

Sow & Grow

Oregano (*Origanum vulgare* subsp. *hirtum*)
Mint family (Labiatae)

SOWING

Seed depth: Just cover
Germination soil temperature: 65–70°F (18–21°C)
Days to germination: 7–21
Sow indoors: 8 weeks before last frost
Sow outdoors: 2 weeks before last frost

GROWING

pH range: 6.0–7.5
Growing soil temperature: 55–80°F (13–27°C)
Spacing in beds: 12" (30 cm)
Watering: Low
Light: Full sun to partial shade
Nutrient requirements: N=low; P=low; K=low
Rotation considerations: Avoid rotating with marjoram and basil
Seed longevity: 1 year

Golden Oregano. Mild flavor, attractive, golden leaf and mauve flowers; both decorative and culinary.
Greek Oregano. Low-growing, strong flavor, very aromatic, with white flowers; a good container plant.

Parsley

Parsley is full of vitamins A and C, carotene and iron. A single planting produces all summer and is often the last plant still producing in the garden, even after a few light snows. You can pot it up (or grow it in a pot right from the get-go) and bring it inside to sit in a sunny window for fresh seasonings all winter.

THE SITE

Parsley needs a fertile, friable, and deeply loosened soil enriched with compost. It prefers the sun but can tolerate partial shade. Parsley can grow anywhere in the garden except with other carrot-family members. Put it at the end of an asparagus or tomato row. Or grow it in a container, either traditional or self-watering, that's about 8 inches (20 cm) deep.

SOWING AND GROWING

Parsley is not at all fussy, but it does have one eccentricity: It takes at least three to five weeks to germinate. When other seedbeds are filled with seedlings, the parsley bed will be empty. If you want to skip the long anticipation, buy small, deep-green plants from a nursery. Transplant to the garden in early spring; parsley can tolerate a light frost.

Parsley doesn't need a lot of water but does have shallow roots, so don't allow the soil to dry out more than an inch or so down. Mulch to maintain soil moisture.

▲ **Patience rewarded.** *Parsley may take a long time to germinate, but it repays you for the wait with beauty, nutrients, and flavor.*

HURRY UP PLEASE, IT'S TIME

You can either live with parsley's slow germination habit, or you can use one or more of the ruses gardeners have come up with to speed the process:

- Soak or refrigerate the seeds for a day before sowing them.

- Freeze the seeds, or soak them and then freeze them.

- Scald the seeds with boiling water.

Sow & Grow

Parsley (*Petroselinum crispum*)
Carrot family (Umbelliferae)

SOWING

Seed depth: ¼" (6 mm)
Germination soil temperature: 65–70°F (18–21°C)
Days to germination: 21–35
Sow indoors: Late winter to early spring
Sow outdoors: Early spring before last frost

GROWING

pH range: 6.0–7.0
Growing soil temperature: 60–65°F (16–18°C)
Spacing in beds: 6" (15 cm)
Watering: Light
Light: Full sun to light shade
Nutrient requirements: N=moderate; P=moderate; K=moderate
Rotation considerations: Avoid rotating with carrot, celery, and parsnip
Seed longevity: 1–3 years

HARVEST AND STORAGE

Harvest as needed, beginning with the larger, outer leaves. To maintain production and quality, harvest the leaf stem along with the leaf blades. If you need a lot of parsley all at once, cut the whole plant a little above the soil level. It will grow new foliage.

For fresh parsley all winter, transplant one or two plants into 10-inch (25 cm) pots in late fall, keep them outside until the first fall frost, then bring them indoors to a sunny windowsill. (Parsley is a biennial and may experience the move indoors as the start of a new year, causing it to bolt. To ensure a winter crop indoors, start some seeds in a container in the fall so the plants will be young when they're moved indoors.)

For extra-seasonal parsley, you can dry it, but not much of the flavor survives. Or you can freeze it. Clip the leaf clusters and pack into pint plastic freezer containers. At the last stages of cooking soup or stew, toss in some chopped frozen parsley for a nice shot of bright green color and a flavor boost.

Root Parsley

All parsleys have roots, but only one type of parsley is called root parsley (aka parsleyroot or Hamburg parsley). Although its leaves taste very good, root parsley is valued more for its large, swollen root. It's about the size of a carrot and the color of a parsnip, with a distinctive taste all its own.

Grow root parsley the same way you grow other parsley. To harvest, dig up the whole plants, remove the tops, and store the roots in damp sand or sawdust, just like carrots. You can also leave them in the garden with a covering of mulch and dig them in spring like parsnips. The roots can also be forced in winter for greens. (Plant the roots in a pot of damp sand or soil.)

Grate parsley root raw into salads or slaw or serve it fried, baked, or boiled or in soups or stew.

VARIETIES

Berliner Bero. Long, white roots that store well and can overwinter under a thick mulch.

Hamburg Parsley. Nutty-flavored roots and zesty leaves.

Trade a Bit of Parsley for a Butterfly

Parsley is one of the favorite foods (along with carrot and parsnip tops, dill, cilantro, and celery) of a caterpillar known as the parsleyworm. After appropriate metamorphosis, the lowly parsleyworm becomes the beautiful Black Swallowtail butterfly. If you find a parsleyworm in your garden, let it be and share a bit of your bounty with it, or move it to some Queen Anne's lace, a wild relative of the carrot.

▲ Flat-out stronger. *Many cooks prefer Italian, or flat-leafed, parsley over curly, for its heartier taste.*

VARIETIES

Curly-Leaved Parsley
These varieties have deeply curled, dark green leaves and mild flavor. This is the parsley you're likely to find on your plate in a restaurant.
Forest Green. Good yield on long stems.
Starke. Good yield, compact plant.

Flat-Leaved Parsley
Also called Italian parsley, this type has flat, celery-like leaves and a stronger, sweeter flavor.
Giant of Italy. Huge dark green leaves and excellent flavor.
Italian Dark Green. Strong, parsley/celery flavor.

Rosemary

Rosemary is a decorative evergreen plant native to the Mediterranean, whose piney-scented leaves are used in cooking and medicinal teas. Its Latin name, *Rosmarinus*, means "dew of the sea." It can be grown from seed but can also be propagated from stem cuttings. Germination is long and at a low rate. I buy the one or two plants I need from a local nursery.

PLANTING

If you're growing rosemary from seed, start the process 22 weeks in advance of when you're planning to transplant to the garden after danger of frost is past. Expect germination to be spotty and take a long time. Or let somebody else deal with this plant's difficult birth and buy a plant or two. (Some seed catalogs offer only started plants anyway.) Space the plants 8 to 24 inches (20 to 60 cm) apart, depending on the variety, and plant in full sun if you can. Rosemary needs light, well-drained soil with a pH of at least 6.0, and does best in more alkaline soil (closer to 7.0).

GROWING

Once it gets past its difficult beginning, rosemary is not fussy. Water only moderately and only when the soil gets fairly dry about 2 inches (5 cm) down. Like many plants with a Mediterranean heritage, rosemary is used to times of little water and responds poorly to overwatering. Rosemary is sensitive to frost and cannot survive below 17°F (−8°C); if you live in a cold climate, it's best to grow the plant in a container and move it indoors for the winter.

HARVESTING

Clip leaves whenever you want them. Or harvest the whole plant before frost and dry the leaves for later use.

VARIETIES

Roman Beauty. Dwarf, trailing rosemary, spreads about 12 inches (30 cm), pewter-green foliage.
Salem. Grows to about 20 inches (51 cm), strong scented, upright growth habit and dark purple flowers.

▲ **Tender but tough.** *Rosemary isn't hardy where I live, so I grow it in a container and bring it indoors for the winter. In areas where it can survive the winter, it's one of the most heat- and drought-tolerant plants you can find.*

Sow & Grow

Rosemary (*Rosmarinus officinalis*)
Mint family (Labiatae)

SOWING/PROPAGATING

Cuttings: Take cuttings from green (not woody) branches, dip in powdered rooting hormone, and stick in a pot of open, loose soil

Seed depth: Just pat the seeds gently into the soil; rosemary requires light to germinate

Germination soil temperature: 65–70°F (18–21°C). Germination is naturally slow, and the rate is low (30–50 percent)

Days to germination: 15–25 days (Note: germination is faster and more uniform with "primed" seed available from some seed catalogs.)

Sow indoors: 22 weeks before transplanting time

GROWING

pH range: 6.0–7.5 but grows best in alkaline soil
Spacing in beds: 8–24" (20–60 cm)
Watering: Moderate and even; do not overwater
Light: Best in full sun, but can tolerate light shade
Nutrient requirements: N=moderate; P=moderate; K=moderate
Rotation considerations: Avoid following cucumber

Sage

Sage has a lingering, slightly spicy aroma that's as warm and inviting as a country kitchen when Sunday dinner is cooking. Generations ago, it was used to restore the body. Today, its fragrant bouquet instills a sense of calm and well-being, while adding beauty and fragrance to the garden. Add it to stuffing, stews, and omelets.

PLANTING

Sage is a perennial that is hardy in Zones 4 to 8. Instead of starting plants from seed, you may want to buy year-old plants from a nursery or garden center. This way, you'll get a rich harvest the same season, instead of the two growing seasons required if you start plants from seed.

GROWING

Sage isn't fussy; plant it in the sun or partial shade in well-drained, moderately fertile soil. It should be lightly shaded in hot weather and south of Zone 8. Water only during dry periods; sage doesn't like wet feet. Don't fertilize; as is the case with many herbs, sage develops a stronger flavor if it's not fed too bountifully.

HARVEST

The leaves can be gathered anytime during the growing season. They seem to be most flavorful just as the flowers begin to open. Purple-leaved varieties tend to be more aromatic than green-leaved types. Use the leaves fresh in recipes or add them sparingly to salads. You can store dried leaves in airtight, dark-colored jars for about a year.

BEST VARIETIES

Berggarten. Aromatic, blue-gray leaves; good in soups and stews.

Purpurea. A beautiful dusky purple, with very aromatic leaves on an attractive spreading plant.

Tricolor. Very pretty, with white, green, and purple leaves.

▲ **Looking good.** *Sage adds grace and style to the garden while repelling harmful pests.*

Sow & Grow

Sage (*Salvia officinalis*)
Mint family (Labiatae)

SOWING

Seed depth: Surface or lightly cover
Germination soil temperature: 70–85°F (21–29°C)
Days to germination: 10–21
Sow indoors: 6–8 weeks before last frost
Sow outdoors: Not recommended

GROWING

pH range: 5.5–7.0
Growing soil temperature: 55–80°F (13–27°C)
Spacing in beds: 12–18" (30–45 cm)
Watering: Light
Light: Full sun to part shade
Nutrient requirements: N=low; P=low; K=low
Rotation considerations: Plants should be replaced every 4 to 5 years. Avoid rotating with basil, cucumber, marjoram, and oregano
Seed longevity: 2 years
Seeds per ounce: 3,400 (120 per g)

Tarragon

Tarragon is a traditional favorite in such French standards as béarnaise sauce and fines herbes. Its delightfully subtle, licorice-like flavor is perfect with chicken and seafood. It's also good for flavoring vinegars. A perennial herb, tarragon is easy to grow and hardy to Zone 4 if well mulched in the winter.

THE SITE

This is the ultimate unfussy plant; it won't smell or taste as good if you pamper it. Pick a spot in full sun, with well-drained but only moderately fertile soil with a pH around 7.0.

PLANTING AND GROWING

"A rose is a rose is a rose" may be true for that fragrant flower, but it isn't for tarragon. There's more than one tarragon, and even with the right one, there's a lot of variability in aroma and flavor. Lesson One: Don't buy tarragon seed. French tarragon, which is the herb you need for cooking, is grown not from seeds but from cuttings and is sold as started plants. Lesson Two: Don't buy Russian tarragon; it's bland and tasteless. Lesson Three: Sniff. Buy the most aromatic plants you can find.

Don't fertilize at all, and let the soil dry out some between waterings; tarragon is amazingly drought tolerant. As the plants age, their flavor declines; when they're three to five years old, remove them and replace them with new plants. Alternatively, you can create new plants yourself by digging up the old plant, cutting off pieces of the roots, and replanting them.

HARVEST AND STORAGE

Gather leaves to use fresh as soon as the plants are in full growth, about a month or two after transplanting. The leaves are most flavorful before plants flower. Use them fresh in chicken and fish dishes, as well as with mushrooms, potatoes, or leeks. Add tarragon late in the cooking process so its aromatic oils don't dissipate.

To preserve tarragon, steep leaves in white wine vinegar (about one part tarragon to two parts vinegar) for about four weeks, or dry it.

▲ **Tarragon for the table.** *Tarragon's narrow, shiny, dark green leaves pack a punch, with their combination peppery and licorice-like flavor.*

Sow & Grow

Tarragon (*Artemisia dracunculus* var. *sativa*)
Sunflower family (Compositae)

SOWING/PLANTING

Plant outdoors: Spring

GROWING

pH range: 5.5–7.0
Growing soil temperature: 50–80°F (10–27°C)
Spacing in beds: 12–18" (30–45 cm)
Watering: Low
Light: Full sun
Nutrient requirements: N=low; P=low; K=low
Rotation considerations: Avoid rotating with sunflower family plants

Thyme

There aren't many dishes with a European heritage that won't be improved by adding some of this very aromatic herb. In the garden, it makes a wonderful ground cover for dry sites, and its purple-pink flowers attract butterflies and bees in the garden.

Like many herbs that share its Mediterranean heritage, thyme thrives on neglect: Don't pay it too much attention, and don't be too nice to it. It doesn't need (and actually doesn't prefer) fertile soil, and it should be watered only sparingly. It's used to going without.

▲ **Thyme for restraint.** *This is one herb that thrives on neglect, so plant it in poor soil and be careful not to overwater it.*

THE SITE

Thyme grows best in full sun. Although its soil need not be fertile, it must be well drained with a pH between 5.5 and 7.0. Sandy soil is best for thyme. If you're dealing with clay soil, add plenty of compost to improve drainage before planting. Alternatively, grow thyme in a container. This way, you can bring it indoors to spend the winter on a sunny windowsill, and you'll have fresh thyme whenever you want it.

PLANTING AND GROWING

Although thyme is often propagated by division, this perennial can also be grown from seed. (I buy started plants at a local nursery or by mail order.) If you'd like to try your hand at starting your own, sow seeds indoors in early spring; germination takes two to three weeks. After the last frost, transplant seedlings into the garden, spacing them 6 to 8 inches apart after. Thyme can survive a light freeze, but if you're in doubt about how cold it's going to get, cover young seedlings with a row cover.

Generally pest and disease free, thyme only runs into trouble with fungal disease if it gets too much water or if the water it gets lingers too long because the soil drains poorly.

HARVEST AND STORAGE

Harvest just before the flowers open, and hang cuttings upside down in a paper bag to dry.

> ### Sow and Grow
> Thyme (*Thymus* spp.)
> Mint family (Labiatae)
>
> SOWING
> **Seed depth:** ¼"
> **Germination soil temperature:** 60–65°F
> **Days to germination:** 14–21
> **Sow indoors:** 6 weeks before last frost
> **Sow outdoors:** Not recommended
>
> GROWING
> **pH range:** 5.5–7.0
> **Growing soil temperature:** 75°F
> **Spacing in beds:** 6–8" (15–20 cm)
> **Watering:** Light and intermittent
> **Light:** Full sun is best, but partial shade tolerated
> **Rotation considerations:** Avoid rotating with cucumber

Thyme is most aromatic when used fresh, but it retains significant potency when dried if it is stored in a tightly sealed jar in a cool place.

VARIETIES

There are many, many varieties of thyme, including some that are more ornamental than culinary. The kinds most often grown as culinary herbs are two variants of common, or garden, thyme: English and French. There is also a creeping thyme that is a good ground cover in addition to being aromatic and a good bee attractor.

Zone Maps

Many catalogs and references use both the USDA and AHS maps to help consumers evaluate plants for their garden. Four numbers describe the hardiness of a plant. The first two numbers, such as "5–8," indicate the USDA zones where that plant will grow. The last two numbers, such as "7–3," indicate the range of zones where it will grow using the AHS data. This means that if your garden is in USDA zone 6 and in AHS zone 7, then the plant will be hardy in your garden.

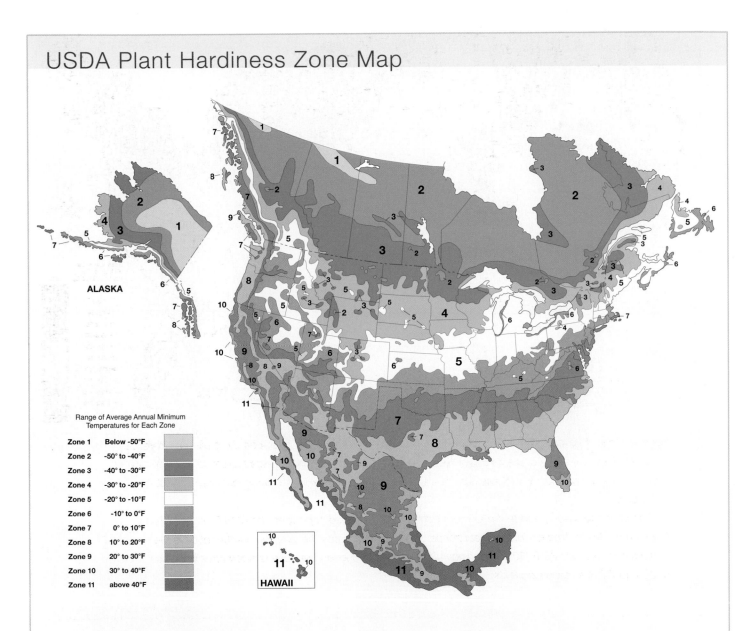

USDA Plant Hardiness Zone Map

Range of Average Annual Minimum Temperatures for Each Zone

Zone 1	Below -50°F
Zone 2	-50° to -40°F
Zone 3	-40° to -30°F
Zone 4	-30° to -20°F
Zone 5	-20° to -10°F
Zone 6	-10° to 0°F
Zone 7	0° to 10°F
Zone 8	10° to 20°F
Zone 9	20° to 30°F
Zone 10	30° to 40°F
Zone 11	above 40°F

ALASKA

HAWAII

The United States Department of Agriculture (USDA) created this map to give gardeners a helpful tool for selecting and cultivating plants. The map divides North America into 11 zones based on each area's average minimum winter temperature. Zone 1 is the coldest and Zone 11 the warmest. Once you determine your zone, you may use that information to select plants that are most likely to thrive in your climate.

American Horticultural Society Plant Heat Zone Map

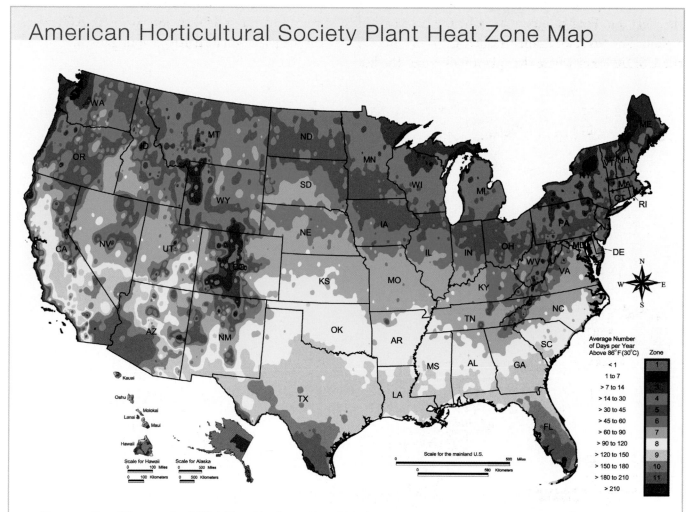

Average Number of Days per Year Above 86°F (30°C)	Zone
< 1	1
1 to 7	
> 7 to 14	
> 14 to 30	4
> 30 to 45	5
> 45 to 60	6
> 60 to 90	7
> 90 to 120	8
> 120 to 150	9
> 150 to 180	10
> 180 to 210	11
> 210	

For more than 30 years, the USDA Plant Hardiness Zone Map (opposite) has been the preferred reference for determining the ability of plants to survive in different regions. That map bases hardiness on minimum winter temperatures. But while these are significant, they are not the only factors in determining a plant's hardiness.

Based on the assumption that maximum temperatures are also important, the AHS Plant Heat Zone Map divides North America into 12 heat zones. Each zone indicates the average number of days the temperature exceeds 86°F (30°C) each year. This value was chosen because temperatures in excess of 86°F (30°C) can damage plants.

A Guide to Plant Families

Plant Family	Vegetable/Herb/Fruit
Amaranth	Amaranth
Beet	Beet, spinach, Swiss chard
Borage	Borage
Buckwheat	Rhubarb, sorrel
Cabbage	Arugula, broccoli, broccoli rabe, Brussels sprouts, cabbage, cauli-broc, cauliflower, Chinese cabbage, cress, horseradish, kale, kohlrabi, mizuna, mustard, pak choi, radish, rutabaga, turnip
Carrot	Carrot, celeriac, celery, chervil, cilantro/coriander, dill, fennel, parsley, parsnip
Cucumber	Cucumber, gourd, melon, summer squash, watermelon, winter squash
Goosefoot	Orach
Grass	Corn
Mallow	Okra
Mint	Basil, marjoram, oregano, rosemary, sage, thyme
Morning glory	Sweet potato
Onion	Asparagus, chive, garlic, leek, onion, scallion
Pea	Bean, pea, peanut
Purslane	Claytonia
Rose	Alpine strawberry
Sunflower	Artichoke, cardoon, dandelion, endive/escarole, Jerusalem artichoke, lettuce, radicchio, salsify, sunflower, tarragon
Tomato	Eggplant, pepper, potato (white), tomatillo, tomato
Valerian	Mâche

Suppliers

A.M. Leonard
800-543-8955
www.amleo.com
General gardening supplies

Abundant Life Seeds
541-767-9606
www.abundantlifeseeds.com
Untreated seeds of hard-to-find varieties

Alberta Nurseries & Seeds, Ltd.
403-224-3544
www.gardenersweb.ca
Seeds for short-season areas

Allen, Sterling & Lothrop
207-781-4142
www.allensterlinglothrop.com
Vegetable seeds adapted to northern
New England

Comstock, Ferre and Co.
800-733-3773
www.comstockferre.com
Many varieties of vegetables,
including many older varieties

Cook's Garden, The
800-457-9703
www.cooksgarden.com
Seeds, some tools, and garden supplies

Fedco Seeds
207-873-7333
www.fedcoseeds.com
Seeds, some tools, and garden supplies

Gardener's Supply Company
888-833-1412
www.gardeners.com
Gardening supplies, greenhouses

Gardens Alive!
513-354-1482
www.gardensalive.com
Organic gardening supplies

Harris Seeds
800-514-4441
www.harrisseeds.com
Seeds, tools, gardening supplies,
greenhouses, compost bins

Heirloom Seeds
412-384-0852
www.heirloomseeds.com
Seeds, tools, and books

High Mowing Organic Seeds
802-472-6174
www.highmowingseeds.com
Organic open pollinated and hybrid
varieties of vegetables, flowers, and herbs

Johnny's Selected Seeds
877-564-6997
www.johnnyseeds.com
Seeds, tools, gardening supplies, cold
frames, compost bins; catalog has excellent
information on sowing, harvesting, and
pest/disease control

Jung Quality Seeds
800-247-5864
www.jungseed.com
Vegetable seeds

Lee Valley Tools
800-871-8158 in the United States
800-267-8767 in Canada
www.leevalley.com
Woodworking and gardening tools,
home and garden supplies

Lehman's
877-438-5346
www.lehmans.com
Fork tiller

Nichols Garden Nursery
800-422-3985
www.nicholsgardennursery.com
Tools, seeds

Park Seed
800-213-0076
www.parkseed.com
Seeds, gardening supplies, and
decorative accents

Peaceful Valley Farm & Garden Supply
888-784-1722
www.groworganic.com
Seeds (including cover crops), tools,
gardening supplies, Deep Spader

Pinetree Garden Seeds
207-926-3400
www.superseeds.com
Wide selection of interesting vegetables
in small packets

Seed Savers Exchange
563-382-5990
www.seedsavers.org
Heirloom vegetable, herb, and flower
seed collections

Seeds of Change
888-762-7333
www.seedsofchange.com
Organically grown seeds

Stokes Seeds
800-396-9238
www.stokesseeds.com
Vegetable, herb, flower, and
perennial seeds

Territorial Seed Company
800-626-0866
www.territorial-seed.com
Organic seeds, cover crops, garden
supplies, Garden Digger

Totally Tomatoes
800-345-5977
www.totallytomato.com
Seeds — lots and lots of tomatoes
and peppers

Union Tools
800-888-4196
www.uniontools.com
Razor-Back brand and other heavy
duty garden tools

Vesey's Seeds Ltd.
800-363-7333
www.veseys.com
Specializes in seeds for short
growing seasons

Virtual Seeds Company
www.virtualseeds.com
Full line of seeds, including vegetables

W. Atlee Burpee Seed Co.
800-888-1447
www.burpee.com
Seeds, plants, gardening supplies,
and decorative accents

Further Reading

Bubel, Mike and Nancy. *Root Cellaring*. Storey Publishing, 1991. Now that you've grown it, learn how to store it.

Coleman, Eliot. *Four-Season Harvest: Organic Vegetables from Your Home Garden All Year Long*. Chelsea Green Publishing Company, 1999. This book is full of useful tips and written in a warm and friendly style. Although its focus is on season-extension, *Four-Season Harvest* is also an excellent source of general gardening help.

Damrosch, Barbara. *The Garden Primer*. Workman Publishing, 2008. An essential reference book for every organic gardener.

Denckla, Tanya. *The Gardener's A–Z Guide to Growing Organic Food*. Storey Publishing, 1994. Full of the specific details (germination and growth temperatures, planting dates, and so on) that can make a big difference in garden success. A good reference book.

Editors of Garden Way Publishing. *Just the Facts: Dozens of Garden Charts, Thousands of Garden Answers*. Storey Publishing, 1994. As the title describes, this book contains valuable information in chart form on everything from compost to frost dates.

Gershuny, Grace. *Start with the Soil*. Rodale Press, 1993. Much of what you need to know about garden soil and how to create the best growing conditions in your garden.

Hart, Rhonda Massingham. *Bugs, Slugs, and Other Thugs*. Storey Publishing, 1991. The tool you need to help identify and deal with garden pests.

Homeyer, Henry. *Notes from the Garden*. University Press of New England, 2002. A book of gardening essays by a seasoned organic gardener.

Hopp, Henry. *What Every Gardener Should Know About Earthworms*. Country Wisdom Bulletin A-21, Storey Publishing, 1978. This concise booklet does just what the title says it will.

Jeavons, John. *How to Grow More Vegetables*. Ten Speed Press, 1982. This book is worth reading, even if you don't end up following all of its rules.

Jenkins, Joseph. *The Humanure Handbook*. Jenkins Publishing, 1999. An excellent book on composting, as well as a profound but humorous introduction to a very important topic.

Stell, Elizabeth P. *Secrets to Great Soil*. Storey Publishing, 1998. An excellent reference on how to understand soil and create better soil in your garden.

Special Thanks to . . .

A number of companies went out of their way to help in the production of this book and deserve special recognition.

Shepherd's Garden Seeds has been a dream come true. Not only did they graciously send loads of vegetable and herb seeds for us to grow, but they also opened their doors to our photographer and editors. We were allowed to wander and photograph the lush trial gardens, where we saw many of the best varieties offered today, as well as a hint of what is to come in future seasons. Thank you, Eliot Wadsworth III, Renee Beaulieu, and Vincent Lawrence.

Gardener's Supply Company took a special interest in the book and did much to help us from beginning to end. The items they supplied, from tools to raised cedar beds, were instrumental in making the book look as good as possible. They are nice people doing what they like to do.

L.L. Bean, Inc. helped the author look his best, supplying well-made, comfortable clothes that not only looked good but held up beautifully all season long.

Lee Valley Tools Ltd. sent us some of the nicest hand gardening tools we've seen. Strong, attractive, easy-to-use, and just about indestructible.

The Cook's Garden provided vegetable seeds and the seed-starter mix to get them off to a great start.

Harris Seeds was very generous to the project and sent us enough vegetable seeds to grow many gardens. They also supplied deer netting, hot caps, and a pH meter. All of these made our jobs a lot easier.

Union Tools sent us an array of gardening tools, from manure forks and trowels to shovels and rakes. They're attractive enough for photo shoots and tough as nails.

Mount Greylock Greenhouses. These very generous people allowed us to photograph their sales and production houses, even though we tended to get in the way.

Interior Photography Credits

© Sylvia Ferry Smith: 5, 17 bottom, 23, 31 top left and right, 40, 41, 45, 65 bottom, 68 right, 82, 84, 95 (circle hoe, farmer's weeder), 106 right, 108, 109 top right, 120 right, 132 right, 147, 148 right, 149 right, 151 top left and right, bottom left, 159, 162 C and D, 164, 165, 166, 169 bottom right, 192, 193, 195, 200, 203, 205, 207 bottom right, 211, 212 top, 215 bottom, 219, 222, 224, 227, 232 top, 234, 237 bottom, 238–241, 243, 244, 246 right, 247, 248, 250, 251, 253, 258–263, 266, 268, 269, 274, 275 left, 276, 277 bottom, 278–280, 281 bottom, 286, 287, 294, 295, 296 top center and bottom right, 299 top, 300, 302, 303, 309 top, 313, 314 top row and bottom center, 323, 324, 330, 333

© Storey Publishing/Giles Prett: 4, 6–7, 8, 10, 12, 13, 15, 16, 17 top, 19, 24, 25, 27, 29, 31 bottom left, 32–38, 44, 46, 49, 52, 56, 59, 60 top and bottom left, 61–64, 65 top and middle, 66, 67, 68 left, 69, 71–80, 83, 85–88, 90–94, 95 (all except circle hoe, farmer's weeder), 96–101, 103, 104, 106 left, 107, 109 top left and bottom, 112–114, 116–118, 120 left, 122–125, 128–131, 132 left, 134, 136–138, 140, 142, 144, 148 left, 149 top and bottom left, 150, 152, 154, 155, 156, 162 A and B, 163, 168, 169 top and bottom left, 170, 171, 185–189, 196–199, 201, 202, 204 top, 206, 207 top and bottom left, 208–210, 212 middle, 214, 215 top, 216–220, 223, 225, 226, 229–231, 232 bottom, 233, 235, 236, 237 top and middle, 245, 254–257, 264, 265, 267, 270, 273, 275 right, 277 top, 281 top and middle, 283, 288, 292, 293, 296 top left and right; bottom left, 297, 298, 299 bottom, 304–308, 309 bottom, 310 top left and right, 311, 312, 314 bottom left and right, 315, 320–322, 325, 327–329, 331, 332

Additional photography by:

© Artville/Jeff Burke and Lorraine Triolo: 42, 127

© Harris Barnes, Jr./AGStockUSA: 272

© David Cavagnaro: 180 bottom right, 212 bottom, 252, 284, 289, 316, 317 right

© Christine DuPuis: 60 bottom right, 249

John Ewing: 102

© Debra Ferguson/AGStockUSA: 184 top right

© Lisa Fletcher/iStockphoto: 271

© Armando Frazao/iStockphoto: 161

© GAP Photos/BBC Magazines, Ltd. 167, © GAP Photos/Claire Davies 285, © GAP Photos/Visions 290, © GAP Photos/J.S. Sira 318, © GAP Photos/Geoff Kidd 326

© John Gruen: 31 bottom right, 310 bottom

© Harold Kaufman/AGStockUSA: 184 left

© Rob Neimy/AGStockUSA: 213

© 2009, Nova-Photo-Graphik/Vienna: 317 left

© Clive Schaupmeyer/AGStockUSA: 182 bottom left

© Howard Schwartz/AGStockUSA: 180 top right, 182 top left, right, 183

© Storey Publishing/Mars Vilaubi: 204 bottom row, all

Wikimedia Commons/Goldlocki: 181 top right

Wikimedia Commons/Rasbak : 181 left

© Dr. X. B. Yang/AGStockUSA: 181 bottom right

© Tom Zitter/AGStockUSA: 180 left , 184 bottom right

© YinYang/iStockphoto: 162 left

Index

Page references in *italics* indicate photographs or illustrations; page references in **bold** indicate main entries.

Other Storey Titles You Will Enjoy

Carrots Love Tomatoes, by Louise Riotte.
A classic companion planting guide that shows how to use plants'
natural partnerships to produce bigger and better harvests.
224 pages. Paper. ISBN 978-1-58017-027-7.

The Complete Compost Gardening Guide,
by Barbara Pleasant & Deborah L. Martin.
Everything a gardener needs to know to produce the best compost,
nourishment for abundant, flavorful vegetables.
320 pages. Paper. ISBN 978-1-58017-702-3.

The Gardener's A–Z Guide to Growing Organic Food,
by Tanya L. K. Denckla.
An invaluable resource for growing, harvesting, and storing
765 varieties of vegetables, fruits, herbs, and nuts.
496 pages. Paper. ISBN 978-1-58017-370-4.

The Herb Gardener, by Susan McClure.
Herb gardening basics for every season, indoors and out.
240 pages. Paper. ISBN 978-0-88266-873-4.

Incredible Vegetables from Self-Watering Containers,
by Edward C. Smith.
A foolproof method to produce a bountiful harvest without
the trouble of a traditional earth garden.
256 pages. Paper. ISBN 978-1-58017-556-2.
Hardcover. ISBN 978-1-58017-557-9.

The Veggie Gardener's Answer Book, by Barbara W. Ellis.
Insider's tips and tricks, practical advice, and organic wisdom for vegetable
growers everywhere.
432 pages. Paper. ISBN 978-1-60342-024-2.

These and other books from Storey Publishing are available
wherever quality books are sold or by calling 1-800-441-5700.
Visit us at *www.storey.com*.